STRUGGLING WITH THEIR HISTORIES:
ECONOMIC DECLINE AND EDUCATIONAL IMPROVEMENT
IN FOUR RURAL SOUTHEASTERN SCHOOL DISTRICTS

INTERPRETIVE PERSPECTIVES ON EDUCATION AND POLICY
George W. Noblit and William T. Pink, **Series Editors**

STRUGGLING WITH THEIR HISTORIES:
ECONOMIC DECLINE AND EDUCATIONAL IMPROVEMENT
IN FOUR RURAL SOUTHEASTERN SCHOOL DISTRICTS

Alan J. DeYoung
University of Kentucky

ABLEX PUBLISHING COPORATION
NORWOOD, NEW JERSEY

Library of Congress Cataloging-in-Publication Data

DeYoung, Alan J.
   Struggling with their histories : economic decline and educational improvement in four rural southeastern school districts / Alan J. DeYoung.
      p.   cm. – (Interpretive perspectives on education and policy)
   Includes bibliographical references and index.
   ISBN 0-89391-817-2
   1. Education, Rural–Appalachian Region–Case studies.
   2. Community and school–Appalachian region–Case studies.
   3. School supervision–Appalachian Region–Case Studies.   I. Title.
   II. Series.
   LC5146.D49 1991
   370.19'346'0974 – dc20   91-16201
                                            CIP

Ablex Publishing Corporation
355 Chestnut Street
Norwood, New Jersey 07648

Table of Contents

v

Acknowledgments

University professors of almost any stripe are relatively rare in and around America's rural school systems. This may especially be the case of professors whose intent is to listen to teachers and administrators, rather than to profess to them. Unlike most educational research, then, the following study came about as the result of listening to rural school teachers, counselors, administrators, and local citizens involved in the day to day life of four different school systems in the American Southeast.

Given the fact that most of what follows has been informed by them, I need to take a moment to formally thank those dozens and dozens of individuals who provided the advice, insights, and perspectives related to aims of this book. To be sure, many of the questions initially posed in this research were ones I set out to answer before I entered Braxton, Charlotte, Clinch, and Cave Counties. On the other hand, many of the questions I ended up pursuing were reframed by people I interviewed; and others were pointed out as perhaps better questions to ask than those I had set out to investigate.

So too, in each of the four counties/school systems, I developed close personal relationships with various "key informants." And this was as much the case in systems where parts of my narrative may appear less flattering as it was in cases where my fieldwork paints arguably more positive images. Many of these individuals still seek me out to talk about their schools and counties now, over two years after most of my fieldwork activities. And in one county I currently have new research in progress, partly because of the personal relationships I have developed there.

All of the people I would like to acknowledge and thank here provided invaluable insight into the concerns and issues discussed in this book. Some became informants because they occupied official offices either of a school system I "studied;" others because they were identified by school people as local citizens who could best answer the questions I was interested in pursuing. Few of these people had to cooperate with me, but each spent the extra time to attempt to determine what I was about and to answer and reframe questions I posed to them. Some I now consider close friends. Within this category of teachers, administrators, and local citizens I interviewed, who provided me with key information and perspectives, and/or who read and critiqued early versions of the case studies I wrote on their school systems and its context, I include Mary Ellen Turner, Karen Huffman, Judy Lacks, Gary Walker, Barbara Cox, Ramsey White, Jim Rogers, Twila White, Mike McCoy, Bobby Howard, Kenna Seal, Paul Stapleton, Roger Fleenor, Otis Lovelace, Dora Bowlin, and Billy Elder.

Equally as important to the larger study were a host of individuals in similar school and community-based roles as those mentioned above, but who requested anonymity for any contribution they might have made to my research. As they read the final version of this manuscript, I am confident they will recognize the value of their input, and I thank them here without specific mention as they requested.

There were also various other individuals who contributed to this study as a function either of their formal involvement with the school improvement projects they were funded to facilitate, or as colleagues of mine who read and advised me on various aspects of my conceptualization and/or writing. Among the former of these contributors were Appalachia Educational Laboratory staff members Craig Howley, Todd Strohmenger, Pam Coe, and Jack Sanders. Among the second group mentioned above are Richard Angelo, Beth Goldstein, Ron Eller, and Jane Bagby. William Link also advised me on portions of my historical sketch of rural education in Virginia.

Finally I want to thank my family, and especially my wife, for allowing me the time away from home which this research demanded. I was "in the field" continuously during 1988, 1989, and early 1990, and am told I was missed. I therefore hope this volume provides a worthwhile contribution to the understanding of rural schooling in the American Southeast, and thus helps to compensate those closest to me who also paid a price for my undertaking it. With these concerns in mind, I dedicate this book to my son, Nathaniel; my daughter, Amy; and most especially to my wife, Patricia.

CREDIT: PATTI DeYOUNG

Abandoned school, Clinch County, Tennessee.

INTRODUCTION

While nationally the Reagan years in the White House saw a period of economic expansion, in rural America (and particularly in the Midwest) the news was much less favorable. As land prices fell and property foreclosures rose, the U.S. Congress rushed through several pieces of legislation aimed at helping to offset the social impact of the 1980s rural economic decline. One piece of legislation sponsored in 1986, as a result of expressed congressional concern over this rural economic decline, focused upon aiding and improving rural educational opportunities across the country. Authorized under the Educational Appropriation Act of 1986 (H.R. 5233; as referenced in H.J. Res. 738; Public Law 99-500 and 99-591), this "rural initiative" for improving America's rural schools made available a total of $4 million for school improvement.

Ostensibly, since there are only a few avenues for the federal government to become rapidly involved in noncategorical school improvement activities, and since Congress was interested in moving quickly to help rural regions experiencing the 1980s economic downturn, it was decided to disburse the dollars earmarked for rural school improvement through the nation's nine already existing research and development laboratories. These nine regional labs are strategically located throughout the United States and are funded and monitored by the Office of Educational Research and Improvement (OERI) of the U.S. Department of Education.

The guidelines for spending special federal dollars for rural school improvement adopted by OERI were relatively flexible for approximately 70% of the total allocation. According to OERI guidelines, "core" proposals eligible for funding would focus upon one or more of the following strategies for rural school improvement:

1. Providing a full range of school services
2. Strengthening students' thinking and reasoning skills
3. Improving achievement
4. Improving the transition from school to work
5. Recruiting good teachers
6. strengthening school–community partnerships
7. helping schools organize for improvement

1

Each of the regional labs was requested to submit a detailed plan outlining why rural schools in its regions needed special help; what sorts of special programs or facilities would be facilitated by funds under consideration; and what sorts of outcomes would be expected as a result of rural initiative expenditures.

Given the relatively open-ended possibilities for eligible intervention/ assistance strategies outlined above, funding awards made for core proposals by OERI went to a variety of different rural school improvement programs. For example, rural school improvement funds allocated the Southwest Educational Improvement Laboratory (SEDL) were spent on various staff development projects aimed at improving "higher order thinking skills." At the Mid Continent Regional Educational Laboratory (McREL), rural school improvement funds were spent on several different programs, including school-based entrepreneurship and community history gathering efforts like those pioneered by Eliot Wigginton at Foxfire (see Wigginton, 1985, or Hobbs, 1988).

RURAL SCHOOL IMPROVEMENT PLANS OF THE APPALACHIA EDUCATIONAL LAB

Rather than focusing directly on improving school or classroom facilities among rural schools in its target states of Kentucky, Virginia, West Virginia, and Tennessee, the Appalachia Educational Laboratory (AEL) chose to concentrate in its core proposal upon OERI categories (6) "strengthening partnerships between rural schools and the community," and (7) "assisting rural schools to organize for school improvement." AEL's focus on these two OERI approved objectives was to be facilitated by constituting a Rural/Small School Program within the lab with three primary objectives, four work strategies, and two basic activities.

These objectives, strategies, and activities were outlined thusly in its formal proposal to OERI:

Objectives

The work of the RSS core project is guided by three objectives, as follows: (1) to involve key in- fluential persons and rural leaders of the Region in AEL's rural school improvement work; (2) to provide information about school improvement and community development to those in leadership positions in the Region's rural, small schools; and (3) to establish demonstrations of how school and com- munity leaders can develop and use information to achieve ongoing school improvement and community development.

Strategies

The work of the RSS core project is guided by four general strategies. First, *advisement* of the program is based on state advisory groups. These are comprised of key influential persons and rural leaders in AEL's Region.. . . Second, the RSS program is *building a data base*—information pertinent to the improvement of small, rural schools. Third, *dissemination* of information pertinent to the improvement of small, rural schools, including community development, occurs through a variety of activities, including publication of a supplement to the Lab's quarterly newsletter. Fourth, the RSS program is undertaking four *School–Community Partnership demonstrations.*

Activities

The work of the RSS core project occurs under the rubric of two activities as follows: (1) advisement, management and information tasks and (2) school–community partnership demonstrations.

As the objectives, strategies, and (particularly) activities overviewed above suggest, a central feature of the AEL's Rural/Small School program focused on the utility of its school/community improvement model, which it planned to "demonstrate" in one site in each of its four designated states. And, as the proposal appeared to meet OERI's guidelines, it was initially funded for the 1987–1988 and 1988–1989 school years.

FUNDING AN "ETHNOGRAPHIC EVALUATION"

In addition to a basic pool of funds for rural school improvement equally disseminated through the nine regional labs, a smaller pool of funds (approximately 30% of the total $4 million) was held aside by OERI for competitive bidding among the laboratories. According to numerous regional Lab staff members, OERI was never happy during the administration of Education Secretary William Bennet in having to deal directly with the Labs. Rather, it had sought to open up competition for federal dollars (including those channeled via the rural initiative) to multiple outside agencies and groups. Yet, as Congressional legislation specifically mandated that rural initiative funds would be spent through the Labs, OERI apparently felt that some form of limited competition between them for a portion of the rural school initiative funding might enhance the quality of some school enhancement programs.

Under the sponsorship of AEL, I formally proposed to evaluate the strengths and weaknesses of AEL's school/community improvement demonstrations using qualitative and ethnographic methods. Each of the Labs was allowed to submit two supplementary proposals for additional funding, and the Ethnographic Evaluation proposal submitted by AEL (to be completed by myself and two graduate students) was rated highly in the competitive assessments. Subsequently this project was funded by OERI under the competitive awards category within the rural school initiative guidelines.

The following monograph is primarily based upon the Ethnographic Evaluation of the AEL School-Community Partnership model formally submitted to OERI in May 1990. Yet the substance of this book has been significantly altered from the original report in a number of ways. The main difference between this work and the OERI report is focus. The primary intent of the AEL project was to demonstrate how school improvement might be positively affected with reference to particular school leadership strategies within (theoretically) supportive community contexts. In other words, providing a model for the ostensible improvement of school *instructional* programs was the official theme of the AEL project, and the "ethnographic evaluation" was to be focused upon contextual factors associated with either its success or its failure.

Yet, while improving instruction in rural school settings was not an uninteresting topic for evaluation staff, it became clear to me that an even greater need within the professional education literature would be some thorough description and discussion of school contextual factors (i.e., the social, economic, and political situation surrounding schools) in the rural Southeast. Even including this work, I would argue, systematic description of rural education contexts in this part of the United States remains underdeveloped. And my conviction that some academically oriented description and analysis of rural school contexts in the Southeast would be an important contribution to the literature grew further as progress on this research continued. Thus, most of the work reported upon here is concerned with the community contexts that surrounded schools in each of the county districts studied, rather than with the actual school improvement effects of AEL.

ORGANIZATION OF THE BOOK

There are six chapters in this work, plus the introduction which is now drawing to a close. Here I have mentioned briefly the impetus for the study which produced this manuscript; and in Chapter 1 I will talk further about the methodologies and focal concerns of the AEL School/Community Partnership Demonstrations. However, the heart of this manuscript is really contained in the four school/community case studies originally completed (though slightly revised) for OERI. In Chapters 2-5, attempts are made to outline the current community and school leadership dynamics of each of the four demonstration project sites, as well as to historically situate each involved county in its economic, political, and sociological contexts.

Chapter 6 of this work includes more general discussions of the overall theme of this book: how previous and current social, economic, and political conditions surrounding the rural schools talked about in the earlier chapters currently affect educational conditions and school improvement strategies/practices. As part of this discussion, most recent (1990) dynamics in each county related to earlier discussions are also included. And importantly, some consideration to the actual school improvement practices attempted by AEL are overviewed and assessed.

While the methodology, "findings," and logic underlying this book will be extensively elaborated upon shortly, I assume that readers specifically interested in the AEL school/community partnership model will contact that organization directly for some of their many relevant publications. I have only attempted here to sketch most of the processes involved. Furthermore, obtaining actual case studies upon which much of the following is based is not possible.

As will be suggested shortly, school leadership issues in at least two of the four school districts studied proved comparatively controversial. As a federal agency charged with improving instruction rather than publishing compromising profiles, AEL chose not to publish the larger Ethnographic Evaluation. Related to this issue, none of the following information, nor my interpretation, necessarily reflects the opinion of the Appalachia Educational Laboratory or of the Office of Educational Research and Improvement.

So too, I decided that "key informants" in the two previously mentioned districts required continued anonymity in these pages. Thus, two of the following case studies deal with county school systems which exist but cannot be identified as such on any U.S. map. While such tactics will make it difficult for the concerned reader to utilize sources I did in these two cases, it is the best compromise I could come up with. For, this is really a book not just about four school systems; it is primarily a book about rural contexts in the southeastern U.S. as they affect educational leadership, teaching, and school functioning.

Randolph–Henry High School, Charlotte County, Virginia.

1
PROJECT METHODOLOGY

As expressed in the Introduction, the work upon which this book is based had two general purposes. Officially, the study which informs this book was completed as an evaluation of four specific AEL school/community partnership demonstrations. Yet, since the literature on formal schooling in rural America (particularly in the southeastern U.S.) is greatly underrepresented among professional accounts of public education (DeYoung, 1987), much of the study was intended to investigate existing issues and concerns in American rural education as such themes manifested themselves in four specific places.

Thus, the contexts even more so than the school improvement projects of the four school systems investigated for AEL are the primary focus of this work. However, in order to provide contextual information regarding how we proceeded methodologically and how we obtained access to the sites we studied, some of the following chapter details specifics of the AEL project per se.

In order to facilitate descriptive as well as analytical objectives on both contextual and evaluative dimensions of this research, several sorts of methodological decisions were initially called for. One consideration was concerned with research methods utilized for the study, and the defense of chosen methods as opposed to others. Inasmuch as the formal title of this project was "An Ethnographic Study," it obviously should come as no surprise that primarily ethnographic and qualitative methods were utilized in the larger report.

While there are several important distinctions even between these methodological approaches (Dorr-Bremme, 1985; Erikson, 1977), one of the primary characteristics common to both methodological schools is that they are less interested in the quantitative testing of specific hypotheses generated by researchers removed from the scene, and are instead primarily concerned with description and understanding of particular cultural settings as interpreted by those who occupy them.

The academic debate between advocates of qualitative vs. quantitative analysis has been particularly keen during the last decade within the American educational research community and is far too complex to be easily reproduced here. Those interested in such discussions might best pursue them in the pages of *Educational Researcher* during the past 5 years, where disputes between contending camps have occupied an impressive amount of coverage (e.g.,

7

Firestone, 1988; Howe, 1985; Peshkin, 1988; Smith, 1983). Discussions about qualitative methods likewise occupy the pages of numerous recent texts and edited collections of essays. These have been put together during the past 10 years (typically by proponents of qualitative methods) and have attempted to explicate the conceptual and methodological distinctions between quantitative vs. qualitative research (e.g., Bredo & Feinberg, 1982; Fetterman, 1984; Guba & Lincoln, 1981; Spindler, 1982).

Given that both the model to be "demonstrated" by AEL was previously untested; that the composition of participant groups was comparatively undefined (particularly those designated by district superintendents); that the choice of innovation projects was open-ended and to be voluntarily participated in by each district; and so on, ethnographic and qualitative techniques were proposed for utilization in this study.

Similarly, while there have recently emerged numerous studies related to the adoption/utilization of educational innovations within American school districts (discussed below), the above considerations, as well as the general lack of descriptive material on contemporary rural schools in the U.S., suggested to the evaluation team that theory–driven and extensive reliance upon quantitative data might miss important aspects of the demonstration model and its potential impact upon the local schools and communities in each setting.

Perhaps the "ethnographic intent" or research aspiration of this study was best suggested by one important educational anthropologist, Alan Peshkin, who coincidentally remains one of the only other educational researchers who has ever specifically targeted contemporary American rural schools for qualitative investigation. According to Peshkin,

> The pre-specified intent of quantitative inquiry contrasts with the relatively un-prespecified intent of qualitative inquiry, which fastens on the ordinary and enormous complexity of the social phenomenon we investigate. Since qualitative inquiry potentially responds to the fullness of the people, events, and settings that we study, it may attend to that which quantitative research is likely to not see or to ignore.

> Quantitative inquiry finds its ultimate strength in the structure of the experiment. Typically, its findings are expressed in the disembodied, formal research report. Qualitative inquiry finds its ultimate strength in the vast opportunity that the holism of being there makes possible. It's findings are expressed in the multitude of forms that convention allows the research report to take; by the use of personal pronouns, its report testifies to the researcher's presence.

> In quantitative inquiry, researchers tend to look hard, but seldom more than once, as in the questionnaire or test performance of a given individual. In this fact is the trimness and orderliness that establishes the economy of this form of research. In qualitative inquiry, however, researchers tend to look again and again, and they

look, moreover, in the varying moods and times of both researchers and researched. (1988, p. 418)

However, describing what follows as *an* ethnographic study is somewhat
misleading (as I have earlier suggested). In the first place, formal ethnographies
per se are typically constructed by social scientists interested in understanding
and describing specific cultures and/or subcultures in a particular geographic
location. Furthermore, perhaps the most important criteria of acceptable ethnographic research is that entering hypotheses and value judgments of field
researchers must be held in abeyance in order for objective observation and
description to take place. Underlying this concern is the belief that, in order to
come to understand a culturally different setting, one must attempt to minimize
as much as possible the cultural categories and ways of interpreting reality
consistent with one's native culture.

On both of these accounts, this "ethnographic study" falls technically and
methodologically short of a "true" ethnography. In the first place, what follows
here are descriptions and interpretations of what the principle investigator and
his research team found important in *four* (rather than one) different cultural
scenes. Naturally, any suggestion that the diverse constituent groups and
interaction patterns evident in even small rural school districts in the United
States can be considered within the framework of one cultural setting would be
seriously misleading. This likelihood proved to be quite true, in our judgment,
by the study's end.

Furthermore, since the intent of this study was an evaluation of a particular
school innovation strategy/process, key aspects of the researchers *neutrality* in
the selection of sites to observe and questions to ask were technically invali-
dated. In a number of important ways, the questions asked in this study were
focused upon school and community leadership issues, as such issues were
suggested by both those who sponsored the school/community partnership
demonstrations and by those in each of the four school districts and communities involved in this study.

On the other hand, while what follows should not be construed as "an
ethnography" of four rural school districts and their communities, much of the
information herein probably falls within the acceptable range of "focused
ethnographies" or ethnographically informed case studies, as such studies have
come to be defined within the qualitative research community (Stake, 1978;
Puckett, 1988). Furthermore, as a number of educational anthropologists have
argued, the actual percentage of acceptable "ethnographies" in educational
research is far fewer than the authors of many would-be ethnographies claim
(Wolcott, 1984). Because most educational research funded today is sponsored
in efforts to evaluate particular programs and/or to investigate specific social
and/or cultural "problems," the best that can be said of *some* ethnographically

oriented research is that it attempts to use qualitative methods toward specific ends. In other words, research which is used primarily to answer questions posed by outsiders (i.e., funding agencies), rather than that which emerges substantially as description and analysis of the concerns and interests of "natives," conceptually violates fundamental prerequisites of ethnographic research.

The following analysis, then, attempted to use a host of ethnographically compatible methods, guided both by an interest in describing the contexts in which the AEL demonstration projects operated (the primary theme of this book), and upon school leadership themes central to concerns of both AEL and the funding agency (i.e., whether and to what extent the demonstration projects were successful in each of the four sites).

In point of fact, a host of research activities and data collection strategies were used in this evaluation project. To be sure, several quintessential ethnographic methods were used, including direct observation, participant observation, open ended interview techniques, and the collection of official documents issued by the school systems and the federal agency involved (Bogdan & Biklen, 1982; Pelto & Pelto, 1978; Spradley, 1980). While the number of contact hours and positions of "key informants" differed from site to site, literally hundreds of hours and dozens of interviews were collected at each site relevant to questions posed in this research.

The case of Braxton County, West Virginia may be illustrative. As of this writing, over a dozen formal and informal interviews were completed with the superintendent of schools, and at least one interview with five of nine building principals was accomplished. As well, almost twenty interviews with the high school counseling staff, four with the head of the vocational programs at the high school, six with high school teachers, three with middle school teachers, four with elementary teachers (including the president of the county teachers' education association), six with central office staff, and two with district school psychologists were completed (and most recorded). In addition, four community business leaders, several high school students, and one school board member supplied interview "data" upon which much of the Braxton County case study is based. The "bias" towards informants at, or centrally involved with, Braxton County High School represented in the preceeding list did not happen by chance: rather (as Chapter 2 will suggest), this school was and remained the center of community controversy throughout the duration of our fieldwork.

As is typically the case with ethnographic research, several well located interviewees in each school district (including Braxton County) proved to excellent mediators/interpreters of local dynamics as they related to interests of the evaluation staff. Naturally, therefore, these "key informants" were relied on more heavily for purposes of this study than others also interviewed. For example, in one county the superintendent of schools quickly recognized the multiple interests of our research focus and proved to be an excellent guide to questions we were interested in pursuing. In another county, a politically

powerful high school teacher became a very central figure in providing information and later critiquing our written interpretation of dynamics in her school
and community context; in a third setting, a central office figure who later
became principal of the high school was a key informant; and in yet another
system, it was an outspoken critic of the school superintendent who served on
the county school board who provided critical information relevant to the aims
of this research. Naturally, more than one key informant in any one county was
relied upon for this work; in point of fact, at least three and more typically four
or five individuals in each county were central figures in the ethnographic work
reported on here.

In addition to interviews, many other data sources were used in this study.
For example, evaluation staff were present for almost all AEL sponsored
meetings in the county (to be described shortly), as well as at numerous other
official and unofficial events. In Braxton County I attended eight school board
meetings, numerous in-service days, two high school "pep-rallies," several school
improvement meetings of teachers and administrators in one middle and one
elementary school; and I participated in three general discussions of school
improvement activities in the central office. Likewise, I traveled with the school
board and/or principals to two regional meetings concerned with statewide
school reform issues, ate lunch in three different school cafeterias throughout
the course of the study, participated in a rural school superintendents' meeting
in the state capital where strategies were being discussed relevant to impending
state school funding legislation, and was given numerous guided tours of current
and previous county school facilities by school and central office representatives.
Such field activities were repeated in likewise fashion (more or less) at each of the
other three sites involved in this study.

CAPTURING A HISTORICAL DIMENSION

Yet, even with all such above listed field experiences and data sources, it quickly
became apparent to me that understanding further the social and economic
context of communities under consideration called for better understanding of
historical and contemporary social and economic factors over and above those
which might be visible in the immediate school contexts and/or occasions where
school and community persons met to carry on the business of schooling and/or
the school based innovations we were charged with monitoring. And as this
research progressed, I became increasingly interested in how the history of rural
economic decline in each county studied came to have long term consequences
for contemporary school dynamics.

So, in addition to what some have described as the historically "flat" tradition
of ethnographic research (Puckett, 1988), I found myself drawn toward investigating previous economic and social forces in each county which typically

affected (in my judgement) current school practice there, including efforts sponsored by AEL. In order to accomplish this facet of our research, the research team involved in this study spent some considerable time collecting both secondary (i.e., scholarly focused) historical documents related to the educational and economic conditions in each of the communities involved, as well as locally produced histories of each county and its school system (where available). In addition, local, regional and statewide newspapers were subscribed to and monitored during the course of our fieldwork, and school archives (where available) were obtained, photocopied, and frequently quoted from when they were found of particular relevance.

A final set of descriptive and statistical data for each district was also made available by AEL as part of their evaluation process. In addition to collecting, tabulating, and providing to us various state and federal data sets on each included school system, AEL collected self-report data on each school system via its Profile of School Excellence. This instrument asked school personnel for information on a host of school–related matters (e.g., significant accomplishments, opinions about greatest local educational needs, etc.).

Inasmuch as Lab personnel were quite generous with responding to our informational requests and in supplying data to us over and above what was required even for their own use, I am extremely grateful. It is also quite likely that the quality of the initial report, as well as of this book, owes something of its substance to the efforts of AEL.

ACTIVITIES IN THE FIELD

One of the primary objectives of the AEL school/community project involved what Lab officials described as "giving ownership" of the model over to the schools and communities which became involved with the project. As will be discussed shortly, an important belief held by AEL staff members was that the particular significance of the school/community demonstration process lay in its functional utility, even after AEL had completed their local involvement. Therefore, Lab staff were particularly interested in explaining and carrying through the very labor–extensive activities involved with the two needs assessment protocols in the model, as well as with innovative activities called for in addressing specific school improvement activities chosen as a result of the processes. The hope being that community groups would "replicate" the model for other school and/or community improvement efforts.

Given this fact, a primary strategy chosen by the evaluation staff for entering each of the four field sites centered upon being present whenever AEL staff members were at one of the four school/county locations. In point of fact, we were fortunate enough to be present for a the vast majority of formal interactions between Lab staff members and members of the school systems involved, and literally hundreds of hours in the field were occupied with observations in such settings. As well, because we were typically viewed as independent of the Lab yet interested in the strengths *and* weaknesses of the process (a status we worked hard to achieve), we were privy to a host of interactions between school officials and community members over and above those organized by AEL staff.

Furthermore, over the course of our 28+ months in the field, a number of school/community themes/controversies potentially related to the long-term consequences of the demonstration projects became of particular interest. Therefore, in several cases the evaluation staff spent a great deal of time in classrooms and schools as interested observers of the day-to-day lives of teachers, students, and administrators in these settings.

In my experience, one of the difficulties university based researchers have faced when attempting to observe and collect data in metropolitan schools and/or those surrounding a university campus is that of entry into the schools of concern. To the contrary, we found this to not be the case at all in virtually any educational context we observed. In classrooms, on the playgrounds, at staff meetings, and so on, both school administrators and classroom teachers seemed quite willing to have outsiders come into their institutions and observe and discuss local issues and the dynamics of their settings.

Ostensibly, then, the lack of interested outsiders typically present in the districts we studied led local educational practitioners to be most appreciative of the aims and concerns of our research and quite willing to contribute to our efforts (with the possible exception of one district). Rather than the following report being potentially weakened by lack of cooperation on the part of the schools and communities studied, it seems far more likely that whatever weaknesses there may be in it would be attributable to the comparatively brief period of time we had to come to know these places, and to the somewhat constraining focus of the evaluation of AEL's school and community partnership model.

THE PERIOD OF STUDY

Field-based research related to the evaluation of the AEL project began in the first week of September 1987 and was to terminate at the conclusion of demonstration activities in May 1989. However, two of four AEL projects remain essentially unfinished even at the time of this writing (July 1990), which has given me the chance to semiofficially stay in touch with each district for over 1 year past the proposed project deadline. During most of this period, the research team involved in the project evaluation spent, on average, 2 to 3 days per week in at least one the four sites (excluding the summer of 1989).

As suggested earlier, many of the actual site visits included time in the schools and in community group meetings relevant to the school/community demonstrations, as well as observation and some participant observation in the many needs assessment processes conducted by AEL which more typically occurred at the central offices of participating districts. Put another way, while the AEL process frequently did not involve each of the schools in each of the four districts, the evaluation team spent some time in every one of the schools in every one of the districts.

A typical visit to the field would include 2 to 3 days visiting and interviewing in local schools and communities, including several hours of observing interactions between AEL staff and the various community and/or school-based groups participating in the needs assessment process. On the other hand, many site visits were "freestanding," that is, did not involve AEL staff at all, and frequently were nondirected (i.e., focused little upon matters specifically related to the AEL project). In point of fact, there were numerous visits made to one or more of the sites where AEL facilitators had not been present for several months.

Related to this last point, it was not unusual for members of the evaluation team to become "interpreters" of AEL interests and concerns in each of the four districts which were part of the demonstration projects. For example, in one of the districts, much of the communication between AEL and the district occurred over the phone between the steering committee leader and AEL staff. In this particular case, the evaluation team was the only visible evidence of the demonstration project/process to many participants during most of the important study and planning phases of the project (see description of the model, below). Predictably, perhaps, we were frequently called upon to clarify aspects of the project which would be deemed acceptable to AEL as we were routinely the only outsiders in attendance during the course of school and community deliberations on the AEL project.

JUSTIFYING THE NEED FOR THE RURAL/SMALL SCHOOL PARTNERSHIP MODEL

According to the AEL core proposal, there exist both school-based and community-based types of needs in small and rural communities of the Appalachian region. On the one hand, studies by the lab and by the National Rural Small Schools Task Force (1987) had determined various concerns of regional educators relevant to funding inequities, poor student performance, and poor school completion rates. As well, rural economic instability/decline in the Central Appalachian area had become a well-rehearsed theme throughout the area and had resulted, according to the AEL, in lack of local leadership related to community and economic development. According to AEL:

> The AEL region—specifically its Appalachian interior—is an area of marginal economic progress and development. Some analysts ascribe the lack of progress in

this Region to "cultures of poverty" that they claim characterize rural communities here. Others explain the Region's lack of progress as an outcome of absentee ownership of land, timber, and mineral resources – resources for which the Region is well known. Whatever the cause, one result is that in most rural communities of the Region, local leaders have been unable to supply the impetus necessary for social, educational, and economic improvement. The power vacuum created by local leaders who direct their efforts toward maintenance rather than moderniza-tion appears to be a critical factor in the Region's educational underachievement and lack of community economic development. However, the educational reform movement that has recently swept the United States seems to have combined with the worsening economic conditions found in the Region's communities to create new interest in school improvement and economic development. It appears that local leaders are now ready to turn their efforts from maintenance of the status quo toward the kind of vigorous social and economic development that the Region so desperately needs. (AEL, 1987, p. 8)

The guiding purpose of the AEL school/community partnership model, then, was to help rural and poor schools improve, while at the same time providing school and other local community leaders with a model for potentially helping to also enhance local community/economic development.

ORIGIN OF THE MODEL

As we discovered in our interviews, the rationale behind the AEL school/ community partnership model and how it was to operate was based upon the ideas of the Lab Executive Director and Associate Director. According to them, the two most important school and community needs for improvement lay in the quality and quantity of data upon which to base improvement, and upon the type of leadership available to affect such improvement. The conviction that rural school and community enhancement ought to be approached in such a manner ostensibly emerged from both their reading of the school effectiveness literature, as well as earlier Lab experience (and deemed successes) in helping to forge educational cooperatives in the Appalachian region.

The school effectiveness literature, as many readers of this document may be aware, places great emphasis upon several key variables that are argued to relate to successful schooling (instructional) outcomes. For example, holding high expectations for pupil performance is a virtual prerequisite for effective schools, according to those who use this language, as is developing and maintaining supportive classroom and school climates. So too, academics and "time on task" are emphasized in this literature as systematically related to improved academic achievement.

At least two other key ingredients of the effective schools literature are also noteworthy, given the objectives of the AEL school/community improvement model and our earlier evaluation of its success. One has to do with constant monitoring of student progress on academic objectives of the school. So too, the effective schools literature places great emphasis on school building leadership, noting particularly the significance of school principals in helping to set curricular goals; facilitating and supporting teacher planning related to the attainment of such goals; and helping to provide the mechanisms necessary for the monitoring of student progress. For overviews of effective schools research and its policy proposals/implications, see, for example, Brookover and Lezotte (1979) and Edmonds (1982).

School improvement, according to effective schools research, must be viewed as a continuous process and must be based upon ongoing, reliable, and valid data. From such data, school and school district improvement strategies involving local building staffs can be led and/or facilitated by building principals, who are the instructional leaders of each school.

The AEL model, then, proceeded under the assumption that some schools had the leadership in place to use extensive data for local school improvement, which the Lab could help to provide (see selection procedures discussion below). Furthermore, the Lab believed that helping to set up steering committees, where school and community representatives could be helped to interpret the data on their schools and come up with a research-based plan for school improvement, would not only provide a model for **school** improvement, but might also provide a model for how local school and community leaders might tackle other **community** improvement projects, like enhancing local economic development.

THE LITERATURE ON OUTSIDE INTERVENTION
IN LOCAL SCHOOL ENHANCEMENT

The literature to which AEL hoped the Evaluation Report would contribute, and from which funding for the OERI project was based, is/was that body of scholarship concerned with "school improvement." Historically, most introductions to innovation in public education began with some discourse on the lack of literature related to whatever changes were about to be attempted in the schools under consideration. In the past decade, however, such disclaimers have become rarer, as the evaluation of effective (and ineffective) educational innovation projects has become virtually a subspecialty within the educational research and development community (e.g., Harriott & Gross, 1979; Guba & Lincoln, 1981; Huberman & Miles, 1984).

Without going into great detail, most of this recent literature suggests that outside intervention into the dynamics of existing schools frequently meets with stiff opposition and/or indifference on the part of those charged with implementing school improvement. At best, externally sponsored reforms legislated and/or funded by federal and/or state governments may have some measurable effect on school dynamics and/or student outcome measures; as long as supplemental funds last; while teaching or accountability standards are tightly monitored by external agencies (which typically also control routine operating funds of the school); and/or if local school administrators accept and encourage teachers and school staff in their efforts to put significant school reforms in place (Huberman & Miles, 1984; Papagiannis, Klees, & Bickel, 1982).

At the other extreme, many designed school improvement strategies have been "blunted at the schoolhouse door" when innovations have been perceived as forced upon a school district, a school, or particular teachers and/or teaching staffs. The perceived ability of many schools to effectively minimize and/or moderate external demands for school "improvements" even led some organizational sociologists in the last decade to view public schools as "decoupled" organizations (e.g., Deal & Celotti, 1980), the implication being that external requirements for internal school reforms can routinely be minimized by the lack of strict bureaucratic control over public schools, which are not and have never been the types of strictly rational bureaucratic organizations in which unequivocal top-down mandates could be achieved (e.g., Firestone, 1980; Wolcott, 1977).

On the other hand, the study of successful and/or unsuccessful rural school innovation suffers from both a dearth of studies specifically targeted at rural school problems, and arguably from the fact that many who have written on rural school change concerns have spent comparatively little time considering the different context of rural schools in their social settings. In point of fact, very little is known about rural school issues and/or problems in general, let alone the dynamics of planned educational change in such contexts (one major exception perhaps being the previously cited work of Firestone).

As some have argued, this appears to be because most study and analysis of schooling dynamics in the U.S. has been targeted at urban schooling issues and urban based reforms (DeYoung, 1987; Sher, 1977). While some attention has been paid to rural education concerns in the Midwest, the Northeast, and the West, perhaps the major focus of interest in the southeastern U.S. has been with regard to racial desegregation concerns; however, even in these cases most available scholarship has dealt with integration issues in large metropolitan areas like Memphis, Birmingham, and Atlanta.

Yet the dynamics of rural communities in a general period of economic decline has garnered some attention in the Central Appalachian and southeastern U.S. over the years, and sometimes this attention has focused upon public schools. There are, for example, interesting accounts of rural schools and rural schooling issues in various historical accounts now available (e.g., Link, 1986; Puckett, 1988). So, too, limited scholarship on educational dynamics in Appalachia and Appalachian schools has become prevalent in the last decade, particularly work attempting to link perceived educational underperformance in the region to failed/inadequate/unequal economic development strategies (e.g., DeYoung, 1985; Duncan, 1986; Page & Clelland, 1978). And there have been interesting regional attempts to trace the impact of school reform efforts since national concern for the "rising tide of mediocrity" in our schools was first declared in 1983 (e.g., Brizius, Foster, & Patton, 1988; Fowler, 1988).

The bottom line of all this discussion, then, is that there is a limited literature on educational innovation which suggests that interested and concerned school leaders can sometimes help to facilitate school improvement efforts—if and when they have resources and ideas for so doing; and if and when potentially innovative efforts are not perceived as coercive. As well, while there is little on rural schooling reform problems and possibilities in the U.S., some of what there is on this topic is related to the general concerns of community and economic development/decline as such factors are related to the status of public education. Such factors and concerns were ones which gave AEL hope that rural school improvement was possible and documentable in their region, and that an ethnographic evaluation of their work would have utility.

AN INVITATION TO PARTICIPATE

Briefly put, the logic behind the AEL school/community partnership model was that inviting rural schools in economically disadvantaged communities to participate in a school based improvement process might facilitate two types of improvements. On the one hand, this process would help local schools and communities to identify mutually agreeable problem areas in the schools, and/or school district, that could be improved by the technical assistance of AEL. Furthermore, designers of the demonstrations also believed that a primary need in declining rural areas is a model for analyzing and addressing the community and economic factors contributing to regional decline. The AEL school/community partnership demonstrations (inasmuch as they were to include both school and community leaders) were hoped to be models that, when once observed and practiced for school based improvements, could be adapted at a later date for analyzing and addressing other compelling needs in these rural communities. While the evaluation staff remained somewhat skeptical that rural economic decline in the Southeast was/is primarily remediable by local community efforts, it appeared quite obvious to us that this focus comprised one central element in the hopes of AEL.

EXTENDING THE INVITATION

Once AEL received OERI approval for initiating the proposed school/ community partnerships, there were several steps required before invitations could be extended. One involved narrowing the number of school districts eligible for consideration. As a number of authors have suggested, definitions of rurality within the rural education literature are myriad (Dunne & Carlsen, 1981; Helge, 1985). For example, many school districts in the U.S. contain both rural and metropolitan areas. Some rural areas are sparsely populated yet actually contiguous to very large municipalities. So too, because "smallness" was of concern to OERI and the Lab, selecting small rural districts for demonstrations became a priority. Naturally, where a cutoff point should be established with regard to such a criterion becomes (and became) a matter of judgement. Some of the rural school districts in AEL's region cover large geographic areas, contain dozens of schools, and enroll thousands of students. On the other hand, there are comparatively small districts in AEL's region which are very rural and at the same time very sparsely populated (Meehan, 1987).

Deciding upon some criteria for poverty is also frequently a difficult process. Poverty levels in the AEL region vary from areas with very little poverty to areas with 70%–80% of households below federal poverty guidelines. And even within some relatively wealthy counties in the region, there are typically pockets of poverty which demand special school attention.

Given these several considerations, the first task pursued by AEL was a compiling of school district data for the four states to be part of the demonstration projects. In the southeastern U.S., the majority of school districts are organized on a county basis, although the governance of such districts may or may not be independent of other county offices (this varies by state and will be discussed shortly). In addition, several types of independent/city/special districts exist in Kentucky, Tennessee, and Virginia, although these are typically not rural and differ from state to state in their organizational form.

Given definitional problems (what is a rural district, what is a poor district, etc.), and given the different organizational types of districts in the region, one of the most important early tasks for the Lab was establishing guidelines for districts which might qualify for project participation on the basis of rurality, smallness, and poverty. In the end, several such guidelines were established for identifying districts which would become statistically eligible to participate in the AEL partnerships. With regard to rurality, AEL decided that eligible districts would have to come from those that, according to U.S. census data were at least 75% rural and not immediately contiguous to any metropolitan area. With regard to poverty, the Lab proposed to target its model at school districts in which greater than 25% of district households were below the federal poverty level. And finally, with regard to district size, AEL determined an adequate school enrollment figure of fewer than 3,000 students should be used for participating county districts, and fewer than 1,500 students for independent ones. Ostensibly, the preceding figures were chosen (like the others) because this would yield a manageable pool of rural, small, and poor schools from which to choose one eligible district in each of the four states. In point of fact, using such calculations, 41 (of 178) Kentucky districts, 16 (of 120) Tennessee districts, 3 (of 130) Virginia districts, and 8 (of 55) West Virginia districts became technically eligible for the AEL partnership demonstrations. Yet, as our later discussions will suggest, modification in the eligibility criteria were adopted in two of the states under review; modifications in one state were completed to increase the number of potential participants; and in the other case to limit potential districts for selection.

USING STATE ADVISORY COMMITTEES TO HELP
SELECT TARGET SCHOOL DISTRICTS

Choosing from among the many eligible districts mentioned above, however, was not performed solely by Lab staff. In order to help select from among them, the Lab formed and utilized advisory groups in each state: and members of these advisory groups came from among what we judged were an impressive array of local and state education officials with whom the Lab had apparently worked for a number of years. The rationale for forming and using state advisory groups (with Lab consultation) for the RSS project was outlined in AEL's initial technical proposal (1987):

> The relationship that AEL has developed with the influential persons who currently lead educational reform and community development in the Region is an important asset that the Lab brings to this work. We have already called upon these resource people in planning our work, and we propose to depend heavily upon them for several dimensions of the work proposed. One of the first steps to be implemented . . . will (be) the creation in each state of a state advisory group (state AG), which will meet once a year. . . . The state AGs will be centrally involved . . . (in) selecting demonstration sites where School-Community Partnerships will be implemented.

> Each of the state AGs will be made up of a key AEL Board member, a state education (SEA) representative, a representative of the governor's staff who is responsible for rural community economic development (or equivalent), and three to five additional state leaders selected for their knowledge of the state's rural communities and schools. We expect that some of each state's most influential leaders in business, agriculture, public television, and special resources such as the Tennessee Valley Authority, the Southern Regional Education Board, and similar enterprises will be selected to complete the membership of each state AG. (pp. 30-31)

> each state's RSS program advisory group will be involved in identifying the rural, small school site where the School-Community Partnership will be implemented. . . . Advisory group members will be asked to assist staff in applying two additional

(i.e., non- statistical) criteria to the process of selecting demonstration sites. The first criterion will be that of accessibility. This criterion will also make the demonstration sites more accessible to others who wish to observe firsthand what has occurred there. The second criterion . . . (is) the interest and willingness of school and community leaders to work with the RSS program staff in implementing the School–Community Partnership Model. (p. 43)

THE ADVISORY GROUPS IN ACTION

Most of the remainder of this book will focus upon the contexts in which the AEL projects took place, and to a lesser degree upon the actual outcomes of the School–Community Partnerships demonstrations. I have spent considerable time to this point outlining the project rationale and procedures, because some readers may be particularly interested in its underpinnings and dynamics. More importantly to the aims of this document, however, I wanted to suggest the complexity of the school improvement "plot" and our (my) involvement in it for methodological reasons. As well, I wanted to suggest the large scope of this project, for, in many ways, my entire academic focus during 1988 and 1989 dwelled on this research and in trying to come to grips with the multiple interests and the multiple perspectives related to "understanding" the implications of community economic decline at the same time that continuous rounds of school reform/"improvement" were occurring.

However, before plunging into actual events in each of the four chosen school systems and counties surrounding them, a few more particulars on selection procedures employed by state advisory groups is called for, as are several comments on the internal transformation of AEL in its rural education directions.

While there were some minor exceptions, in general the processes of site selection for each of the four school districts statistically eligible occurred as stated in the earlier description. In most cases, a full day meeting was held in a central location of each state for the respective advisory groups to aid RSS staff in district selection (with evaluation team representation in three of the four meetings). The agenda for each of these meetings involved a thorough introduction to the School–Community Partnership model, and to the rationale developed by the Lab for site selection. The West Virginia site was chosen first because of its proximity to AEL. Subsequently, a site in Kentucky was chosen. And, as promised in the technical proposal, these two locations became the targets for the first of the 2-year projects under discussion. In the second year of the project, advisory groups were formed and helped the Lab choose districts in Tennessee and Virginia.

Following the outline of statistical protocols for site selection in each of the state advisory group meetings, advisory group members were typically asked to help narrow the search for a target district with reference to three (as opposed to two) additional criteria. Geographic location was indeed of concern to RSS staff present at these meetings, yet not exactly as outlined in the technical proposal. In the Kentucky case, for example, certain technically eligible districts were excluded from consideration because they belonged to a consortium of school districts where significant school improvements were (theoretically) already occurring. Unfortunately, these school districts were arguably among the neediest in the state, but because they fell within the fifth U.S. congressional district, and belonged to *Forward in the Fifth*, they were "redlined" by RSS staff early in the site selection process. AEL believed it had to show some impact from its model, and interfering projects, it believed, would weaken any claim AEL might have made to have improved local school functioning.

Other slight deviations from the AEL technical proposal occurred in later project stages. For example, accessability to each demonstration site was an early concern which became less so by the project's second year. Instead, population complexity became of later interest, as racial composition of target districts in Tennessee and Virginia emerged as important to RSS staff. The first two demonstration sites selected were primarily White, and attempting to locate and invite a district with a sizeable Black and/or Native American population became of interest to RSS staff, as expressed to Tennessee and Virginia advisory groups.

Furthermore, by the second year of the project, RSS staff had decided that one or more relatively isolated school districts ought to become part of the demonstrations. This appears to have been an interest with both the West Virginia and Kentucky county districts chosen for participation, because they were transected by relatively new interstate highways and were thus judged advantaged (with regard to future economic development possibilities) compared to other more remote counties/ communities.

Another factor which became quite central in much of the RSS and state advisory group deliberations focused on the quality and stability of leadership in each of the districts that were eventually invited to participate, a factor earlier mentioned. Though not stated in the technical proposal, RSS staff sought to locate in each state a school district with both a reputation for educational excellence and/or recent school improvement, **and** one in which the district superintendent was a prominent, stable, and respected member of the local community. In the first place, such leadership would be important for implementing a school improvement plan which would take some time even to define. Furthermore, it was hypothesized that only a school leader well respected in the larger community could facilitate long-term community improvement efforts which lay officially outside of the jurisdiction of the school system.

In addition to the several preceding discrepancies between what typically transpired at advisory group meetings and what was proposed to occur, the actual composition of advisory groups in each of the states was not exactly as billed: knowledge about actual school and community issues in eligible counties was visibly limited in several advisory group proceedings; and on more than one occasion, not all invited participants attended the advisory group selection meetings. Some of these technical difficulties are discussed later in this analysis, and all were discussed at some length in the OERI final report.

AEL'S RURAL, SMALL SCHOOL STAFF

The "story" of the first four demonstrations completed by AEL as part of their Rural and Small Schools initiative also importantly involved some discussion of a growing national interest in rural education and the internal transformation of AEL as it has become involved in this larger "movement" in the late 1980s. To put it most succinctly, the success AEL had in 1987 through 1989 in obtaining further funding for its rural education initiatives had a dramatic impact on the organization of its rural education staff. Perhaps describable in Spring 1986 as a bootstrap operation within the Lab, by Spring 1989 the Lab's rural component had become one of the major AEL programs, both in terms of numbers of projects undertaken and in terms of Lab staff assigned to one or more rural education activities.

While AEL has a long tradition of working with rural and poor school districts in its region, a focus on rurality per se, coupled with special possibilities (and funding) for such efforts, was a new field for them in 1986. Not surprisingly, the opportunity for working with four rural and poor school districts, and the funding which made this possible enabled the Lab to reassign and reallocate several staff positions already within the Lab.

In essence, RSS program funding created a new internal division and director of this division, who was reassigned from other duties in the Lab. Additionally, a second Lab member also already "on board" was also assigned to the Rural and Small Schools Program (of which the School–Community Partnership Demonstrations was a major feature). All of this was quite fortunate for AEL, given congressionally initiated budgetary cutbacks for regular OERI funding to all of the Labs. On the other hand, funding of the rural initiative may have brought about an even better utilization of some talents within the Lab, as each of the staff members assigned primary duties on the RSS projects had extensive interest and expertise in rural schooling issues. Rather than having to find the right persons to staff the School–Community Partnerships on short notice, the Lab had on hand what evaluation staff believed were knowledgeable and committed individuals to start the project(s) once approved.

However, the continued success of AEL in obtaining funding for its work in rural education may have had a few (if predictable) negative consequences for aspects of the demonstrations under discussion. As mentioned, the first year of the demonstrations involved extensive needs assessment and continuous contact with several school and community groups in the first two sites of the project (West Virginia and Kentucky). In essence, these assessments and contacts between the Lab and the first two districts occurred between the months of September and May 1987. During Spring and Summer 1987, however, AEL was successful in obtaining a second round of funding for the RSS Program **and** was awarded the federal contract to become the national ERIC Center for Rural and Small Schools.

Predictably, the Rural and Small Schools Program suddenly had become a "hot spot" in the Lab, and the interest and excitement generated by the program seemed to have generated as well some internal staffing issues and dilemmas. Since many (if not most) of staff members in the Lab have various amounts of their time allocated to two or more of the (seven) different Lab programs, various staff members volunteered to be reassigned to the RSS program and/or the ERIC system. As well, for the first time in several years, the Lab actually had several new positions to fill. For example, while AEL employed 25 staff members in 1986, by 1989 the Lab had grown to 35 employees—many of whom went to work on rural-schools-related projects. Reassignment of existing staff, in other words, could not accomplish all of the many new duties and tasks promised by AEL in its successfully obtained new rural programs.

Furthermore, as the Lab had rapidly become part of a newly emerging rural education "network," trips to national conferences and to Washington, D.C., increasingly began to fill up the time of the RSS director. Instead of providing workshops on computer applications for the schools (a major function of the RSS director's role before the rural initiative was funded), or being directly involved in necessary fieldwork in two rural and poor school districts as part of the first year funding for the RSS projects, AEL's Rural Small Schools Director found himself by 1988 an active participant in national discourse on rural education as well as a major actor in the transfer of an ERIC Clearinghouse to a new location and with a new staff.

Additionally, the research and development specialist initially assigned to the RSS project began to find the strain of travel and multiple rural assignments within the Lab somewhat more than he wanted to deal with. And since some of the ERIC duties (e.g., in technical writing and editing) were also of much interest to him, he was given the opportunity of playing perhaps the major role of getting the ERIC Clearinghouse on Rural and Small Schools in Operation.

All of which is therefore to say that the two principal actors from AEL in the school partnerships began to play, by the second year of the project, a much lesser role than they had in the first year. And instead, a variety of other R&D specialists (with various amounts of interest and expertise in rural education) began to take on activities of the RSS project by Summer 1988.

For example, during the first 10 months of the School–Community demonstrations, the only two actors "on the scene" in either of the first two districts were the RSS director and the R&D specialist just mentioned. And even they (on paper) were only assigned a part-time commitment to the demonstration projects. Supporting their part-time commitment to the RSS project were a half-time secretary and the limited services of the Lab's evaluation specialist back in Charleston. However, by the second year of this project, neither of the two principals were primarily involved in either of the school improvement dynamics in the first two districts, or in many of the events in the two districts which began the process during the second year. By 1989, nine (rather than four) AEL staff members had assignments in the RSS programs (including the ERIC Clearinghouse); the RSS project had moved from two separate offices in the Atlas Building of downtown Charleston to two large suites on one of the upper floors of the same building; and the principle RSS operators in the School–Community Partnership demonstrations were both newcomers to classroom and school life in the rural Southeast (although not new to issues in rural America per se).

OPERATIONALIZING THE SCHOOL/COMMUNITY PARTNERSHIPS

The School–Community Partnership demonstrations primarily involved two needs assessment processes coupled with a formalized process for "steering" each of the four target school districts toward specific school improvement strategies related to findings of the needs assessments. The role of the Lab in this process was (a) to identify and invite districts to participate, (b) to administer and organize the two needs assessments, (c) to perform data analysis and synthesis of needs assessments, (d) to help organize and instruct a standing ("steering") committee with regard to possible innovation strategies for each district, and (e) to provide support services for implementing the innovation(s) chosen.

Of the five general tasks described above, some attention has already been given to the first, and a full elaboration of the others is readily available in a variety of AEL documents. However, at this point, some overview of the demonstration process requires attention.

As the heading of this section suggests, a needs assessment based upon characteristics identified by the effective schools literature was used by the RSS staff in each of the districts that volunteered to participate in project demonstrations. Entitled the *Profile of School Excellence* (Pro-S/E), this instrument is copyrighted by the Deputy Executive Director of AEL (among others) and typically costs interested school districts between $4,000 and $8,000 to be administered and scored (depending on the number of schools/students involved). As part of the RSS project, however, participating school districts paid no fee for the assessment of their schools using this instrument.

The Pro-S/E was administered to all central office staff in each of the four districts under consideration; to approximately half of all school teachers (except in the smallest schools where all or most teachers completed the instrument); and to approximately 10% of all students within each district school. Questions asked and scores obtained on the Pro-S/E fall into 11 categories, as guided by the effective schools literature (according to it's authors). These subscales are entitled: needs basis, objectives, expectations, roles and responsibilities, conditions and resources, instructional time and task orientation, use of assessment, rewards and reinforcement, code of behavior, school climate, and parental support and involvement.

According to explanations supplied to school personnel, school **excellence**, rather than effectiveness, was the key word to use when thinking about the meaning of the assessment protocols. That is, low scores on effectiveness can have a more negative connotation than low scores on excellence, and may cause school leaders to become defensive rather than improvement oriented as a result of a Pro-S/E assessment.

According to Pro-S/E instructions, excellent schools develop a system to determine students' instructional needs; have formal objectives or goals for student learning, which are communicated to them; convey high expectations to students that they can achieve such objectives; have clearly demarcated roles and responsibilities for students, teachers, and staff; have adequate and well-organized resources in classrooms and schools; make efficient use of school time for instruction and learning tasks; make effective use of assessment protocols in assessing student academic performance; make systematic use of rewards and reinforcements for rewarding such performance; develop fair codes of behavior for managing student interaction in classrooms and schools; have supportive and nurturing school climates; and have active parent involvement and support of students' the parents.

For each of the demonstration sites in the School–Community Partnerships, then, a Profile of School Excellence was developed using school personnel themselves as reporters on specific questions related to the above dimensions. For each of the four school districts that participated in the RSS demonstrations, a final report was written by the Lab, which assessed both the strengths and weaknesses of each school in the district and the district as a whole. In addition, based upon the same information, assessments of district and school level (elementary, middle, and/or high school) needs were reported. For example, in most of the schools assessed in the RSS demonstrations, strengths of the schools far outweighed their weaknesses. Given that each of the school districts that participated had been identified as ones strong on academics and innovation, this was perhaps no surprise. On the other hand, in each of the four districts "moderate" needs in one or more of the 11 areas just mentioned were identified by the Pro-S/E. For example, at the high school level several districts reported low parental support and involvement, and in two cases such needs eventually came to be addressed by the steering committee in terms of a formal school improvement project.

THE COMMUNITY NEEDS ASSESSMENT

In addition to the school-based and highly focused Pro-S/E, a community needs assessment was administered in each of the four school districts that served as demonstration sites for AEL. This needs assessment process was initially entitled the *DAP process* (for descriptive, appraisive, prescriptive) but, by the third demonstration, was no longer referred to as such. And in fact by late in the second year of the RSS project, the community needs assessment process was referred to as "the community needs-sensing study" in official Lab descriptions.

In many respects, it was the community needs assessment process whereby significant community members outside of the school were to initially become partners in school and community development and improvement. Not only were community members theoretically removed from influencing school-based decisions asked to talk about and identify problems in the schools from their perspectives, but many members of the steering committee (which would weigh the results of both the school and community needs assessments) would eventually be drawn from the community group assembled for this phase of the demonstrations.

The DAP process (as it was initially termed) is a needs assessment procedure which AEL claims to have used numerous times since the mid 1970s. In the four demonstrations organized by the Lab for the RSS demonstrations, approximately 30 members of the communities contiguous with each of the four school districts were invited by each school superintendent to participate in a half-day session (typically an evening session) for the needs assessment process.

In each of the demonstration sites, the composition of these groups varied substantially. For example, in one site retired schoolteachers, middle management officials, and several white-collar employees of small businesses were invited by the superintendent to participate. Ostensibly, this was because each district school had a school–business partnership, and each of these businesses was asked to send a representative (who typically was an employee of the organization, rather than a senior official). In another site, even fewer significant political and/or business leaders took part in the community needs assessment process. In this setting, a variety of retired school personnel, housewives, and recent newcomers to the area comprised most of the assembled group. Significantly, few key players in either county's "power structure" were part of either of these processes, for reasons which may become clearer later.

On the other hand, in two other community needs assessment meetings the ranks of those in attendance was a virtual who's who of the county political and economic leadership. Attending these sessions were officers of both counties' banks, a county judge executive, ministers, major private employers, and other prominent citizens already identified with school reform efforts of years immediately preceding the RSS demonstrations. Significantly, in each of these two sites a school board member was also in attendance at all needs assessment activities. Furthermore, most members of both these groups appeared quite familiar with one another, and in one setting a participant specifically alluded to the fact that many members present "were always called upon" by the superintendent for school improvement and sponsorship activities.

Perhaps based upon the dissimilarities in the composition of these four groups, it was decided by RSS staff that more pointed guidance to the school superintendents ought to be given in future demonstrations. And by the second year of the RSS project, more specific guidelines for selection of community needs assessment members became part of the information packet distributed to those interested in replicating the process.

Parenthetically, one similarity observed in all four sites was that a significant percentage of community needs assessment participants were also related (as husbands or wives) to school employees (many of whom had already participated in the Pro-S/E assessment). This appeared to be the case, not necessarily by design, but rather because the school districts in each of the four sites in question were the largest employers in each county and were thus situated in most households where an interest in school improvement could be relied on by each county superintendent.

As mentioned previously, the half-day session given to the community needs assessment initially involved a highly structured **process** for helping participants understand what a needs statement was and how to write such a statement. However, Contrary to the Pro-S/E, no prespecified **focal areas** of school weaknesses and/or need were built into the process. Rather, step-by-step protocols were handed out by RSS staff, and approximately 2 hours were spent given and illustrating what a suitable needs statement would look like, once generated by participants themselves.

Following these individual and group exercises, the approximately 30 members of each group broke into smaller groups of from five to six members for the generation of needs statements. This process involved soliciting from each member of the group as many needs statements as they volunteered, and all such statements were recorded by a group secretary. Not surprisingly, the actual number of such statements generated by different groups at different times and at different sites varied greatly. As well, it became quite evident in each of these processes that some invited participants thought the local schools needed many improvements, while others had fewer preconceived notions of what sorts of problems the local schools had (if any).

After the first attempt at generating need statements within the groups, a final edited and precise list from each group was called for by RSS staff. Importantly, participants were urged to generate as many needs statements as possible, subject only to their technical suitability as needs statements (as opposed, for example, to prescriptive statements). Following the final compilation by each group secretary, all lists were handed over to RSS staff, who then proceeded to enumerate and organize them while community members were hosted to a sit-down dinner, typically in another location.

Upon the completion of dinner, community group members were returned to the site of the needs statement generation process for a rating session. In this briefer encounter, all needs statements generated by each subgroup were presented via an overhead computer display for each participant to rate. At this point, RSS staff asked all participants to assign a grade/score to each need statement, where an "A" was worth five points, a "B" four points, etc. The lowest possible scored given could be an "E", worth one point. This activity concluded the community needs assessment process, as RSS staff then collected all individual rating sheets for future scoring procedures.

ISSUING TWO SUMMARY REPORTS

One of the most polished aspects of the RSS demonstrations was the impressive quality of all handouts and reports distributed by the Lab in each site. The centerpieces of these reports were undoubtedly the two issued as results of the school based and community based needs assessments. The Pro-S/E data collection and reduction efforts by the Lab were reported back to the school district and the steering committee in such a report. Furthermore, item responses for each school were tabulated by the Lab for more extensive utilization by each superintendent (assuming some interest on their part).

Results of the community needs assessment were also fed back to relevant groups via a document entitled by the Lab: *Taking the Pulse: A Community Conference to Gather Information About School Needs in (District Name, State)*. In order to complete the community needs assessment process, RSS staff also returned to Charleston with the data collected at each of the four demonstration sites. However, unlike the Pro S/E scoring procedure, RSS staff had more difficult data reduction problems with needs statements and their ratings than was the case with the Pro-S/E. Since the object of the demonstrations was to have school district steering committees select from a short list of potential school improvement projects, reducing the multiple needs articulated at each site (for example, 68 such statements were generated and rated in the Virginia district) into a smaller set for consideration was a major project.

Several strategies were employed by the Lab in suggesting each community's expressed needs. One was to report means and standard deviations of all generated needs statements. However, as even this procedure typically yielded dozens of highly ranked needs, a factor analysis procedure was used to sort similar needs into categories. Subsequently, these factors were also assigned some numerical equivalent. And each of these strategies for reducing need statements to some comprehensible picture was presented and explained in the *Taking the Pulse* document.

FUNCTIONS OF THE STEERING COMMITTEES

All of the above notwithstanding, RSS personnel took great effort to suggest that the Lab had not "determined" the "true" school-based or community-based needs of each of the demonstration projects. Rather, RSS staff compiled for each school district two needs assessment reports for use by a steering committee in each site. These steering committees were to be comprised of approximately 10 school-based personnel (from local schools and/or the central office), and approximately 10 community members. Again, invitations to participate on this committee were issued by each school superintendent, and while technically its members did not have to come from either of the two groups who participated in either the school-based or community-based needs assessments, in each of the four sites the vast majority of steering committee members had so participated.

According to AEL's technical proposal, each school–community steering committee was to be the heart of the demonstration project. These were the committees that reviewed both needs assessments previously compiled; that were to seek out from school leaders information which might verify or disconfirm generated needs (in other words, needs for which improvement strategies may have just recently been put into place already); that were to discuss and choose potential school improvement projects for implementation; that were to review materials provided by the lab on the best possible improvement strategy to implement; and that were to monitor and help facilitate chosen school improvement plans.

In order to accomplish these many objectives, the steering committees in each demonstration site were carefully instructed by RSS staff in their multiple duties. As well, in each case careful instruction was given to the steering committees to select a school improvement plan which could be attained and assessed within the time frame of the funding period. Furthermore, in each site (and as elaborated upon at length in both the technical proposal for the school–community partnerships and in the handouts given to each steering committee), the several functions assigned to the steering committee were primarily carried out by particular subcommittees rather than by the any of the entire committees. In none of the four cases did the decisions of any subcommittees in the demonstration projects have their recommendations overruled in larger group discussions.

Of the multiple duties assigned to steering committees in each site, a careful division of labor was completed. For example, from each steering committee **study groups** were formed (each comprised of from eight to ten members) to review and decide which of the needs outlined in the two reports might be best addressed in a school improvement project. And considering that needs even within the same report could be quite divergent, arriving at a consensus on which two or three needs were both the greatest and best addressable from two reports typically consumed a great deal of time and effort.

Following selection of two or three (and sometimes four) most important needs by each study group, the study group reported back to the larger committees upon their deliberations. In actuality, the study groups typically contained the most active participants in the steering committees, and elected chairs of the steering committee were also primary actors in each study group. Therefore, by the time the steering committees were typically reconvened for approval of a school improvement strategy, members of the study group were the majority of those in attendance anyway. In point of fact, in other words, in most of the demonstration sites there were fewer than a dozen active participants in later stages of the process, even though twice that many were technically involved. Not surprisingly, therefore, recommendations of each study group were usually accepted without much debate, and later meetings of the steering committees were proforma affairs.

Following the selection of a need to be addressed by study groups and their steering committees, **planning groups** were established for selecting a school improvement strategy to address such needs. Again, RSS staff played a prominent role in defining the missions of the planning groups and in providing materials for consideration by such groups.

The mission of the planning group was to consider and formulate a school improvement strategy which would address the need agreed upon by the larger steering committee as of most significance for the school district. Furthermore, and again as emphasized by RSS staff, whatever school improvement strategies were selected, both had to be manageable within the timeframe of the demonstrations, and needed to be evaluated for OERI accountability purposes.

Once the steering committee had targeted a need and formed a planning committee, RSS staff began to search the published R&D literature for products/ practices/strategies used in other places which might have relevance for each demonstration site. Even before the first meeting of each planning group (in two sites at least), RSS staff had forwarded to each member of these groups a collection of articles and/or product reviews believed of relevance.

THE LOCAL RESOURCE CENTER

According to the AEL technical report, a local resource center was to be established within each district to house both of the needs assessment studies, together with an account of the deliberations, proposals, and plans of the study group, the planning group, and the steering committee. However, unlike other aspects of the RSS demonstrations, these "centers" appear not to have been developed as originally intended.

This is *not* to suggest that important R&D based information was not provided to each site during study and planning group processes. In fact, it might be said that in all four sites more information was supplied than could have been digested by steering committee subgroups in the time frame required for them to finish their allotted tasks. All in all, we judged the data compilation and reduction methods of the Lab rather extensive and complete. And as will be presented shortly, much of this data corroborated qualitatively oriented analyses completed by evaluation staff.

SUMMARY

The remainder of this book is divided into five chapters. Four of these are comprised of essentially separate case studies of each demonstration site included in the RSS program. As stated before, our close working relationship with AEL during the 2½ years of this project saw important changes in "the model" over this time frame; some of which are mentioned in the final chapter of this monograph.

More important for this document, however, are the case studies themselves, for in many ways they each locate the immediate school improvement projects undertaken within specific historical, social, and economic contexts. Not surprisingly, from my perspective, the scope and extensiveness of most local economic and social issues proved too complex and deep seated for remediation by the school/community demonstration projects/models attempted. This being one of my overall "conclusions," I believe the case studies presented may help those interested in better understanding rural schools and their settings. And such a discussion, also from my perspective, would be far more helpful (and academically interesting) than would be a discussion of instructional benefits (or lack of same) that might be attributed to the RSS project proper. For, as stated earlier, there appears precious little on rural schools and/or rural school life available in the scholarly literature on rural education.

Following the four case studies, I move to some more explicit discussion of the common (and unique) economic and social factors/issues which continue to exist in each of the four counties earlier profiled. In this final chapter, I also bring up to date each county "story" as of July 1990 and discuss briefly the strengths and weaknesses of the RSS school/community demonstration model as we found them for OERI.

With the possible exception of the knowledge/deliberations of advisory groups just discussed, most of the conceptualization and proceedings of the RSS demonstration model appeared to evaluation staff as well thought out, documented, and put into practice. We were particularly impressed with the great range of coverage and exposition of the school improvement literature as it was potentially related to demonstration projects attempted.

On the other hand, while most of the technical proposal and actual field-based efforts of RSS staff appeared highly polished and well-informed, evaluation staff were somewhat surprised to find comparatively little literature and/or staff expertise in the domain of community and/or economic development, as such themes were argued relevant to "second order" hopes of AEL. As the technical proposal suggested, one hypothesized outcome of the Lab's efforts in each of their chosen sites would be a new problem-solving strategy for use by local communities to upgrade their efforts at community and/or economic improvement. In point of fact, the dearth of literature on school and community relations of any type in the professional education literature, as represented even by AEL's literature review, gave rise to the particular ambition of this book.

In response to an interview question posed to one Lab informant, "our leader" and his early rural school innovation work was the practical basis for much of the model as constructed. However, one of the findings of evaluation staff was that there does indeed exist a rather complex yet extensive literature on rural regional development strategies/issues which has developed over the past several decades (see, for example, analysis/discussion/critique of many such projects in Cobb, 1982; Lewis, Johnson, & Askins, 1978; Plunkett & Bowman, 1973; or Whisnant, 1980). Yet examples from such extensive literature were little mentioned in any Lab documents. Furthermore, RSS staff who later visited and worked in the four demonstration sites appeared to spend relatively little time investigating earlier local efforts in these areas.

Interestingly, several community economic development projects involving "leadership training" were discovered in the very counties chosen by AEL for demonstration sites – which is not to suggest that the hopes of AEL were necessarily misguided related to the possible utility of the school/community partnership for addressing nonschool community issues, but rather that little information/literature on such possibilities was demonstrated by RSS staff or available in the educational R&D literature.

All of this being said, and knowing that most of the themes raised to this point will be readdressed in some fashion in the pages ahead, we turn now to the first of our case studies.

REFERENCES

AEL. (1987). *Technical proposal for the AEL Rural, Small Schools Program.* Charleston, WV: Appalachia Educational Laboratory.

Bogdan, R., & Biklen, S. (1982). *Qualitative research for education.* Boston: Allyn and Bacon.

Bredo, E., & Feinberg, W. (1982). *Knowledge and values in social and educational research.* Philadelphia: Temple University Press.

Brizius, J., Foster, S., & Patton, H. (1988). *Education reform in rural appalachia.* Washington, DC: State Research Associates publication, sponsored by the Appalachian Regional Commission.

Brookover, W. B., & Lezotte, L. W. (1979). *Changes in school characteristics coincident with changes in student achievement.* East Lansing, MI: Michigan State University, College of Urban Development.

Cobb, J. (1982). *The selling of the South: The Southern crusade for industrial development, 1936-1980.* Baton Rouge, LA: Louisiana State University Press.

Deal, T., & Celoti, L. (1980). How much influence do (and can) administrators have on classrooms? *Phi Delta Kappan, 61,* 471-473.

DeYoung, A. (1987). The status of American rural education research: An integrated review and commentary. *Review of Educational Research, 57*(2), 123-148.

DeYoung, A. J. (1985). Economic development and educational status in Appalachian Kentucky. *Comparative Educational Review, 29*(1), 47-67.

DeYoung, A. J. (1983). The status of formal education in Central Appalachia. *Appalachian Journal, 10*(4), 321-334.

Dorr-Bremme, D. W. (1985). Ethnographic evaluation: A theory and method. *Educational Evaluation and Policy Analysis, 7*(1), 65-83.

Duncan, C. (1986). Myths and realities of Appalachian poverty: Public policy for good people surrounded by a bad economy and bad politics. In R. Eller (Ed.), *The land and economy of appalachia: Proceedings from the 1986 Conference on Appalachia.* Lexington, KY: The Appalachian Center.

Dunne, F., & Carlsen, W. (1981). *Small rural schools in the United States: A statistical profile.* Washington, DC: National Rural Center.

Edmonds, R. R. (1982). Programs of school improvement: An overview. *Educational Leadership, 40*(3), 4-11.

Erikson, F. (1977). Some approaches to inquiry in school-community ethnography. *Anthropology and Education Quarterly, 8*(2), 58-69.

Fetterman, D. (1984). *Ethnography in educational evaluation.* Beverly Hills, CA: Sage Publications.

Firestone, W. A. (1980). *Great expectations for small schools: The limitations of federal projects.* New York: Praeger.

Fowler, F. (1988). The politics of school reform in Tennessee: A view from the classroom. In W. Boyd & C. Kercher (Eds.), *The politics of excellence and choice in education* (pp. 183-197).

Guba, E.G., & Lincoln, Y.S. (1981). *Effective evaluation: Improving the usefulness of evaluation results through responsive and naturalistic approaches.* San Francisco: Jossey-Bass.

Harriot, R., & Gross, N. (1979). *The dynamics of planned educational change.* Berkeley, CA: McCutchan.

Helge, D. (1985). *Establishing a national rural education research agenda.* Bellingham, WV: National Rural Development Institute.

Hobbs, D. (1988). *Community economic development innovation: The key to rural school improvement and rural revitalization.* Aurora, IL.: Mid-Continent Regional Educational Laboratory.

Howe, K. R. (1985). Two dogmas of educational research. *Educational Researcher, 14*(8), 10-18.

Huberman, A. M., & Miles, M. B. (1984). *Innovation up close: How school improvement works.* New York: Plenum Press.

Lewis, H., Johnson, L., & Askins, D. (1978). *Colonialism in modern America: The Appalachian case.* Boone, NC: Appalachian Consortium Press.

Link, W. (1986). A hard time and a lonely place: Schooling, society and reform in rural Virginia, 1870–1920. Chapel Hill, NC: University of North Carolina Press.

Lortie, D. (1975). The balance of control and autonomy in elementary school teaching. In A. Etzioni (Ed.), The semi-professions and their organization. New York: Free Press.

Meehan, M. (1987). A demographic study of rural, small school districts in four Appalachian states, (Occasional Paper 025). Charleston, WV: Appalachia Educational Laboratory.

National Rural, Small Schools Task Force. (1987). Building on excellence. Washington, DC: Council for Educational Development and Research.

Page, A., & Clelland, D. (1978). The Kanawha County textbook controversy: A study in the politics of lifestyle concern. Social Forces, 57(1), 265-281.

Papagiannis, G., Klees, S., & Bickel, R. (1982). Toward a political economy of educational innovation. Review of Educational Research, 52(2), 245-290.

Pelto, P., & Pelto, G. (1978). Anthropological research: The structure of inquiry. Cambridge, UK: Cambridge University Press.

Peshkin, A. (1988). In search of subjectivity—one's own. Educational Researcher, 17(7), 17-22.

Plunkett, H.D., & Bowman, M.J. (1973). Elites and change in the Kentucky mountains. Lexington, KY: University of Kentucky Press.

Puckett, J. (1988). Foxfire reconsidered: A twenty year experiment in progressive education. Urbana, IL: University of Illinois Press.

Schlechty, P. (1976). Teaching and social behavior. Boston: Allyn and Bacon.

Sher, J. (1977). Education in rural America: A reassessment of the conventional wisdom. Boulder, CO: Westview Press.

Smith, J. K. (1983). Quantitative vs. qualitative research: AN attempt to clarify the issues. Educational Researcher, 12(3), 6-13.

Spindler, G. (1982). Doing the ethnography of schooling. New York: Holt, Rinehart and Winston.

Spradley, J. (1980). Participant observation. New York: Holt, Rinehart and Winston.

Stake, R. (1978, February). The case study method in social inquiry. Educational Researcher, pp. 5-8.

Whisnant, D. (1980). Modernizing the mountaineer. Boone, NC: Appalachian Consortium Press.

Wigginton, E. (1985). Sometimes a shining moment. Garden City, NY: Anchor Books

Wolcott, H. (1984). Ethnographers sans ethnography: The evaluation compromise. In D. Fetterman (Ed.), Ethnography in educational evaluation. Beverly Hills, CA: Sage.

Wolcott, H. (1977). Teachers vs. technocrats: An educational innovation in anthropological perspective. Eugene, OR: Center for Educational Policy and Management, University of Oregon.

Braxton County High School

At Braxton County High School, almost all students come by bus.

This is Eagle Country: Braxton County West Virginia.

2

Braxton County, West Virginia

As one with great interest in issues and concerns of rural education, and as one who has authored a number of studies and essays on such matters, the opportunity to help evaluate RSS demonstration projects for AEL came as quite a pleasant one for the principal investigator. Furthermore, as much of my contact with rural schools in the Southeast has been "contact" with official state department data sets (rather than actually in many of the schools and school districts I have written about), I viewed the RSS demonstration project as both an opportunity to help evaluate this project for AEL and OERI, as well as an excellent opportunity to better view the rural education dynamics I have long considered of special interest.

As others who have completed case studies in rural schools have testified, and as some of my previous work in a variety of schooling contexts augered, I found the four school districts chosen by AEL (in conjunction with its four state advisory groups) to be quite similar in many respects yet significantly different on a variety of concerns, contexts, and policies related to the assessment activities and school improvement hopes previously outlined.

So too, establishing relationships and attempting to understand each of the counties and school districts that were the focus of this study was easier in some cases than it was in others. This is not to suggest that any of the evaluation staff believe (in retrospect) that we really "know all about" each of these places and institutions. Rather, we have each developed feelings about which of schools and school systems we felt most comfortable being in, which places we believed honest and insightful answers to our questions were most easily arrived at, and which places had informants and/or sources of information which we felt able to consult for reliable feedback and input. This being said (and illustrations of these issues will become clear later on), the concern of this section of our report deals primarily with social, economic, and political context of the first of four school districts chosen for RSS demonstrations, Braxton County, West Virginia.

THE BRAXTON COUNTY SETTING

As mentioned in Part I of this report, the order of invitation to participate in the School/Community improvement demonstrations of the Rural Small School

Program of AEL was determined by the Lab. And, by default, so was the order of our selected field sites. The first district worked in was Braxton County, West Virginia; the second Cave County, Kentucky; the third Charlotte County, Virginia; and finally, Clinch County, Tennessee. As it turned out, however, by the time this evaluation was really underway, virtually every site was simultaneously "in process," even if two are yet to be completed.

On the other hand, both the second and third counties formally approached in the demonstration process finished their projects rather quickly. Thus, the order of presentation followed in this report was somewhat subjective: depending upon where RSS staff were most intensely working following the completion of a preceding district, such districts typically became the site of our case study. Viewed historically (and historical emphasis in our study even further intensified following our research on Charlotte County, Virginia), it probably would have made greater sense to begin our discussion with the Virginia site. For as the reader will soon see, each of the following case studies begins with a consideration of local provision of public education from earliest times. And Charlotte County's educational dynamics precedes all of the others and at the same time partly suggests an educational philosophy rejected as elitist by early education advocates in each of the other locations. Yet, since our first endeavors at trying to untangle the "rural context" of a local district began in AEL's first demonstration site, this is where our first case study begins.

Most of the first-hand experience upon which the Braxton County evaluation is based comes from on-site visits of the principal investigator. As this site was the first chosen and contacted by the Lab, the start-up activities of the project evaluation by the University of Kentucky followed by several months the field activities of AEL. Even before the principle investigator was able to obtain the services of advanced graduate students at U.K., therefore, contractual agreements called for in the OERI award demanded my immediate immersion in site activities in West Virginia.

For those unaware of the literature on Appalachia and Appalachian education, the stereotypes of schools in this region are notoriously full of negative images (e.g., Branscome, 1978; DeYoung, 1985, 1987; MACED, 1986). At worst, some of the (limited) scholarship on Appalachian education charges that schools there are co-conspirators with external agents and are designed to help reproduce failure and inequality in the region. At best, the negative educational images of the region are attributed to a "culture of poverty" brought on by dependence on declining extractive industries, where not only the people but also the institutions of the region have few resources for helping to alleviate their economic and educational conditions.

Therefore, with some apprehension, I approached Braxton County and its schools with several guarded but preconceived notions about what I might observe. After all, while Braxton County is not among the West Virginia counties (to the south) reputed to be the worst off economically, it is still a comparatively poor county and in the heart of Appalachia (as is all of West Virginia, according to the Appalachian Regional Commission). However, while I did find much poverty as well as evidence of significant community "decay" there, I also found historical and educational trends much different than what I had expected.

Succintly put, the history of West Virginia is one inextricably bound up with two major 19th-century political, economic, and social events: the Civil War and the Industrial Revolution. Like many other rural regions of the nation, those initially settling in West Virginia in the early 19th-century came from the east into this hilly and mountainous region. However, unlike many of the other rural settlements in America, agricultural opportunities in West Virginia were more limited in the size and scope. The available evidence suggests that small scale farming in the "hollows" of thousands of rivers and streams in West Virginia led to a more marginal/subsistence lifestyle than was available in better located agricultural settings to the east and to the west in the U.S. (Rice, 1985).

According to some, the isolation of the mountaineer in West Virginia, where few easy contacts with the outside world were available in the early 19th century, led to increasingly inner-directed economic, social, and kinship systems somewhat unlike the social organization of production and reproduction in other regions of the U.S. (Eller, 1982). However, by the middle of the 19th century, economic and political developments outside of the area began to have significant consequences for inhabitants of the region now known as West Virginia.

As mentioned previously, the economic and political changes brought about by industrialization and the Civil War influenced greatly most residents of (then) western Virginia. For example, unlike most other Virginians, residents of many counties in the western part of that state did not support Virginia's succession from the Union in the early 1860s. While some clearly did support the Virginia cause, the lack of slaves and the agricultural base upon which slavery had developed throughout the South no doubt played a major role in the refusal of many western Virginians to enlist in the Confederate armies.

At about the same time, America's Industrial Revolution in the Northeast called for increased timber and mineral resources, which were readily available among the forests and coalfields in many of these same rural western Virginia counties. Accordingly, the general popular dissatisfaction with Virginia's cause, coupled with aggressive political leadership by entrepreneurial statesmen located primarily in what are now the northern panhandle counties of West Virginia, led to its secession from Virginia in 1863.

One of the Virginia territories which seceded from Virginia at that time to become part of the new state of West Virginia includes what we now know as Braxton County. Braxton County was named after one of the Virginia signers of the American Declaration of Independence, and the county lies geographically in the middle of the state, and has a 19th- and early 20th-century history in some ways similiar to many of its sister counties in either direction.

Unlike many rural regions of the Southeast (and others among the AEL demonstration sites), Braxton County appears to have been geographically and economically fortunate in the 19th and early 20th centuries. Specifically, while Braxton County's 19th-century history importantly includes early dependence upon subsistence agriculture, several navigable rivers linking the county with the outside world enabled a number of successful commercial activities to develop there. In addition to the establishment and operation of several grist mills on the county's rivers, commercial ventures in tannery, lumber processing, salt manufacture, and pottery enabled the county to grow and become economically diverse throughout its early period. So too, because of transportation possibilities, a cannery and a creamery/bottling plant operated in the county later in the 19th century.

Concomitantly, since the Elk and Little Kanawha Rivers provided sites for economic activities like those mentioned above, several small settlements situated on these rivers grew into important towns during this period. The first of these was the town of Sutton, named after John Sutton, who was an early settler and one of the largest landholders in the county. Sutton came to Braxton County in the early 1800s from Alexandria Virginia. Somewhat later, Burnsville was formed on the Little Kanawha river, and was the site of a large sawmill.

The commercial importance of these two towns, which grew throughout the early 19th century, appears to have been significant, not only for the economic diversity and vitality of the county, but also for the social and political diversity which they helped to engender. Since the county was comparatively accessible, and since the river transportation system appears to have encouraged early commercial markets, a number of "mainstream" churches were established there throughout the 19th century, including Methodist, Catholic, Presbyterian, and Baptist congregations. With some commercial and agricultural success, a viable middle class appears to have developed there, too. Several communities in the county had hotels by the end of the 19th century. As well, competing newspapers emerged in both Burnsville and Sutton during this period, suggesting an aggressive and diverse county citizenry.

Perhaps reflecting the growing civic consciousness and "moral respectability" of Braxton County, schools there appear to have become increasingly important social institutions following the Civil War. As the numerous smaller communities in the county grew and prospered, early 19th-century subscription schools gave way after the Civil War to a system of public education as advocated by many of the county's civic leaders.

According to a compilation of early school oral histories, neighborhood schools were voluntarily constructed by county residents early in the 19th century. And instruction in piety and basic literacy skills appeared important:

Spelling, reading, writing and arithmetic were the (subjects) taught. The Bible was the text used in the reading class. In arithmetic, if the single rule of three (now called simple proportion) was understood, it was thought that the person possessing such knowledge was competent to teach school. (Dick, 1922, p. 24)

However, by mid-century, the influx of more highly educated individuals began to change rural schooling practices, according to this same source:

During the decade between 1846 and 1856 many persons who had received a very good education beyond the mountains, and in Greenbriar County, moved into the Elk Valley. They greatly aided in the establishment of schools in neighborhoods in which they settled. The old-time teachers were usually deficient in educational qualifications, yet they did a noble work and prepared the way for the introduction of the free school system in West Virginia.

THE CIVIL WAR AND ITS ECONOMIC CONSEQUENCES FOR BRAXTON COUNTY

Much of the progress suggested above occurred before the Civil War and before Braxton County became a county of West Virginia. Unfortunately, even though Braxton County was far removed from major battlefields of the war, the strategic location of Sutton on the Elk River caused both Union and Confederate troops to consider it of some military importance. Therefore, not only were many of its young people involved in military pursuits away from the county (on both sides of the conflict, we assume), but contending military forces occupied the surrounding area at various times throughout the mid-1860s. And the town of Sutton was burned to the ground during this period.

Rebuilding after the Civil War appears to have been onerous for Braxton County citizens but not insurmountable. While the industrial revolution in the north experienced recession in the late 19th century, and while Southern states were experiencing rebuilding problems associated with defeat in the Civil War (see a discussion of such factors in Chapters 3 and 5), Braxton County's still viable agricultural base and lack of political problems associated with reconstruction governments to the south appear to have eased local rebuilding conditions, which other areas experienced more fully. Towns, houses, and bridges were rebuilt, and problems attendant with freed slaves were infrequent, as the population of Braxton County has historically remained almost entirely White.

While most Braxton County manufacturing industries (other than timber) appear to have served primarily regional markets during the 19th century, new "opportunities" presented themselves to Braxton County residents around the turn of the 20th century. Specifically, coal and natural gas discoveries brought much attention and outside investment into central West Virginia, including Braxton County, between 1880 and 1930. Much of the early timber and mineral exploitation in the county was made possible by short rail lines built into the hollows, where such resources could be economically extracted. However, unlike many other central West Virginia counties, the emerging rail industry and continuing transportation possibilities provided by the county's rivers engendered more than just resource-extraction job opportunities for local citizens. Rather, regional manufacturing and processing of timber, coal, oil, and gas were all made possible in the county and provided many skilled and unskilled jobs, not only for local citizens, but also for growing numbers of workers coming into the county (see Table WVA-1).

At least part of the reason for early 20th-century prosperity in Braxton County was the demand for industrial chemicals in the Northeast, a demand which was particularly intensified by the First World War. Particularly important to county growth and development during this period and up until the 1940s was the chemical plant built in Sutton. These were the days when wood by-products were a mainstay of American chemical production, and such by-products were more than readily available in Braxton County.

On August 5, 1920, the *Braxton County Democrat* ran an illustrated "Booster-Industrial" series on manufacturing, business, and residential opportunities and benefits of life in central West Virginia, including a long story on the (then) largest county chemical plant located in Sutton. Part of the story read thusly:

> The large plant of the Sutton Chemical Company, which was nearly two years in building, was put in operation April 27 of this year (1920). Charcoal, acetate of lime and wood alchol are manufactured.. . . The plant consists of a number of large and substantial buildings, among which are the retort builder, the dryers, coolers, loading sheds, tube still houses, machine shop, settling pans, boiler and pump house, transfer shed, charcoal storage, acetate storage, office building, warehouses, ensign house, sawmill plant, etc. The company has its own electric light plant and all the buildings are electrically lighted. (sect. 2, p. 9)

Unfortunately, as was the case of many 20th-century West Virginia economic development projects, outside ownership of this facility was an important factor, and it depended on both local "extractable" resources and distant but changing markets:

> The plant has a capacity of eighty cords of wood daily. The wood is obtained from a large tract of timberland on Wolf creek, to which a standard guage railroad has been built, and smaller tracts owned by the company in this section. All the timber in these tracts suitable for lumber is cut in the company's sawmill, (and) the waste is converted into chemicals.. . . When in full operation the plant employs 150 men and from 200 to 400 are employed in the woods. Henry M. Miner, of New York, is president of the company; A. Cameron of Chicago is vice-president, Chas. L.

Read, of Newark, N.J., is secretary, and Harold T. Edgar, of New York is treasurer. L.D. Hawkins, of New York, is assistant to the president and spends (only) a portion of his time here. (sect. 2, p. 9)

"QUALITY OF LIFE" PROSPECTS IN BOOMING BRAXTON COUNTY

In his travels up and down the Elk River between 1880 and 1925, Mr. W. E. R. Byrne gave an impression of the dramatic growth of the town of Sutton during the early 20th century, a growth which was mirrored throughout the county.

Sutton (in 1885) was a small shoestring village, closely built up on either side of the Weston and Gauley Bridge turnpike, a mud road running east and west from Old Women's Run down the Elk River on the north side, about one third of a mile to where it turned to the left at right angles to the bridge spanning the Elk, with a few scattered buildings farther down on the north side and over on the south side of the river; the buildings were all of wood construction excepting the new courthouse, which was of brick, and the ancient jail, which was of massive cut stone. It was 44 miles from the nearest railroad which was a narrow gauge at Weston. A very different place indeed from the very citified and up-to-date metropolis of exactly central West Virginia (in the mid 1920s), equipped with all the modern conveniences and improvements, such as two railroads, two paved highways, paved streets, water works, ice plant, natural gas, electric lights, the buildings modern in every particular, and a population a dozen times greater than it was in April 1885; greater in number, yes – greater in spirit, no – and this goes for Braxton County as well as the county seat – no finer class of citizens could then or can now be found in the state of West Virginia or elsewhere, than those I found in the year 1885. (Byrne, 1940, pp. 146-147)

Similar sentiments were recorded in the Booster-Industrial issue of *The Braxton Democrat* (only one of the still remaining papers). According to this admittedly pro-development edition, all three of Braxton County's then-incorporated towns (as well as the smaller village of Flatwoods) were thriving and growing:

There are more opportunities open to the people of Braxton county than in any other section of the coming great state of West Virginia. This may seem strange to some, but nevertheless it is true. . . Come to Braxton County, West Virginia, the land of milk and honey, insofar as this world's goods are concerned. You will be made welcome. If you are seeking a place on which to locate a manufacturing plant, we can help you; if you are looking for a good home, we can accommodate you; if you are trying to locate yourself where you will have all the advantages that a good school system will make, come to Braxton; if you want to buy a home and live in perfect contentment, come to Braxton; or, if you are desirous of buying one of the best farms to be found anywhere, come to Braxton County, West Virginia. We have all these and more. We invite you again to come—come and see if what we have told you is not true. Fact of the matter is that your investigation will prove to your own satisfaction that we have just what you are looking for and more than we have enumerated. (sect. 1, p. 1)

THE IMPORTANCE OF BRAXTON COUNTY'S RAILROAD INDUSTRY

As suggested before, the coming of the railroad in Braxton County had perhaps greater significance there than in most other West Virginia locations. That is, the several major train lines through the county (by 1917) were primarily constructed in the early years for the transportation of timber and coal from local and southern West Virginia forests and coalfields to the industrial North. However, citizens of the county were able to take advantage of the railroads in terms of the shipment of produce and manufactured goods out of the region. As well, travelers on the *Coal and Coke Railroad* appear to have been frequent visitors to towns in Braxton County, as both passenger and freight trains stopped there. Thus, while the various negative consequences of the coal industry in West Virginia (such as the physical dangers of mining and its "boom and bust" nature) did effect Braxton and its sister counties, Braxton County fared somewhat better during the years when its easily extractable timber and mineral resources were being "developed," because of its multiple transportation possibilities.

Furthermore, not only did several rail systems pass through Braxton County, but one line established a major switch yard and repair facility for its trains, which turned out to be of major economic importance there. Henry Gassaway Davis (later an important state political figure) purchased a large tract of land in southern Braxton County for this purpose, and a third prominent county town was born in the early 20th century, which local citizens named for him. It is probably fair to say that, in the early 20th century, this Braxton County town of Gassaway was the fastest growing and most "modern" in the entire region, due almost entirely to the employment of hundreds of skilled workers in occupations directly related to railroad operations and maintenance.

Gassaway is one of the most substantially built little cities to be found anywhere; its houses are modern in architecture; its business buildings are substantial; its churches are numbered among the best and most attractive of any community; the school buildings are replete in every sense that the word implies, and coupled to this fact the town is so situated and so arranged that it shows every building to its best advantage. The environments to this little city are enchanting and hold the admiration of every stranger who enters its confines. The railroad company seems to take a keen pride in the town and have so arranged its station and the surroundings that it appeals to all who are permitted to view it and its surroundings.. . . (its) shops, it is said, (also) employ several hundred men and give steady employment the year around. (*The Braxton Democrat*, 38(27), p. 3)

LOCAL HISTORIES IN THE 1930s, 1940s, AND 1950s

During the course of our research, we typically found few locally produced volumes of local economic, social, or educational histories (or booster newspaper editions) for Braxton County like those earlier produced. Rather, oral histories of the county, combined with statistical information over the past five decades, gave us most of the few "pictures" of community life there we could locate. This lack of locally produced written histories perhaps not coincidentally occurred during years of community and economic decline.

Perhaps the best series of state histories relevant to 1930s and 1940s economic, political, and educational issues in West Virginia (and, in fact, each of the states included in this book) was published by the Works Progress Administration. Also, in West Virginia separate community histories for each of Braxton County's three small towns were also underwritten by the WPA through the West Virginia Writers Project. In each of these late-1930 or early-1940 works, Braxton County towns are described in glowing terms, and were similar to public pronouncements like those we cited from 20 years earlier. For example, the "social progress" to be found in Gassaway is described thusly:

> The location of Gassaway is a beautiful one, surrounded as it is by entrancing mountain scenery. It may be properly termed an agricultural center, serving a large area of fertile and well kept farms. Also, a splendid citizenship resides near the town in the Otter Creek and Elk River valleys. The surrounding communities have good schools and churches, and many other organizations that wield an important cultural influence. . . . City services include sewerage, six miles of paved streets, fire department, police and other features of present-day towns, and a public library. An active chamber of commerce organized in 1920 is made up of local business men whose object is to promote the best interests of the town and surrounding community. (West Virginia Writers' Project, 1941, p. 5)

HARD TIMES COME TO BRAXTON COUNTY

All of the above notwithstanding, the data suggest that, at least 10 years before the Writers Project description was published, Braxton County was already in economic decline. While some absent landowners may have cared little for the economic fortunes of county residents (Eller, 1982), local business leaders no doubt sensed that their future was jeopardized by the lack of roads and highways even as far back as 1920. Unfortunately, building roads in mountainous, rural central West Virginia has never been easy or affordable. And the lack of a viable state highway system, combined with the rapid mid-20th-century erosion of extractive industries, spelled the doom of hopes and dreams of many in Braxton County's local communities.

The impending erosion of the local economy was presaged in yet another story tucked away in later pages of the 1920 Booster-Industrial edition of the *Braxton County Democrat*.

> Although we in West Virginia are living in the twentieth century, we do not have two county seats in the state connected with a hard surface road. Our farmers can haul their products to market only at certain times of the year. Hauling costs amount to 37 cents per ton mile as against 10 and 12 cents in states that have improved roads. Thousands of bushels of fruit rot each year because it cannot be hauled to shipping points; schools in some sections are in session only four or five months each year because roads become impassable; in fact, practically everything that is deplorable in our state can be traced directly or indirectly to our bad roads. (sect. 3, p. 8)

By 1960, Braxton County, West Virginia, had joined the ranks of most economically depressed regions of the country, where unemployment was high, wages were low, and where dramatic outmigration of many of its citizens had been occurring for at least two decades. This is a sobering fact, considering that, for almost 100 years, the county was witness to vigorous growth and inmigration of individuals seeking the positive advantages of life in its several towns and outlying areas.

During the past several decades a number of economic conditions appear to have brought about this economic decline. Tables WVA-1–4 document a number of these employment, income, and population trends. Initially, of course, the century-long decline of small-scale and regional agriculture in much of rural America also affected Braxton County. As noted before, the percentage of arable land in central West Virginia is minimal, due its mountainous nature. Therefore, the larger and larger land holdings and transportation systems necessary to compete successfully (and nationally) in large-scale farming appear never to have been a 20th-century possibility there. As Table WV-1 suggests, the percentage of working Braxton Countians in (undoubtedly small-scale) agriculture in 1930 was over 60% while comparable figures in 1980 show it at less than 3%.

So, too, the rapid decline of the coal industry in West Virginia following World War I appears to have undermined most local mining operations, as well as numerous others in surrounding counties. Of even more significance, however, was the decline of the railroad industry in central West Virginia, upon which much of Braxton County's 20th-century progress was built. The decline of southernWest Virginia coalfields, coupled with increased highway construc-

WVA-1. EMPLOYMENT INDUSTRIES.

	YEAR					
CHARACTERISTICS	*1930*	*1940*	*1950*	*1960*	*1970*	*1980*
Total persons employed 14 or 16 years old.	6,710	5,236	5,034	3,290	2,827	3,814
% in AG.	60.3	57.8	41.8	17.4	2.7	2.2
% in Mining	3.5	3.6	10.5	9.7	4.6	0.5
% in MANFG	10.2	4.2	4.1	11.1	14.6	10.8
% in TRANS/COMM	6.8	4.8	8.1	7.4	10.2	8.4
% in RETAIL	4.2	6.0	9.3	15.1	11.3	18.3
% in FIN/INS	.53	.43	.65	.9	1.3	1.3
% in SERVICES	10.0	15.0	11.2	15.0	21.7	23.7

WVA-2. INCOME CHARACTERISTICS.

	YEAR					
CHARACTERISTICS	*1930*	*1940*	*1950*	*1960*	*1970*	*1980*
Median income of						
All families	–	–	1,378	2,610	4,502	12,072
All households	–	–	–	–	–	10,286
Families with own-children 18 years						12,843
Married couples	–	–	–	3,788	3,560	13,515
Female householder (no husband)	–	–	–	–	–	7,016

tion outside of the state, appears to have doomed the commercial utility of the railroad system in the county. Thus, the (then) *Baltimore and Ohio Railroad* for all intent and purposes abandoned the Gassaway trainyard and guaranteed Braxton County's quickening economic downslide.

With the demise of the railroad, hundreds of employees lost their jobs, visitors no longer traveled by rail into and through the county, and markets for the few agricultural and manufactured goods still being produced in the region became even harder to reach. Furthermore, by the 1950s, those once the most vigorous supporters of civic affairs and projects in the county (including officers and employees of the B&O Railroad) were no longer in a position to financially help such projects. As Table WVA-3 indicates, outmigration of the citizenry of the county was dramatic between 1920 and 1970, when the population declined from almost 24,000 to fewer than 13,000.

WVA-3. POPULATION CHARACTERISTICS.

CHARACTERISTICS	YEAR								
	1900	1910	1920	1930	1940	1950	1960	1970	1980
Total Popln	18,904	23,023	23,973	22,579	21,568	18,082	15,152	12,666	13,894
Male	–	–	12,411	11,731	11,113	9,170	–	–	6,902
Female	–	–	11,532	10,848	10,545	8,912	–	–	6,992
White	18,717	22,606	23,361	21,498	17,971	15,079	12,666	13,894	
Black	187	221	273	188	160	111	75	–	–

WVA-4. LABOR CHARACTERISITICS.

CHARACTERISITICS	YEAR				
	1940	1950	1960	1970	1980
Labor Force:					
Persons 16 yrs and older	14,763	12,422	10,458	8,925	10,390
Male 16 yrs and older	7,604	6,250	5,087	4,259	5,071
% in labor Force	77.0	71.9	60.7	53.1	58.0
Females 16 yrs and older	7,159	6,172	5,363	4,666	5,319
% in labor force	10.7	11.4	13.5	19.4	28.3
Females 16 yrs/older (with children 18 yrs)	–	–	–	878	1,060
% in labor force	–	–	–	16.4	39.2

While the statistics in Tables WVA-1–4 in one way document Braxton County economic decline and outmigration, other images of the human meaning of this process are available in the county. Many former 20th-century residents appear to have felt strongly about the Braxton County towns they had to leave in search of employment, for local homecomings and reunions of families no longer living there (but who return yearly to celebrate) are frequently highlighted and advertised in the pages of both remaining county newspapers. An additional measure of interest, for the purposes of this book, is that sometimes community reunions and homecomings are held by former graduates in old (but voluntarily restored and maintained) one-room schools which still stand in various county locations. So, too, editors of both local newpapers (the *Braxton County Democrat* and the *Braxton County Citizens-News*) report more subscriptions are held by out-of-county (former) residents than by those who still live there.

Each of the three still-declining Braxton County towns also has annual homecoming days. The town of Gassaway, for example, sees "Gassaway Day" celebrations late every summer. In August 1989, a former resident extolled the days earlier in this century when this town was one of considerable importance in central West Virginia, and yet another picture on the rise and demise of the several communities in Braxton County:

> Some towns become ghost towns mainly because a location is not suitable for what the city was for, like the ghost towns out west after the gold was all mined and like so many towns in West Virginia and some other states. This beautiful little town of Gassaway was my hometown for many years and is still dear to my heart. . . . Gassaway was built mainly because of the railroad, due to shops being needed to build and repair the cars and locomotives. Trains were replacing stage coaches at that time, and a railroad was being built to connect Charleston to the North-eastern part of the state and Gassaway or what became Gassaway, was an ideal place to build a large shop to repair the trains.. . . The years passed and the Town of Gassaway prospered and grew. But through the years it had bad times along with the good. I remember when I was going to high school here. The Great Depression came and the shops almost closed and many of the workers who were residents of Gassaway almost completely cleared the hillside across the river from the shops and planted large gardens of corn and potatoes. They had the determination to carry on. Then World War II came along and the shops probably employed more workers than ever before. (Yet), as our highway system expanded, the trucking industry grew and grew until many branches of the railroad couldn't compete and were abandoned. The shops at Gassaway fell by the wayside and what (residents) are left in Gassaway have to go out of town to their jobs. (Dean, 1989, sect. 2, p. 2)

Finally, I offer an "official" version of the current state of economic affairs in Braxton County, as issued by the state economic development bureau summary in 1985. The transition of the county from a rather prosperous one to its current state of impoverishment is clearly suggested in this passage:

> Braxton County lies in the center of the state and, like its neighboring counties, suffers economically from this geographic handicap. Until the building of Inter-state 79, the county was isolated to a considerable degree from even more metropolitan areas of the state. Even with the completion of the interstate highway in the 1970s, the expected growth and development has been limited.. . . The population of Braxton County declined steadily between 1940 and 1970. The county claimed 21,658 residents in 1940 but only 12,666 in 1970, a population loss of 41.5% in 30 years. This tremendous loss occurred as individuals were literally forced by economic considerations to abandon hillside farms and seek employ-ment in the factories of Ohio, Michigan and other industrial states. (West Virginia Department of Employment Security, 1985, pp. 5-6)

ECONOMIC DECLINE AND SCHOOL
CONSOLIDATION ISSUES

During the early 20th century each of the three larger towns in Braxton County appear to have been quite aggressive with regard to the improvement of public schooling in the region. The county was divided into four magisterial districts, each with its own school board. The number of one-room schools, as well as "graded" schools, in these four districts numbered well over 100 in the 1920s. As well, three of the four districts each had their own high school. In addition, both Sutton and the small town of Flatwoods had their own independent districts and were financially separate from the four magisterial districts.

From evidence available to us, and contrary to much conventional wisdom about the inadequacy of public education in Appalachia, public schools and formal education appear to have been very important concerns of many Braxton Countians by the early 20th century. Hypothetically, this interest may have been explained by the relative affluence of the area during its boom years, and by the high expectations for schooling probably demanded by growing managerial and skilled laboring classes of parents. In each of the larger towns of Burnsville, Sutton and Gassaway, for example, new and "modern" high schools were built in the second decade of the 20th century. And according to some we interviewed, a healthy competition existed between these towns with regard to which community had the best high school.

Furthermore, population growth in Sutton in the early 20th century led to the construction of, not one, but two new and larger schools during the first quarter of the 20th century. As it turns out, almost before the first new high school was constructed, increased enrollment demands made the structure obsolete, and a second had to be built. In yet another WPA publication, public works and public education (with a clear Deweyian tone) in Sutton just preceding its rapid decline are extolled:

> Sutton is situated on the beautiful Elk River, 100 miles east of Charleston and 70 miles from Clarksburg. A rich farming region surrounds the city and contributes to its economic welfare. The river which divides the town, and the hills on all sides provide a scenic background for the thoroughly up-to-date homes and business houses of the Braxton County seat. . . . City services include sewerage, paved streets, motorized fire department, police and other features of present-day towns. . . . Forward-looking yet anxious to preserve its atmosphere of rural peace while taking advantage of every facility of the age, Sutton has combined the old and new in a delightful blend of easy living and progressive building. . . . The schools of 1941 are an example of this attitude. Special emphasis is placed on social adjustments and vocational guidance. Clubs and intramural activities instruct the pupils in social living. With 300 students, the Sutton High School in its 36th session is representative of the best in modern education. . . . In 1941, Sutton can proudly boast that it has taken full advantage of twentieth-century developments, without losing its character as a pioneer community motivated by pride in its past and present and faith in its future. (West Virginia Writers Project, 1941, pp. 34-35)

As the preceding discussion suggests, the economic development of Braxton County appears to have led to the establishment of a strong middle class with high hopes for public education by the 1920s and 1930s. Yet, since most of the county was still primarily rural, and since subsistence and small-scale farming was a primary economic activity for many county residents, it seems probable that formal schooling through high school was not seen essential for all children's success. The fact, for example, that the total enrollment of the county's three small high schools averaged fewer than 800 students during a period when the total population of the county averaged over 23,000 clearly suggests that educational expectations for many families did not include high-school attendance. And the strong emphasis upon vocational programs for many of these students further suggests the vocational and technical interests of both students and teachers. Yet support for local small schools appears to have been high, and a demand for increased educational opportunities seemed to be growing until the economic collapse of the county.

In many ways, educational decline in Braxton County appears to have begun at about the same time as it did in the rest of the state: just after the larger national depression of 1929. During the early 1930s, many large tracts of land held by outside interests were forfeited to the state for nonpayment of taxes (taxes which were used at least partly to education). And because in-state residents also feared loss of their property as a result of potentially escalating tax assessments, a constitutional amendment was passed in 1932 that placed a cap on these assessments and also had a predictably negative effect on revenues available for local school programs.

Not surprisingly, the erosion of school revenues in the state due to such economic concerns led to significant educational problems. Due to lack of funds, many teachers remained unpaid, and school terms were either shortened or the schools themselves closed altogether. The following year, in partial response to the school-funding crisis, the state's 398 school districts were consolidated into 55 districts to coincide with county units (although they remained financially independent of the county political structure).

In Braxton County, therefore, the six previous county and independent districts were combined into one, and the county superintendent and county school board became its governing authorities. In so doing, the state of West Virginia took on significant financing of schools in the 55 county districts, while local resources became of somewhat less importance. Unfortunately, it appears that the rapid decline of Braxton County's economic picture, coupled with a generally low state tax support system, led to decades of cost cutting practices by local education officials in their efforts to maintain schools.

Since the 1940s, school histories in Braxton County have remained just as scarce as they were earlier. Part of this may be due to the fact that no subsidized writers like those affiliated with the WPA operated there. Furthermore, as previously suggested, writing histories of declining economic areas and declining schools may be less appealing to local historians than writing upbeat narratives like those we found from Braxton County's "boom" years.

On the other hand, some documentation of the various types of problems related to economic decline and population outmigration are available in the county between the 1940s and 1980s. Perhaps the one most helpful in describing the consequences of these two trends was completed by an advisory group brought in from Pennsylvania by the Braxton County School Board in the mid-1960s. In this document, a tale of rural school closings throughout the 1950s and 1960s is described in some detail. The document outlines a general population decline in outlying areas of the county, and the movement of many remaining county children into the larger towns. Such trends led to the abandonment of schools undersubscribed in the outlying areas, particularly given the increasing state programmatic and physical requirements for accredited educational programs and facilities.

Illustrative of the language of this report is the following:

> The population change in Braxton County as a whole has been one of decline over the last years. Most of the loss has been at the expense of the more rural and isolated areas with areas such as Sutton declining also, but at a much slower rate. Part of this rural decline has occurred because some of the people who are leaving the outlying areas are moving into or near towns such as Sutton. . . . Within the Sutton Attendance Area, elementary school enrollment dropped from 1122 in 1957-58 to 870 in 1963-64. This was a loss of 252 students or 22.5 percent of elementary enrollment. In this same period, enrollment at the Sutton Elementary dropped from 485 in the 1957-58 school year to 340 in the 1963-64 school year. During this period, the schools of Windy Run, Stoney Creek, Maymond, Bug Ridge, Wolf Creek, and Marpleton were closed and their pupils transferred to the Sutton Elementary school. (Weston, 1967, p. 7-4)

Without belaboring the point, consultants to the Braxton County Board of Education talked at length in the planning document referred to here about the inevitability and desirability of continued school closings and consolidations in the county, and made special reference to the inability (and unwillingness) of county residents to vote for increases in taxes for enhanced school programs and teacher salaries. What they also suggested was that recreational facilities attendant on the construction of a new dam in the county might provide some jobs for county residents, thus potentially stabilizing the pattern of outmigration in the county by the 1970s.

Furthermore, in the planning document of 1967, reference is made to the construction of a new high school facility in the county which would "enable" the consolidation of the three county high schools into one facility. Another potentially useful result of this development would be that the three former high schools might become sites for handling the overflow of elementary children coming into the three towns as remaining one- and two-room schools in outer areas continued to be consolidated (according to the report, 44 schools had been so consolidated in the few years just preceding their survey).

1988 EDUCATIONAL FINANCE CONDITIONS

To a great extent, the nightmare of economic decline and inadequate school funding continues to be a fact of life in Braxton County even into the 1990s. As noted earlier, the building of a new interstate through the county occurred in the mid-1970s, but once the highway was completed, the many short-term construction jobs associated with it were finished as well. Furthermore, even though two man-made dams now lie in the county, the lakes which they form have not attracted the type of tourist industries some thought they would, according to local sources. Ironically, according to an economic development expert with whom we spoke, one of the lakes now covers the best agricultural land in the entire county, no doubt one of the few areas which enabled some economic success in an earlier era.

As Table WVA-1 indicates, most income earners in the county today are employed in services industries, many of which depend upon transfer of payments from state and federal income sources. The school system is currently, and has for some time, been the largest employer in the county. So too, services to the aged, unemployed, and sick generate some income to various welfare agencies, hospitals, etc.

Of late there have arrived a number of retail outlets for goods produced outside of the county and the state. There are several supermarkets and franchised restaurants, including the one where the AEL community needs assessment was held for Braxton County. Otherwise, many of the industries, hotels, and restaurants described in earlier days in the county are currently out of business (and their buildings still remain empty).

Symbolizing perhaps the declining financial possibilities of the district is the location and condition of the School Board office in Braxton County, now housed on the second floor of an early 20th-century building which once contained a Sutton hardware store. The building sits across the street from the county courthouse, and on the main street of the county seat. Outside, the street is paved in the direction of Gassaway (to the south), but the residential portion of the street in the other direction is of ancient brick. And the roadbed turns to gravel as it takes a sharp left turn into a hollow less than a mile from the county courthouse.

This is not to suggest that either the building or the old street are in a state of disrepair. Both are actually quite attractive, considering their age. So too, the three old high school buildings in the county at Sutton, Gassaway, and Burnsville are still attractive structures on the outside. Of course, the inside of each building has been "remodeled" so many times (to comply with changing space needs, energy savings requirements, and state regulations) that their original builders would probably no longer recognize them. Importantly, none of these buildings serves as a high school anymore: rather, each houses either middle school populations of grades 5 through 8, or, in one case (Burnsville), kindergarten through eighth grade.

Illustrative perhaps of decades of practice in making do with fewer resources, the maintenance and upkeep of each of the old schools is a note of particular pride in Braxton County. Unlike many more affluent school districts, which typically contract out new building construction projects, building maintenance and affiliated service personnel of Braxton County schools have been turned into building construction and remodeling crews on several occasions during the past decade.

For example, rather than consolidating one outlying small elementary school due to low attendance and substandard facilities, the superintendent decided (after much negative publicity over his consolidation strategy) to have these crews build a new wing onto an existing structure and perform extensive remodeling to existing facilities. By not contracting most of this work out, a considerable savings was achieved for the district. As well, extensive site preparation and elaborate new playground equipment has been installed adjacent to several county elementary schools where level ground was available. And most of this work was done by school maintenance personnel rather than by outside contractors.

Another important theme related to the above is the strength of the public school "service workers" organization in West Virginia and Braxton County. In West Virginia the Service Workers' Union represents bus drivers, cafeteria workers and custodial staff. Not coincidentally, staffing ratios mandated by the state for each county school system guarantee minimum (and maximum) numbers of service workers to be paid out of state funds, as well as the minimum salaries which they can be paid. And compared to other schools discussed in this study, the number of noninstructional staff in Braxton County is quite high.

Put another way, (relatively) generous numbers of service positions are almost automatically built into the budget of all West Virginia county educational systems by state legislation, and one important theme in Braxton County, while we observed there, had to do with systematic and concerted efforts by the school administration to motivate/induce all technically noninstructional employees of the system into systematic "support" of instructional objectives. As will be discussed later, at both the county and state levels we observed protracted struggles over school-funding issues in West Virginia; and this struggle raged between school administrators, the West Virginia Education Association (teachers), and organized service workers.

In Braxton County, formal evaluation procedures were an important mechanism used by the central office to insure the efficient utilization of bus drivers, cafeteria workers, and custodial staff (as well as teachers and principals) in the pursuit of instructional objectives. Which is how the central office probably managed to induce custodial workers to help remodel the building facilities previously mentioned.

As some of this discussion might suggest, one of the most important components of leadership exhibited by the school superintendent in Braxton County centered on his ability to manipulate available funds (and personnel paid out of these funds) for the school district into creditable educational programs. In the several dozen interviews performed in Braxton County relevant to citizen and school personnel assessments of county school leadership, invariably we received positive accounts of the superintendent and central office staff. When pushed to suggest why the superintendent was held in high regard, the first answer almost always given typically lauded his ability to handle the financial assets and accounts of the district at a time when other districts in the state and the region were under scrutiny from government and public spokespersons for mismanagement of funds.

In point of fact, some suspicion existed regarding the finances of Braxton County schools during the 1987 school year. In the state legislature the year before, a bill had been passed which tripled state funds for handicapped children in each county district. Since such funding could be used for more than direct services to the handicapped, some superintendents apparently became extremely aggressive in testing and classifying special needs students in their districts. And the superintendent of Braxton County was one of these aggressive superintendents.

Braxton County's superintendent also earned high marks among some employees and most board members for other significant cost-saving programs (in addition to building remodeling via existing personnel, and his reputation for manipulating state funding formulas). For example, an early critic of the superintendent's who ran one of the local papers (begrudgingly) began to criticize other government bodies for fiscal waste and mismanagement. And to do this, he illustrated what things ought to cost with reference to the school superintendent's published expense accounts.

As well, during 1988 the state of West Virginia itself became (again) financially strapped. And since disbursements to county schools and funding of state pension and hospitalization programs were among the primary recipients of state allocations, delaying as long as possible transfers from the state treasury to these government agencies became commonplace. Not surprisingly, many county school systems (including larger and more affluent ones) operated close to the line financially, and when the state fell two and/or three months behind in payments to local schools, some counties could not make their payrolls on time. In Braxton County, however, the financial acuity of the superintendent and his budget supervisor made this a nonissue. Throughout the well-publicized state budget crisis, Braxton County had enough money put away in interest-bearing accounts to compensate for the tardiness of state payments. And since such budget records (available to the public) clearly showed ample margin (compared to many surrounding districts), it was quite easy to find teacher and public accolades for the financial prowess of the central office, and gratitude for the job done by the superintendent. On more than one occasion, individuals both inside and outside the school, who may have disagreed with aspects of the superintendent's educational philosophy, agreed that "we are lucky to have him."

THE EDUCATIONAL CLIMATE OF BRAXTON COUNTY SCHOOLS

While the handling of fiscal and personnel matters in the school system appears to have been the primary concerns of most citizens outside of the school (and of the school board), our research team was also somewhat impressed by the pedagogical sophistication/enthusiasm of Braxton County schools and the central office there. We had expected, for example, that a school system experiencing the kind of financial problems Braxton County was would quite likely find it difficult to entertain seriously various types of school improvement efforts. Much to our surprise, however, we discovered in Braxton County serious pursuit of a variety of such efforts on the part of teachers, principals, and central office supervisors.

At least part of the attention to learner outcomes and the educational climate which makes them important in Braxton County probably has its origin in the state "Master Plan" for school reform, developed in 1983. The Master Plan was developed in the early 1980s as a consequence of a state court case (Pauley v. Bailey) that ruled that the provision of education in West Virginia prior to this time had been inequitable and thus unconstitutional. Judge Arthur Recht ruled in 1982 that the Lincoln County public schools had not provided a "thorough and efficient" education to five of its students: an education which is deemed a constitutional right in West Virginia.

Following this decision, a 99-member advisory committee was assembled to construct a state plan which would guarantee "thorough and efficient" educational opportunities across the state. And this plan was formally adopted in March of 1983.

> The West Virginia Master Plan provides that all of those programs and activities required for a "thorough and efficient" system of education must be available to **all** students. The plan identifies the following elements of a thorough and efficient system: 1) standards for high-quality programs; 2) required administrative and instructional practices in the areas of personnel, facilities and supplies; 3) a suggested method of funding; and 4) accountability, to assure the public that a thorough and efficient system of education is provided. (Truby, 1983, p. 285)

Yet, while subsequent development of the Master Plan identified, and specified many, "standards, practices, and accountability" measures as instructed by the court, the monies for implementing the Master Plan have rarely kept pace with the costs of implementing them, according to local informants: and a "suggested method of funding" them has never been fully developed. For example, most early efforts to guarantee equal provision of education in West Virginia have focused on such items as pupil–teacher staffing ratios, curricular content, minimum amounts of classroom instructional time, and so on. However, at the same time as requirements were standardized and increased, declining state revenues (once again) derailed efforts to increase the taxes necessary for fully supporting their implementation.

> The timing was bad, however, in the sense that the master plan for high-quality education was developed when West Virginia was in the middle of a depression. During the last year (1982), West Virginia had the highest percentage of unemployed workers in the nation. It is unfortunate that the Recht decision, which could have helped West Virginia become a "Mayo clinic of education" for the rest of the U.S., came at a time when nearly 20% of West Virginians were out of work. (Truby, 1983, p. 284)

In our interviews with Braxton County central office staff and principals, reference to "the Master Plan" as the source of curricular planning for the local district was frequently mentioned. Yet it's one thing to accept state mandates regarding "thorough and efficient" school programs; it's quite another to be aggressive in attempting to live up to the intent of such legislation. And we judged the intent of providing a quality education (broadly defined) quite apparent throughout the system in Braxton county.

For example, our first interview in one of the County's middle schools was with a principal surrounded with file drawers full of test scores and background information ostensibly related to student performance in his school. As it so happened, this principal was in the midst of extensive data analysis relevant to the prediction of student underachievement, data which he was eager to share with us. Furthermore, the language he used in discussing his school's status and direction was not the language of defeat, low expectations, and/or decline, but rather included phrases like "alterable elements," "time on task," "school climate," and so on.

Continuing in the interview, it turned out that this principal had recently been sponsored by the County to attend the West Virginia Principals' Academy, along with two others from the district. According to the principal (and at least one other), all of the "big names" in the "effective schools" movement had been at this Academy, and he was sold on the notion that assessment of student performance and systematic emphasis on school improvement activities based upon the Effective Schools literature was **the** way to go in his school.

Having been apprised by someone at the central office that Braxton County was collaborating with AEL in potential school improvement activities, several principals appeared skeptical: As one phrased it, "they (AEL) probably view us like Mayberry, and are coming in to help us . . . when we have already done most of what they could help us with." As this principal viewed it, the primary obstacles to continued improvement efforts in his school were lack of state funding for programs and a teacher tenure system which restricted some of his efforts to motivate "less enthusiastic" teachers.

Parenthetically, not all district teachers were as enamored by continued emphasis on school improvement as championed by several building principals (or the superintendent). In numerous teacher interviews, individual school principals were castigated as unrealistic in their expectations regarding how much teachers could do with children from particularly impoverished home environments. One elementary principal, for example, was described around the system as a "little Hitler;" and he too was one of the principals infected with a continuous drive for school improvement based on Effective Schools research.

Yet familiarity with the themes of school improvement and school effectiveness pervaded most of our discussions with school administrators in Braxton County. One supervisor, asked why she thought Braxton County had volunteered to become a demonstration site, responded that this was a good way of "showing others what a good school system we have." Yet another person in the central office was unsure why AEL was present at all. She could only assume that the folks from Charleston were coming in to learn **from** Braxton County how to develop effective programs, rather than the reverse.

In later interviews, the rather aggressive attitude toward school improvement activities suggested by the principal previously mentioned, as well as by sentiments of central office staff, was echoed by at least two other principals in the system. At these two schools, the first thing principals did when we walked in the door was to pull out extensive data sets and begin some discussion of their school improvement plans, based on the Effective Schools literature. Apparently, when I, the principal investigator of the evaluation study, introduced myself as a professor of education, both of these individuals assumed my familiarity with and interest in the effective schools research, and they were eager to discuss their schools and school improvement activities with me.

SUPERINTENDENT AND SCHOOL BOARD RELATIONS IN BRAXTON COUNTY

While a number of important expectations regarding what I would find in this study were disconfirmed during over 2 years (off and on) of site visits, there were several which appeared to be accurate. For example, I had assumed that school systems identified by state advisory committees as academically progressive and with stable and effective school leadership would have school boards equally as committed to processes of school improvement and innovation. Furthermore, I had assumed that, as central as a school superintendent was to the processes of running a school system, his or her leadership efforts would importantly depend upon solid support for his/her academic programs among school board members. What I saw in several of the counties involved in the AEL study, however, were school superintendents whose educational agendas appeared to be relatively independent of the direction and/or concern of board members for whom each (theoretically) worked. And the Braxton County superintendent provided an excellent illustration of this point.

Perhaps like many other rural school superintendents, the Braxton County superintendent came into office following the election of a new school board and the dismissal of a head football coach in 1976. Even though the superintendent had nothing to do with either of these events (as he did not reside in the county at the time), his early tenure as the Braxton County superintendent experienced some "aftershocks" related to these earlier factors.

As suggested earlier, few occupational opportunities of a "professional" or white collar nature exist in Braxton County today outside of the school system, which makes hiring and firing decisions virtually life altering situations there. Combined with the fact that most workers are organized and routinely defended by their union organizations, dismissing (or demoting) staff members is done with extreme care. And, since most residents in rural counties are well known and interract with each other in a varity of nonschool settings outside of work, the "impact on the community" appears an important factor in hiring and (especially) firing considerations.

So, too, sports programs appear to be extremely important in Braxton County (as they were in all RSS sites). For example, each of the three middle schools as well as the high school participate in a variety of interschool athletic leagues in several sports. And each school has a boosters club heavily supporting such activities. Not surprisingly, competitions between schools at all levels are well attended by local parents and other community members, and high school boys and girls football and basketball games are even broadcast on the local affiliate of the West Virginia public radio system.

To move perhaps belatedly to the point, most topics visible on the agenda of Braxton County School Board meetings during the fieldwork phase of our study involved either reports on expenditures and the condition of school finances, or involved discussions of hirings, transfers, and/or possible termination of employees for disciplinary reasons. Occasionally, the status of the athletic teams (and the coaches) in the county was also on the agenda of these meetings. However, rarely was there any overt discussion of the academic programs of the county. Nor, for that matter, was there any serious discussion of the AEL project among board members in the approximately dozen or so occasions when I was there. Significantly, when I was there, I was typically either the only one outside the board in attendance, or one of two or three.

Yet, in my judgment, it was the academic programs, social concerns, and educational philosophy of the county school system that were so interesting. Furthermore, by the time we had become involved in the county, the emphasis upon academic programs we observed in several of the schools we had visited (and suggested in AEL's Pro-S/E report) had become recognized statewide. Rankings of all counties in the state on academic skills (particularly at the elementary and middle school levels) showed Braxton County to be high on the list. And even the *Charleston Gazette* ran a lead story (with photos) profiling how one poor and rural school district (i.e., Braxton County) could be excellent even without an average resource base.

SCHOOL DISTRICT LEADERSHIP IN BRAXTON COUNTY

As the above description ought to suggest, leadership of the academic (and social) programs in Braxton County was not a major concern of the school board. However, perhaps to their credit, the board seemed content to allow the superintendent of schools to run the system as he desired. This is not to argue that the superintendent was unaware of the ultimate power of the board, for he was concerned about its composition and not eager to have to deal with potentially disruptive members who might be elected. Such an occurrence did not happen during the primary phase of fieldwork completed for this book, and even when a new member was elected in Spring 1990, the superintendent suggested this person would not cause any substantial shift in "my board" or district policy.

As I have already mentioned, the academic programs of the district we found to be innovative and aggressively pursued. And in many respects, at least according to the observations and interviews we made in Braxton County, these academic programs and the educational philosophy supporting them in the district were primarily a function of the superintendent's interests and concerns, as executed by building principals in most schools of the county.

I have also suggested some of the significant academic school programs and awards which the district "won" during the period we were present for this study. These would include above average rankings in elementary reading and math CTBS achievement scores (compared to state averages) in 1987 and 1988, and a state award for Sutton Middle School as an exemplary school for 1988. At the high school level, several specific teachers/programs were recognized for academic and literary prowess, including a state award to the high school journalism teacher for producing the best school newspaper in the state, and recognition of the high-quality drama program of Braxton County High School (BCHS) which performed in the state capital.

In addition, the active sponsorship of district principals to the West Virginia Principal's Academy, and pursuit of "effective schools" agendas in several schools, documented for us the seriousness of the academic agendas in Braxton County schools. Reflective of this last point, perhaps, was the response typically given by Braxton County principals to a Pro-S/E query, while only occasionally suggested by principles in other school districts involved in this study. When asked about how each Braxton County principal viewed his or her role as a school principal, virtually every one of them responded that "instructional leadership" was their function. In none of the other districts of this study was such a answer given across the board as the typical response.

This heavy academic performance emphasis was also very evident among central office staff in the county. For example, high CTBS reading scores appeared a particular point of pride among those in the central office assigned to supervisory duties of elementary and kindergarten children. When asked to explain why these scores were so high, the immediate answer was that district teachers had made extraordinary efforts in reading classes. And such an emphasis was demanded, they claimed, because all of later education depended upon successful reading skills and experiences in the early grades.

Such a "professional" response to this question (as well as others) also was echoed in discussions and interviews with the county superintendent. In his office, professional journals were quite prevalent on his desk and in his book-cases. Furthermore, on numerous visits to his office these journals appeared to actually have been read (or else intentionally strewn around the room). And contrary to discussions with some superintendents later in the AEL study, the Braxton County superintendent would frequently lapse into educational dis-course more common perhaps to educational researchers than to educational administrators.

Yet an academic emphasis was only one of the characteristics of a good school system, according to the superintendent. And a concentration solely upon academics, he argued, would not necessarily serve all parties of the community equally. Used as many in the county appear to be to the significant outmigration of county children upon high school graduation, the superintendent argued that schools which did not serve all in the community were essentially "cutting their own throats." That is (as he put it), "when the more able and better skilled students leave the county for a job or for college, only less-skilled and ambitious kids are left." When this happens, he suggested, "if they've had bad school experiences, how can we expect them to support the schools as adults?"

Accordingly (apparently), Braxton County schools supported and/or spon-sored a large number of alternative and community education efforts. For example, adult/community education programs were widely advertised and taught through the high school, and the part-time adult education director seemed always at the high school (next to the motel where I frequently stayed, and where we had numerous long interviews). At the other end of the age spectrum, aggressive head start and "prekindergarten" programs were initiated in hopes of identifying children whose special needs required attention even before regular teachers would begin working with them. As well, the county sponsored and housed a sheltered workshop for handicapped students and citizens; partially funded three community libraries in Sutton, Gassaway, and Burnsville (for use by students as well as by the public at large); and financially supported the county 4-H programs and recreation agencies.

As each of these examples suggest, the educational philosophy of the county (supported primarily by the superintendent) entailed more than school-based "excellence." Significantly, most of the programs just mentioned fell outside what the Braxton County School District was **obliged** to support by state law, and this significance is even further underlined by the relative paucity of funds available to fund the total school budget.

Again, just as the central office emphasis upon academic programs appeared outside the active involvement of the board of education there (although they did approve funding for such initiatives), so too the support of various community education projects outside the formal school curriculum appeared to result from the conviction of the superintendent. For, unlike some other counties in West Virginia, no "excess levy" or voluntary financial support for the school system's budget has ever been voted in by its taxpayers, many of whom appear to have received a number of school benefits from the minimum input of taxpayer dollars.

Again, as best we have been able to ascertain, academic and community service programs have been so aggressively pursued in Braxton County apparently through the efforts and grantsmanship of the county superintendent. In interviews with him (as corroborated by interviews of his staff), the superintendent argued that it is the function of the public school system to provide a host of social services to the community which otherwise would not be available, **in addition to** a heavy emphasis upon academic programs and basic skills for students in school.

As he viewed it, public schools in West Virginia had not only to provide **educational** services to children, but also **social** services. According to the superintendent, the decade of the 1980s saw an important erosion of the social "safety nets" earlier provided by the federal government. And his opinion was that social services to children, like providing early health care and subsidized breakfast and lunch programs, had to be the duty of the schools, since they had been so greatly cut back in other sectors.

In the course of this study, I had the occasion of sharing with the superintendent of Braxton County an article by James Coleman (1987) on the concept of "social capital" and the importance of active community and parent support and involvement in school affairs for learner outcomes. Furthermore, I suggested that nowhere in our assessment of the factors associated with the seeming success of the schools in Braxton County had we discovered the type of social capital which Coleman describes. He concurred, adding that he and his staff were trying to replace the loss of significant community support structures in

Braxton County at the school level and by forming school–business partnerships with each school. Subsequently, he shared the Coleman article with a number of staff members in the system and would often allude to this topic in later interviews.

SIGNIFICANT ISSUES AND UNDERTAKINGS IN THE 1988 AND 1989 SCHOOL YEARS

As suggested in much of the earlier discussion, we perceived a great amount of building autonomy in the nine total schools of the Braxton County system. That is, in the county building principals saw themselves and were encouraged by the central office to see themselves, as "instructional leaders." Significantly, principals too were carefully evaluated by the superintendent with regard to the success of their instructional leadership (a situation somewhat unique among the four systems studied for this book). And we were not surprised to find out that school-based information supplied by the AEL project became a data source later used by the superintendent in his principal evaluations. Interestingly, in the three schools run by "graduates" of the West Virginia Principals' Academy, putting together and coordinating "school improvement teams" seemed to be a favorite leadership strategy.

Of course, not all principal-run "school improvement" efforts ran as smoothly as much of the previous discussion would imply. For example, significant opposition to some of the school improvement efforts of the award-winning middle school principal surfaced among a few teachers in our early interviews there. So, too, as mentioned before, late 1989 saw a number of teachers in one of the elementary schools "revolt" against some of the school improvement strategies of the principal there.

According to his data, lower SES children were scoring comparatively poorer on achievement tests in the school, and differential teacher expectations must have been the cause. Some of the teachers, on the other hand, countered that there were limits to how much they could compensate for poor home learning conditions in the classroom. After all, they argued, they had already been working diligently on school improvement teams for several years and were familiar with what the effective schools literature said. But perhaps this literature was wrong, or its costs too high.

In another instance, the comparatively extreme concentration on academic skills emphasized in one elementary school caused community-wide controversy. Inasmuch as "time on task" has been empirically correlated with higher achievement test scores, more instructional time has been added in each of the Braxton County elementary schools during the past several years. While the (new) principal there pointed out that such an emphasis was crucial for maintaining high test scores for the school (and dictated anyway by the West

Virginia Master Plan), a number of parents began to question whether all of this academic concentration was robbing children of some of the fun they ought to be experiencing in elementary school. In particular, they noted that children only got one relatively brief recess period per day in this school, and had little opportunity to go outside and play. Not only was this concern voiced to the central office in the county, it also occupied center stage at least one school PTO meeting and was prominent in several "letters to the editor" in local papers.

Yet, most of the issues in Braxton during 1988 and 1989 have revolved around the continuing loss of revenues to operate the schools and issues and problems at the county high school.

As suggested earlier, the state of West Virginia is the primary funding source for most state schools. And this source of funding is even more crucial for poorer counties who have not voted in excess levies, like Braxton County. Given the statewide decline in revenues during the late 1980s, the West Virginia legislature began (predictably) to look for cost-saving possibilities throughout state budgets. Not surprisingly, school budgets quickly became a favorite focus.

At the same time, public perceptions of general school functioning in West Virginia were low. For example, a national campaigner against (what he claimed were) abuses of nationally standardized achievement tests was from West Virginia, and some of his heaviest criticisms were directed at the great number of schools in his state whose students tested "above average." Furthermore, both the national and statewide presses were full of stories during the period of this project with stories of local school inefficiency, waste, and incompetence. In West Virginia, many stories in the prominent *Charleston Gazette* profiled corrupt school systems, tales of poor teaching, and what they perceived as poor management practices.

Continuing to experience state treasury shortfalls, the state legislature went after county school system budgets during this period, apparently sensing that the time was right to reform public school accountability methods while at the same time saving money. In 1987, a bill in the legislature with a variety of cost-saving provisions targeted at county school systems was barely defeated. However, Senate Bill 14, passed in 1988, was an even more drastic measure intended to reduce programmatic and personnel expenditures funded under state equalization formulas (Ceperley, 1989).

In Braxton County, for example, no longer were special education students eligible for triple funding—a funding source used extensively for supplementing many school programs in addition to those for handicapped students. So, too, the number of central office staff and school administrators (including curriculum supervisors) funded under state equalization formulas was reduced by formula in Senate Bill 14, as were the number of teachers which would be paid for out-of-state sources. However, as the Braxton County superintendent saw it, the real targets of Senate Bill 14 were school administrators, as mandated minimums of classroom teachers rose in proportion to the total number of professional educators allowed per district.

> The state funds minimum salaries for professional educators, up to 55 per 1,000 students (adjusted enrollment). Before the passage of Senate Bill 14, at least 49 of the 55 professional educators were required to be instructional personnel (classroom teachers, librarians or counselors). SB14 increased the minimum instructional personnel to 50, beginning July 1, 1988, and in 1990, it will increase to 51 out of 55 professional educators. (Ceperley, 1988, p. 4)

In addition to specifying exactly what types of educational professionals and service personnel would be funded by the state, SB 14 also altered procedures for adjusted enrollment calculations. As mentioned earlier, Braxton County had relied on triple funding for all identified special education students, to boost its adjusted enrollment figures upwards. Senate Bill 14, however, specified that, by 1990, adjusted enrollment figures could not include more than the state average (16.2%) of special education students for any local district. According to such provisions, Braxton County schools were due to receive a financial cut in their state appropriations of over $1 million (out of an earlier estimated budget of $8,877,000).

In response, a number of rural and poor school systems around the state began to complain that loss of revenues for educating handicapped students, and declining administrative/instructional leadership personnel necessary for small and isolated schools, unduly affected the provision of education in their districts. School superintendents of the 25 most rural counties in the state (including Braxton County) formed a rural schools task force, issued a substantial statistical document that documented how funding formulas of Senate Bill 14 adversely affected the most sparsely populated school districts of the state, and spent several months in early 1989 lobbying for special financial considerations with Senate and House leaders in Charleston.

Importantly, Braxton County's superintendent was a primary spokesperson for this group, speaking directly with both House and Senate Education Committee chairs on such issues, as well as with the newly elected governor of the state. And just as importantly (for consideration in this study), AEL, through its earlier association with the Braxton County superintendent, became an important supplier of information to the rural task force. And the Rural Director of the Lab became a member of the task force.

CONCERNS AT BRAXTON COUNTY
HIGH SCHOOL

While fiscal concerns of a seemingly deteriorating school funding base increasingly began to occupy the attention of the superintendent in Braxton County, another long-standing concern of his began to fester at the high school. As may be true in a variety of other rural counties, the consolidated high school in Braxton County appears to have received the same kind of community support as the three previous high schools which now house other grades.

Several factors appear related to county-wide frustrations over the consolidated high school. In the first place (and perhaps intentionally), the high school is situated on the interstate near Flatwoods and is not in any of the three larger county communities. Apparently, in order convince county residents of the desirability of a new high school (and in order to get them to vote in favor of special bond money for its construction), many optimistic promises were made.

Unfortunately, according to our sources, few if any of the proposed advantages of the new high school were realized. For example, a large gymnasium and an auditorium were to have been part of the new building, as promised by the school board in the early 1960s. As well, since high school sports remain cornerstones of many Braxton Countians' interest in local schools, high hopes for combined teams was supposedly a selling point for high school consolidation. Yet hopes of becoming a state athletic power by merging three small but good (boys) high school teams into one for basketball and one for football (in addition to wrestling, which is another BCHS sport) have never been realized in the 20-year history of the county high school.

In addition to whatever poor planning may have been behind the consolidation plans from the beginning, money problems appear to have plagued the consolidated high school from the start. Soon after construction began on the new building, the original architect died, and county funds ran out before even the basic building was completed. Furthermore, the gym was scaled back so that there isn't enough room even for all parents to watch basketball games there: Instead, home games for all major indoor BCHS interscholastic sports are held in the National Guard Armory several miles away, between Sutton and Gassaway. In order to seat all students and/or hold school related public meetings at BCHS, the moveable wall between the cafeteria and the gym must be opened up and chairs spread out across both the lunchroom and gym floors.

This is not to suggest that important activities/programs are not present or observable at the high school. In accord with district-wide emphasis on diverse educational programs, four of its most highly successful offerings/activities are noteworthy even though they cannot be assessed in achievement score terms. For example, not only have the drama and journalism programs won statewide awards, but community education and vocational education offerings appear to be extremely strong and diverse. So too, the BCHS marching band is a strong source of local pride among students and administrators alike. Parenthetically (again), the commitment given vocational programs at the high school seems related to the fact that the superintendent has his doctorate in vocational education and has himself a penchant for such undertakings as rebuilding cars in his own shop at home.

Yet, even given the multiple emphases on a variety of curricular opportunities at the high school, and even given the proven track record of district students on achievement tests in earlier grades, the dropout rate of students in Braxton County High School has hovered between 20% and 30% during the past decade. And, with the possible exception of attempting to maintain local programs already in place-with fewer state dollars (discussed above), the "battle" at the high school has probably garnered the most recent attention in the Braxton County school system.

To make a long and complex story short, there occurred throughout our primary fieldwork activities in Braxton County a protracted war between the district superintendent and the principal and teachers at BCHS. In accord with the superintendent's earlier expressed philosophy, his conviction is that the high school must attempt to retain all of its students by providing different sorts of programming for all of them. And while advanced coursework and creative academic undertakings are readily available in the high school, it is the non-college-bound students whom the superintendent is particularly concerned about. The superintendent makes no bones about it: It was a vocational teacher in the school system who gave him the encouragement to succeed in school. And fully 90% of the current students in the high school take at least some coursework in the vocational wing of the building.

Put another way, college-bound students will likely succeed if the right programs are available to them in school, according to the superintendent. But since there are relatively few local jobs in the county for Braxton County High School graduates, working with these children (and with the psychological and social problems many bring from impoverished backgrounds) must be equally important in a rural and poor county.

Yet many teachers, and the high school principal, do not see their mission in quite the same terms. Rather, school discipline and academic attainment in core curricular areas are (predictably) espoused by many teachers, who believe that students who can't measure up to school achievement and attendance policies ought to be suspended/expelled as their performance dictates.

In order to attack the perceived dropout problem at the high school, several important strategies have been advanced. We have mentioned previously that relatively comprehensive and innovative vocational programs are run at BCHS, including (for example) a building trades program whereby many students spend half-days off-campus actually building/renovating (with formal supervision) houses/offices for various community groups. So, too, the drama program, school publications, and band undertakings have high priority at the central office level.

Yet even such programs did not appear to be denting the dropout rate at BCHS, and in 1987 monies from Job Training Partnership Act and Appalachian Regional Commission were obtained for an innovative dropout prevention program called "Context III." The Context III program was developed by two professional educators with long histories of research and development efforts in public education. Based importantly on the Slavin (1986) cooperative learning approach, the logic behind Context III is that "student blockages" are the primary reason behind student decisions to drop out of school. Furthermore, according to the program, dropping out of school is but the final event in a student's career, an event that can be negated if and when teachers and other school based staff undertake the task of analyzing and remediating the causes of such blockages

Without going further into the details of this program, the underlying assumption is that reducing dropout rates in the school demands a systematic and proactive stance by building leaders and teachers in the remediation of the blockages which can lead to dropping out. And the attention to potential student blockages must begin in the elementary school, not just in the high school. Furthermore, according to the program, forming groups such as "student advocacy teams" to investigate and alleviate student blockages related to future possible student decisions to leave school is essential. Standing by and claiming that the school cannot overcome "student backgrounds" which predict dropout rates, or even worse, actually "pushing out" students who are perceived as unable/unwilling to accommodate to academic discipline, is deemed unacceptable in the Context III philosophy.

As I am not particularly well versed in the myriad number of programs designed for school dropouts, it is perhaps the case that the Context III program is not all that unique among programs of its type (although I personally am in agreement with much of its underlying logic). Yet what we found most compelling about the program was that the superintendent himself was personally committed to its implementation in the Braxton County school system, and that he was equally well versed in its aims, objectives, and underlying premises as were the several high-school-based counselors/advisors who coordinated the program throughout the system.

Which brings us the heart of the matter: Try as they might, neither the superintendent nor his several "agents" in the high school (the curriculum coordinator, a dropout prevention counselor, and the vocational director) were able to muster unanimous support for the Context III program at the high school in the 1987–1988 and 1988–1989 school years. True, there were in-service programs specifically dealing with how to use the program, there were dropout-prevention public relations "blitzes" on the radio, and school-climate improvement pronouncements were available from counselors and the central office. Yet some teachers, and the high school principal, were ostensibly more interested in running an orderly and academically respectable high school than they were in devoting extra time and energy to keeping all "at-risk" students.

This being the case, the county superintendent began to use what we suggested before was his strongest tool for gaining personnel compliance in the system: highly formalized evaluation procedures. As suggested before, firing school employees is hard to accomplish in Braxton County. What the superintendent **does** use evaluations for, however, are forms of staff evaluation in which low ratings are used by the central office to submit extensive "self-improvement" plans for remediating poorly judged performance.

Not surprisingly, the superintendent in Braxton County defends the criteria for personnel evaluation and required remediation with reference to state guidelines for so doing. As well, recent cutbacks in appropriations for teaching and administrative positions has enabled him to differentially reassign teachers to different schools/grade levels etc. as he decides. In Braxton County (as is perhaps true throughout West Virginia) being "put on transfer" means that one's job next year is only guaranteed depending on future enrollment figures and instructional requirements, primarily *as interpreted/determined by the superintendent.*

Not happy with BCHS's response to the Context III program (or others designed to enhance positive school climate at the high school), the superintendent sent in several central office staff to evaluate teachers there. Two events technically enabled him to do this: On the one hand, around the system elementary and middle school teachers had begun to notice/complain about the fact that their performance was constantly under scrutiny by principals, yet they saw no similar actions being undertaken at the high school. At the same time, the principal at the high school (who had been there for 8 years) was diagnosed as having cancer of the liver and perhaps understandably had little interest in the extra effort which formal evaluation of teachers would imply.

Predictably, perhaps, central office evaluations of teachers met with great resistance, especially when some teachers were evaluated by central office staff who had never taught at the high school level, and when the evaluations were actually made after the date when district policy said they were to be made.

When the results of the evaluations were returned to teachers at the high school, a number of them appealed their assessments (with suggestions for remediation) to the superintendent and the school board. So too, a formal petition was drawn up and signed by 41 teachers proclaiming the "unfair" evaluation procedures of the central office. As it later happened, the superintendent formally acknowledged the technical violation of district policy regarding high school evaluations; but according to him, "they know now that I've got my eye on them." And notice had been served that he was displeased with a number of specific teachers, several of whom, not coincidentally, were later placed on transfer when the ramifications of Senate Bill 14 finally hit home in Braxton County.

LOCAL SCHOOL AND COMMUNITY
DEVELOPMENTS IN THE SUMMER OF 1989

Fieldwork related to the AEL Rural/Small School School/Community Partnership Model (the results of which are briefly discussed in Chapter 6) were essentially completed in Braxton County by Spring of the 1989 school year. Yet, in writing up the "final report" on field activities for OERI, I completed a short postscript several months later. In this postscript (which is also further extended in Chapter 6), I noted several additional developments

On the one hand, I observed several very visible economic developments in the county. For example, a new MacDonalds restaurant was built at the Flatwoods exit of I-79 in 1989, and quickly proved too small for the overflow crowds it attracted off the interstate. Within 6 months it had already been remodeled and enlarged.

Next to the MacDonalds we observed that another chain steakhouse and another motel were also under construction, and all of these developments were adjacent to, and visible from, the high school. Ironically, all of this development had and was taking place on the original estate of John Sutton, now owned by John Skidmore, and the old family home was torn down to make way for a gas station, motel, and the MacDonalds.

Two other potential economic "developments" were also on the drawing boards as we left Braxton County in 1989. The District of Columbia had entered into an initial agreement to build a large correctional facility for D.C. prisoners in Gilmer County, just to the northwest of the Braxton County line. Should this prison be built (a project that earned general disapproval among Braxton Countians when the target was their county), hundreds of new jobs would be created in the region, many of which would theoretically provide employment for people living in the Burnsville area. Meanwhile, at the other end of the county (and further away from the interstate), the town of Gassaway continued to decline. And even the auto dealership which has been the business "partner" of Davis Elementary had abandoned downtown Gassaway and moved further up route 4 towards Sutton and I-79.

Coincidentally, the state of West Virginia was also attempting to "regionalize" a number of social services throughout the state, including both prisons and schools. Regional Educational Service Areas (RESAs) were being asked (and expected) to expand their services for county school systems, including services to Braxton County. Importantly, Braxton County already had an extensive history of involvement with its RESA, which was unique among the districts we performed fieldwork in.

As well, a regional jail potentially involving 6 counties was being openly discussed for central West Virginia, and in 1989 the southern end of Braxton County was a favored locale of the committee instituted to select a place for the regional jail. Perhaps due to the business acuity the Braxton County superintendent was reputed to have (although his part-time business manager performs many of the actual accounting functions), he was a member of the regional jail site selection committee.

As well, the superintendent served on a number of other commissions which he himself described were composed of "wild groups of do-gooders," a term many native West Virginians reserve for "ex-hippies" from the Northeast who migrated into the state in the 1960s and 1970s. In addition to the Rural Task Force earlier mentioned, the superintendent served in 1989 on the Governor's Task Force on Children, Youth and Families. Put together ostensibly to suggest to Governor Caperton a comprehensive strategy for addressing the plight of children in the state (half of whom, according to the superintendent, are born into families below the poverty line), the final report of this committee apparently stopped short of recommending additional funding for recommended new programs. Subsequently, the superintendent joined a(nother) new group of "do-gooders" and "former hippies" who were interested in "monitoring" (and perhaps publicly criticizing) what they initially perceived as a half-hearted public relations gesture on the part of the governor.

At the same time as the superintendent was worried about the future of the system under the then standing state legislature (according to him, "Jesus Christ himself won't be able to run this system in a couple of years"), and he has increased his regional and state-wide visibility in various social causes. So, too, the general mood of the teachers in the district remained quite low due to the various financial problems of the state and cutbacks related to SB 14.

Yet perhaps the biggest system-wide issue other than funding continued to be the condition of the high school and its leadership. In Spring 1989, the high school principal received "a brutal evaluation" (according to the superintendent), and the shortening of his annual contract, which used to extend beyond the end of classes into the summer. Technically, the reduction in days the principal was compensated for was due to SB 14 budget cutbacks, which also affected almost every administrator in the system.

After losing an appeal to the School Board over the reduction of his contract period, he left town for his summer vacation the day before school ended in 1989 and did not reappear until the first week of classes for the fall. Not surprisingly, given the principal's illness and the financial problems of the district throughout the 1988–89 school year, improving the climate of the high school and the dropout rate were issue virtually lost in the shuffle at BCHS.

And things didn't get any better in Fall 1989 at the high school. District wide, the system appeared to regain some composure as a result of the various cutbacks put in place by the central office (and various retirements, etc.), which saved enough money so that no personnel were actually laid off. Of course, several teachers in the system who had received (consistently) poor evaluations somehow did not end up in the same places they had occupied before the crisis hit.

But the battle for control of the high school remained undecided at the end of the 1989 school year. Upon the reappearance of the principal in the fall, it was discovered that his cancer was once again active. And as the OERI evaluation report was being submitted, administrators and the central office were all biding their time, waiting for some final resolution of his illness. According to the superintendent, "we're desperate to do some school improvement at the high school, but I'm not sure [the principal] can handle it right now. We'll have to wait for [leadership] change." And this change became possible in 1990.

REFERENCES

Branscome, J. (1978). Annihilating the hillbilly: The Appalachian's struggle with America's institutions. In H. Lewis, L. Johnson, & D. Askins (Eds.), *Colonialism in modern America: The Appalachian case*. Boone, NC: Appalachian Consortium Press.

Byrne, W. E. R. (1940). *Tale of the Elk*. Richwood, WV: Mountain State Press.

Ceperley, P. (1989). *Senate Bill 14—1988 changes in funding education in West Virginia*. Charleston, WV: Appalachia Educational Laboratory and the Office of Educational Research and Improvement.

Coleman, J. (1987). Families and schools. *Educational Researcher, 16*(6), 32-38.

Dean, D. (1989, August 14). Gassaway Days speech. *Braxton's Citizens' News*, sec. 2, p. 2.

DeYoung, A. J. (1987). The status of American rural education research: An integrated review and commentary. *Review of Educational Research, 57*(2), 123-148.

DeYoung, A. J. (1985). Economic development and educational status in Appalachian Kentucky. *Comparative Educational Review, 29*(1), 47-67.

Dick, D. (1976). *Echoes from the West Virginia hills*. Charleston, WV: West Virginia Retired School Employees.

Eller, R. (1982). *Miners, millhands and mountaineers*. Knoxville, TN: University of Tennessee Press.

MACED. (1986). *Would you like to swing on a Star?: Opportunities to improve education in Kentucky's Fifth Congressional District*. Berea, KY: Mountain Association for Community Economic Development.

Rice, O. (1985). *West Virginia: A history*. Lexington, KY: University of Kentucky Press.

Slavin, R. (1986). *Using student team learning* (3rd ed.). Baltimore, MD: Center for Research on Elementary and Middle Schools, Johns Hopkins University.

Truby, R. (1983). Pauley v. Bailey and the West Virginia master plan. *Phi Delta Kappan, 65*(4), 284-290.

Weston Community Planning Commission. (1967). *Sutton, West Virginia: A comprehensive development plan*. West Chester, PA: WCPC.

West Virginia Department of Employment Security. (1985). *West Virginia profiles*. Charleston, WV: Labor and Economic Research Section.

West Virginia Writers' Project. (1941). *Sutton on the Elk*. Charleston, WV: Works Progress Administration.

3

CHARLOTTE COUNTY, VIRGINIA

As explained earlier, school systems discused in this book were not chosen at random, by the evaluation staff of the earlier report, or by me for this book. Rather, AEL set up an elaborate procedure for so doing which was discussed in Chapter 1. In the evaluation report, we paid special attention to two interesting site selection procedures in Virginia. One had to do with the comparative paucity of eligible districts under the guidelines of site selection laid out by AEL. According to rurality, district size, and poverty rate, only 3 of Virginia's 137 school districts were technically eligible for the school/community demonstration project, and eligibility criteria had to be moderately adjusted to enlarge the pool to 5. Furthermore, and apparently to the surprise of RSS staff, school districts in the western (i.e., Appalachian) part of the state were not among even these five: rather, all five districts were in the southern and eastern parts of the state. And all had sizable percentages of minority (Black) students.

Part of the reason so few districts were eligible in Virginia stemmed from the fact that most are quite large. Also, compared to other states in AEL's region, Virginia districts are comparatively affluent. According to the southern regional education board, the financial condition of most Virginia school systems (1986–1987) is higher across the board than are those of the states of Kentucky, Tennessee, and West Virginia. Their figures particularly suggest significant discrepancies in per pupil costs and teacher salaries among these states, as well as important differences in the percentage of students continuing their education beyond high school. Virginia students as a group have much higher post-secondary-school attendance rates compared to the other three states, even though SAT scores for Virginia students are no higher than those of Kentucky, Tennessee, and West Virginia students (SREB, 1987).

While Appalachian Virginia school districts ended up not being technically eligible for the RSS demonstrations, this lack of western Virginia school districts actually appeared of little real concern to AEL representatives at the site selection meeting held in Roanoke on June 17, 1988. As will be discussed in Chapter 4, it was hoped that at least one demonstration site from the four state area would have a sizable minority population. Yet the Tennessee Advisory

73

TABLE VA-1.   DATA ON EDUCATION OF POOR CHILDREN IN
CHARLOTTE COUNTY, 1832–1860 (FROM SHEPARD, 1938, p.49)

Year	Number common schools in county	Number poor children in county	Number poor children in school	Per capita cost	Total cost tuition & other purposes
				Per. da.	
1832	8	300	95	$.04	$360.16
1834	26	300	88	.04	382.06
1837	24	400	229	.04	720.68
1846	26	400	146	.04	423.91
1847	23	396	145	.04	460.18
1848	20	398	101	.04	373.90
1849	20	385	163	.04	511.14
				Per. yr.	
1851	18	–	110	3.96	390.02
1852	18	331	128	3.37	431.30
1854	14	308	103	4.00	496.47
1855	19	332	146	4.66	681.36
1858	17	298	147	7.43	1155.52
1859	–	341	152	7.50	1195.36
1860	–	341	174	5.59	1014.69

Group (which met two weeks before the Virginia AG) failed to nominate any. Therefore, the RSS director expressed some interest in drawing from among the five technically eligible Virginia districts: for they all represented a different student population than participating districts in the other states.

However, as matters turned out, at least one member of the Virginia AG resisted selection of any of these five (believing that none of them had any chance for success according to AEL guidelines). Furthermore, since three of the four who attended the site selection meeting in Roanoke resided/worked in western Virginia, none of the "advisors" in the Advisory Group could give much advice on the five districts in question. And none claimed even to have been in the county eventually chosen to participate.

Each of the five eligible districts (or "divisions," as they are called in Virginia) were contiguous with county geopolitical organization. That is, no town, city, or special districts which exist in Virginia were among the five considered on June 17. Furthermore, unlike the earlier case of West Virginia, Virginia school divisions must interact more extensively with county government representatives: for example, minimum funding formulas are essentially locked into place in West Virginia (without a public referendum), while school budgets are under more variable and annual control of county boards of supervisors in Virginia. And the superintendent of schools in Virginia counties must formally appear before these boards to have budgets approved, a responsibility of extreme importance in states with such a system of school finance.

The five divisions technically eligible in Virginia according to AEL guidelines were Brunswick, Cumberland, Charlotte, Northampton, and Southampton. By a process of elimination, several were rather quickly demoted in the ensuing discussion. Two primary (and interrelated) reasons appeared to play heavily in the minds of the AG during the afternoon site selection discussion: whether and to what extent race relations were problematic; and to what extent private academies were prevalent in or near each county. On these criteria, Brunswick and Northampton were discounted. Furthermore, both Southampton and Cumberland were alleged to have divided Black and White communities, although recent evidence of this was not brought forward. Only Charlotte County seemed to escape serious criticism of community dynamics related to schooling—yet this escape was also based primarily on lack of information (other than statistical information provided by AEL), rather than first-hand experience.

Stable leadership was also discussed as important for consideration, as suggested by RSS staff in attendance. Both Brunswick and Southampton were alleged to be administered by "custodial" (i.e., noninnovative) superintendents. Yet the superintendent of Charlotte County was still an unknown, having just begun his superintendency there in 1988. One member of the advisory group knew of the Charlotte County superintendent, as it turned out he was from, and had been a principal in, a western Virginia school system. Yet he had no feedback on the superintendent's first 6 months on the job in Charlotte County. And the other two divisions were not seriously talked about further at this meeting, the consensus being that any county which had a significant private academy would never muster the type of community support necessary for an effective school/community partnership. (The historical and contemporary significance of private and typically White academies in Virginia and much of the South will be developed in later pages of this chapter.)

For purposes of this discussion, further details related to final selection of Charlotte County for the RSS project are not presented here. From our vantage point, the most interesting observation of this process was that most members of the Virginia Advisory Group assembled by AEL knew little about the local leadership of rural school divisions in Southside Virginia, and most had rather negative impressions of school functioning there. This was particularly true of the AG representative from the Governor's office, who was convinced that no Southside school division had the potential for school improvement as envisioned by AEL.

Instead of selecting a school division in Roanoke on June 17, it was decided that a second AG meeting would be held in the state capital (Richmond) on June 23 for further deliberation. And it was decided that personal appearances/ presentations from each of the three divisions still under consideration would be the best way to make a final selection. The Richmond Advisory Group meeting was a one-of-a-kind occurrence for the school/community partnership demonstrations. Meeting in the state capital under the technical sponsorship of the governor, two- and three-member delegations from Brunswick, Southampton, and Charlotte Counties made a pitch to be included in the AEL demonstrations, even though they could only have received scant and piecemeal information about the program they were volunteering for, and even though none present really understood beforehand what the mission of AEL was in the region.

At this meeting, the Southampton superintendent and one of his board members made the first "presentation" to the Advisory Group, arguing that the RSS demonstration project would help him put the local private academy in his district out of business. The Charlotte County superintendent made the second presentation: the private academy in his county had in effect just been put out of business, and the minority community was unanimously behind the new spirit in the county for enhanced educational opportunities there. He further described not only the positive academic programs of Charlotte County (which the Southampton superintendent had also gone out of his way to mention), but also the aggressive minority teacher recruitment programs just instituted there, and the special programs designed to keep minority and poor students in school.

Brunswick County was last to petition the group. Arguing that one of the biggest problems there was loss of enrollment, the superintendent talked about both his previous innovative programs and his desire to build/consolidate schools for more effective age groupings in the years ahead. Unlike each of the other two superintendents, the Brunswick County superintendent appeared to have a plan requiring outside public relations aid, which he perceived the RSS project might contribute to.

Unfortunately, the "plan-in-mind" orientation of the Brunswick County superintendent seemingly caused his district to be eliminated by the Virginia AG in post-presentation discussions. And the Southampton superintendent was judged perhaps somewhat overly optimistic regarding the success seen in that county on the race issue. Instead, Charlotte County was recommended by the state AG (with the full concurrence of the RSS director) as one where not only good things were beginning to happen, but where fresh energy, and no preconceived agenda, existed. So, by the late afternoon of June 23, Charlotte County had been chosen, even though its superintendent left convinced that no rural and poor district like his would ever attract an outside interest like that of the AEL school/community demonstration project.

CHARLOTTE COUNTY:
THE ANTEBELLUM CONTEXT

Charlotte County, Virginia, lies in the south-central region of Virginia known as the Southside. Initially, Southside Virginia was considered to include most of rural Virginia south of the James River, where the capital of the state (Richmond) lies, and to extend from the Atlantic coast to the Cumberland Plateau of the Appalachian mountain range. In current fashion, one can drive less than three hours in either direction from Charlotte County to either the ocean or to the foothills of the mountains. So too, several hours of driving to the northeast will put one in the nation's capital, while an even shorter drive in a southerly direction will bring one into the Research Triangle "hub" of North Carolina's economic activities.

Charlotte County is bounded by the Staunton branch of the Roanoke River on the southwest, and lies one county south of the Appomattox River. Currently contiguous counties to Charlotte are Appomattox and Prince Edward to the north, Campbell on the west, Halifax to the south, and Mecklenburg and Lunenburg to the east. Charlotte County contains almost 500,000 square acres, with its greatest width being 25 miles and its greatest length 50 miles. Its topography is described in county economic development brochures as of "moderately high plateau," and is traversed by numerous creeks and streams. The surface of the county is primarily rolling and hilly, and is currently over half-forested (Center for Economic Development, 1988).

Early development in Virginia lay to the north and east of Charlotte County, and to the west lie those counties of the state more similar in topography, history, and economic development forces to Braxton County, West Virginia, which we have just discussed. While by no means the earliest developed area of the state of Virginia, the first settlements in Charlotte County preceded that of Braxton County by over 70 years, and incorporation as a county unit within Virginia occurred in Charlotte County probably before what is now known as Braxton County had even been fully explored.

As in all other counties of this study, Charlotte County was formed from several other counties within an already existing state. In the early 18th century, the area which would eventually become Charlotte County lay on the western frontier of Virginia, and a number of efforts and inducements by the Virginia House of Burgesses were instituted to settle the south-central and western areas of the state. One motivation for such settlement was to provide a western buffer zone to the south and west of the more established coastal and northern piedmont regions of Virginia, which by the end of the 17th century had already become thriving centers of agriculture and commerce.

In point fact, what would later become the county seat of Charlotte County was once a munitions location fortified by the state of Virginia for militia action during the French and Indian War. Even before this (circa 1715), Governor Spotswood's famous "Ride through the Blueridge" went through Charlotte County, and its strategic location for later inroads into Indian territory was noted. The fortification established during the French and Indian War was first called Magazine, and later became Maryville. Later this town became Charlotte Courthouse when the county of Charlotte was formed in 1764 (Ailsworth, Keller, Nichols, & Walker, 1979).

The typical organization of Virginia counties, as was the case later in West Virginia, Tennessee, and Kentucky, was for settlements locating in wilderness areas to petition state governments for incorporation as county units once population growth achieved sizes which local citizens believed would enable them to form more local county governments. Therefore, during the 18th century, the land area which was to eventually become Charlotte County was included in four different and ever smaller counties. Once belonging within the boundaries of Charles City County, this area became "subdivided" during the early 18th century, first into Prince George County, then into Brunswick County, into Lunenburg County, and finally into Charlotte County in 1764.

As the names of each of these counties might suggest, a variety of New World practices and customs were inherited in 18th-century Virginia from the mother country. Charlotte County itself, for example, was named for the German Princess Sophie Charlotte of Mecklenburg-Strelitz, who wed King George III of England when she was 17 years old. So, too, many procedures of early county units of government in Virginia, as well as most important economic and political aspects of life within these places, were adopted directly from England and English political and organizational forms.

For example, political units of government in Virginia up until the time of the American Revolution were both formally and informally tied to the Church of England. And while the justice system formally belonged within the jurisdiction of secular authorities, social services (which would later include public education) were early on considered primarily a function of the church. Furthermore, those who administered secular duties of early Virginia counties were expected to participate extensively in church-related activities as well, in order to represent the moral responsibilities of their positions. According to the "official" history of the county:

> County government in early Virginia was separated into two factions. The parish was the religious district with church wardens or vestrymen carrying out specific duties which dealt chiefly with the welfare of parish members. The county court was the other governing body, responsible for administering justice and providing the officials that performed services not entrusted to the parish. These governmental positions were positions of honor, prominence and power. Although the fees received by some officials were more than nominal, the rewards for most measured in prestige rather than money. (Ailsworth et al., 1979, p. 64)

In 18th-century Charlotte County, then, church and state were clearly intertwined. Property boundaries, for example, were surveyed and monitored by church officials, as tithes for support of church activities (like supporting the poor) were mandatory. Furthermore, many other aspects of both private and public life were constrained to some form of administrative regulation by either the court system or the church before the Revolutionary War in early Virginia. For example, the county courts of Virginia licensed and set fees for local businesses and occupations. They appointed persons responsible for maintaining rural roads, for authorizing ministers to perform marriages, for registering "free Negroes," and so on.

However, by the late 18th century the formal hold of the church upon county social and civil procedures had greatly eroded. For example, in order to stimulate settlement of the western region of the state, a number of colonies not earlier recognized by the established Episcopalian church were recognized as legitimate. In Charlotte County, an important Presbyterian Colony, which had historically rejected and been persecuted by the "Established Church," flourished in the Cub Creek area before 1750. Thus, a precedent of religious toleration was evident there even before the Revolutionary War.

So, too, various acts of the British parliament, which attempted to constrain trade and business activities of the colonies apparently led to serious political activism among Charlotte Countians by the late 18th century. For example, Charlotte County was reputed to be either the first or second county government in Virginia to vote in favor of independence from Britain in 1776.

During the American War of Independence, Charlotte County saw several military skirmishes and contributed militia to a number of engagements against British armies. As favorite places to cross the Dan and Staunton Rivers lay just south of the county, frequent crossings of these rivers by various forces occurred throughout the Revolutionary War period. In point of fact, local histories of Charlotte County still proudly document the importance of citizens and local government leaders to the cause of independence during this period. Two of the most important statesmen of the local area were John Randolph and Patrick Henry, both of whom had Charlotte County ties in the late 18th century. Parenthetically, the consolidated high school (opened in 1939) of the county is not named after the county (as is the case in other school districts of this study), but instead is named Randolph-Henry High School. And the nickname of the athletic/academic teams of the school is the "Statesmen."

With victory over the British achieved in the 1780s, a number of important changes in the political structure of the county occurred. At the state level, for example, more autonomy for local decision making appears to have been granted to individual counties. Furthermore, whereas Charlotte County representatives to the House of Burgesses had been virtual newcomers before 1776, by the turn of the 19th century a number of important Virginia statesmen could claim Charlotte County as their home.

Perhaps just as importantly, the loss by Great Britain to the United States meant the end of formal church and state interrelationships in Southside Virginia. Since most formal church (Episcopalian) positions were officially tied to England, the loss of its armies in the colonies caused the "recall" of its ministers back to England. So, too, given the great amount of religious toleration in places like Southside Virginia, many citizens of the area were quite happy to formally cut their ties with the Church of England and to transfer many of the nonspiritual duties of the former church back to secular government offices. In point of fact, the historical evidence suggests that within a few years after the end of the Revolutionary War, the Episcopalian Church was a minority denomination in Charlotte County, having been replaced by the middle of the 19th century with numerous Baptist, Methodist, and Presbyterian congregations.

CHARLOTTE COUNTY'S ECONOMY BEFORE THE CIVIL WAR

The economy of most of eastern and central Virginia, including the Southside, has historically depended on agriculture, with tobacco as the major cash crop. In fact, the potential for tobacco growing in Charlotte County was one of the major reasons why large landowners came to the area, and one of the major reasons why they stayed. Furthermore, the importance of tobacco in the state economy is documented by the fact that this commodity actually had formal exchange value during the 18th and early 19th century. For example, in order to entice reluctant "investors" to settle on the Virginia frontier during the middle of the 18th century, the House of Burgesses passed a "Southern Boundary" act in 1738.

> there were three provisions of the of the 1738 Act that greatly enhanced the appeal of leaving the devoloped Tidewater section of Virginia to make a permanent settlement in the boundary counties of Virginia. Part II of the act contained a provision which made all settlers exempt from taxes for a ten year period beginning in 1738, if they would settle on the Roanoke River. . . and the lands lying between the northern and southern branches of the Roanoke River. (Ailsworth et al., 1979, p. 32)

Furthermore, since payment of fees for land and commodities in rural Virginia were historically made in tobacco weights, this 1738 act was viewed as innovative because it allowed for the purchase of land with money *instead* of tobacco:

> Many colonists had been reluctant to risk the possible financial difficulties that a move to the Virginia wilderness might cause if their former occupation would not support them once there. Part II of the 1738 Act allowed the settlers to make all payments in current money, as well as pay all fees and taxes after the ten year exemption period in currency. Because raising tobacco had become the most feasible source of income for Tidewater plantation owners, tobacco was the accepted means of exchange in the colony.. . . . Thus, lifting the requirement that all exchange had to be made in tobacco would allow settlers plenty of time to develop a means of income in the frontier area. (Ailsworth et al., 1979, p. 32)

Like the already "developed" areas of Virginia, Southside Virginia too proved to be an excellent location for the growing and harvesting of tobacco. Therefore, it wasn't too long before a full-fledged "plantation economy" was in existence there. And in fact, there was concern in Richmond that too many large estates were forming in the Southside which might prohibit the population growth they hoped would occur.

Yet, as we have discussed, smaller settlements by less wealthy immigrant groups not tied to the landed aristocracy of Tidewater Virginia also took up occupancy in the area which was to become Charlotte County. So too, transportation difficulties involved with tobacco trade in the late 18th century appear to have precluded Charlotte County's sole dependence on tobacco. While the Roanoke River did border the county to the south, it emptied into North Carolina, which was a rival colony of Virginia before the Revolutionary War, and other means of transportation to coastal markets were relatively underdeveloped. Therefore, much subsistence farming occurred in Charlotte County prior to the Civil War. Cash crops of more regional utility (e.g., grains) also appear to have been raised in the area, as well as livestock.

THE IMPACT OF THE WAR BETWEEN THE STATES

Southside Virginia appears to have been a flourishing region of the U.S. by the middle of the 19th century. The tobacco trade was still strong, and the arrival of the railroad in the county enabled a variety of agricultural markets to be even better reached from the Southside by the 1850s. Somewhat later, the timber industry of Charlotte County was boosted appreciably by availability of rail shipment (an industry which currently provides one important agricultural alternative to tobacco and cattle raising there).

Yet tobacco growing is an extremely labor intensive process, and the plantation economy which emerged in the county during 18th century was heavily dependent upon slavery. Thus, during the Civil War, all of Southside Virginia backed the Confederacy. And when the war ended, so too did the heyday of political and economic vitality of Charlotte County.

As in its earlier history, historians of Charlotte County during the Civil War era enthusiastically tell the stories of local heroes from the county and how they contributed to what would become the "Lost Cause." While only one pitched battle occurred in the county during the war, troop movements and occupations during the period from 1861 to 1865 were significant. Not only did the county supply several units to the Army of the Confederacy, but the local militia turned out numerous times to help repel Union army units in surrounding counties during the conflict.

At the conclusion of the war, Charlotte County was politically, socially, and economically in ruin. Since the Union had blockaded all Southern ports during the war, and since many of the physically able White males had gone off to fight in the conflict, the tobacco economy of Southside Virginia had completely collapsed. Also, since whatever available agricultural surplus was either procured by the Confederacy or donated to the war effort, by the end of the war even those living on Southside farms were hungry. And, not surprisingly, units of both armies passing through Charlotte County towards the end of the war helped themselves to whatever was left.

> By April of 1865 the county had run out of food and other important items. Also, there was little, if any, hope among its citizens. The surrender at Appomattox created such a state of confusion within the county, that there were no entries in the Court Order Books from April to August. When the books were continued again however, the first entries called for new elections for public officials. This was the result of northern interference, and the beginning of one of the worst periods in our country's history, reconstruction. (Ailsworth et al., 1979, p. 245)

FORMAL EDUCATION IN THE SOUTHSIDE

As opposed to educational undertakings in many other parts of the U.S., public education in Charlotte County has in many respects only been a viable entity during the 20th century. That is, in most of Southside Virginia, education was viewed strictly as a private affair and not an undertaking to be financed from public coffers. To be sure, there has always been a highly educated class of citizens in Virginia and the Southside. However, up until the 20th century there was little agreement on a common curriculum for all public school students, and even then the secondary school curriculum of the state appears to have been a dual track system until federal desegregation efforts of the mid-20th century.

In essence, during the antebellum period wealthy plantation owners either hired private tutors for their own children or set up private academies with other landowners for the mutual benefit of their boys and girls. For the landed gentry, typical schooling experiences for boys would include private tutoring in Virginia and, potentially, a liberal arts college education in England. The education of elite girls would frequently follow the same early pattern, although attendance at a private girls academy might more typically conclude formal instruction for women.

At the other extreme were the children of poor farmers and slaves. Of course, slaves had no political rights, and neither did their children. Therefore, what individual slave owners did with them was deemed their own business. Furthermore, since it was assumed that sound character training and specific skill instruction would best benefit poor White children, apprenticeship programs for nonfarm Whites and pauper schools supported by philanthropic efforts (and the church) for the poor were set up in the state. Unfortunately, inasmuch as only orphans and the children of indigents were seen as requiring public assistance in their education, public schooling soon became an enigma within most of Virginia, including the Southside. And even the formal instruction of these classes of children was severely hampered with the return of many of the clergy to England during the 1780s.

> (In Charlotte County) Education was available for the children of the planter class and for orphans and pauper children. For others it seemed to be a hit or miss affair in which many children missed! When the revolution began, more than two-thirds of the "Parsons," who constituted the only group professionally qualified to teach, returned to England. This left a scarcity of men competent to teach, thus the few schools that were established often had difficulty in obtaining a teacher. (Ailsworth et al., 1979, p. 176)

Furthermore, even when teachers were again available in Southside Virginia, students who attended public schools were deemed second-class citizens:

> Unfortunately, association of free primary education with the poor orphan produced what has been called an "orphan fixation," which for more than 200 years proved an obstacle to the development and general acceptance of a public school system and even after 1869 prevented a wholehearted support of free education for all classes. (WPA, 1940, p. 119)

On the other hand, while popular support for public schooling was slow to come in most of the state, in many respects Virginia actually pioneered several educational undertakings. For example, Thomas Jefferson, as Governor of Virginia, proposed in the late 18th century a system of public education specifically designed to alter the elite system which existed in the state at that time. Among his proposals were the implementation of free primary schooling for all White citizens in Virginia, followed by free secondary schooling for those who proved able in their primary education undertakings, followed by free higher education for those gifted few who would be leaders of the Commonwealth as adults. Unfortunately, since the funding for this plan was dependent upon the local taxation (which landowners were little interested in performing), even when parts of the plan were made law by the Virginia legislature in 1796, there was little local implementation.

Another piece of early 19th-century legislation which was approved in Virginia, and which appears to have had some early impact on education there, was the establishment of a state Literary Fund in 1810. Such a fund was theoretically instituted for promoting education at primary, secondary, and higher education levels, and monies used for such purposes came directly from state levied fines and property confiscations. However, since the funding of projects from the Literacy Fund were typically to be used in conjunction with locally collected taxes, only a few of Virginia's counties used these funds for establishing a *system* of public instruction. Furthermore, rarely were any of the programs which received this money at the secondary level. Rather, higher education programs which benefitted primarily the elite, and primary educational programs participated in by the poor, were the major beneficiaries of the Fund. And linkages between primary and college educations remained completely underdeveloped until just before the Civil War.

> The Literary Fund was dubbed "Virginia's Pauper System" because it benefited only those children of the poorest class. In addition to its unpopularity, the system was virtually ineffective. Funds appropriated were inadequate to operate a school without the aid of private tuition, and well-to-do parents did not want to pay to have their children educated with the poor. Some schools therefore had to close. Many parents unable to pay tuition still considered free schools as charity and refused to allow their children to attend. Teacher prejudice against the poor also affected enrollment.. . . (Yet) Despite its failures the Literary Fund Plan with minor changes was used for over fifty years. (Ailsworth et al., 1979, p. 177)

Unfortunately, just as Virginia appeared to be ready for a major overhaul of its public education institutions, the Civil War arrived. By the middle of the 19th century, several metropolitan Southside communities experimented with jointly funded (public and private) Lancasterian systems. As well, the religious revival movements of the early and mid-19th century spurred the development of a "pan-protestant" Sunday School Movement orchestrated by several protestant denominations throughout the state (Tyack & Hansot, 1982; WPA, 1940).

Of further significance (and related to our earlier discussion about Braxton County, West Virginia), the public school movement, which began to take hold in Virginia just before the Civil War, appears to have been spearheaded in the nonplantation regions in the western part of Virginia, not in the Southside.

> A growing sentiment in favor of extending educational opportunity was reflected in the (state) educational conventions of 1841, 1845, 1856, and 1857. In the western counties a rising middle class was founding schools and colleges and demanding a State-supported system of free schools. The descendants of Scotch and Scotch-Irish settlers were the most powerful factors in this movement. Official recognition of free education actually came in 1851. Then through revision of the constitution it was provided that one-half of the capitation tax might be applied to free primary schools. (WPA, 1940, p. 120)

PUBLIC EDUCATION DURING THE RECONSTRUCTION PERIOD

As suggested earlier, many public institutions in the South, including Virginia, took years to recover from the Civil War and the Reconstruction Era. Perhaps

Table VA-2.. Curricular descriptions of two Charlotte County private academies advertised in the *Lynchburg Virginian* in 1837 & 1842. Note the almost exclusively pre-college orientation. (From Shepard, 1938, pp. 22-23)

Classical School at Charlotte Court House, Virginia

The subscriber will open a classical school at Charlotte Court House the 1st of February next, for the reception of pupils. The scholastic year will be divided into two Sessions—the 1st ending the 30th of June, terminating the 24th of December. The course of study will embrace all the branches necessary for taking the degree of Master of Arts in the University of Virginia, and the method of imparting instruction will be similar to that adopted in that institution. All branches of Mathematics will receive especial attention in this school. In order to make the study of Chemistry more interesting to the student, most of the experiments will be exhibited before the class. The subscriber has prepared himself almost entirely at the University of Virginia, in which institution he has taken the degree of Master of Arts.

Terms of tuition.

Forty dollars per annum, half in advance. For the Modern Languages, French and Spanish,there will be an additional fee of $5 per Session.
References --- Faculty of the University of Virginia. Wood Bouldin, Charlotte C.H., Va. Board can be obtained inthe village.
  C. H. Barksdale, A.M.

Madison Academy

THE SECOND SESSION of this institution, situated at the Red House, in the County of Charlotte, will commence the 15th of February 1838, and terminate the 24th of December following, with a vacation of two weeks in summer. The course of instruction, in addition to the ordinary branches of a good English education, will include such elementary information in the Greek and Latin Languages and Mathematics as will constitute a thorough preparation for College. The discipline will be mild, depending entirely on moral influence; it will nevertheless be firm. Orderly deportment and a fair and reasonable degree of mental exertion will be the conditions on which every pupil's continuance in the school must depend. The following list includes the principle Test Books: the Malte-Brun School Geography, Tyler's Elements of History, Davies' Arithmetic, do. Bourdon's Algebra, do/ Legendre's Geometry, Fisk's Greek Grammar, Adam's Latin, do. Brown's English, do.

Terms

For tuition in the Greek and Latin Languages, Algebra and Geometry $30 per session, in the other branches $20. Board may be obtained at the Red House, or in the neighborhood on reasonable terms. In regard to the qualifications of the teacher, MR. M. Lewis, employed by the Trustees to conduct this school, they would remark that they have in their possession and will show to any who desire it, written testimonials, from literary gentlemen, entitled confidence. Relying upon these, and upon the experience of the present session, they respectfully invite the attention of parents and guardians to this school, as one in which the business of education will be conducted with fidelity and skill.
  Sam'l Branch
  Chairman of the board of Trustees.

symbolic of this fact are the public sentiments of many (white) citizens in Charlotte County, who even today confide that "history stopped in the Southside in 1865." And the county history upon which much of the previous discussion has been based ends with the Civil War period. (Perhaps also symbolically, the second volume of the county's history has been talked about for over a decade, but there appear to be too few funds available locally to get it off the ground.)

Of course, Charlotte County has experienced a rich and interesting history since Reconstruction, and in many respects its current and future economic and educational prospects may be far better than those in other counties included in this book. Yet the persistent problem faced in Southside Virginia (and the South in general) has been the problem of deinstitutionalizing a class- and race-based educational system atypical of the educational institutions in other rural areas of the country.

Three primary and interrelated problems emerged during Reconstruction in Virginia, which contradicted over 200 years of previous history in the state. The first, naturally, involved the leveling of the landed gentry throughout the old slave-holding South, and the collapse of all institutions which depended upon local taxes for operation. At the same time, the emancipation proclamation had legally proclaimed all negroes to be free, and the 14th Amendment formally entitled them with similar rights as Whites. And particularly related to the emancipation of the slaves were aggressive philanthropic and federally funded initiatives from outside of the region to "improve" the education of freed slaves throughout the South and in the Southside. Not surprisingly, such interventions under the control of outsiders was a difficult pill to swallow in most of rural Virginia.

> At the close of the War between the States, Virginia was too impoverished to educate even her white children. It was then that the Freedman's Bureau and the Peabody Fund, both Northern Philanthropies, gave money and moral support for Negro education.. . . Negro education in the South (was also) vitally assisted by four funds established by Northern philanthropists. The Slater Fund, the earliest, provided $1,000,000 for Negro rural schools and the training of Negro teachers. . . . the Jeans Fund, endowed in 1905 by a Philadelphia Quaker, Miss Anna Jeans, financ(ed) supervisors for rural schools. The Phelps-Stokes Fund, founded by Miss Caroline Phelps-Stokes in 1909, aid(ed) the public rural schools of both races. (and) The Rosenwald fund for rural Negro education, with a magnificent endowment of $22,000,000, was founded by Julius Rosenwald of Chicago. (WPA, 1940, p. 126)

In Charlotte County, the years just following the Civil War saw some vestiges of private schooling which had existed before it. Just before the War, most of these private academies concentrated on "Classical" subjects to prepare students for enrolling at the numerous private colleges in Virginia. Afterwards, there appear to have been a number of short-lived efforts to reestablish some of these academies. And on more than one occasion it appears that former plantation owners sought to form academies both to preserve elitist educational ideas as well as to help generate some income in the face of personal economic hardships

(Shepard, 1938). Yet, since few of the previous landowners could now afford to enroll their children in the academies, and since public monies could not be used for such educational purposes, in Charlotte County these academies appear not to have fared well.

Furthermore, while we have only circumstantial evidence that Charlotte Countians opposed the introduction of schools for newly freed Blacks during reconstruction, the general mood of Virginia and the South was that the outsiders who were endowing and supporting Negro education were using such schools to indoctrinate students with "yankee" ideas (Perkinson, 1968). Naturally, most White constituents detested such schools as outposts of oppression rather than as locations upon which to build a new future for Virginia. And, as stated before, inasmuch as there was little money for establishing alternative educational opportunities, some have argued that the schoolhouse during Reconstruction was a symbol of all that was foreign and repressive into the early 20th century (Perkinson, 1968; WPA, 1940).

On the other hand, while publicly financed formal education for all Virginians was not generally available immediately after the Civil War, the rudiments of such a system appear to have been in place by about the turn of the century. Discussions about the importance of public education for the state's future appeared in legislative debates in the late 1860s, and in 1870 a state educational bureaucracy was set up with a paid state Superintendent of Public Instruction. According to many, this first State Superintendent (Reverend William Henry Ruffner) was responsible for actually helping to bring about local school implementation and innovation in a state with a long history of local inattention to state initiatives (Link, 1986; Shepard, 1938).

While the format for public education had been laid out by the Virginia legislature in 1870, the actual establishment of public schools (particularly secondary schools) in much of rural Virginia did not occur until the turn of the century. Since newly empowered local school districts hesitated to tax what remained of value in rebuilding rural areas, and since state revenues from the Literary Fund were diverted away from educational projects by the Legislature during the late 1870s, the only major new schooling initiatives visible were typically sponsored by outside groups like those previously mentioned.

> The period from 1870 to 1906 was a period of transition in the educational system of Charlotte County. A state wide free school system had come as a product of the notorious Underwood Convention. People of the county were slow to give up their private schools; for the idea of public free schools still carried the stigma of the "pauper schools,". . . however (there was) a gradual growth of public school interest. The first public high school in the county was established in 1891. This two- teacher school had to compete with Bonair and other private schools. However, sentiment was growing in favor of public schools, and in 1902 this school was moved to a larger building. (Shepard, 1938, pp. 68-70)

AGRICULTURAL DIVERSIFICATION AND
20TH-CENTURY ECONOMIC GROWTH

Following the end of statehouse turmoil during the Reconstruction period, the state of Virginia appears to have become quite aggressive in helping local regions to diversify and take advantage of the agricultural possibilities statewide, and certainly in the Southside. In addition, the completion and rebuilding of county infrastructures (i.e., railroads, highways, and bridges) appears to have benefitted places like Charlotte County greatly.

In a locally published and widely disseminated early 20th-century "booster" document extolling the virtues of the county, a variety of benefits are held up as reasons why outsiders might want to relocate near the towns of Charlotte Courthouse, Keysville, or Drakes Branch. Of course, the proud history of the county was offered as a primary benefit. So, too, the sound character of its residents was held up as demonstrating the positive quality of life available there:

> The people of Charlotte present that type of Virginia character which is formed upon the Cavalier and Established Church of England as the basis, into which has been infused the Scotch-Irish, Puritan and Huguenot strains of blood. Hence, as might be expected, no more conservative or orthodox people can be found, nor one more homogeneous in thought, sentiment and action.. . . the people of the county are noted for their intelligence, morality, hospitality and general thrifti-ness. That they are law abiding is amply demonstrated by the fact that with a population of 15,355 it is no uncommon occurrence that the county jail is without inmates; and as an evidence of their thrift, the report of the superintendent of the county poorhouse for year ending July 1, 1906, shows there was an average of only eleven inmates. (Carrington, 1907, p. 25)

In this publication, a great variety of agricultural products produced in the county were discussed, as well as why the local climate, rainfall, soil, and market conditions of early 20th-century Southside Virginia were so favorable. Several types of locally produced tobacco (dark-fired, flue-cured, and burley) were profiled. And a good portion of the 1907 document reproduced (probably) solicited testimonials form farmers who seemingly moved into the county and made overnight fortunes on relatively moderate investments in tobacco and other agricultural products. Apparently, a good reason why economic returns on tobacco agriculture were so good in the early 20th century had to do with the very low land prices at the time. As well, the comparatively good rail system in Charlotte County enabled Drakes Branch to become a regional tobacco sales and marketing center in the early 20th century—a fact that is easy to believe, considering the large number of ancient and largely abandoned tobacco ware-houses along the railroad tracks in this once thriving town (many of which were torn down during 1989 and 1990).

However, many other types of produce were also extolled in the 1907 document. For example, letters to the Charlotte County Board of Supervisors (which published the book) talk about how easy the raising of cattle, hogs, and poultry were in the county. So, too, the possibilities for fruit orchards, the raising of oats, corn, and wheat, and bee keeping were aggressively documented.

Interestingly, in a section later in the book, the "desirability" of subdividing remaining larger farms in the county is discussed. Specifically (and unlike several economic development foci of Braxton County), the future of Charlotte County in 1907 appeared to local and regional leaders to depend upon the diversification of agriculture rather than in industry or manufacture. As stated in the 1907 *Charlotte County* handbook:

> Because we have lands greatly in excess of population, it is desireable from every standpoint that our large landed estates should be subdivided in order to meet the demands of the present day farming. The process of subdivision has been going on to some extent with the most beneficial results both to the seller and the buyer, the one disposes of his surplus lands and the other acquires all the land he needs at moderate prices; and it has (almost without exception) been demonstrated that the portions sold off to industrious settlers soon render their owners independent and rival the parent heads in productive qualities. Farming upon a moderate scale brings results which are not realized from hardly any other legitimate business. This has been amply shown from the few testimonials given in this book. They could be multiplied by the score. Then, too, being brought into close contact by railroad facilities all over the county, diversified farming is destined to play an important part. Trucking, canning, vineyards and orchards will be found profitable and often followed instead of crop raising, according to the tastes and inclinations of land owners. (Carrington, 1907, p. 134)

Another indication that turn-of-the-century economic progress was real in Charlotte County stems from the fact that two of its most important (though currently declining) rural towns there were only incorporated following the reconstruction period. The rail system apparently enabled both Keysville and Drakes Branch to become early 20th-century regional marketing centers, and they incorporated as cities in the decades just before and after the turn of the 20th century. As well, the (now) very small community of Phenix emerged between 1900 and 1930 as a thriving center of commerce, where a large pickle-packing plant provided employment for hundreds of workers.

POVERTY AND RACE ISSUES IN SOUTHSIDE VIRGINIA

While local boosters and county administrators could (and did) praise the economic possibilities of rural Virginia in the early 20th century, much less local

VA-3. EMPLOYMENT INDUSTRIES.

	YEAR					
	1930	1940	1950	1960	1970	1980
Total persons employed 14 or 16 years old.	4,877	4,808	4,855	4,409	4,116	4,676
% in AG.	66.0	67.8	49.5	35.2	18.5	10.0
% in Mining	–	–	.4	.1	.6	.3
% in MANFG	12.2	10.4	44.2	51.8	43.0	38.0
% in TRANS/COMM	2.4	2.3	3.2	5.3	2.6	4.6
% in RETAIL	4.0	4.4	7.0	8.3	5.3	11.0
% in FIN/INS	.5	.3	.8	1.0	1.4	2.0
% in SERVICES	10.7	11.4	8.2	11.6	14.6	18.0

writing on the enduring poverty of poor Whites and Negroes was apparent. Yet we know from a variety of sources that the economic conditions of both of these groups throughout most of the South improved little during the late 19th and early 20th centuries (Cobb, 1982; Flynt, 1979; Wright, 1986). Furthermore, as will be discussed shortly, race relations in Southside Virginia played an increasingly important role in the evolution of local public schools.

In general, the aftermath of the Civil War in the Southside rewrote contractual relationships between former plantation owners and both subsistence farmers and newly freed slaves. Since most incomes in rural Virginia were dependent in one form or another upon tobacco sales of the large plantations, the demise of the production and distribution system of this crop in places like Charlotte County adversely affected all classes of people. Freed negroes who were once the unpaid labor source for the plantation owners were allowed/forced to enter into a market economy where they could sell their labor at just the same time as there was no money locally available for such employment. Similarly, the lack of locally available cash for seasonal employment, coupled with severe weather conditions during the late 1860s, led to two types of "solutions" to economic problems of the day.

By the late 19th century, the rural poor of both races had begun a century-long outmigration from the south in search of urban based employment opportunities. This "redistribution of population" related to perceived employment opportunities outside of rural Virginia was clearly visible in all of the Southside counties (including Charlotte) that depended upon agriculture. And this general trend was particularly true for negroes (see Table VA-5).

For example, the total population of the County in 1900 was 15,543, yet by 1980 it had been reduced to 12,266 (and is still declining). Furthermore, while the White population of the County experienced a slight increase from 1900 to 1920 (perhaps because of the benefits in agriculture and low land prices extolled in the previous pages), Negro outmigration continued unabated throughout the

VA-4. INCOME CHARACTERISTICS.

	YEAR					
	1930	*1940*	*1950*	*1960*	*1970*	*1980*
Median income of						
All families	–	–	1,362	2,864	5,838	12,776
All households	–	–	–	–	–	11,070
Families with						
own children 18yrs	–	–	–	–	–	14,984
married couples	–	–	–	4,638	5,031	16,637
Female householder	–	–	–	–	–	4,286

VA-5. POPULATION CHARACTERISTICS.

	YEAR								
	1900	*1910*	*1920*	*1930*	*1940*	*1950*	*1960*	*1970*	*1980*
Total									
Popln	15,543	15,578	17,540	16,061	15,861	14,057	13,368	11,551	12,266
male	–	–	8,899	8,151	8,163	7,228	–	5,759	6,009
Female	–	–	8,641	7,910	7,698	6,829	–	5,792	6,257
White	6,798	7,419	9,987	9,305	9,169	10,271	7,978	6,200	7,518
Black	8,545	8,335	7,537	6,742	6,692	3,789	5,351	4,599	4,737

VA-6. LABOR CHARACTERISTICS.

	YEAR				
	1940	*1950*	*1960*	*1970*	*1980*
Labor Force:					
Persons 16 yrs and older	10,719	9,654	9,170	7,859	9,068
Male 16 yrs and older	5,573	4,984	4,621	3,886	4,380
% in labor Force	81.0	82.0	73.6	70.0	67.0
Females 16 yrs and older	5,146	4,984	4,621	3,886	4,380
% in labor force	11.4	18.0	25.0	38.0	43.4
Females 16 yrs/older	–	–	–	869	871
(with children 18 yrs)					
% in labor force	–	–	–	22.0	70.0

20th century. In 1900, approximately 55% of Charlotte County residents were Negro. However, by 1980, this percentage had fallen to 39%.

Many of those whot did remain in Charlotte County following the Civil War became sharecroppers or tenant farmers on the former plantations of owners now too poor to reimburse these workers with cash payments. Even though land costs were low, there were few avenues for either poor Whites or Negroes to borrow and/or earn enough money to buy land. Therefore, as some Southern historians have argued, before the Civil War plantation owners were laborlords, but afterwards they became landlords (Wright, 1986). And rather than charging rents to poor workers on their lands, percentages of marketable crops were extracted as payments for farm tenancy.

> The share-wage system arose primarily, as several scholars have pointed out, because many planters lacked the resources to pay cash wages, because the disruption of the credit institutions during the war had dismantled the familiar means of financing planting operations, and because former slaves, for reasons that remain indistinct in most historical accounts, preferred it. For planters, the use of what one historian terms "retained wages" offered certain other distinct advantages. From the planters' point of view, the share-wage system not only resolved the cash shortage problem but also, perhaps more importantly, provided the means of access to black labor least suggestive of change in the nature of the antebellum plantation system. Planters believed it would, at the same time, encourage greater industry from the former slaves by giving them an interest in the output. The freedpeople would continue to work and live as before, receiving their compensation at the end of the year in shares of the crop. (Glymph, 1985, p. 52)

While we have found no satisfactory income figures for 19th- and early 20th-century citizens of Charlotte County, we have heard of no large Negro landowners or affluent farmers/merchants in the county in the course of our interviews. Furthermore, the generally marginal and nonassertive status of Negroes in Charlotte County early in the 20th century is suggested in another passage of the 1907 boosters edition earlier mentioned, as is some additional insight as to why schooling must have been increasingly viewed as of particular benefit by local Negro leaders:

> Under the new Constitution of Virginia the right of suffrage is based upon an educational qualification and but a limited number of negroes enjoy this privlege, the electorate thereby being purged of the ignorant, venal class of negroes. This has had a marked and happy effect upon the complexion of political affairs, and has redounded to the good of society generally. No county in the State has a more orderly or law abiding class of negroes than Charlotte, and the relations existing between the two races are exceedingly friendly. Separate schools are provided for both races, each race has its own churches, and the statute law forbids intermarriage. While these restrictions exist there is no reason far any fricton between the races and there is no apprehension felt by anyone that there will be. The negro spends much of his time on public works and is not so accessible as formerly, but, withal, is the best suited labor for our section that has ever been tried. (Carrington, 1907, p. 29)

EARLY 20TH-CENTURY SCHOOL REFORM

Between 1906 and the late 1930s, Charlotte County experienced a boom in public education. For example, while in 1870 fewer than one third of all Charlotte County children attended any school at all, by 1905 almost two thirds of eligible children in the county were enrolled. And, by 1935 this percentage had risen to almost 72% (Shepard, 1938).

Furthermore, for the first time in Charlotte County, public *secondary* education seemingly became an important institutional cause. While at the turn of the century there were no public high schools in the county, by 1935 there were seven small (white) high schools located in the most prominent county towns of Charlotte Courthouse, Keysville, Drakes Branch, Madisonville, Saxe, Phenix, Wylliesburg, and Aspen. In addition there was a consolidated Negro high school at the county seat (Charlotte CourtHouse), and a very small private (Baptist) high school for Negroes.

Considering the fact(s) that mandatory attendance in high school was not required (or at least enforced), that children of elite families still typically were sent to private academies outside of the county, and that the provision of education for Black children appears not to have been a major local concern in Charlotte County (for example, the county did not pay for the transportation of

VA-7. "PROCESS OF THE PUBLIC SCHOOL SYSTEM IN CHARLOTTE COUNTY, 1870-1906" (FROM SHEPARD, 1938, p. 69).

Year	No. schools wh.	cd.	Average no. months taught	No. taught wh.	cd.	Average monthly salary	Average attendance wh.	cd.	Percent school population enrolled wh.	cd.	No. taking higher branches	Per capita cost per month per pupil enrolled	Total cost public education
1871	21	15	4.29	21	16	27.90	406	397	39	29	6	.67	5589.51
1874	23	17	5.	31	10	27.12	386	506	41	24	50	.98	7659.46
1877	22	19	5.40	28	15	29.89	407	605	42	28			7047.38
1880	22	16	5.5	26	13	24.93	468	557	52	21.5	138	.56	6386.76
1883	29	25	5.9	36	16	26.94	648	964	63	32	247	.73	13364.55
1886	34	24	5.77	34	19	26.50	702	716	71	30	285	.76	12252.41
1889	37	29	5.6	38	28	26.42	765	850	67	36	140	.71	12028.70
1892	45	31	5.61	45	31	26.25	670	866	56	33	67	.75	12189.01
1895	52	27	5.53	56	22	25.18	833	309	67	36	154	.68	11864.69
1898	54	26	5.86	58	22	22.70	861	860	64	36	133	.64	11686.14
1901	54	26	5.79	54	26	23.41	778	950	60	39	144	.70	12384.56
1904	58	30	5.26	58	30	24.38	771	930	72	52	326	.77	12686.29
1906	54	27	5.91	54	27	34.85	783	782	71	71	538	.86	15721.26

children to the Negro high school), the 1935 high school enrollment figure of 506 students suggests a major turn-around in local appreciation for the possibilities of a high school education (Shepard, 1938).

At least two separate state and national forces, consistent with the local context in Charlotte County, appear to have motivated rural Virginians in the Southside to undertake serious school reform early in the 20th century. On the one hand, the Virginia state department of education continued in its efforts to upgrade local educational conditions and opportunities. Importantly, as in other states of the nation, middle class school reform advocates in Virginia's urban areas also appear to have played a major role in influencing the state legislature and the state department of education with regard to the importance of system-wide reform (Link, 1986; Tyack, 1972; Woodward, 1951).

The net effect in rural Virginia was that low-cost loans and special school building funds were established for school districts wishing to undertake school construction projects, particularly secondary school construction projects (Shepard, 1938). During this same period, school programs and facilities came under increasing scrutiny of state accrediting procedures.

So, too, with the passage of the Smith-Hughes Act of 1917, special funds for agricultural and home economics programs in the rural South became available. And in Charlotte County, these programs and monies appear to have been eagerly accepted for programmatic implementation in most of the local high schools.

As noted previously, many early 20th-century county development efforts in the Southside appear to have been based on the benefits and possibilities of agriculture. Ostensibly, curricular programs in the high school related to scientific agricultural development were (and continue to be) a main focus.

> When the high schools (in Charlotte County) were first established the dominating aim of instruction was preparation for admission to college. Training of teachers for elementary schools and vocational instruction in agriculture and home economics forced an entry into the program of studies, enlarging somewhat the purpose of high school instruction. The personnel of the student body had changed from the original select group of prospective doctors, lawyers, teachers, and preachers to include also pupils whose vocational destiny would locate them in the home and in agricultural pursuits. (Shepard, 1938, p. 95)

However, it wasn't very long before the dramatic increase of interest in enhancing educational opportunities in each of the small Charlotte County communities ran afoul of increasing accreditation guidelines and costs associated with attempting to provide the wide variety of curricular offerings suggested above. For example, each of the town high schools apparently attempted to offer courses preparatory to regional and state colleges, as well as coursework designed specifically for vocational and home economics futures. However, none of the seven public high schools had consistent enrollments of over 100 students, and perhaps the largest high school was the Negro school in Charlotte CourtHouse, which concentrated on a narrower industrial arts curriculum (then the focus of most secondary education for negroes (Link, 1986).

Therefore, teachers in each of the seven small high schools taught multiple subjects, and advanced coursework in most schools was not available. Furthermore, principals in each of the high schools were actually teaching principals, and were unable to satisfactorily perform the supervisory duties suggested by the state department of education.

Throughout the late 1920s and all of the 1930s, then, Charlotte County saw an escalating debate regarding the desirability of consolidating many of its (then 52) schools. Arguments in favor of so doing included the benefits of curricular diversity that such a move would bring, and the fact that by 1930 a fairly well established county highway system was in place which would enable efficient

VA-8. Comparative Data for Charlotte County High School (White) and Charlotte County Training School (Colored) for the years 1929-1937. The 1929 year was the first year for any Black public secondary schools in Charlotte County, and even in the years covered here there are clear educational inequalities for attending students (From Shepard, 1938, pp. 77 & 98).

	YEAR	No. grades in high school	No. full time high school teachers	No. part time high school teachers	No. high school pupils enrolled	Average daily atten- dances percent	No. days taught	Average monthly salaries	High school per capita cost	No. graduates
	1936-37	4	3	2	67	96	160	$138.00	$70.51	16
	1935-36	4	3	2	58	95	160	100.37	79.17	13
	1934-34	4	3	2	65	97	160	106.75	68.73	17
CHARLOTTE	1933-34	4	3	2	75	97	160	118.12	55.53	15
HIGH	1932-33	4	3	2	74	96	160	101.25	59.50	15
SCHOOL	1931-32	4	3	2	70	96	160	138.	77.00	9
	1930-31	4	3	2	68	96	170	143.	69.25	11
	1929-30	4	3	2	76	94	180	140.	83.68	13
	1928-29	4	3	2	71	89	180	137.50	77.53	13
	1936-37	4	3	2	88	96	160	$ 94.50	$34.08	10
	1935-36	4	3	2	109	96	160	118.25	27.47	12
CHARLOTTE	1934-35	4	2	2	89	93	160	93.78	32.30	17
COUNTY	1933-34	4	3	2	76	95	160	65.00	30.00	13
TRAINING	1932-33	4	3	2	79	93	160	65.00	33.52	11
SCHOOL	1931-32	4	4	0	71	97	167	69.00	51.55	8
	1930-31	4	2	1	68	95	180	80.00	31.76	5
	1929-30	3	1	1	36	92	180	75.00	18.75	0

VA-9.   CHARLOTTE COUNTY (WHITE) HIGH SCHOOLS, CIRCA 1937
(FROM SHEPARD, 1938, p. 114).

1	*2*	*3*	*4*	*5*	*6*
School	*High school enrollment*	*Total high school salaries*	*High school per capita cost*	*Elementary per capita cost*	*Ratio of high school to elementary cost*
Charlotte	67	$4512	$70,51	$18.93	1-4
Keysville	80	4592	59.64	30.22	1-3
Wylliesburg	90	4179	43.54	19.37	1-2.5
Drakes' Branch	68	4179	65.31	20.81	1-3.25
Madisonville	77	4187	57.36	22.86	1-2.6
Phenix	97	4267	45.40	19.17	1-2.5
Aspen	27	1500	48.00	21.80	1-2.3
Total	506	27416	55.68	20.46	1-2.75

transportation of students to more central school locations. On the other hand (as was the case in Braxton County), each of the smaller towns wanted to keep its own schools intact.

However, while local attachments to secondary schools appear to have blunted several state- and county-wide proposals for school closures and mergers, the general economic decline of agriculture in the 1930s led the Charlotte County Board of Supervisors to become extremely conservative with regard to appropriating tax monies for public education. During most of the 1930s, Charlotte County appropriated fewer tax dollars for such purposes than did any of the surrounding counties in the Southside (Shepard, 1938).

In addition to the general financial stress level of the county in the early 1930s, a particular emergency appears to have had an impact upon later decisions to consolidate county secondary (and elementary) schools. Specifically, the main high school building at Phenix burned down in 1937, and most of its students had to attend classes in stores and homes in the year immediately following. Efforts to arrive at a more cost-effective system of secondary school education, which would help to solve both the Phenix High School situation and accommodate the accrediting demands of the state department of public education, appears to have caused a complete rethinking of requirements for public schooling in the county by 1939.

AGRICULTURAL DECLINE AND REGIONAL
ECONOMIC DEVELOPMENT

As documented earlier, Charlotte County's agricultural undertakings did appear to be moderately successful in the 1920s and 1930s. According to the 1930 and 1940 census, approximately two thirds of those employed in the county worked in the agricultural sector, and serious population decline appears not to have begun in earnest until late in the depression era.

Yet, during the 1930s and 1940s, national agricultural trends moved to more mechanized farming methods, which in turn called for new large-scale investments in land and machinery. The net result of such processes appears to have doomed the prospects of small-scale farmers such as those who had just begun to experience some success in Southside Virginia. The erosion of agricultural markets for small-scale farmers, coupled perhaps with immediate employment opportunities related to the World War II war industry (e.g., one of Americas largest shipbuilding yards lies just 2 hours east of Charlotte County) appears related to the gradual county population loss that has continued to today.

Furthermore, job creation in Charlotte County following World War II appears to have proceeded as it did in much of the rural South in the middle of the 20th century. As Table VA-3 shows, employment in agriculture dropped dramatically between 1930 and 1960, while the percentage of those employed in manufacturing industries increased during the same period from approximately 12% to almost 52%. Meanwhile, employment figures for women suggest that, increasingly, they became part of the workforce in Charlotte County, which they had not been before. For example, as Table VA-6 shows, fewer than 12% of County women were technically employed in 1930, but by 1970, this percentage had almost tripled. As Cobb suggests:

> By the end of World War II migrating industries had moved away from the practice of creating a factory or mill village and were instead choosing sites that would allow them to draw form a rural area's farm-based labor surplus. Promoters courted low-wage industries with descriptions of sturdy folk who were willing to work for less because they supplemented their incomes and food supplies by farming. A typical Mississippi ad noted "with plenty of space gardens will be found at practically every home, supplementing cash income." In addition to the fact that they grew their own vegetables, Mississippi workers also had less need for cash income because, typically, they were "wives, sons and daughters and farmers living on the farm." Therefore their wages, even if meager, would nonetheless "mean extra dollars over and above the accustomed existence." (Cobb, 1982, p. 112)

In essence, the ability of the majority of the population in places like Charlotte County to rely on agriculture for a livelihood seems to have disappeared by 1950 (which of course parallels the case of Braxton County). However, the availability of low-level manufacturing jobs in relocating textile, clothing, and lumber-processing industries in surrounding Southside locations appears to have prevented the massive exodus out of Charlotte County, which was more typical of the Appalachian region.

Charlotte County attracted textile mill branch plants and a modular home construction industry of its own in the 1950s and 1960s. Two of the biggest national names in the textile industry came into the area during this boom period: Armstrong Industries, and Evans and Black. However, we have found no specific accounts of relocation strategies of Northern low-skilled industries in Southside Virginia, nor have we been able to trace local officials claiming responsibility for helping to bring in such factories. Nevertheless, anecdotal accounts from local civic leaders regarding reasons why various garment-related industries came into Southside Virginia and Charlotte County corroborate the general development analysis given by various Southern labor historians.

As suggested above, most of these accounts argue that many declining Southern agricultural regions of the U.S. advertised themselves and/or were identified by many large Northern companies as good locations to set up branch textile and apparel-manufacturing plants. Prime reasons for the relocation and/or creation of such plants was that large supplies of cheap and unorganized labor existed there. As well, since many local and/or regional leaders sought to diversify the dwindling agricultural fortunes of places like Southside Virginia, low taxes and infrastructure costs were assured to potential incoming manufacturers (Cobb, 1982; Wright, 1986).

Southside Virginia attracted many semiskilled jobs related to textiles and clothing in the 1940s, 1950s, and 1960s. And given the more than adequate transportation system linking towns and cities in the Southside (and beyond), employment in industries other than agriculture increased dramatically during these decades. In Charlotte County, companies then and now involved in the garment-related industries offered relatively low-wage jobs to some men, but perhaps more significantly, to women and high-school-age girls. As well as seasonal employment in tobacco harvesting, many men and boys have continuously worked (since the 1950s) in constructing prefab housing parts and in the several county lumber mills.

Another very visible remaining industry in the county is tree harvesting. Specifically, many acres of Charlotte County appear to be under tree "cultivation," where cut-over hardwood forests are replanted with pine trees for harvesting 20 or 30 years hence. In addition to large out-of-state land holdings by wood-processing companies, the easy road access to most county acreage enables local tree farmers to clear-cut large stands of timber, selling off cleared land and/or the historic homes which once were surrounded by forests to incoming lumber speculators or retirees looking for old plantation houses to restore. And this process appears to have been occurring for several decades.

Yet, while the lumber industry may have remained healthy in Charlotte County for much of this century, the branch textile plants previously discussed have not remained safe employment opportunities during the entire period. Just as outside companies came to the Southside during the middle of the 20th century, so, too, have they apparently begun to move to even cheaper labor sources during the 1980s. When we first arrived in the county, we were advised that one local factory had changed corporate ownership several times in the previous 2 years. And local people not working for its most recent owner (WestPoint Pepperell) appeared to have difficulty remembering who owned the company at the beginning of our fieldwork there.

EDUCATIONAL CHANGES BETWEEN
1939 AND 1969

As stated earlier, documentory histories of Charlotte County's 20th-century developments are almost nonexistant. While changes there appear statistically dramatic during the past few decades, very little local description is available relative to them. Surprisingly (and this has proven true in most of the cases overviewed in this study), neither has Charlotte County's school division kept very good records on the changing nature of its students and schools.

The one (and only) detailed account of education in Charlotte County upon which much of our earlier discussion was based concluded with the year 1938. In this (Shepard) study, the author suggested that, by 1937, County residents were coming to agree that consolidation of schools would be necessary in the not-to-distant future. Apparently, some mood favoring school consolidation rose quickly in the county, for only 2 years after Shepard published his study all of the (White) high schools in Charlotte County were merged into Randolph-Henry High. While little in writing is available on the opening of this school, local residents recall vividly that Randolph-Henry was touted as a showplace for how to consolidate small high schools state-wide. According to several interviewees in our project, Charlotte County was one of the first consolidated high schools in the state, and other Southside school divisions only slowly began to follow their lead in the following decade.

Ostensibly, the consolidating of secondary schools in Charlotte County depended upon the two primary forces earlier responsible for Southside educational reform: local consensus that action was required, and the availability of low cost loans and grants for school construction made possible through the state Literary Fund. During the 1940s and especially the 1950s, many of the remaining one- and two-room schools throughout the county were combined into larger facilities. Although such consolidations must have been resisted (as they appear to in many rural school districts), few current educators in Charlotte County can remember pitched battles over school closings during this period. Perhaps, since the secondary schools were consolidated first, it appeared more reasonable to many county residents for such consolidations. On the other hand, since true public education came relatively late in Virginia, perhaps attachments to local schools was less well developed in Charlotte County than in other places (like Braxton County) with longer public school traditions.

Another likely reason, however, that school closings and/or consolidations might have been accepted more favorably in Southside Virginia, compared to such events in other states, was that typically new schools with more modern facilities were constructed as a result of aggressive state funding programs. As suggested earlier, this is a very different dynamic than was the case in Braxton County, where students were transferred to other existing facilities (after limited renovation) and old buildings abandoned during several decades of consolidation. Aggressive school building programs sponsored by the state in Virginia remained an important difference seen at the county level in the four districts visited for this book. And, in fact, a popular governor of Virginia in the 1950s is still remembered in Charlotte County for his aggressive sponsorship of school building projects when he was in office—known in the county as Governor Battle's "Battleplan."

Yet, as was the case early in the century, the aggressive school building campaigns seen in Southside Virginia actually became a stumbling block to later reforms there. When local towns built and/or obtained new school buildings after 1906, it soon became obvious that such decentralized projects were inefficient for secondary school curricular diversity. And most of these schools became abandoned in later years.

Likewise, given that, prior to the 1960s, Virginia schools were *segregated*, the dual school facilities constructed in the 1950s and 1960s in places like Charlotte County cost the state and local governments far more than they would have were all children to attend the same community schools.

Early in the 20th century, reputation has it that schools built for Negroes were far inferior to those built for Whites. And current administrators in Charlotte County who inherited schools built for Negroes prior to the late 1950s are quick to point this out. One of these current Charlotte County principals who has inherited a former Black school building argued that he could "put my fist through most of these supposedly brick walls."

On the other hand, in the years just after the 1954 school desegregation decision of the U.S. Supreme Court, many new school construction projects were dedicated specifically to consolidating and improving "Negro" schools. In a number of Southside Virginia counties, compliance with the Brown vs. Topeka decision was attempted by offering the locally infamous "Freedom of Choice" plan, where Negroes could "choose" to attend previously White schools if they wanted to. However, in order to discourage such attempts, many school divisions apparently decided that improving the material conditions of Negro schools would dissuade such an interest on the part of Black parents.

In Charlotte County, the late 1950s saw the construction of two new schools for Negroes: one in Bacon (magisterial) District, and one near Phenix. As well, a new high school building was constructed in Charlotte CourtHouse for Negroes. And only one new White school was built (also near Phenix) during the 1950s.

While potential race issues related to total school integration appear to have been minimized temporarily in this way in most Southside counties, in others there were more difficulties. In fact, Charlotte County's larger and more affluent neighbor to the north became a national hot spot with regard to race and education issues. In Prince Edward County, prominent citizens, the Board of Supervisors, and the School Board refused to comply in any manner with school desegregation, and they closed their public schools completely for half a decade (Smith, 1965). Rather, suggestive of the older private school tradition in Virginia, many White citizens there helped to form and send their schools to Prince Edward Academy. And the poorest of Whites and all negroes were virtually excluded from any public instruction there between 1959 and 1964.

The story of Prince Edward County Schools and Prince Edward Academy is not mentioned here just as interesting historical information. Rather, these events had consequences both then and now for residents of Charlotte County. For example, Charlotte County schools did educate some Negro students who crossed over the county line in the 1960s. On the other hand, many families who were unhappy with Charlotte County's "liberal" adoption of the Freedom of Choice plan began to transport their children up to Prince Edward Academy. Furthermore, the reinvigorated academy model for White students first launched in Prince Edward County led soon in Charlotte County to the establishment of Patrick Henry Academy in Charlotte CourtHouse. While the popularity of Patrick Henry Academy waned during the decade of the 1980s, even today school officials estimate that approximately 80 children of comparatively affluent White parents are still transported up to 50 miles north every morning to attend Prince Edward Academy.

CURRENT ECONOMIC CONDITIONS IN CHARLOTTE COUNTY

State and local industrial development organizations have a long history in much of the South, and Southside Virginia appears to be no exception. We have already discussed local boosterism efforts early in the 20th century. Similarly, various local and regional economic development associations operate in Southside Virginia today, and these several groups often hold their meetings in the regional community college in Keysville. So, too, published documents about why Charlotte County and other Southside locations are entrepreneurially desireable are also locally and regionally available (e.g., Center for Economic Development, 1988).

For example, the Charlotte County Industrial Development Foundation issued a "Community Profile" in 1989 which contains a host of current topographical, economic, population, and climate data on the county. Most of these data (on climate, location, history, and so on.) we have mentioned before. In addition, updated infrastructure and tax rate data are supplied in this profile, as are data on employers, types of current employment, and so on. Interestingly, real estate, sales, and use tax rates in Charlotte County still remain quite low, ostensibly as inducements for outside investments.

"Major Employers" in 1988 Charlotte County were still primarily involved in the same industries as they were in the 1950s and 1960s. Three of the largest four companies are branch textile plants owned by out of state companies which (combined) employ almost 900 people. Six of the remaining top 10 are typically much smaller operations involved either in lumber processing, modular home construction, or children's apparel. Only one employer (with but 12 employees) has anything to do with agriculture, the former economic staple of the county.

Parenthetically, Charlotte County is the only one of the four counties targeted in this evaluation which has a single company having more employees than the public school system. Unfortunately, most of these employees (of J.P. Stevens) perform shiftwork at low-paying textile related jobs. Typical goods produced in such industries include bathroom rugs, toilet bowl covers, towels, and some apparel.

Perhaps even more unfortunately, viewed locally, is that WestPoint Pepperell announced in May 1989 that it would soon be closing its Keysville facility. Arguing that its plant facilities there were inefficient by contemporary standards, it announced that almost all of its 150+ employees would be laid off by October 1989. The county paper announced the plant shut-down thusly:

> The Keysville plant of WestPoint Pepperell, Inc. shut its doors for the final time last week following an announcement in May that the move was planned to consolidate local production with that of the company's Scottsboro, Alabama plant. . . . Keysville's Mayor Howard Hanmer called the plant's closing a real tragedy for the town of Keysville. "They've been mighty good citizens over the years," he said. "We sure do hate to see them close." According to the mayor, the closing could mean a loss of up to $40,000 annually in the town's water/sewer and tax revenues.

In what probably will result in an empty gesture, WestPoint Pepperell further announced that laid-off workers would be given the option of applying for employment at other (out of state) company plants. However, we suspect that most native Charlotte Countians would not be going along with this previously important local employer to work for the (low) wages typically paid by that company.

Another recent "economic development" pattern in Southside Virginia (and particularly in Charlotte County) involves the increasing number of out of state residents moving into the region to retire. Seemingly attracted by low land costs, available older homes very minimally priced, and by the low tax rates previously mentioned, "folks from New Jersey" (as many Charlotte Countians describe them) keep moving into the area. Many local (school-based) interviewees decried this development, arguing that retirees on fixed incomes would not only be little willing to vote for tax increases necessary to improve local schooling, but would also not help falling attendance rates (since they would typically bring no school-aged children with them).

Furthermore, this inmigration has not occurred by chance. Aggressive real estate marketing of the historical, climatological, geographical, and low tax "benefits" of Charlotte County are almost impossible to escape the casual visitor to the area. Local restaurants and motels in the several Southside counties we passed through had stockpiles of real estate brochures profiling local properties they claimed were the essence of slow, easy, and inexpensive retirement living. Most of these brochures also had detailed maps showing the route to the Southside from Washington, D.C., New York, and (yes) New Jersey. And according to many we interviewed, the "marketing" of the retirement advantages of Southside Virginia is quite aggressive in distant Northeastern cities; one doesn't have to pass through the area, they claim, in order to find out about it.

Yet currently lagging local economic development patterns of late (other than real estate) are perhaps not quite as devastating in Charlotte County as they have been in Braxton County. Unlike more mountainous regions to the west, Charlotte County is rural but not really isolated. To be sure, the county has no stoplights, no chain restaurants, no discount stores, and few other retail establishments with nonfamily employees. Yet there is a county bank with several branches, and there are several branches of larger state banks. So, too, there are miles and miles of well-maintained, paved state and federal highways criss-crossing through the county (or around its boundaries), as well as many more miles of unpaved but drivable rural roads. In other words, the economy of Charlotte County appears in many ways a *regional* economy, with local residents frequently working and shopping in towns surrounding Charlotte, and commuting back to homes in the county after work. Good-sized towns (and small cities) to which many Charlotte Countians commute include Farmville, South Boston, and even Lynchburg. Each of these cities lies less than an hour's drive from most Charlotte County communities, and each also has a hospital and a variety of shopping and cultural facilities approximating those of larger metropolitan areas.

THE (CURRENT) SCHOOLS OF
CHARLOTTE COUNTY

In 1968, the "Freedom of Choice" plan in Virginia was ruled unconstitutional, and most school divisions voluntarily integrated their schools (including Charlotte County) during the 1968–1969 school year. Unfortunately, what this meant in Charlotte County was that several physically adequate and well-supported community schools had to be consolidated, since the dual facilities previously maintained in order to "insure" racial segregation were no longer cost effective. Ironically, given that, in at least two cases, the best facilities were those of former Black schools (which had been built in an effort to maintain segregation), it was the older White schools which were closed down, and White students moved to these formerly Black schools during elementary school consolidation.

At the same time, county administrators and school personnel had become attracted to the curricular possibilities of a junior high school for the County. Coupled with the mandated consolidation of elementary schools, what all of this amounted to was a grand reshuffling of virtually every local school. Not only were grades combined between formerly racially segregated schools, but entire secondary school grade levels were shifted during 1968.

For example, prior to full integration, Randolph-Henry High School housed White students in grades 8–12, and Central High housed the Black students of the same grade levels. However, since both student bodies could not be combined quickly into Randolph-Henry (in 1968–1969), only White and Black students in grades 10–12 were initially taught there, while the Central High School facility became the new junior high school, containing grades 8 and 9.

According to many in the central office in Charlotte County, national curricular trends also pointed the way to further school reform and consolidation 10 years later. At this time, the national "swing" to middle schools was in full force, and administrators in Charlotte County once again shuffled grade levels. This time, however, grade level changes occurred at virtually every school, not just in grades 8–12. Specifically, the Charlotte County School Board placed all seventh and eighth graders in Central Middle School in the 1979–1980 academic year, which meant, not only high school reorganization (i.e., ninth graders went back to the high school), but also the loss of all county seventh graders to remaining elementary schools.

The loss of seventh graders to elementary schools, coupled with plans for also adding sixth graders to the middle school as soon as possible, and with a general enrollment decline throughout the division, led quickly to even further school consolidation pressures. And once again, the availability of low-cost loans for school construction throughout Virginia was seized upon by the Charlotte County School Board (and Board of Supervisors), which began to discuss the construction of a more central elementary school for the County.

As mentioned previously, most interviewees in the county could not remember community debates from the wave of school consolidations done in the 1940s and 1950s, although we are sure there must have been some. However, the location and naming of the most recently constructed elementary school at Eureka apparently caused much antagonism in Charlotte County during the early 1980s.

The ostensible need for constructing the new school (as has been the pattern) involved the savings in operating costs to be achieved by consolidating the two elementary schools at Keysville and Drakes Branch. Also, while we have no data on this possibility, it seems quite likely that state accreditation forces helped to close one or more of these smaller county elementary schools (see an even more recent version of this dynamic in Chapter 5). In this light, it was probably argued that paying the interest on state-subsidized low-cost loans for a new building would quickly prove more efficient than maintaining and staffing two schools with continually declining enrollments anyway. However, each of the communities in which the schools were to be closed wanted the new facility built closer to them, and many wanted the new school to retain the name of their respective communities.

Yet the "planning committee" involved in site selection chose a "neutral" site between Drakes Branch and Keysville, near the very small community of Eureka. Even then, however, controversy surrounding the site continued, because the owner of one piece of the target property refused to sell, and it took legal action for the School Board to acquire it.

In 1984, however, Eureka Elementary opened in mid-year, combining the students from Drakes Branch and Keysville. And while some local residents are still bitter about its location and construction, the architectural design and attractiveness of Eureka Elementary far exceeded any of the other elementary schools in the four demonstration sites of the AEL project. For example, virtually across the board each of the schools in the four demonstration projects contained ultimately functional floor designs, with an occasional addition of either attached classrooms or mobile units in an adjacent parking lot.

Eureka Elementary, however, contains a variety of aesthetic touches and common areas rarely seen in even the most affluent school systems. In addition to fully carpeted halls, naturally lighted walkways, a large and modern dining room, and an attractive library, classrooms in the building are grouped in numerous pods around several large common areas containing a host of "modern" shared curricular holdings and audio-visual equipment. Furthermore, an acoustically designed music amphitheater is located in the rear of the school, which also frequently serves as meeting place for various school and school/community meetings (like several held for the AEL project).

Even though the facilities of Eureka Elementary appeared quite advantageous to our evaluation staff (compared to others we visited), local residents still appear to have mixed feelings about the planning and placement protocols made by the School Board at its inception. Such feelings were perhaps further aggravated when yet a third elementary school (Charlotte Elementary) was closed in 1985–1986, and children from that school bussed to Eureka. Again, while each of these school closings appears not to have produced the trauma visible in other locations, it still appears that the loss of community schools at Drakes Branch, Keysville, and Charlotte CourtHouse contributed to some irritation directed at the Eureka location.

Other functioning elementary schools faced rather interesting grade-level solutions to the perceived duplication of school facilities following full integration. For example, between 1968 and 1978 the (previously) White Charlotte Elementary and the (previously) Black Central Elementary were run as a single school, with the combined K-3 being held in the former Central building and the combined grades 4–7 held in the Charlotte building. However, declining enrollments and the move of the seventh graders to Central Middle School led the School Board to close the older Charlotte Elementary building and consolidate all remaining students into Central Elementary (the former Black school) in the 1979–80 academic year. Furthermore, with the addition of the sixth grade to Central Middle School and yet further enrollment declines among elementary age children in the Charlotte CourtHouse area, Central Elementary became an annex (housing primarily sixth graders) to Central Middle School, and remaining K-5 students were consolidated into Eureka Elementary.

Importantly, as some of the above discussion ought to suggest, official grade-level groupings for elementary, middle, and high schools have been part of Virginia mandated school reform initiatives (see the later discussion on Virginia's "Standards of Quality" Program) during the past two decades. Thus, trying to balance declines in daily attendance in the division while (re)organizing institutional levels has in some ways exacerbated problems with use of existing facilities first brought about by desegregation mandates.

While the majority of the "action" in the shuffling of students during the last two decades occurred in the most centrally located areas Charlotte County, important school consolidations also occurred in the furthest "corners" of the county during the late 1950s, sites which were further removed from the county seat but which in essence had the most modern facilities until the construction of Eureka Elementary.

In the southern part of the county, the older White Wyliesburg school was closed down and its students transferred to the previously Negro but newer Bacon District School. Currently, this school still serves perhaps the most impoverished group of the county's children, whose parents are more typically Black tenant farmers on (still) numerous large farms. Not coincidentally, according to some school officials, it is from some of these large estates in Bacon District where most of the White children who attend Prince Edward Academy reside, and whose more affluent (White) parents appear little interested in matters of the local school and/or the school division.

While in general the race and education theme appears a nonissue to most school officials and community leaders with whom we have been in contact, it is in the Bacon District School where the residue of segregation and criticism of previous low expectations for minority children can be heard. The current (White) principal there has been a steady advocate for special programs for disadvantaged children during the past decade, and has been a vocal advocate for both an instructional program for 4-year-olds and an agitator for getting the school board to talk with and meet the needs of Bacon District parents.

Since much of the focus of our AEL study related to the notion of school district instructional leadership, some brief mention of the Bacon district principal is probably called for. Among elementary school principals, it appeared clearly the case to us that the Bacon District principal best represented Charlotte County's version of an effective "instructional leader" in 1988–1989. At Eureka Elementary, the first year principal was a newcomer to elementary education, having served at the high school for several years. And at JMJ and Phenix, the (female) principal spent much of her time attempting to administer two different school facilities. Furthermore, both of these principals appeared to primarily define their jobs in terms of improving community relations and teacher morale.

Yet the Bacon District principal chose voluntarily to leave his administrative position in Charlotte CourtHouse (where he had served in several capacities over 15 years) to intervene in the southeastern end of Charlotte County. Importantly, families served by Bacon District almost all come from its most rural part: All other elementary schools include some or many students from the county's remaining small towns. However, according to the principal of Bacon district, "60% of the students here are at risk because they are poor and have no experience with the wider world." Also, he claimed that "many, many children who go to school here live in abandoned farmhouses without plumbing. . . and (which) in many cases don't even have floors or windows." In his judgment, most of the attention in the county prior to the 1989–1990 school year had been directed towards schools in its "upper" region: and he felt somewhat angry at this attention, believing that special concerns of Bacon District required more focus than they have been given by community leaders and the school board.

In response to such "facts," the Bacon District principal seemed to talk/behave in ways reminiscent of some of the Braxton County principals discussed earlier. In addition to the programs he championed above, the Bacon District principal (seemingly on his own) appeared to us well rehearsed in the national school improvement literature and was in the midst of implementing a variety of innovative programs even as the rest of the district had been involved in other (noninstructional) leadership issues and/or in adapting state-wide school programs.

For example, the Bacon District principal knew about the "effective schools" literature, had used "assertive discipline" techniques; still had a file on the "Effective Rural Schools Program" run by the state of Virginia "some years back;" had introduced various curricular enhancement programs for disadvantaged readers in his school; and gave workshops himself around the state for teachers of "at-risk" students. Most recently, Bacon District school has been chosen as a national "model program" for showcasing the Developmental Skills Program, which is based on the "cognitive instruction" techniques developed by Joan Fulton (1987). Monies utilized to fund this program have come from a major electronics sales chain (not located in the county).

Meanwhile, on the west side of the county, two new (small) schools were built in the late 1950s, one ostensibly for Whites and one for Negroes. However, since neither of these facilities was big enough to hold all area students, and as each was in too good a state of repair to close, elementary education in the Phenix area was subdivided into a K–3 operation at Phenix and a grade 4–7 organization at J. Murray Jeffress. In most respects these two facilities still operate as a unit, with a shared principal, shared staff meetings, etc., although now the grade levels served are K–2 at the one institution (with some prekindergarten students) and 3–5 at the other.

According to the Phenix/JMJ principal, most students from her school are from families who work intermittently on their own small land holdings, supplemented by outside income from textile employment either in the county or in one of the small plants in adjacent counties. This fact, she suggests, sets her students and her school(s) apart from those of Bacon district some 30 miles distant.

THE VIRGINIA "STANDARDS OF QUALITY" PROGRAM

One of the difficulties of talking about contemporary local school leadership and curricular dynamics we found in our evaluation study revolved around trying to disentangle state mandates from local initiatives. Yet, since local interpretations of state mandates and local actions taken in accord with (or taken to evade) state directives can vary greatly, the "disentangling" process can be (and was) a very time consuming one.

Yet, as we believed that the West Virginia Master Plan importantly influenced much local educational focus in Braxton County, so too does it appear that the Virginia Standards of Quality Program (first introduced there in 1970) has strongly affected schooling practices in Charlotte County during the last two decades. Furthermore, coupled with monies for school construction made available from the state's Literary Fund, it might be argued that much of the relative success of schooling in Charlotte County can be traced to the impact of these state initiatives. Yet we are unwilling to credit all of the division's school innovation/development to state-wide programs, given that much local pride and concern for education goes back even before World War II.

Nevertheless, some mention of the Standards of Quality Program initiatives are worthy of discussion here, as many contemporary dynamics in Charlotte County (to be discussed shortly) are called for, or made available by, this program. The Standards of Quality Program has been updated several times since 1970, and its regulations are part of the state constitution; that is, unlike many states in the region, the Virginia Board of Education is not charged with relatively diffuse tasks like providing an "adequate" and/or "efficient" system of education. Rather, very specific mandates have been given the State Board, and the updating of these "Standards of Quality" occurs routinely. The most recent upgrading (established in July 1988) focuses on seven different topics.

Standard 1, for example, specifies that state Board will establish educational objectives or basic competencies required for "success in school and for a productive life in the years beyond, which shall be known as the Standards of Learning." Furthermore, Standard 1 mandates that students will be tested with regard to the mastery of the Standards of Learning, and those found deficient will be required (with partial state subsidy) to undertake programs of remediation in the local division.

Standard 2, among other things, mandates that the state School Board and local divisions will provide support services adequate for the attainment of the Standards of Learning, including pupil guidance, staff development, in-service training, development of appropriate facility plans, etc.

Standard 3 specifically addresses academic and staff accountability issues, calling on the State Board to institute accreditation guidelines and develop for use pupil criterion reference tests (as well as selecting for application nationally normed achievement tests). Subsequently, local divisions must adhere to accreditation formats and timetables and must test students as the State Board requires.

Standard 4 mandates that, in order to obtain a regular high school diploma, all students must first obtain a "Literacy Passport" certifying the reading mastery required to enter ninth grade. Satisfactorily obtaining a Literacy Passport must be accomplished in addition to completing the regular high school course of study required by local high schools and the State Board for high school graduation.

Standard 5 mandates much of what many professional education groups already call for: continuous training and professional development activities for almost every official in each divisional school system. Included in this mandate for continuous staff development are local board members, superintendents, principals, teachers, and central office program coordinators. Furthermore, all of these staff development activities (covering personnel, curriculum, and current educational issues) must be monitored and/or coordinated by each local division.

Standards 6 and 7 were particularly interesting, given the concerns of the AEL project, as they both called for extensive public/community involvement in program planning and outreach activities for each local division. Standard 6 specifically calls for (among other things) biennial revisions/adaptations by both state and division school officials of their mandated 6-year school improvement plans. In other words, each division is required to be almost continuously involved in the process of self-study and school improvement. And community groups are specifically required to part of this ongoing process.

Standard 7 further specifies that each local division must maintain and have available a division policy manual, which includes policies governing staff evaluations, student conduct and attendance requirements, policies for involving the local community, and soon. Standard 7 also requires that this policy manual be readily available to all parents and school employees.

SECONDARY EDUCATION IN CHARLOTTE COUNTY

Ironically, while much concern and change discussed previously has been in evidence throughout Charlotte County elementary and middle schools (more on the middle school follows shortly), Randolph-Henry High School appears to be the consensus "flagship" of the county school system. The irony in this particular case refers, not to any unimportance of elementary education there, but rather to the fact that, throughout the state (including Charlotte County), public secondary education was of such marginal concern until comparatively recently. Yet, compared to all of the other three high schools discussed in this report, the academic, vocational, and sports programs at Randolph-Henry have commanded much public support and interest for decades.

As mentioned earlier, Randolph-Henry High was the first division-wide consolidated school in the region and thus was widely touted by local and state officials in the 1940s as the model which the rest of the state ought to follow. Furthermore, given that most current adults living in the county attended Randolph-Henry, the school appears a strong focal point for community pride in a region with few other 20th-century historical institutions. Such an interpretation appeared easily confirmed during our fieldwork, for Randolph Henry was celebrating its 50th anniversary in 1989, and monthly celebrations at the high school, in cooperation with the high school PTO and various community groups occurred throughout the 1989–1990 school year.

Yet the tradition which the high school represents is not the only source of local interest. Rather, the diverse academic curriculum, athletics programs, vocational/agriculture programs and extracurricular vocational and academic teams and clubs are very visible throughout the region. For example, while multiple extramural sports teams compete at the high school level, the boys baseball (not basketball) team almost always has a winning season, successfully competes in state tournament play, and is widely recognized throughout the Southside for this prowess. Parenthetically, the fact that the high school has such a winning baseball program was arguably the only fact correctly recalled by the state AG members in Roanoke when site selection for the RSS study was first discussed.

In addition, several of the academic programs and numerous vocational programs have also won statewide recognition during the past several decades. The Forensic (debate) Team is widely supported in the county and has won regional awards. So, too, several of the vocational programs in home economics and agriculture are widely subscribed to by students, and many state-wide competitions have been won by Randolph-Henry students. Significantly, the Future Farmers of America have a strong chapter in Randolph-Henry High, and their presence is much more visible there than in any of the other districts of this study.

In addition to a very diverse set of curricular offerings and numerous extracurricularly innovative and successful club activities, a number of individual student outcome measures are impressive, given the low-income levels of many Randolph-Henry students. For example, even though Charlotte County has a high percentage of students coming from low-income families, and even though both property values and taxes on such properties are low compared to the rest of the state and the nation, the percentage of high school graduates from the high school is relatively high (approximately 70%), while the official yearly dropout rate is less than 5% (VA Dept. of Educ., 1988). Furthermore, one of the main reasons why some students either delay completing their schooling or drop out of school altogether is because they enter into local employment in the regional textile/garment factories (a fact which irritates many teachers and central office staff).

THE SIGNIFICANCE OF HIGHER
EDUCATION IN VIRGINIA

To be sure, school reform and improvement in Charlotte County appears to have been impressive, especially considering its early 20th-century status. Some of these local improvements and levels of student attainment can no doubt be attributed to the hard work of local educators and community leaders (more of which will be discussed shortly). However, in Charlotte County a variety of late 20th-century extralocal educational and economic factors also appear systematically related to comparative strengths of the school division.

For example, as mentioned earlier, Virginia as a state ranks higher than each of the others in this study on most educational indicators. For instance, Virginia has higher teacher salaries, greater per-pupil expenditures, and greater numbers of students continuing their studies after high school graduation than any of the other three states, even though measured student performance is typically no higher (SREB, 1987).

I have already made mention of the state subsidized building funds which appear to have played a prominent role in the lives of Charlotte county schools since the early 20th century. Similarly, basic accountability and provision of services mandated throughout the state (via the Standards of Quality) have been mentioned earlier in this report (even prior to the round of current school reforms following on the national *Nation at Risk* study).

However, another factor which appears to explain how and why so many students throughout Virginia and Charlotte County persist longer in school than appears to be the case in other states involves the excellent and diverse nature of higher education institutions in Virginia. According to state statistics, almost 67% of all Virginia high school graduates attend some form of college after leaving high school. And this figure significantly exceeds both national and regional averages (SREB, 1987).

Furthermore, Virginia's commitment to higher education is well grounded historically, as we attempted to suggest earlier in this case study. As one group of authors phrased it:

> higher education has always been Virginia's favorite child, while the free or public school (was previously) left like Ishmael to sojourn in the desert. (WPA, 1940, p. 124)

And the forceful state-wide emphasis on higher education also appears to have significantly influenced the educational attainment of many Charlotte Countians. For example, the presence of several institutions of higher education surrounding Charlotte County appears to provide both cultural and instrumental support for post-high-school ambitions of many Randolph-Henry students. Within 90 minutes of most of Charlotte County lies virtually every type of higher education institution in the U.S. These include several state universities (including the University of Virginia) and state colleges (including Longwood College, just up the road in Farmville). At either end of the higher education continuum, the elite liberal arts college (for men) of Hampden-Sydney borders Charlotte County on the north (close to Longwood), and a branch of the state community college system is housed in Keysville.

Perhaps worthy of particular note is that Hampden-Sydney College and nearby Washington and Lee University (formerly Liberty Hall Academy) were both started as academies in the Southside under the sponsorship of the Presbyterian Church. And the original meeting where decisions were made to undertake both institutions was held in Cub Creek Church in what later became Charlotte County.

In any event, not only are higher education institutions *highly visible* in the Southside, but they literally appear to *compete* with each other for students at all levels in places like Charlotte County. For example, college recruiters informally mingled with students at Randolph-Henry in the cafeteria during one of our visits to the high school. During this visit, the principal volunteered that "almost any student who graduates from here can go to college for free if he or she wants – except perhaps for some of the White boys."

A visit to the high school guidance counselor's office at the high school likewise suggests that post-graduate education is typically expected in the county for most students (even though "only 50% or so" continue some form of schooling, which is lower than the state average). Along the back wall in one of the biggest offices in the school, the counselors have extensive holdings of regional, state, and national university catalogues. We were even encouraged to send one from the University of Kentucky.

The significance of post-high school expectations at Randolph-Henry lies in the facts suggested earlier: that Charlotte County is a poor and rural place by national statistical definitions. Yet various forms of post high school instruction are available for vocationally interested students. While approximately half of the graduates of Randolph-Henry go on to 4-year colleges, many others enroll in advanced vocational and technical programs at places like Keysville Community College. Importantly, Keysville Community College also has direct access to high school students in Charlotte County via a partnership with Randolph-Henry to offer dual enrollment/credit courses in both academic and vocational/technical subjects. It is conceivable, in other words, that some students in several advanced curricular areas can virtually complete both their senior year of high school *and* their freshman year of college while at Randolph-Henry. And high school students can take up to two dual enrollment courses a semester in Randolph-Henry, *paid for by the public school division.*

A CONCLUDING NOTE ON THE MIDDLE SCHOOL

Inasmuch as Central Middle School in Charlotte County later became the focus of RSS school improvement activities there, particular discussion of its strengths and problems in our evaluation report was to be held back in the OERI report until the concluding chapter. However, as frequently happens in ethnographically informed studies such as this, we decided to insert several paragraphs on the middle school in the case study and now here, after the principal there (who was one of our "key informants") read and severely critiqued an early draft of the evaluation document. More accurately stated, perhaps, it wasn't what *was* said about the county or its school system which drew the ire of the principal, but rather what *wasn't* said. And in an extended interview in late September 1989, the principal spoke his mind about what was missing in our discussion of Charlotte County's educational system.

Put briefly, what was lacking in our first draft on Charlotte County, according to him, was an adequate discussion of the curricular advantages and significance of Central Middle. The principal, who is a lifelong resident of Charlotte County (and who has been principal there for almost a decade), argued that our quite positive detailing of programs and opportunities at Randolph-Henry High School failed to acknowledge the similar sorts of curricular importance of his school. As we have argued, the high school in Charlotte County appears to us virtually synonymous (symbolically) with education itself there: as the division superintendent put it, "Randolph-Henry is the heart of the community." And while such a possibility has been suggested elsewhere as perhaps typical of many rural school systems (e.g., Peshkin, 1978), it is probably the only such example in our four-site study.

Yet, according to the principal of Central Middle, programs and opportunities at his school were and are at least equally as impressive as those at the high school, and were that way even when things weren't going quite so well at the high school earlier in the decade. During the "minilecture" given the principle investigator on September 24, the middle school principal overviewed a host of school programs and activities perhaps unique among the many middle schools in the districts involved in this study. Not only did Central Middle have a host of sports programs (including baseball, of course), but it had its own band, systematic instruction in computers, a large (78 students) program in Agriculture/ Home Economics, and foreign language instruction in French, Spanish, and even Latin.

Furthermore, Mr. E was particularly concerned that our high school discussion mentioned its forensics program as so impressive; however, according to him, the forensic team at Central Middle had an even better regional reputation than the high school's. His school, he argued, competed in several regional Forensic competitions in such areas as extemporaneous speaking, after-dinner speaking, and one-act plays. Furthermore, successfully competing in other regional math and science competitions was a testament to how innovative and strong Central Middle was in academics, a strength he did not perceive in our overall discussion of Charlotte County's educational system.

And he was also quick to point out that his school's strong reputation in academics was not an accident. Rather, his teachers (he claimed) were on the cutting edge of professional practice. New techniques and organizational strategies were frequently put into place at Central Middle. A new team-teaching approach, developed by the sixth-grade teachers, had just been instituted at Central Middle. And attendance and presentations at various middle school staff and leadership institutes was the norm for his school rather than the exception.

SCHOOL LEADERSHIP ISSUES IN
CHARLOTTE COUNTY

To this point, a general history of the economic and social histories of Charlotte County has been pursued to inform the reader about the previous local contexts as related to school functioning and change. As well, we have spent several pages attempting to overview contemporary educational issues and dynamics at each school level in the county. To conclude this chapter, however, we would like to briefly overview current district-wide school issues, problems, and dynamics, paying special attention to school leadership and/or governance concerns. Again, this focus has been chosen, not because it necessarily represents the only topic worthy of more particular discussion, but rather because the AEL project under review was concerned primarily with school and community leadership and how such leadership might be enhanced through participation in the RSS school/community partnership model. This discussion will be relatively brief, however, because the new superintendent's career and the division's then positive climate were both very recent developments during the 1988–1989 school year. Later developments are profiled in Chapter 6.

As indicated earlier, school and community leaders in Charlotte County were and remain quite proud of a number of their state and local traditions. And some of the local judicial and legislative practices in Charlotte County date back to its antebellum history. For example, county-wide meetings for the discussion of important community concerns happen routinely in Charlotte County: in 1987, a controversy over the way the previous school superintendent handled several high school personnel matters prompted an open forum of just this type at Charlotte CourtHouse, in the courthouse. So, too, widely announced County policy-making events (like meetings of the Board of Supervisors) are also held in the old but meticulously maintained courthouse, a structure originally designed by Thomas Jefferson.

Parenthetically, public forums on two (locally opposed) economic development "opportunities" were held at Charlotte Court House during 1989. One involved an out-of-county company which wanted to build and operate a biological waste incinerator in nearby Pamplin. County residents were greatly concerned about air quality deterioration related to such a facility, and the Board of Supervisors passed a zoning ordinance which prohibited this facility from being built.

During the same period, a state power company proposed to build in Charlotte County a major new plant on the Staunton River, a project which would probably create upwards of 3,000 construction jobs over a 5-year period, as well as adding some long-term employment for county citizens. However, concerned with environmental impact (damming and flooding of the river which now includes a wildlife refuge), public meetings (at the courthouse) convinced the company to seek a new site in Halifax County. Yet, since the new site is still contiguous to Charlotte County, residents now fear they may still get all of the negative consequences of this development without *any* benefit. Therefore, Charlotte County citizens are appealing the potential building of the power plant to a regional development board. And several prominent citizens even want to use the auditorium of Randolph-Henry to hold the next meeting on this public issue, as the courthouse is alleged to be too small for such a gathering.

In any event, public meetings and visible local leadership on important issues is easy to see in Charlotte County, which may be why the old courthouse still remains the way it must have been throughout this century. As best we can tell, there are only two functions of the Charlotte Courthouse beyond actual twice-weekly court cases held there: to house memorabilia (pictures, documents, and statues from the county's early history), and to serve as a meeting place for the discussion of public issues like those mentioned above. There are no offices in this building, and most of the time there are no people there, for most county officers are housed in other small (historic) buildings behind the courthouse proper. And in no other county included in this study was there a counterpart to the freestanding and symbolic courthouse in Charlotte County, or to the visibility of public meetings (including those which had to do with the schools).

So, too, a number of school governance protocols in Southside Virginia differ from school practice in much of the remainder of the country (and from most practices at all other other districts in this study). For example, unlike Braxton County, which was discussed earlier, the school operating budget in Charlotte County is not decided upon by the local school board or (technically) dictated by the state. Rather, school budgets are only recommended by the local boards (and the division superintendent), as ultimate approval of operating budgets are decided upon by the county Board of Supervisors. Of course, minimum appropriations are required at the local level in order to qualify for state supplements to the Standards of Quality programs. And Charlotte County, like many other rural counties, has typically taxed local citizens at minimum rates during the last several decades.

Perhaps another important anomaly visible in Charlotte County (and ostensibly throughout the state) is that its seven school board members (as opposed to five in Braxton County) are not directly elected by county citizens. Rather, a school board Selection Committee is appointed by the (Piedmont) District Judge, which in turn appoints theoretically interested citizens to the school board. At the current time, six of seven members of this board are male (one is Black), all have had at least some college education, and all either have large farms in the county and/or have been career professionals or owners of their own small businesses.

Naturally, such a system has (and had, as the case of Prince Edward County demonstrates) some built-in biases against aggressive local school improvement efforts in Southside Virginia (moderated, we are sure, by mandates built into the Standards of Quality Program). Inasmuch as primarily wealthier and White citizens in a region skeptical of public schooling were historically charged with deciding upon local school policies and budgets, both conservative academic and fiscal decisions appear to have occurred in Charlotte County during the century. And, according to our interviews, climates for educational upgrading versus eras in which school board interests favored providing minimum school services by keeping taxes low seem to have alternated during the past several decades.

We assume that, as county school boards in the Southside were probably drawn from typically conservative political and cultural elites, there probably were confrontations between them and middle class sponsors of town school systems, especially in times of economic stagnation. Perhaps relatedly, there currently is some state-wide interest in replacing the nonelected boards of education in Virginia with popularly elected boards, ostensibly so that more aggressive local school improvement efforts (with attendant higher costs) can be achieved.

In any event, a traditionally powerful respect for education does seem visible in Charlotte County with regard to the esteem with which teachers seem to be held in there. Unlike the negative perceptions of teachers very visible in other southeastern states (including to some extent each of the three states discussed in this study, and especially West Virginia), teachers in Virginia appear to have historically been held in high regard by most citizens. While historical skepticism of the need for extensive educational opportunities for poor and/or Black children, coupled with little taxable wealth for running local schools, may both have influenced local hesitancy for greater school support in Southside Virginia, nowhere in our experiences, interviews, or readings have we been able to find systematic condemnation of inept teachers or corrupt leadership practices at local school levels. Further, as 1989 was an important election year in Virginia, we were greatly surprised to hear in local radio "spots," in state and regional newspapers, and on television a host of pro-education ads by almost every candidate running for public office. In some contests, it appeared to be that "who had done the most to increase educational spending" was an underlying theme. And public endorsements from the Virginia Educational Association were proudly announced by some politicians, endorsements which were not made public to our knowledge in the other three states during our field experiences.

In fact, it might well be argued that challenges to the esteem and prominence of school teachers in Charlotte County was a critical factor in the replacement of the previous superintendent, who had angered many teachers during the final years of his tenure. Organized teachers, in point of fact, were one of the groups which complained loudest about the educational malaise and lack of communication they perceived in Charlotte County during the 1986–1987 school year.

Currently, according to almost every one of our informants, there exists in Charlotte County an aggressive school improvement climate not seen there for a number of years. Symptomatic perhaps of the current reform and improvement minded concerns of the Charlotte County Board of Education was the recent hiring of its new division superintendent.

The previous superintendent served for 11 years and had a state-wide reputation as an effective school leader. However, according to several of our informants, his leadership efforts began to seriously decline during the last several years of his tenure, at least partly as a function of his advancing age and declining health. By the mid-1980s, the former superintendent was approaching 60 years of age, and he had survived two strokes. As a career superintendent about to become eligible for state retirement benefits, and as one who expressed few professional goals he had not already achieved, a number of his subordinates increasingly came to consider him a "retirement superintendent" by 1985 or 1986; ostensibly interested in maintaining the Charlotte County system until he could retire, rather than seriously undertaking any (new) school improvement efforts.

Furthermore, according to many teachers we interviewed, other Southside school divisions were obtaining grants and acquiring equipment in the early 1980s not available in Charlotte County, apparently because the former superintendent was not as aggressive in their pursuit as other superintendents. And this "fact" appears to have bothered a number of classroom teachers in contact with such systems, as well as at least one administrator who was further chagrined with the former superintendent's efforts always to turn back to the Board of Supervisors extra money budgeted but not spent during the fiscal year.

Outside of the school, the former superintendent apparently was also rarely visible at athletic or social functions sponsored either by his school system or by other community agencies. And the visibility of the division superintendent in a variety of social settings surrounding the school was argued to be a major concern of the school board, which replaced him just prior to AEL's involvement in Charlotte County.

The "straw that broke the camel's back" in Charlotte County (at least with regard to the issue of school leadership there) appears to have been the handling of teacher reassignments following the 1986-1987 school year by the superintendent. Even though financial circumstances had remained difficult in the county, job security and school reassignments for tenured teachers and principals appear to have been openly discussed, and resolved matters in the county during the 1970s and 1980s. And even today, career administrators and teachers in the Charlotte County system appear to move around somewhat; yet it appears that mutual agreement (perhaps as "suggested" by the superintendent) underlies most reassignments. However, this pattern appears to have been broken during the 1986-1987 school year in Charlotte County, when several teachers at Randolph-Henry (including the baseball coach) were reassigned teaching duties without their consultation or consent.

Forced reassignments, coupled with already low teacher morale, perceived lack of community visibility, and consistently mediocre test scores in the division led the Charlotte County School Board to seek a new superintendent for the 1988-1989 school year. And in order to "ease out" one superintendent while "easing in" a new one, the current superintendent was hired as a deputy superintendent for the first half of the 1987-1988 school year and assumed full responsibilities beginning in January 1988.

According to school board members and central office staff we interviewed, the newly hired school superintendent was chosen on the basis of how well he got along with individuals and groups in the community, as well as how he was perceived to relate to teachers. He was not chosen specifically to be an instructional leader, or because of his vast administrative experience. In point of fact, the newly hired superintendent was the only finalist for the position who did not have a doctoral degree, central office experience, or any regional reputation, which each of the other two finalists had.

Rather, the new superintendent appeared to have been hired in an effort to help rebuild bridges between the school division, its teachers, and the surrounding community. In order to accomplish this task, personal qualities like openness, energy, enthusiasm for community involvement, and listening to the wishes of teachers and school staff members appear to have played a crucial role.

1988 AND 1989 ISSUES AND TRENDS IN CHARLOTTE COUNTY SCHOOLS

Once hired, the several objectives mentioned above appeared to play an important part in the "duties" taken on by the current superintendent during his half-year as deputy superintendent, and later as the division head. According to our interviews, the incumbent went during his first 6 months in the county to virtually every church, community meeting, and county teacher assembly to introduce himself and hear about local wishes and concerns. He also is reported to have attended almost every high school athletic function during the past 2 years and frequently speaks at many community public forums. Having witnessed his "performance" in a number of contexts, to say that "Mr. S" is a high-profile person in the county would not be an understatement. Importantly, the current superintendent appears to be widely accepted and appreciated in Charlotte County, even though he is not a native.

Yet Mr. S appears to also have an experience-based concern for school improvement which goes over and above his community "networking" expertise. Building somewhat upon the mandates of the Standards of Quality program, the current superintendent of Charlotte County schools issued a "call to arms" in Spring 1989, whereby various educational excellence themes and their potential (extra) cost to the taxpayers of Charlotte County were published.

According to this document, accountability, professional development of teachers, new curricular initiatives (like the new program for 4-year-olds, dual enrollment courses in the high school, vocational and adult education opportunities, etc.), and avenues for parent and community involvement in the schools were advertised and described. Of particular note, with regard to the minority community, the Charlotte County Board of Education has entered into a special agreement with Longwood College for minority teacher training. Specifically, Black graduates of Randolph-Henry High School interested in returning to teach in Charlotte County are (virtually) automatically admitted to Longwood College and have been promised immediate employment in Charlotte County when they are through with their studies.

Importantly, Mr. S believes that he was hired to enable the community (including its Black community) to once again become involved with the system, to improve the morale and professional development of teachers, and to better the overall performance of the system, objectives which he views as closely interrelated. Importantly, although the superintendent confesses to having read a few professional journals, his school improvement efforts appear to be based on his own experiences:

> basically, (school improvement) goes back to what you have seen and how you thought it worked. I've been involved in a number of (projects) as teacher and principal. . . . What you need to do is to add on to these as common sense suggests. I don't see myself as a grand innovator. Sometimes the (innovations) I'm interested in coincidentally coincide with what I've read in the literature. But only rarely have I tried something based primarily on what I read in the (professional) journals.

Yet, the long term positive trend in the school division was not necessarily guaranteed by the "honeymoon" period visible there during the year and a half of our initial fieldwork. Strong criticism of some school leadership practices remains present, and, even though it was criticism of previous events in the school division, Mr. S appears wary of the possibility of its reemergence.

One harbinger of future system problems in Charlotte County had to do with new funding patterns announced by the state legislature in 1988 (and a problem in all four of the districts studied for this book). For example, as Virginia funds the Standards of Quality Program on an Average Daily Membership basis, falling enrollments have cost over a dozen staff and administrative positions since Mr. S came into office. And the new accounting procedures put into effect by the Joint Legislative Audit and Review Committee (JLARC) were particularly biased against the needs of rural and small school districts, according to the superintendent.

In the short run, retirements and reassignments enabled the system not to lay anyone off in 1989–1990. And, in 1988, many parents actually lobbied the Board of Supervisors to increase local taxes for support of school programs. However, as projected enrollments also suggested future losses of students (the division had declined in enrollment by about 200 students in the 4 years before 1989), it is unclear how long the system can internally correct itself without angering particular schools, teachers and/or parent groups.

In any event, Charlotte County at the end of the 1988–1989 school year seemed to be "on the move," both in terms of its local constituents and the national mood for improving schools. There appeared to be some lingering problems regarding minority pupil success in the system (as mentioned in our overview of the Bacon District situation), and the "poor stepchild" perceptions of some teachers and parents at the middle school remained of concern to them. Both of these themes were among the "expressed needs" picked up in the AEL

Community "Needs Sensing" process, completed in the spring of 1988. How such themes played themselves out in the AEL project, as well as important events of 1989-1990 that related to the previous discussion, are more particularly discussed in Chapter 6 of this book.

REFERENCES

Ailsworth, T., Keller, A., Nichols, L., & Walker, B. (1979). *Charlotte County: Rich indeed.* Charlotte County, VA: Charlotte County Board of Supervisors.

Appalachian Regional Commission. (1988). *Education reform in rural Appalachia.* Washington, DC: ARC.

Carrington, J. (1907). *Charlotte County Virginia: Historical, statistical and present attractions.* Richmond, VA: Hermitage Press.

Center for Economic Development. (1988). *The logical location, south central Virginia.* Keysville, VA: Southside Virginia Community College.

Charlotte County Industrial Development Foundation. (1988). *Charlotte County, Virginia: Community profile, 1988–89.* Charlotte County, VA: C.C.I.D.F.

Cobb, J. (1982). *The selling of the South: The Southern crusade for industrial development 1936–1980.* Baton Rouge, LA: Louisiana State University Press.

Flynt, J. W. (1979). *Dixie's forgotten people.* Bloomington, IN: Indiana University Press.

Fulton, J. (1987, November). What's next in instruction? *The effective school report.* Richmond, VA: Virginia Department of Education.

Glymph, T. (1985). *Essays on the Postbellum Southern economy.* College Station TX: Texas A&M University Press.

Link, W. (1986). *A hard country and a lonely place: Schooling, society and reform in rural Virginia, 1870–1920.* Chapel Hill, NC: University of North Carolina Press.

Perkinson, H. (1968). *The imperfect panacea: American faith in education, 1865-1976.* New York: Random House.

Peshkin, A. (1978). *Growing up American: Schooling and the survival of community.* Chicago: University of Chicago Press.

Shepard, L. (1938). *Secondary education in Charlotte County, 1764-1937.* Unpublished thesis, University of Virginia.

Smith, B. (1965). *They closed their schools: Prince Edward County, Virginia, 1951-1964.* Chapel Hill, NC: University of North Carolina Press.

Southern Regional Education Board. (1987). *A progress report and recommendations on educational improvements in the SREB states.* Atlanta, GA: SREB.

Tate, L. (1929). *The Virginia guide.* Lebanon, VA: Leland Tate, Publisher.

Tyack, D. (1972). *The one best system.* Cambridge, MA: Harvard University Press.

Tyack, D., & Hansot, E. (1982). *Managers of virtue.* New York: Basic Books.

Virginia Department of Education. (1988). *Facing up.* Richmond, VA: Department of management information services.

Work Projects Administration. (1940). *Virginia: A guide to the old dominion.* New York: Oxford University Press.

Woodward, C. (1951). *Origins of the New South, 1877-1913.* Baton Rouge: LSU Press.

Wright, G. (1986). *Old South, new South.* New York: Basic Books.

Bowlins Ford School, Clinch County, Tennessee

Buses behind Clinch Central School

4

Clinch County, Tennessee

In Chapters 2 and 3 I briefly traced two rural county histories, with particular reference to the evolving status of public education in each. In both of these cases I suggested, based on a variety of historical materials and from multiple contemporary artifacts/interviews, that interest and commitment to the possibilities of schooling either does or did run high. Furthermore, I noted that financial/funding difficulties of schools in each system seem to have had chronic 20th-century problems, subject to (brief) periods of "remission" when particular reforms and occasional building enhancements/consolidations in each district were possible.

The third county/school district surveyed for the AEL study and for this book, however, appears to have developed differently in terms of both the local commitment and funding patterns discussed in the Virginia and West Virginia cases. As well, Clinch County, Tennessee, schools also have a significantly different economic and political history than those earlier discussed. The primary difference between Clinch County and the others centers upon its legacy of economic marginality and isolation from the rest of the U.S., and in fact from much of its own state. According to the 1980 census, Clinch County was among the poorest counties in Tennessee. And according to local officials, per capita income there during the past several decades has placed it among the 10 poorest counties in the U.S., and it is one of many in the Southeast identified as a persistent poverty county.

Related to such facts, local ability/interest in maintaining a strong public school system appears to have wavered significantly in Clinch County during the 20th century. As in the earlier cases, 20th-century written accounts of educational practice/concerns in the county are fragmentary and scarce. Part of the reason for this probably stems from a lack of literate citizens in the county (especially given the large number of outmigrants) with the time and/or interest in writing about local education. The 1980 U.S. Census of Population, for example, showed that just over 1% of Clinch County residents have completed 4 or more years of college, and only 61% are high school graduates.

In addition, some suggest that the educational system in Clinch County has historically been tied to politics and patronage, and few insiders with relatives in the schools may have been interested in "going public" with their stories.

Finally, a major fire at the county courthouse in Sealsville (the county seat) in 1929 destroyed most locally available documents potentially related to the history of public schools there. Rarely in what exists/survives about public schooling in Clinch County is there any reference to systematically effective schooling practices, staffing, or outcomes. Rather, funding inadequacies and political intrigue tend to dominate the historical evidence as well as its contemporary dynamics. Fleshing out the details of perpetual difficulties there follows shortly.

SELECTING A TENNESSEE DISTRICT

On May 25, 1988, the advisory group for helping to select an appropriate Tennessee school district for AEL to invite as a participant in its school/community demonstration project met in Nashville. In addition to the two principal AEL Rural/Small School staffs in attendance, a representative of the Tennessee Valley Authority, an education professor from Tennessee Tech, a member of the Tennessee State Department of Education, and a representative from the Governor's Office were present. Of the four advisory members, two were already familiar with AEL's intent and project objectives, and two were not. Therefore (as in all other site selection cases), several hours of the full day's meeting were occupied with overviewing the RSS mandate and its intentions.

Qualifying statistically as demonstration sites in Tennessee were seven primarily rural and poor schools. Criteria for eligibility remained as before (see Chapter 1). Given that Tennessee from east to west is such a geographically and economically diverse state, it was perhaps inevitable that none of the four state advisory appeared familiar with all seven districts, as they ranged from one in the far western part of the state on the Mississippi River to several in the Appalachian region of East Tennessee.

Of the seven eligible districts, one was quickly eliminated by the advisory committee because it lay close to one of several large metropolitan areas in Tennessee. Of the six which remained, the issue of school leadership and its stability became a focal concern, particularly since most Tennessee school systems have popularly elected superintendents. Therefore, initial discussions among steering committee members focused on reputations of current superintendents on school leadership concerns, followed by questions about whether forthcoming local elections in some districts would produce changing leadership. AEL representatives argued persuasively that it would do little good to identify and invite a school district's superintendent to participate in the R/SS demonstration project if that superintendent then lost his or her local election bid.

In day-long discussions over the six eligible districts, several were rather quickly eliminated. Two superintendents were well known by two advisory group members, who judged them poor choices on leadership criteria. As well, a third district at the extreme western portion of the state was recommended as too remote for AEL staff to get to efficiently. Thus, only three of the original seven appeared to remain under serious consideration.

As had been the case in Virginia, none of the Tennessee advisory group knew much about two of the remaining three districts or their leadership. One county familiar to (the same) two advisory group members was viewed as not particularly strong on improving student performance or effective leadership. This county (as well as one other) were close to Tennessee Tech and thus of potential interest to the advisory group member from that institution. She, in fact, was already working on a project compatable with (and partially funded by) AEL in this district: therefore, critical discussion of which district ought to be recommended to AEL for its school/community improvement project focused on "her" district and one further east in central Appalachia.

As suggested, knowledge about school functioning in the east Tennessee district was minimal among all advisory group members. Statistical data as available on 1980 census (and later updates), as well as school district performance indicators supplied by the state department of education, indicated both counties were rural and poor, and that some test scores had risen in both counties. However, the issue of continued leadership became a penultimate concern by the late stage of deliberation, and the advisory group broke so that phone calls to people potentially familiar with each county's forthcoming political races could be made.

Half an hour later, feedback from the calls was available to the group. One superintendent (in Clinch County) had won his county's primary election and faced little opposition in the August general election. On the other hand, the superintendent of the second county, though well thought of, was rumored to be retiring before the next school year.

In a final vote, Clinch County was recommended to the AEL representatives. As had been the case in other advisory group meetings, second, third, and fourth choices were listed in case Clinch County chose not to participate. The selection round of the Tennessee Advisory Group's participation in the R/SS project was completed by 5:15 p.m. the evening of May 25, and AEL staff promised to contact the Clinch County Superintendent during the following week.

INVITING CLINCH COUNTY'S PARTICIPATION

Inviting Clinch County to participate in the RSS demonstration turned out to be a time consuming, complex, and revealing process. Even getting in touch with the Clinch County Superintendent took 2 weeks, and setting a date to come present the AEL proposal to the superintendent and several central office staff took an additional 2 weeks.

According to notes on this meeting provided by RSS representatives, Clinch County's superintendent expressed some interest in becoming a demonstration site for AEL, as did one or two central office staff members. Furthermore, according to the RSS director, the superintendent felt sure that the Board of Education would likewise agree to become involved in the RSS project. Unfortunately, procuring an agreement with the Clinch County Board of Education was more difficult to obtain than had been suggested.

Initially, this difficulty seemed based on the fact that school was in recess for the summer, and regular board meetings had been postponed several times due to illness of the board chairman. As it turned out, however, school board policy matters in Clinch County in 1988 were frequently politicized, and complying with the superintendent's wishes/advice was rarely a commonplace occurrence.

After cancelled/postponed monthly board meetings in June, a meeting was called for July 14, 1988. Furthermore, since the U.K. evaluation staff were eager to travel to Clinch County, AEL staff members decided that we could just as easily serve as witnesses to board deliberations as they, and RSS staff did not attend the July 14 meeting. Instead, I journeyed from an unrelated workshop in western Kentucky on July 14, arriving in Sealsville approximately 10 minutes before the 7:00 p.m. board meeting was about the begin.

As it turns out, it was just as well I had been through completed phases of two RSS projects prior to arriving at the Sealsville meeting, as agreeing to become involved in the AEL demonstration appeared more problematic than I had been advised. Suggestive of this interpretation was that, although my attendance at the board meeting had been described as only one of observation, no sooner had I walked through the board office door than I was turned to by the superintendent for a full public explanation of the RSS demonstration's focus, process, and intended benefit to the county.

Following a 20- or 30-minute (extemporaneous) overview of the AEL project, a vote was taken by the several board members on whether or not to participate. Notably absent from participating in either discussion of the possibilities of the project for Clinch County schools was the superintendent or most board members. One member of the board did speak favorably about having access to the professional literature related to school improvement (i.e., access to a resource center), yet he was the only one who seemed enthusiastic about the project although a unanimous positive vote was recorded.

As it turns out, the vote to participate in the RSS demonstrations was the only unanimous vote seen at the Clinch County Board of Education meeting the night of July 14. The hour-and-a-half meeting held that evening in a sweltering summer heat saw a number of personnel and budgetary votes passing and failing by typically 4–3 margins. Importantly, in most of these cases the majority ruled against the recommendations of the superintendent.

A BRIEF HISTORY OF TENNESSEE EDUCATION

As will become clear soon, two focal sets of concerns stand out in Clinch County that require discussions relevant to serious consideration of school improvement activities there. One of these involves the implications for school functioning in a rural and poor county which has always been rural and poor. As well, while it is difficult to verify the extent to which political factionalism has historically dominated school policy making in Clinch County, this element much more clearly appeared to have influenced its school dynamics and policies than it does (or did) in either Braxton County or Charlotte County.

The historical accounts we reviewed suggest that most of Tennessee has suffered in this century from educational "underinvestment" and "underperformance" compared to the other three states covered in this report. Furthermore, as most **East** Tennessee counties were sympathetic with the Union during the Civil War (and many remain aligned with the Republican party), Democrat-controlled statehouses appear to have been even less forthcoming in supporting social and educational services there than in other parts of the state.

Tennessee (among other southeastern states) had and has a strong tradition of elite versus populist views on the goals and processes of formal education. For example, antebellum academies and universities for the children of large land (and slave) owners in Tennessee mirrored many of those in Virginia and North Carolina. And many, if not most, "public" schools in Tennessee were also typically used as pauper schools and clearly regarded as charity institutions by landed gentry who helped set them up.

Extensive settlement of Tennessee followed by almost 100 years the earlier colonization of Virginia and North Carolina. Importantly, much early settlement in Tennessee was accomplished by poor farmers and rural immigrants from those two states unable to find suitable settlement possibilities in these older colonies. As well, large tracts of Tennessee lands were obtained by westward-moving elites, a story detailed further in Chapter 5.

As in Virginia, public education in the rural South rarely generated a strong following (or strong advocates) until after the reconstruction period late in the 19th century. Before this time, Tennessee elites around Nashville and Knoxville collaborated to build prestigious universities, while the fate of schools for the lower social classes remained enigmatic.

In 1806, the federal government intervened in boundary and land ownership disputes between North Carolina and its previous "colony" to the west, Tennessee. Part of the federally mandated settlement stipulated that 640 square acres in every six square miles of the new state of Tennessee needed to be set aside for public schools. "Squatters" (without formal land titles) occupying lands set aside for county academies (and two state colleges), as well as the general public, could purchase parcels of this set-aside acreage, as long as proceeds went back into school operating costs of the purchase of other properties for school building.

Apparently, however, assessing subsistence farmers even one dollar an acre for comparatively marginal farm lands (frequently acquired at great personal cost from the Indians), became a political football which few legislators wanted to touch.

Therefore, the state government neither compelled most settlers to forfeit lands ostensibly set aside for schools, nor collected from them the tax monies necessary to establish and run schools, county academies, or colleges:

> Indeed, James Knox Polk revealed in 1823 that although the total amount of land made available to the state for educational purposes in 106 amounted to nearly 450,000 acres, only 22,705 acres had been realized by the schools by 1823. Polk, then a member of the state house of representatives, argued that all of the good lands had been occupied by settlers, and that which remained in "great part...consists of barrens and mountains that is not worth the annual tax required to be paid to the government." (Folmsbee, Corlen, & Mitchell, 1960, p. 431)

Because those interested in establishing and funding schools could not acquire from the state legislature enough money to build and operate them before the Civil War, most formally established public (secondary) academies became "quasipublic." That is, interested counties formed boards of trustees to raise money and establish programs independent of the state, save for whatever small amounts were forthcoming from land sales and taxes mentioned above. As was the case in Virginia, since most county academies charged tuition and were oriented towards college preparation, it was primarily only more affluent citizens who were interested in supporting such academies and thus able to send their children to them.

Children of subsistence farmers without means appear to have been little interested in public elementary schools, such as they were. As in Virginia, free schools carried the stigma of poverty, and rural Tennesseans who had struggled in the late 18th and early 19th century to take up a fragile occupancy on this frontier appear to have been quite resistant to notions that they were somehow inferior to large landholders. And this resistance to accept the charity of public schools appears to have been strong through various funding reform initiatives passed by the Tennessee legislature in the 1820s, 1830s and 1840s.

In 1834 significant school reforms were implemented in Tennessee which seemingly had the potential of putting the state in the education forefront in the South. These reforms included larger appropriations for public schools and the creation of a state superintendent to oversee both tax appropriations and expenditures. Unfortunately, this first superintendent was charged with misappropriating collected revenues in the late 1830s and ordered by the state to make (partial) restitution.

According to several state historians, this scandal damaged the prestige of the public schools; and, two marginal state superintendents later, Governor James

C. Jones recommended the abolition of the office. The duties of the superintendent had been largely fiscal and were transferred to the state treasurer; there they remained until after the Civil War. One student of the times has characterized the period of 1839–1848 as one of "reaction" against public education:

> The swing of the pendulum in the other direction was accelerated by the misfortunes of the system's first superintendent, by the failure of the laws passed to bring about the immediate and complete betterment of conditions...and by the increasing gravity of those never-ending financial difficulties that so hampered and harassed the state of Tennessee all through the antebellum period. (Folmsbee et al., 1960, p. 438)

Apparently, it took over a decade (into the 1850s) before further important pro-education legislation passed in the state legislature, with the backing of Governor Andrew Johnson. During this period, both (minimal) poll and property taxes were added to the various school funds from property forfeitures and school land use taxes used to fund public education. As well, early attention was given in 1853 to teacher certification guidelines, to be monitored by county courts throughout the state.

In general, however, public schools fared poorly in Tennessee prior to the Civil War, due to the several factors already described. Lack of funds, hostility among the rural poor to paying for schools through taxes used by wealthier students, divided sentiments among politicians regarding who should lead the charge for increased school spending, skepticism regarding the agricultural utility of public schooling among small farmers and the rural poor, and malfeasance in office of significant early school leaders all appear to have been important. And, as in Virginia, the Civil War wiped out even the few gains made in the provision of public education in the decades which immediately preceded it.

THE CIVIL WAR AND ITS CONSEQUENCES

As in the earlier case of Virginia, the Civil War had a dramatic influence on the political, economic, and educational dynamics of Tennessee. And, except for the liberating potential of schooling for Negroes which followed the war, most of its immediate consequences were negative.

As much of Central and West Tennessee relied on plantation agriculture, the state succeeded from the Union in 1861. Accordingly, monies earlier supplied by the state legislature for public education were diverted to the war effort, and all schools but a few elite academies shut down.

Following the war, political and economic reforms sponsored by reconstruction forces were vigorously resisted by most Tennesseans. Most reform proposals discussed and enacted at the state level during the late 1860s were seen (as in Virginia) as efforts by Yankees to establish alien institutions and alien ideas into the minds of Tennessee's children.

> State-mandated systems of public schools in the South began to operate in earnest only after the stain of Reconstruction, as perceived by Southern white Redeemers, was removed from them. This cleansing action required the repeal of Radical-inspired public school legislation and, after a decent interval, the creation of less ambitious systems of schools by Conservative Democratic legislatures. Throughout the South, with few exceptions, for at least the next two generations, public school systems existed mainly on paper.. . . Tennessee exemplifies the region's experience. The law establishing a state system of public schools enacted by the Radical Reconstruction Legislature in 1867 was repealed with the return of the Conservative Democrats to power in 1869; in 1874, however, the General Assembly passed a school law which is the foundation of Tennessee's present public school system. (Allison, 1983, p. 27)

However, some externally inspired school reforms managed (belatedly) to take hold in Tennessee.

> In the years of Reconstruction public attention was centered on repairing material damage and little thought could be spared for the problems of education. (Later) while the Republicans controlled the State, the post of superintendent of public instruction was created, county superintendents were appointed, school taxes were levied, and special schools for Negroes were put into operation. As soon as the Democrats returned to power, in 1869, these measures were repealed. In 1873, however, the legislature passed bills which substantially incorporated the earlier measures. (WPA, 1986, p. 124)

By the end of the 19th century, educational concerns had begun to be significantly improved through both private and public means. Of particular note in Tennessee appears to have been the impact of philanthropic and church-sponsored school building and staffing initiatives. As in Virginia, funds for Negro public and vocational schools came from a variety of sources. So, too, funding from such individuals and organizations as Cornelius Vanderbilt, the Peabody Educational Fund, the Methodist Episcopal Church, and the American Missionary Society become central in an aggressive and impressive higher education expansion throughout Tennessee.

However, public school links to higher education were still underdeveloped until after the turn of the 20th century. Following an economic upturn in the state in the late 1890s, public schools finally appear to have become a more serious interest:

> Prior to the beginning of the new century, education had not entered deeply into the politics of the state. It was not that education might not have been a good

political issue, but the people had been more interested in the restoration of state control to the ex-Confederates, and then the small farmers of the state turned on the Bourbons and wrested political control from them. Control, in many respects, was simply more important than issues. Therefore, with improved economic conditions and the battle for political control reasonably well solved, the less privileged people of the state started thinking in terms of improved educational opportunity for their children. Benton McMillin, elected governor in 1898 on a platform calling for better schools, brought about the passage of a Uniform Text Book Law, which served the valuable purpose of stimulating the interest of the people in education. (Folmsbee et al., pp. 243-244)

EARLY 20TH-CENTURY ECONOMIC AND EDUCATIONAL DYNAMICS

By 1909, one-fourth of all of Tennessee's revenues were being allocated to public education. On the one hand, given the skepticism and intrigue related to public schools during the 19th century, such a fact seems quite impressive. On the other hand, Tennessee was still a relatively poor state whose plantation economy (in much of the state) had collapsed into primarily tenant farming, and where most poor White farmers in Central and East Tennessee were barely surviving. Furthermore, as in Virginia, public schools for both Whites and Blacks appeared to have posed endless political and economic complications, all during the early 20th century (Perkinson, 1976).

One of the most important early 20th-century legislative packages to have lasting educational implications in the state was the educational "campaign" of 1903, guided by the then state superintendent.

It would probably be well to examine the status of the schools when Superintendent Mynders took office. Five months was the length of school term prescribed by law, although it would appear that this law was not being enforced in most counties. There were 6,758 primary schools, 1,069 secondary schools, and no high schools operating in the state. The scholastic population, as defined by law, numbered 771,965, of which 484,63 were enrolled in schools, with 341,538 in regular attendance. Thus, it may be seen that less than fifty percent of the eligibles were in regular attendance. The average monthly salary of teachers was $28.86 with a low in Van Buren County of $18.50 and a possible high in Shelby County of $40.72. The training of the teachers appears to have been commensurate with the salaries. There were no state colleges for teacher training, although the state did appropriate in 1901 a total of $55,600 for teacher training. This money went to George Peabody College for Teachers, into scholarships for teachers, and in the holding of teacher institutes. The University of Tennessee received no appropriation from the state. Schools appear to have been of short term, poorly attended, poorly financed, and poorly housed. (Folmsbee et al., 1960, p. 244)

To address such problems in the 1903 campaign (echoed in later "campaigns" of 1906 and 1908), an eight-point platform was developed by Mynders and a group of collaborating county superintendents. This platform sought to address perceived issues and problems not infrequently heard in Clinch County, which will be discussed more specifically in the pages ahead.

> The eight point platform that this group adopted is probably typical of all future education platforms in the numerous campaigns of this century. In brief, it called for: an increased state school fund, local taxation for education, school consolidation, better training for teachers, establishment of teachers' and school libraries, establishment of one or more high schools in each county, elimination of politics and nepotism from the schools, and intelligent and economical expenditure of school funds. (Folmsbee et al., p. 244)

A series of educational campaigns, supported by over 1,000 citizen school improvement associations led to the General Education Bill of 1909, argued by many as the major school funding formula of the 20th century. And this legislation systematically tied state funds to most of the perceived building and staffing inadequacies mentioned above.

On the other hand, public education in Tennessee continued to receive mixed reviews in rural counties, particularly those counties where populist and religious fundamentalist feelings ran high. It was, for example, in the state of Tennessee where famous anti-evolution school laws and court cases first became popular within the Southern states. Some have argued that the rapid push to "modernize" Tennessee public schools in the first three decades of the 20th century caused a backlash against such modernization, exemplified in concern among many rural people about the secular teachings of public school science instruction.

> Tennessee's anti-evolution law and the Dayton trial that was its aftermath are best understood if viewed as indications of a social problem caused by the swift imposition of a system of public education, compulsory and uniform, upon a people long accustomed to private and denominational education—or to no education at all. When the Tennessee fundamentalist found himself compelled by law to send his children to a tax-supported State school, where doctrines were taught that seemed to him a denial of Scripture, he rebelled. This rebellion, characteristically blunt and straightforward, led to the adoption of prohibitive legislation. On March 21, 1925, the General Assembly passed a bill sponsored by John Washington Butler, a farmer, making illegal the teaching in tax-supported institutions of any theory concerning the creation of man which disagreed with Holy Scripture. While discussions of the bill in the legislature were extremely facetious, and the sponsors of the Scopes test case did not themselves take the matter too seriously, the popular tension which followed indicated much support for the law. (WPA, 1986, pp. 125-126)

THE TENNESSEE VALLEY AUTHORITY
IN EAST TENNESSEE

While parts of Tennessee no doubt experienced some success at small-scale farming as Charlotte County, Virginia, did, much of rural East Tennessee never achieved the agricultural prosperity hoped for. Furthermore, increased population pressures and lagging implementation of "scientific" agriculture programs appears to have doomed many East Tennessee counties into a federally recognized "depressed region." This situation was of course further exacerbated by the great depression.

In order to attack problems of underdevelopment and regional poverty in the Tennessee River basin, Congress approved funding in 1933 for a large-scale development effort now known as the Tennessee Valley Authority. According to regional scholar David Whisnant:

> In the three or four decades prior to the advent of TVA, much of the great valley of the Tennessee River, stretching over six hundred miles from Knoxville through northern Alabama and then northwest to the Ohio at Paducah, Kentucky, had been reduced by waste and neglect to an economic and ecologic disaster area. Annual floods, abetted by the clear-cutting of forests and unrelieved years of row-cropping, carried irreplaceable topsoil down the river, destroyed farms and towns, and wasted valuable hydroelectric potential. Forest fires consumed thousands of acres of timber annually. Sixty- two percent of the valley's 3 million people scratched out a bare subsistence on 350,000 small (70-acre average) farms scattered over 41,000 square miles in portions of seven Appalachian states. Unaided by electricity or progressive farming techniques, their efforts earned them an average annual income only 44 percent of the national average. Even the river itself was a largely wasted resource. Frequent shoals, narrows, rock reefs, and gravel bars restricted navigation to a fraction of the river's total length, and little of its hydroelectric potential had been developed. (Whisnant, 1980, pp. 44-45)

TVA projects had national, state, and regional significance with respect to this discussion. On the one hand, as a national attempt to subsidize regional development, it quite clearly signalled (to the dismay of TVA critics in Washington) an emerging federal involvement in economic development. Rather than one of many WPA projects (of which many were seen in Tennessee), the TVA initiative was argued to be a model for the complete transformation of a rural and agriculturally depressed region into one whose cheap energy would lead to new manufacturing possibilities, as well as improving both agriculture and tourism.

Regionally, of course, this project enabled much of Tennessee (including East Tennessee) to attract branch manufacturing plants and small industries, as had Charlotte County. And as we shall discuss shortly, a variety of TVA efforts appear to have had moderate (if indirect) impact on the economy of Clinch County, Tennessee.

According to Whisnant, one important aim of the TVA was to help "modernize" the mountaineers of East Tennessee. As suggested, flood control was argued to be an important goal of the systems of dams and lakes created during the 1930s and 1940s. As well, the hydroelectricity capacity of dams constructed yielded inexpensive power, which was distributed through rural electric cooperatives also facilitated by the Authority. Inexpensive power not only provided "opportunities" for previously rural residents to modernize their homes and living standards, but also created markets for domestic products and incentives for industries to relocate in rural states, where such cheap energy was being subsidized by federal investments. Coupled with (still) falling farm product prices and aggressive campaigns to attract Northern industries into low-wage areas of the south, the TVA by most all accounts did have significant effects on the entire seven-state region in which it still operates.

UPS AND DOWNS IN POST-DEPRESSION SCHOOL FUNDING

The late 20th century still finds Tennessee a state of contrasts. As the three stars on the state flag symbolically indicate, there are three Tennessees. One in the west on the Mississippi River still approximates the deep(er) South, and which is oriented towards Memphis. Central Tennessee, organized around Nashville, is home, not only to country music, but also to agriculture and significant amounts of industry. Still attractive to foreign investments because of low wage and rent costs, Central Tennessee has seen the importation of Japanese auto production during this decade. Meanwhile, East Tennessee grows industrially along its main transportation corridors and with the help of infrastructure investments like those of the TVA, except, of course, for places which, because of their geography and remoteness, inhibit development at all.

With regard to education, the period from the 1930s to the 1970s saw a continuous battle between proeducation advocates and those seeking to balance continual state budget problems via freezes/cutbacks in public education expenditures. In 1936, an "Eight Point Program" was passed in the state legislature with systematic backing from the Tennessee Education Association. The TEA had by the 1930s become a powerful player in garnering public and legislative support for school reform. Monies dedicated to school improvement in 1936 went to all levels of education, and promises were made to fully fund a state equalization formula earlier outlined. However:

World War II brought havoc to the public schools of the state. Large numbers of young men and women left the teaching profession to enter the armed forces.

Countless others left the schoolroom to accept more remunerative employment in defense plants. As the legislative session of 1943 approached, Governor Cooper adhered to his program of economy and the members of the assembly accepted his recommendations. There appeared to be little comprehension by those in authority of the tragic condition of the schools. The elementary and high schools received little increase in funds and the institutions of higher learning fared little better. Numerous teaching positions were filled with untrained and uncertified teachers. The plight of the schools became the object of so much concern among the people that Governor Cooper called the general assembly to meet in special session on April 10, 1944. This special session appropriated $3,200,000 to give each elementary and high school teacher as raise of $20.00 per month. The relief was temporary as the rising cost of living soon consumed this small raise. Education barely held its own during the six-year tenure of Governor Prentice Cooper. Perhaps, the greatest contribution of the Shelbyville governor was the inauguration of a program of textbooks at state expense. (Folmsbee et al., 1960, p. 265)

In addition to protracted struggles over school budgets in Tennessee, race and education became an important theme in state-wide school reform in the 1950s and 1960s. While it seems quite possible that desegregation issues may have run hot in various rural Tennessee counties, the state histories we have read play down most racial conflict in public schools. However, integration problems did attract national attention at Memphis State University, in Clinton and in Nashville—areas for the most part in Central and West Tennessee, where Negro populations were highest.

SCHOOL REFORMS OF THE 1980S

State-wide school outcome and expenditure efforts continue to document the comparative educational disadvantages of Tennessee schools. In many educational categories, Tennessee places almost at the bottom (see Table TN1-4). Following the various school reform reports of 1983, Tennessee became one of the most active states (at the legislative level) in mandating various types of administrative and professional restructuring (State Research Associates, 1988).

Much of the reason for a significant educational reform crusade in Tennessee appears to have taken place in a systematic attack on the politics of education practiced in state and local education agencies by Governor Lamar Alexander. Alexander himself came into office following the indictment of his predecessor on political corruption charges. Public education also remains highly politicized in the state, according to one veteran Anderson County teacher who described conditions this way:

Education in Tennessee is riddled with politics from top bottom—a situation which is encouraged by governance structures at state and local levels. At the

Attention: Alumni of Greene Mathis School

The faculty and students of Greene Mathis have begun a project to re-floor the school. This will be a major project and quite costly. We feel that our school has played a major role in the development of children over the past 60 years and should be given the opportunity to do so in the future. With a little effort on all of our parts, Greene Mathis can continue to serve the children of Clinch County. Any contribution that could be given will be greatly appreciated. Contributions of $50.00 or more will be listed and displayed in the hall for years to come. Please forward your contribution to . . .

Figure TN-1. Clinch County relies heavily on voluntary support for many building and extra equipment. The above notice/appeal appeared in the local shopping news, which is the only publication produced for (but not in) the county. This item appeared throughout the summer of 1990, and sought contributions for the smallest elementary school in the system, which was also in need of serious renovation. The superintendent believes it will eventually be consolidated with Clinch Central.

beginning of the reform movement, the head of K-12 education in Tennessee was a commissioner of education who was appointed by the governor and served as a member of his cabinet. The governor also appointed the State Board of Education (SBE), of which he and the commissioner were members; indeed, the commissioner chaired the Board. The SBE was weak and susceptible to political influence. It had no staff and depended administratively on the (SDE)—which the commissioner also headed. . . . In 1982 the SDE had 459 staff members who worked directly with K-12 education. Since SDE employment is not based on civil service examinations, and there is little job security, the SDE is susceptible to influence from above and below. Staff members closely follow policy lines laid down by the commissioner. At the same time, knowing that they might otherwise lose their jobs, they try to maintain good relations with local school districts. (Fowler, 1987, p. 184)

More specifically, Fowler alluded to political dynamics at both state and local levels, which in her view harmed educational possibilities in many districts:

Tennessee has 142 school districts. In them, 110 school boards and 80 superintendents are popularly elected. Both the school board and the superintendent are elected in 70 districts (including Clinch County). The school system is a major employer in many rural counties; thus political factions seek control of school boards and superintendencies. Because Tennessee's tenure law provides no job security for non-certified personnel and protects certified personnel only against dismissal, it is possible to run a Tennessee school system as a patronage machine. This situation is, in fact, by no means rare. As a result, the educational establishment in Tennessee is characterized by political distrust. Educators at all levels tend to evaluate new policies from a political standpoint, and they value tenure as an essential protection against political game playing. (pp. 184-185)

Governor Alexander used his political and educational connections to help usher in a major school reform package in 1984. Among the objectives of the Comprehensive Reform Act of 1984 were: the introduction of a statewide career ladder system, new evaluation and training mandates for school superintendents and board members, new early childhood program funding, upgraded academic high school graduation requirements, new competency testing programs, new teacher competency testing, and moderate tax increases to help pay for many of these programs (Fowler, 1987; State Research Associates, 1988).

Significantly, Governor Alexander argued that weaknesses in Tennessee schools (and others in the South) were responsible for the declining economic fortunes of his state, and he was quite active in the early 1980s in spearheading gubernatorial support around the nation for state and national education reform (National Governors' Association, 1986).

ECONOMIC AND EDUCATIONAL DEVELOPMENT
IN CLINCH COUNTY

As suggested to this point, various statewide educational and economic developments in Tennessee echo those of states previously discussed. Economic marginality, problems of race relations, and equivocal popular sentiment regarding the utility of public education are all themes visible in Tennessee history. As well, while the former group of themes are also visible in other states of this evaluation, the politics of school provision/reform appear to be more often discussed in historical documents on the status and development of Tennessee schools compared to both West Virginia and Virginia.

Importantly, all of these themes appear to have their specific counterparts in the evolution of public schooling in Clinch County. Clinch County was originally settled from the east by both "squatters" and formal land title holders (from North Carolina and Virginia) who came through the Appalachian Mountains into the numerous large valleys of East Tennessee. Politically, the county was formed out of two adjacent counties in the mid-1840s, and the county seat was named in honor of the attorney who litigated the county's independence.

Clinch County approximates both Braxton and Charlotte Counties in important ways, yet the primary difference between Clinch County and the others centers upon the its economic marginality and isolation from the rest of the U.S. and in fact from much of its own state. While such isolation per se may not have hindered economic development prior to industrialization, in many ways the 20th century has passed Clinch County by. Virtually since the U.S. Bureau of the Census has recorded employment and income figures during this century, such figures have found Clinch County among the poorest counties in the U.S.

According to the 1980 Census of Population, Clinch County remains one of the very poorest in Tennessee. Updated projections of county incomes and income sources suggest (for 1986) that county residents earned just over half as much as most state residents ($6,040 vs. $11,995). Furthermore, sources of income for Tennessee for 1986 show that 70.5% of state incomes were generated from actual earnings, while 13.8% came from dividends, interest, and rent; transfer payments accounted for only 15.7%. Residents of Clinch County, on the other hand, reported only 54.9% of per capita incomes coming from actual earnings, compared to 11.4% from dividends, interest and rent, and 33.7% coming from transfer payments from state and federal sources (all data supplied by the Tennessee Valley Authority).

Geographically, Clinch County is bounded on the north by Virginia, and to the west, south, and east by three different Tennessee counties. The county also lies just to the southeast of the Cumberland Gap, where the states of Kentucky, Virginia, and Tennessee all come together. Importantly, much of the economic and social history of the county, and many family and church allegiances, cross state boundaries there.

Running across the northern part of the county is the Boone River, and running from the northwest and out the southwest of the county is the Clinch River. While never fully commercially navigable, these rivers historically provided both economic advantages and disadvantages prior to the coming of the TVA. On the one hand, the primary "boom" period in the local economy was made possible by turn of the century logging operations; yet this activity was only made possible when the river rose high enough to float logs downstream to market.

On the other hand, local agriculture used to be threatened by damaging floods in the 19th and early 20th centuries. Now, as a result of TVA construction, both rivers are dammed and drain into Norris Lake to the west. The several counties adjacent to Norris (and Cherokee Lakes) have dubbed themselves "the Lakeway Region," and while few recreation activities are available in Clinch County, these adjacent counties have experienced moderate economic development activities associated with tourism.

If the rivers running through the county have never been of consistent utility for transportation into or out of the county, neither have other transportation mechanisms which have so importantly influenced commercial developments in other regions of the South (including all other counties investigated for this book). There isn't now, nor has there ever been, a railroad into or through Clinch County. Paved highways only came here in the 1950s (even those are few and far between). And the closest commercial airport is about 90 minutes away.

Clinch County, in the view of many who live and/or visit there, is one of the most beautiful yet rustic places imaginable. It contains a number of long and majestic ridges that run from the southwest towards the northeast. The hillsides are typically heavily forested, with second-generation timber along mountain crests, and the long and flat Clinch River Valley is a place where sunset watching ought to be required.

Yet the rugged beauty of this Appalachian location also suggests how and why the economic fortunes of its people have been historically so marginal. These same ridges have kept major roads and railroad passes out. The rocky hillsides, which are so picturesque to behold, have obviously broken many a plow and many a mule. And while second-growth timber looks pretty on the hillside, it appears to have little marketability for its owners.

Some suggest that Clinch County provided an adequate economic base for its population prior to the industrial era. Yet its economic marginally throughout the 20th century has been noted by many recent scholars. Our first encounters with several school officials found them describing local dynamics and economic conditions as a function of the onerous distinction that "we're the third (or seventh, or eleventh) poorest county in the United States."

While the very early history of the county suggests that some early landholders there were relatively prosperous, and that several of these were prominent Tennessee statesmen, Clinch County appears never to have had either the concentration of landed gentry of a Charlotte County, nor the aggressive middle class of a Braxton County. As mentioned earlier, most of the recorded history of Clinch County was destroyed in the 1930s.

Furthermore, nowhere does there appear to exist a good comprehensive history of the county from secondary sources such as I quoted heavily from in earlier chapters of this work. Thus, most of what's available on the history of Clinch County comes from oral histories, many of which focus on particular institutions or people of the region. In addition, a "vanity" publishing company which appears to target rural locales sponsored a county history book in Clinch County in 1988–1989. However, the result of this undertaking was focused on family genealogies in which the forbears of every well established county citizen (including those who have migrated) is represented. While this document proved somehwat useful for generating leads to questions we pursued in our fieldwork, its primary purpose was to sell thousands of book copies to descendants of earlier county residents (which it did).

In any event, most available evidence on the history of Clinch County (none of which is cited here for reasons suggested in Chapter 1) basically speaks to the predominance of subsistence agriculture and rural poverty throughout the county's history from at least the end of the 19th century. Even the county seat had only 300 inhabitants until the 1920s. Yet this is *not* to suggest that little of the county's history is interesting or without color. To the contrary, anthropologists, historians, Appalachian scholars and magazine writers have been drawn to Clinch County continuously over the past hundred years either to "study" one identified ethnic group and/or folk characters from the region, or to help mediate forces of poverty and inequality frequently equated with the very name "Clinch County, Tennessee."

THE MELUNGEONS OF CLINCH COUNTY

Of particular interest to almost anyone who has written on Clinch County (and a number of contiguous counties) appears to be the story of the "Melungeons," and the relationships this "ethnic" group had with the rest of the region's population. Like most rural areas of the Southeast, the numerous river/creek bottoms and flattest portions of Clinch County were the first places claimed in the late 18th century. However, according to several early accounts, a "race" of dark- (or coppery) skinned individuals had taken up residence in many of these better farming areas before others of Scotch-Irish ancestry descended into Clinch and surrounding counties.

While typically described as darker than most other Clinch County settlers, these people also were said to have such Indian characteristics as high cheekbones, dark eyes, and straight black hair. Furthermore, this group (or members of it) appears to have settled in the County decades before the discovery of safe passages into the area were well known and popularly traveled.

Throughout the 19th and 20th centuries, considerable attention was paid to solving the "mystery" of the Melungeons, although most of these attempts appear to have been rather unsystematic by contemporary standards. Early attempts typically focused upon trying to ascertain the cultural origins of these people, who, while they spoke English and were Protestants, somehow either identified themselves or were identified by others as of Indian, Phoenician, Moorish, or Hebrew origin. Later, this minority group became the intermittent attraction of various state and national romance/popular cultural writers in the late 19th and early 20th centuries who also intermittently journeyed to isolated places like Snake Hollow, Fleenor's Ridge, and the Bluewater Valley to write feature stories on this "strange race" of rural Americans.

By the mid-20th century, more academically based geneticists and physical anthropologists also appear to have become interested in the physical differences and genetic spread of the Melungeons as they appear to have intermarried with other "races" in East Tennessee. Today, at least in our observations in the county (and according to most residents), no "true" Melungeons appear to exist, although many Clinch County citizens claim to be of partial Melungeon descent. Rather, intermarriage and migration back to North Carolina, Virginia, or Eastern Kentucky are cited as places where any remaining true Melungeons must have gone.

While attempting to solve the mystery of who exactly these people were and where they came from became a prominent preoccupation of many county and regional investigations in the late 19th and throughout the 20th centuries, by most accounts the Melungeons (and those individuals who bore Melungeons surnames) were greatly discriminated against by others in the county throughout both of these centuries. Perceived as somehow different and clannish (and also owning some of the best agricultural lands in the county), the Melungeons appear to have earned much animosity among many later-arriving settlers.

Accordingly, Clinch County lands settled by Melungeons in the late 18th and early 19th centuries were frequently claimed by later settlers, as those arriving later argued that non-Whites were not entitled to land ownership in the Tennessee territories. Faced with growing racial tensions throughout the state in the decades before the Civil War, state court decisions were used in the confiscation of Melungeon properties in Clinch and surrounding counties. In 1834, many Melungeons were legally defined as "free persons of color" and thereby systematically stripped of many voting and property holding rights in Tennessee. According to the Tennessee Census of 1830, 385 of the residents of Clinch County were "free colored persons." Since there have been relatively few Negroes historically in the county (even before the Civil War), local writers suggest that most of these free persons of color were Melungeons. And while this state of affairs was legally remediated following the Civil War, various sorts of segregation and discrimination against Melungeon families was practiced up until quite recently throughout much of East Tennessee, including Clinch County.

Discrimination and segregation practices in the county appear to have pushed most Melungeons into very marginal economic and political situations by the end of the 19th century. Thus, when popular interest in these peoples emerged at the turn of the century, remnants of this group could only be found in its most isolated and impoverished reaches.

Dynamics like those just described were phrased in these terms by a later Melungeon descendent:

> Early in the last century, when the white folks first came here, the Melungeons was already here, a"hold" of all the good land in the creek bottoms. The white folks was covetous of that good land, but didn't want to just take from the Melungeons brutal-like. Well, it wouldn't a'been no trouble if the Melungeons was ordinary heathen Indians. They woulda' just kicked 'em out. But here they was sorta' livin' like civilized folks, and they was speakin' English, an' on top o'all that they was believin' Christians. But their skins was brown on account o' their Injun blood. So the white folks begin sayin' they had nigger blood in 'em, too. Then they passed a law sayin' nobody with nigger blood could vote, or hold office, or testify in court. Then they went to court and before long they got hold o' that good bottom land. So there wasn't nothin left for the Melungeons to do but move up on the ridges.

RURAL APPALACHIAN LIFE IN EAST TENNESSEE

Were there a prototypical setting in Appalachia where popular images of poverty, subsistence agriculture, isolation, lack of communication, and political intrigue could (still) be found, Clinch County would probably serve as a good example. Except for the plague of heavy extractive industries on many other Appalachian economies, Clinch County has most of the stereotypical difficulties associated with Appalachian underdevelopment.

One of the stereotypical difficulties experienced in Clinch County has to do with a lack of internal communication. As the county is comprised of several large valleys separated by ridges, towns outside of the county, yet in the same valley, are (and historically have been) frequently the source of information and social activity, rather than the county seat of Sealsville. For example, it is much easier to travel to Jamesville, Virginia, for residents of the Hickory Valley than it is to go over Fleenors Ridge to Sealsville. For county residents on the east side of Clinch County, social activities in neighboring Rogersville are much easier to attend than they are over the ridge in the county seat.

Agricultural possibilities have also always remained problematic in much of East Tennessee, compared to the non-Appalachian South. Large landowners in Clinch County did and do exist, yet the value of these lands for commercial agriculture has typically been marginal, due to the hilly terrain and rocky condition of the soil. Around the beginning of the 20th century, logging apparently improved the economic fortunes of many, and introduced for the first time a "cash crop" to the region. On the one hand, unlike many regions of

Appalachia, difficulties in transporting timber out of the county appear to have deterred outside exploitation of timber resources. Thus, local landowners and their families (who could wait for the rivers to rise) appear to have prospered most from external demands for lumber.

When desirable timber was gone, linkages to the outside market economy appear to have withered for many. Most large landowners have generated only moderate economic surplus from agriculture since the 1920s by raising hay and cattle. The only other consistent sources of income for many farmers in the county this century appears to have been from burley tobacco, while for many subsistence farmers a few dollars appears to have been earned in making and selling of "moonshine" whiskey to surrounding locales. In addition, the mining of zinc in eastern Clinch County has employed modest numbers of local citizens in an on-again, off-again pattern during the past several decades. Yet this operation appears never to have been a major factor in the economic fortunes of most county residents.

As mentioned by David Whisnant earlier, many of the poorer mountaineers of East Tennessee lived in very basic housing, suffered dietary inadequacies, and were far removed from many basic health and social services until most recently. While comparative prosperity may have been visible in some Clinch County homes near Hickory Gap and Sealsville in the 19th and 20th centuries, by far the greater majority of those living on subsistence agriculture on the County's ridges and in its hollows lived in conditions which appeared to shock visitors from more cosmopolitan areas of the state. One feature writer journeyed to Fleenors Ridge to do a story on the Melungeons in the 1890s and wrote graphically about the squalor she perceived that many of these families lived in. Later researchers claimed that her accounts of daily life on the Ridge probably reflected not an indictment of the Melungeons per se, but actually pictured lifestyles of many of the rural poor in Clinch County until at least the 1920s.

> Their homes are miserable hovels, set here and there in the very heart of the wilderness. Very few of their cabins have windows, and some have only an opening cut through the wall for a door. In winter an old quilt is hung before it to shut out the cold. . . . Many of their cabins have no floors other than that which nature gave, but one that I remember had a floor made of trees slit in half, the bark still on, placed with the flat side to the ground. The people in this house slept on leaves with an old gray blanket for covering. . . . Their dress consists, among the women, of a short loose calico skirt and a blouse that boasts of neither hook nor button. Some of these blouses were fastened with brass pins conspicuously bright. Others were tied together by means of strings tied on either side. They wear neither shoes nor stockings in the summer, and many of them go barefoot all winter. The men wear jeans, and may be seen almost any day tramping barefoot across the mountain.

As suggested earlier, Clinch County was historically "decentralized," and very small communities at Treadway, Hickory Gap, Bowlins Ford, and dozens

of other crossings and crossroads that no longer appear on the map characterized settlement patterns there. More affluent 19th-century landowners who may
have lived in Sealsville or in surrounding counties would rent out or sell, on
some installment plan, steep hillsides and other marginal agricultural lands to
pioneers coming into Clinch County, who then attempted to live off this
beautiful but austere land. Thus, even though the county is small, a town vs.
countryside mentality appears to have developed there, with most (if few) public
and commercial amenities available only (if belatedly) in the county seat.
According to several regional researchers, class divisions as well as ethnic ones
appear to have multiplied in the early 20th century:

> There seems to have been some ethnic and class problems between the Me-
> lungeons and the Scotch-Irish from the early days. The timber boom period was
> (also) marked by the emergence of a new sociological problem — a predominantly
> two-class society. At the top were those entrepreneurs who had profited from the
> timber boom and had expanded their land holdings. At the bottom were those
> who had not benefitted from the sales and those who worked for wages. As so
> often happens, those who did well became very conservative. Now they live well
> but contribute little to the welfare of the community. Some of the present (1967)
> noticeable tension between the residents of Sealsville and the county's farmers
> issues from this older class problem.

One of the most famous folk characters from Clinch County was a wood-
worker and renowned craftsman profiled in numerous state and national
publications. As he describes it, life was very hard for the average rural resident
of Clinch County even into the 1930s. In a biographical account of his life
authored by an Appalachian historian, he talked of the typically hard times on
Fleenors Ridge:

> I know a little something about hard times, son. I came up with a whole lot of it.
> But of course they was a whole lot of folks that had it a whole lot harder than we
> did. . . . It's miserable to think about how some folks lived. They lived in little
> one-room pole cabins and you could throw a dog through the cracks. They'd have
> dirt floors and I've seen them when they didn't have a stick of furniture in the
> house - not a bed to sleep in, a chair to set in, nor a table to eat off of. In
> summertime most of them would sleep around in the woods, on the ground. Now
> people think I'm lying when I tell them this, but I swear it's the truth.

Because most county residents were too poor to own their own livestock, and
their lands were too poor to raise much of a crop, mountain winters frequently
were critical seasons in the struggle for survival in rural Clinch County until
recently:

> (many families would) make it purty good in the summer and fall, but along up
> towards Christmas they was up against it. I'll tell you they shore did see trouble.

One feller, he lived right over yonder on that ridge, came over and begged (a friend's father) out of a cat. He took that cat home, killed it and fed it to his family. Now he shore done that. He was a Collins. Well, when you get to thinking about it, a cat is a lot cleaner than a 'possum, or even a chicken. They ain't no kind of carrion that a chicken won't eat.

Before the Second World War, according to the just-cited artisan, there were only several ways to escape the hard life in rural East Tennessee. One was by working hard and somehow taking advantage of the relatively few opportunities for self-advancement. More typically, he suggests, were the other two "solutions": an early death, or outmigration to better farming and work opportunities elsewhere.

SOCIAL UPLIFT AND POVERTY PROGRAMS OF THE 20TH CENTURY

Of the various war on poverty programs discussed by Whisnant earlier, Clinch County appears to have received a fair share. The TVA has historically worked in and around Clinch County, and has sponsored various studies and local assistance iniatives. Even before that, however, it appears that New Deal programs sponsored by the Works Progress Administration and the Civilian Conservation Corps (among others) appeared in Clinch County. The County Clerk-Masters office in the Clinch County Courthouse, for example, displays a collection of photos from the early 20th century. And several of these show tent camps of the CCC which must have housed hundreds of young men who worked on "infrastructure" developments in the 1930s.

Development programs for rural and poor Clinch County are also clearly visible in the county's school system. For example, the largest county elementary school (K–8) was built in the early 1930s by the WPA. And except for several modifications for physical education and lunchroom services, the building remains essentially unchanged. The original plaque detailing the federal involvement in helping out Clinch Countians by building their school, in what is arguably the most affluent part of the county (Sealsville), still remains.

In addition to regional, state, and federal subsidies to county institutions and institution building, external philanthropic efforts to intervene in 20th-century poverty and uplift programs are also very visible in Clinch County. So, too, the role of local churches also appears to have been historically important. In particular, Baptist and Presbyterian outreach efforts appear to have reached out to Clinch County in important ways during the past hundred years. One of the most widely known county schools outside of Sealsville, for example, was the Vardy School, founded and operated on Fleenors Ridge by the Northern Presbyterians in the early 20th century. While we have found no particulars on reasons for its founding, it appears that this institution was instituted to serve the educational needs of Melungeon children—Melungeon children, we suppose, who were deemed uneducable by county leaders during this time period, particularly as funds for education were rarely adequate anyway.

Baptists associations also appear to have been socially and institutionally active even earlier than Presbyterians in Clinch County. For example, early in its history Clinch County had one of Tennessee's first private academies in Sealsville (as discussed earlier). However, either because not enough children attended and/or could afford to go this academy, it appears to have been sold to the Baptist church and run as a denominational school late in the 19th century. Only when state funding was made available to the county in the early 20th century did this school finally become a public high school (sometime around 1909).

(MORE) RECENT ECONOMIC DEVELOPMENT PATTERNS

While the earlier quotes sound severe, census data throughout the 20th century at least partially confirm these first-hand perceptions (see Tables TN 1–4). Even though the U.S. Census reports little measurable income from agriculture in Clinch County before the mid-20th century, over 85% of all "employed" persons in the county were engaged in some sort of agriculture as late as 1940. Furthermore, even given that average family income must have been extremely low in this same year, population figures suggest that more people were living in such a subsistence mode in 1940 than had done so any other time in the 20th century. County leaders claim that population figures were even higher in the mid-1940s than they were in 1940.

TN-1.   EMPLOYMENT INDUSTRIES.

CHARACTERISTICS	YEAR					
	1930	1940	1950	1960	1970	1980
Total persons employed 14 or 16 years old.	2,881	2,960	2,522	1,997	1,574	2,055
% in AG.	85.9	86.1	79.1	57.7	22.1	17.3
% in Mining	.24	.64	.47	3.6	1.7	–
% in MANFG	2.46	1.28	2.14	9.4	29.5	36.3
% in TRANS/COMM	2.7	.60	.55	1.10	1.20	2.9
% in RETAIL	.86	1.04	3.4	7.0	9.4	7.8
% in FIN/INS	–	.13	.19	.20	.38	1.9
% in SERVICES	5.5	4.5	6.2	8.9	19.1	21.0

TN-2.   INCOME CHARACTERISTICS.

	YEAR					
CHARACTERISTICS	*1930*	*1940*	*1950*	*1960*	*1970*	*1980*
Median income of						
All families	–	–	835	1,442	2,683	7,830
All households	–	–	–	–	–	6,693
Families with own-						
children 18 years						8,754
Married couples	–	–	–	–	2,101	9,491
Female householder	–	–	–	–	–	6,121
(no husband)						

TN-3.   POPULATION CHARACTERISTICS.

	YEAR								
CHARACTERISTICS	*1900*	*1910*	*1920*	*1930*	*1940*	*1950*	*1960*	*1970*	*1980*
Totl Popln	11,147	10,778	10,454	9,673	11,231	9,116	7,757	6,719	6,887
Male	–	–	5,294	4,931	5,705	4,573	–	–	3,388
Female	–	–	5,160	4,742	5,526	4.543	–	–	3,499
White	10,874	10,295	10,195	9,495	10,997	4,489	7,652	6,719	6,887
Black	273	481	256	162	234	52	–	–	–

However, as the Census data also shows, the percentage of Clinch County workers primarily engaged in agriculture dropped dramatically between 1940 and 1980. While USDA extension agents appear to have helped local farmers improve farming techniques and introduce such specialty row crops as straw-berries, tomatoes, and peppers during the past several decades, such efforts appear to have succeeded only marginally. Thus, small plots of labor-intensive tobacco growing remains as perhaps the only agricultural "common denomina-tor" in the county today. Relatedly, as agricultural production has proven so marginal during the past 50 years, population decline in Clinch County also accelerated during this period, from an official high of 11,231 in 1940 to less than 6,900 in 1980. And current estimates by school officials suggest that the population in the county currently is below 6,500.

Explaining the turnaround in employment patterns and population trends from 1940 can be partly interpolated from census data presented in the four Tennessee tables. On the one hand, there have been a great deal of manufac-turing and retail startups since World War II in several counties adjoining Clinch. Many currently employed residents of Clinch County work in low- and semi-skilled jobs in and around small towns to the east and west, which are located on

TN-4.   LABOR CHARACTERISITICS.

	YEAR				
CHARACTERISITICS	1940	1950	1960	1970	1980
Labor Force.					
Persons 16 yrs and older	7,202	6,024	5,331	4,661	5,110
Male 16 yrs and older	3,663	3,054	2,641	2,248	2,458
% in labor Force	82.3	40.0	69.0	55.3	50.7
Females 16 yrs and older	3,569	2,970	2,694	2,413	2,652
% in labor force	4.7	5.3	8.79	18.2	32.7
Females 16 yrs/older (with children 18 yrs)	–	–	–	919	484
% in labor force	–	–	–	53.2	42.0

U.S. 23E, 23W, 9E, and 11W. These roads have historically served as primary arteries connecting Tennessee, Virginia, and Kentucky, and now are examples of "strip development," where small industries and branch plants are located adjacent to chain stores and fast food restaurants along the main arteries through East Tennessee. Unfortunately, even most of these employment opportunities involve healthy commutes over difficult ridge passes for many Clinch Countians.

In addition to furniture, modular house construction and garment factories located "over the ridge," a few Clinch Countians (fewer than 200) have found work in several furniture factories and a small motor assembly plant in the county. Thus, full time employment in agriculture fell to just over 17% there in 1980, and low wage manufacturing jobs now employ just over 36% of remaining workers (a pattern similar to that in Charlotte County). To supplement meager manufacturing wages earned in the private sector, most Clinch Countians still tend small vegetable plots near their homes from which they raise over half of all their household produce, and tobacco growing would appear to be a primary cash crop for most landowners in the county, judging by a drive on any county road during the growing season. As mentioned earlier, median household income in Clinch County was among the lowest in Tennessee (and the lowest among the four counties studied for this book) at about $6,700 in 1980.

Another category of employment which has become significant in the County during the past several decades has been in the services area. Importantly, according to local officials, the number of retirees in Clinch County is quite high, and health services for them, as well as for poor families, has facilitated the expansion of hospital and social services. Fully 21% of all employed persons in Clinch County were engaged in such services in 1980. Significantly, Clinch County public schools are the largest employer in the county, and the school system also has the largest budget: spending over $3,281,000 during the 1987–1988 school year (Tennessee Department of Education, 1988).

CLINCH COUNTY TODAY

Development efforts funded by regional, state, and federal agencies have occurred frequently in the County since the war on poverty days. A most recent effort was the staging of a drama about the county's Melungeons during the 1970s. Several external funding sources were used to start up this production, which was envisioned to attract, not only tourists from throughout the state, but also "homefolks" seeking a good occasion to return to the county for a visit. Unfortunately, attendance at this outdoor drama waned within several years and was canceled in the early 1980s.

A major reason this probably occurred once again echoes the historic problem of isolation and lack of transportation into the county. It just isn't easy to get to Sealsville from anywhere else in the region. Neither the county seat nor any of its other small communities is on the road to anywhere else. And once a visitor gets there, there isn't anyplace to stay (except in a very small "motel" over one of the county's downtown beauty shops).

To be honest, Sealsville is the only place in the county that in 1989 even looked like a town. There are numerous crossroads with small groceries and a gas pump out front, but many of these appear to have closed down over the past three decades as people left the county. Perhaps symbolically, the major road in from the west had an old gas station very close to where that highway hooked up with the road in from the east. Yet this abandoned two-story concrete block building was covered with Kudzu vines, and obviously hadn't been open for business for many years when we arrived in 1989. Arsonists later set it on fire, and it was razed in 1990.

Two ridges away, in the Hickory Valley, several stores/gas stations sit next to the Hickory Gap Baptist Church, historically one of the most important institutions in Clinch County. And right up the hill from there, Hickory Gap Elementary sits looking very much as it must have in the 1940s when it was first built. It is undoubtedly fortunate that many residents of the county have a history of being able to make due with that which they themselves produce, for only in Sealsville are almost any of the amenities assumed to exist in middle class metropolitan America even visible.

Yet even Sealsville has no chain stores, major gas station outlets, or recognizable restaurants. There are a few good places to eat (like Mike's Drive-In). And there is a supermarket located down past the old jail (towards the high school). But most of town's main street has vacant stores, and even the county courthouse looks from the street like it has been out of business for a few years.

Some activity is visible, though, in and around Sealsville. There is a new drug store behind the courthouse, and the local bank still sits on Main street. As well, a new branch bank from an adjacent county has been built just out of town. However, none of these inducements appear to have helped the local pageant, which folded, or other smaller efforts to attract tourists. According to local spokespersons, the lack of amenities in or near Sealsville appears to have been a main cause for falling attendance at the county's outdoor drama in the early 1970s. In essence, outsiders had nowhere to eat and/or stay when they took the long ride off the main highway into Sealsville. Some also claim that outsiders were given most major roles in the play, and many local folks lost interest after the first several years.

Most recently, there have been two business opportunities in Sealsville which suggest either mixed or ironic blessings for the county, depending on one's perspective. On the one hand, Summer 1989 saw the opening of a Hardee's fast food restaurant near the high school, which has brought convenience foods a bit closer to home for many county residents. Importantly, this establishment created a number of part-time jobs for local high school students/graduates and a new gathering place for many county residents.

The other recent development, however, perhaps best underscores the dilemma of being a poor and rural county in an age of increasing costs for provision of public services. As will be discussed shortly, the funding of public social services (like education) in the county has few sources in Clinch County. In addition to those funds coming from state sources, local governments have to provide revenues from various categories of private property (e.g., taxes on real property, gasoline taxes, and automobile registrations, or *wheel taxes* as they are called in Tennessee). As well, "local option" sales taxes have been enacted in some municipalities and added to state sales taxes. Under this arrangement, some local governments have been able to supplement county school budgets throughout the state.

Many counties/municipalities in Tennessee have dedicated increasing property value assessments and the abovementioned local option sales taxes to the operation of their schools. However, the value of Clinch County property has not kept pace with funding requirements for local schools, and increasingly, Clinch County residents shop out of the county (when visiting or coming home for work). Therefore, stable real property values, and *declining* retail sales receipts, are claimed by Clinch County leaders to be undermining their ability to fund schools (among other services) adequately. And even increases in personal income (were they to occur) would not directly improve local coffers, for Tennessee does not allow state or local income taxes.

Competition for county tax dollars has turned many local County Commission meetings into protracted lobbying sessions by county agencies seeking adequate funding. One result has been that the county school superintendent has turned to the state board of education to compel the local government to provide the minimum appropriation necessary to receive state funding supplements. In addition, Clinch County was one of 66 school districts (now 73) that sued the state for its alledged unconstitutional funding patterns for public instruction (see the updated discussion of this suit in Chapter 6).

More on the politics of local school funding will be discussed shortly. Of particular county-wide economic development interest have been the most recent county initiatives to raise extra tax dollars for the provision of local school services. Earlier in this decade the state of Tennessee began placing criminals convicted in state courts in county jails, depending upon county jail space and interest. As the state also paid counties funds in excess of what they typically spent to house prisoners (especially if their jails were undersubscribed), many counties began to take such prisoners on.

Furthermore, when long-term contracts between the state and individual counties became possible, some counties began specific jail-building programs to insure positive cash flow from county jails to other public service needs. Clinch County was one of numerous Tennessee counties that in the mid-1980s, entered into state prisoner housing contracts. At the same time, Clinch County built a new county jail to house these prisoners. The new jail facility (capacity: 67 prisoners) was built in the county seat, where existing water, sewage, and electricity was available, and replaced perhaps the only remaining building of historical significance in the county: its old four-room jail.

Even so, this development was not enough to head off the current financial crisis in Clinch County, and in 1988 the County Commission (under the sponsorship of its County Executive) entered into a contract with the District of Columbia to house hundreds of D.C. prisoners in an even further expanded jail facility in Sealsville. County Commissioners explained to increasingly concerned local citizens that funds generated by the housing of D.C. prisoners were the only salvation for the county in meeting its funding requirements, particularly its mandated school-funding requirements.

However, this possibility was blocked by county residents in the Spring 1989 through petitions and public demonstrations, leading to (among other things) the county's current financial crisis. The irony of this entire episode (articulated more fully in the pages ahead), as in the cases of Braxton and Charlotte Counties, is that, while small, poor, and rural counties in the Southeast have typically been derided as backward and deficient by cosmopolitan elites and business leaders of the nation's urban centers, various external groups appear to have no compulsion against sending garbage, body parts, or prisoners to be disposed of or incarcerated in these same locales.

THE EVOLUTION OF SCHOOLING IN CLINCH COUNTY

As mentioned earlier, the eastern counties of Tennessee were primary supporters of "public" schooling in the state's early history, and the town of Greasy Rock (later to become Sealsville) is acknowledged as having one of the state's first academies (by 1838). However, also as mentioned earlier, within a few decades this institution appears to have fallen on hard financial times, for the Baptist Church is said to have "reopened" the school as a private academy in 1876.

As appears to have been the case in each of the rural school schools in this report, personnel details of the county academies/high schools is not too difficult to find. The names of principals and teachers of Greasy Rock Academy from the early years are recorded in what are otherwise very thin overviews of county schooling. Details of whatever primary (or "crossroad") schools existed in Clinch County are not nearly as available as are lists of those attending or teaching/administrating in secondary schools. In Clinch County, it appears that this situation existed because of the distinct class structure there, where children of tenant and subsistence farmers either did not go to school at all or were deemed of little educability by county elites who could afford to send their either to Greasy Rock Academy or to others in the region. Of course, had the county courthouse not burned down, perhaps more about 19th-century schooling throughout Clinch County could be ascertained.

In any event, even the Baptists eventually gave way to Presbyterians in 1902 at both county private schools. As mentioned earlier, Melungeon children were discriminated against in Clinch County, and many were forced to attend the few Negro schools provided. Yet, as Melungeon families had retreated to the most isolated areas of the county, and as they resisted being categorized as Negroes, very few Melungeon children attended school at all in the 19th and early 20th centuries. The Vardy School built by the Presbyterian Church appears to have been specifically targeted for the benefit of this population. As one account explains:

> In the spring of 1892, two Presbyterian ministers . . . stopped at the Old Sulphur Springs Baptist Church (where) a (church) meeting was in progress. . . . They (explained) that their purpose of being in the Valley was not to disrupt any already organized church, but to make them better by the process of education. They then announced that they would hold services some place in the Vardy Community. Everyone was invited to attend. They inquired around for a suitable place to hold "meetings." For a time it looked as if they would be unsuccessful. Finally, Batey Collins, grandson of the original Vardy Collins, agreed to let them hold services at the Vardy Springs. They held several services there and then promised that they would send some workers into the valley for the purpose of giving them a basic education. Up to that time education was almost nil in Vardy Valley.

Yet there were some small county elementary schools before the turn of the century in Clinch County. Typically located at dusty (or muddy) rural cross-roads, they were frequently named after (and probably maintained) by local families or small churches nearby. According to some of our interviewees, many "schools" were actually held in church buildings. School names like Hurley's, Sunnyside, Alder's Chapel, Greene-Lawson, Howard's Pond, Panther Creek, Bowlins Ford, and Dry Branch are illustrative. Technically supervised by an elementary board of education, the curriculum, staffing, and day-to-day operations of such schools were probably only loosely coordinated by outside forces, although we have no records for determining this. Yet we do know that the school year was typically a short one: For those choosing to pay a very modest tuition for schooling opportunities (or barter produce/services), the academic year rarely ran more than 3 of 4 months.

While I have already mentioned the importance of religious participation in East Tennessee, it probably needs to be emphasized again that the small rural churches in places like Clinch County have played a large informal (and formal) role in public education there. Many early one- and two-room schools built in Clinch County were constructed very close to such churches, and visits by local ministers to schools were probably commonplace until quite recently, especially when both were held in the same place. A not uncommon practice in Eastern Kentucky was for local (frequently untrained) ministers to augment their limited incomes by maintaining technically public facilities (schools) while watching out for their churches right next door (Smith, 1988).

Also, it is still the case in Clinch County that church functions (like weddings) too large for existing rural churches are sometimes moved into current consolidated schools on the weekends. For example, the high school gymnasium in Clinch County is not infrequently used for weekend gospel sings by regional church groups who bring in national gospel singers to the county. According to the school board, schools are community centers and are available for other public events in addition to classroom instruction. Furthermore, local preachers are still welcome to speak and/or lead students in prayer preceding official school programs or assemblies. And after-school activities are very rarely scheduled on Wednesday nights, on Sundays, or in competition with occasional outdoor church revival meetings held throughout the year.

Like most houses in rural Clinch County, rural schools there before the 1930s were probably as described in other chapters of this study: typically, a one-room log building with a puncheon (unfinished) wood floor, no electricity, and no indoor toilet facilities or plumbing. Being a student in such places usually involved gathering wood (or coal) for the stove, oiling and sweeping the floor on a routine basis, and sitting on home made log benches during seat work when time was finally available for academics. Paranthetically, even today many students at Clinch County's small outlying schools are still involved in various building maintenance functions (like mopping the floors) during the school day.

According to Smith (1988) and local sources, much of the life of rural Appalachian schools revolved around playtime in the schoolyard during various daily recess periods. A catalogue of boy's self-organized play activities is discussed by various authors. The local source, for example, describes the following games:

Games in those days were sometimes very rough, one of the toughest games was "Bull Pen." One side was outside and the other in a ring or pen formation. The outsiders would throw a hardball at the insiders. If they hit anyone, he went to the other side, until all of them had been hit. . . . There were two or three base games. But stinkbase was the most popular. Two leaders would choose up and were about thirty feet apart. Boys on either side would try to run around the other side without getting caught. If he was caught, he was put in the "stink" near the other side. If his side was able to retrieve him, he would go back home again. . . . "Ante over" was a ball game in which one side would get on one side of the school house and the others would get on the other side. One side called out loudly, "ante over" and the other side called "ready" and threw the ball. Then, they ran around the house and threw the ball in the crowd. Whoever was hit had to join the other side. . . . .

SCHOOL REORGANIZATION IN THE
MID-20TH CENTURY

Given the persistent poverty of Clinch County, its geographical isolation, the apparent social cleft between Sealsville and the rest of the county, the lack of an adequate road system, a historic lack of funds for maintaining strong formal institutions (like schools), and the willingness of small churches and families to maintain local one-room schools in the face of funding deficiencies, it has only been in the last three decades that (partially) graded consolidated schools have become the norm here. And this turn of events has only been made possible by increased state and federal financial aid for local counties since the 1960s.

Prior to the 1960s, three one room schools for Blacks existed in the county, in addition to approximately 50 1-room schools for Whites. Slowly, since the mid-1950s, these schools have been consolidated into six. Significantly, compared to other systems covered in this report, only one completely new school building has been constructed in Clinch County since the 1940s, and this was the consolidated high school built in Sealsville. The other five school buildings still in operation in Clinch County are upgraded and modified structures originally built between 40 and 60 years ago.

> In 1953, there were forty-seven schools in the county with thirty of these being one-teacher elementary schools, eight two-teacher elementary schools, six three-teacher elementary schools, one four teacher school embracing grades one through ten, and one eighteen-teacher school embracing grades one through twelve. These have been consolidated into the present system of five elementary schools.

Importantly, just as the federal government had a hand in constructing what was then called Sealsville Elementary back in the 1930s under New Deal legislation, so too did the federal government make possible a major renovation of that structure in the mid-1960s, as well as provide major equipment for the new high school built in 1966. Both of these physical plant improvements/

additions were made possible by the federal Elementary and Secondary Education Act.

The largest of the (now) elementary schools is called Clinch Central, and it is still the only elementary school in the system with homogeneously graded classrooms and at least one teacher for every grade level. The enrollment at Clinch Central in 1988 was approximately 520, with 20 teachers. Central is overcrowded, and rooms underneath the board office across the street (as well as several mobile classrooms) are used currently to hold the overflow.

The other four elementary schools (Hickory Gap, Bowlins Ford, Greene-Mathis, and Flat Gap) are all multigraded and range in enrollment from approximately 60 to 100 students. Hickory Gap Elementary, for example, originally built in the 1940s, served first as a combined elementary and junior high (grades 1–10). With the opening of Clinch County High School in the mid-1960s, Hickory Gap became an elementary school. During the 1988 school year its enrollment varied from about 90 to 100 students. Staffing the four "regular" classrooms were four teachers: one for the combined K–1 class, one for grades 2 and 3, one for grades 4 and 5, and a teacher for grades 6, 7, and 8. Furthermore, the teacher for grades 6 through 8 was also the school principal. Additionally, the school had two special teachers: one for special education students and one for Chapter 1 reading and math.

The other three outlying elementary schools actually have lower enrollments than Hickory Gap and have occasionally during the past several years been the subject of further improvement and/or consolidation discussions. The smallest and oldest of these, Greene-Mathis, appears particularly in need of general reconstruction compared both to others in the county and in surrounding locales. With an attendance of approximately 60, it has no indoor athletic facility and has only had indoor toilets since 1985. The physical condition of this structure is less than ideal: made of wood, it sits on a concrete slab foundation with bowed, unfinished floors and cracked, unpainted plaster in classrooms and hallways. While local parent support for the school (or at least its perennially good basketball team) is argued to be quite high, its attendance has experienced a general decline. The number of teachers assigned to it has also: in 1988 this building had only three regular classroom teachers for grades K–8, in addition to Chapter 1 reading and math teachers.

In general, schools in Clinch County only appear to have become "modern" by mainstream educational standards since the late 1960s, as federal and state programs and program guidelines became instituted. For example, even in 1965 there were 28 county schools, only four of which had indoor plumbing. As well, many teachers up until the mid-1960s taught without regular certification, and there were almost no instructional resources (e.g., filmstrips, movies, record players, school libraries, etc.), according to local sources.

The high school, too, has also historically been criticized for its comparatively limited academic and vocational programs, and is even today. In 1965, approximately 420 students were enrolled at Clinch County High, and the teaching staff was numbered at 17. However, no advanced mathematics courses or foreign language instruction was then available. As well, no guidance counseling related to college attendance or vocational careers were provided by the county. Related to this last point, the high school has been criticized at various times for its high dropout rate, its perceived failure to provide appropriate vocational training, and failure of its either nonexistent or understaffed guidance personnel to identify post high school career avenues for its students. Many of the documents outlining educational deficiencies in the Clinch County system, we found, were put together by school system administrators themselves (or their wives).

For example, until the late 1960s, only vocational agriculture programs were available for non-college-bound students at Clinch County High School. Yet, as earlier tables suggest, "careers" in agriculture were well in decline by this period. Currently, the high school has about the same number of students it had 20 years ago, but with an almost 50% increase in the number of classroom teachers. Some of these now teach in an expanded vocational program; yet even today, complaints continue to be voiced about comparatively limited occupational programs in the vocational wing of the high school. It's not that vocational classes don't exist (say school critics), but rather that the range of programs related to emerging technological requirements are underrepresented.

Improvements in school programs made possible by outside funding sources appear also related to school consolidation efforts in the county. The mid-1960s saw a complete transformation of the school organization when the new high school was built and space became available for more elementary students at Clinch Central. Not coincidentally, perhaps, the current superintendent was quite intent on building a new middle school with money he hoped to acquire from the federal government during the 1988–1989 school year.

The principal investigator's first private contact with the superintendent (August 1988) involved a lengthy discussion about the impact of a low-income federally funded housing project on the school population in Clinch County. According to the superintendent, federally subsidized and rent-controlled housing units built in Sealsville this decade have drawn dozens of poor families and their children from more rural parts of the county into the county seat. This has lowered the population base of the four rural elementary schools and raised by 20% the number of elementary and secondary students attending the two schools in Sealsville. In the superintendent's view, the impact of this development qualified Clinch County for federal assistance under Public Law 81-815, whereby federal initiatives sponsored by one federal agency (in this case public housing), which had adverse affects on other social services (like schooling), could qualify local agencies for even further federal assistance.

The superintendent had filed a report with Washington on the impact aid he sought and had lobbied both of his county's Washington representatives to help him obtain these funds (in excess of $1 million). Arguing that local taxpayers would not and could not come up with any money for new building projects, he suggested that at least one elementary school would be closed were he to obtain impact funding, as well as alleviating the crowding problems faced by Clinch Central.

Actually, other than in private discussions with the superintendent, open talk about further school consolidation in Clinch County was not heard during our 2 years there. On the one hand, this was somewhat surprising, as bussing from the most distant parts of the county is already accomplished for high school students. Also, Clinch County (surprisingly) has no mandated attendance area policy, so that many students bypass the school closest to them and ride to Sealsville to attend classes at Clinch Central. Thus, while we certainly would not argue in favor of further school consolidation in the county, it seems strange that some local residents and/or the superintendent haven't pursued this possibility more aggressively. Adding several more busses to bring in all county students to Sealsville would seem administratively desirable, especially given that the school system has operated in the red for several years. Yet the superintendent only talked about such a likelihood were a middle school to be built in Clinch County. According to him, such an event would clearly provide the incentive and an opportunity for closing one or more of the smaller elementary schools.

Other interviewees in the county pointed out different reasons why further consolidation would be problematic if attempted. For one thing, all seven school board representatives have at least one school now in their covered districts, and since each of the seven board members in the county uses his local school as a power base, it seemed unlikely that such a precedent would be actively voted in by sitting board members.

Until recently, road repair throughout Clinch County has also been an emotional subject. As in other areas, funds are limited for blacktop repair and graveling on county roads. And some residents of the county still remember the days when the only guarantee of good road surfaces in its more remote parts was to have a public school nearby. Such roads have to be maintained according to state law, and were therefore less likely to be subject to the political whims of the county road commissioner. Yet, while some suggest that road maintenance is not a political issue curently, memories appear to linger long in Clinch County (see Chapter 6).

CLINCH COUNTY'S PROFESSIONAL EDUCATORS

According to our completed interviews and the various documents/testimonials discovered in our fieldwork, political intrigue and patronage dynamics appear to have historically influenced school policy and decision making in Clinch

County schools. However, depending upon who was asked, some county citizens believe that the current political climate is either improved or briefly in a state of transition/reorganization.

Some claim that, unlike several previous administrators, the current superintendent has an interest in education as well as considerable political ambition. Sometimes in our 1988–1989 discussions with him, he talked openly about his "political future" in the county. At other times, he expressed guarded interest in perhaps working somewhere in the state department of education. Yet to talk of the Clinch County Superintendent as a "professional educator" on the order of the other superintendents profiled in this report appears to us misleading: for while Mr. A is a shrewd and alert individual, his language and concerns suggest a preoccupation with gaining educational resources and enabling schools to stay open, not with leading instructional programs or even insuring that the county's teachers were aware of the research base and professional literatures that might inform their practice. For example, of all four districts included in this study, only Clinch County failed to take advantage of **any** AEL/ERIC informational resources offered by RSS staff during the course of their local involvement.

As mentioned earlier, most of our discussions with Mr. A revolved around money and funding issues. Perhaps because his earlier teaching experience in the high school was in driver's education, and undoubtedly because he was trying to keep the Clinch County system running on a shoestring, educational philosophy discussions with the superintendent were usually rather brief in our interview encounters. Neither the superintendent's personal office, nor the outer lobby of the board office, showed any signs of professional journals or books, as was the case in districts previously discussed. Instead, state department of education guidelines and assorted unmarked notebooks lined the bookshelf behind the superintendent's desk.

The Clinch county superintendent was clearly the only one of the four superintendents in this study who appeared to view himself as at least as much a politician as an educator. Several times during the course of our visits he talked about how his views on obtaining and providing the (material) educational needs of the county, if successful, would "cost me my political career." He made this point several times whenever he talked of potentially building a new middle school, should he be successful in gaining federal impact aid (a possibility which seemed to fade during the course of the 1988–1989 school year).

With regard to dynamic educational leadership, we heard many times in our interviews that Clinch County schools were either "bad," "poor," "better than they used to be," or "inert." Typically, complaints against the system targeted either the political situation in the county or "uncaring" or "unmotivated" teachers (particularly at the smaller outlying schools or the high school). One or two individuals in the central office (specifically the special education director and the curriculum supervisor) were identified frequently in our interviews as committed teachers/supervisors. Other central office staff (like the director of food services) were more widely known outside of the school system for their alleged nonschool political involvements than for their educational roles. Importantly, several central office personnel were directly involved in either the city or county governance structures, which was not true of educators in any of the other three districts of this study.

Unlike each of the other counties studied for the AEL project, systematic teacher enrichment/development undertakings engaged in either spontaneously or under sponsorship of the county central office were conspicuous by their absence in the case of Clinch County. Part of the reason for this appears to be the comparative lack of professional education courses/seminars offered by the regional community college in Morristown. And while there are several higher education institutions within 90 minutes of Sealsville, their actual presence in the county appears much more remote than in either Charlotte or Braxton Counties.

There is no bulletin board in any of the Clinch County schools outlining off-campus courses of potential interest to county teachers, nor has any public university recently ventured into Clinch County to help upgrade the skills of county teachers. Furthermore, the community college just mentioned is a 2-year institution and is really not chartered to provide the kinds of professional development courses required by certified classroom teachers, especially since many of the fewer than 80 teachers in the system already have a master's degree. Again, our informants suggest that the incentive for attaining a master's degree in Clinch County comes from a state subsidy of an extra $1,000 per year in teacher salary.

To the best of our knowledge, the primary professional development iniatives locally available in Clinch County typically come in the form of "motivational speakers" available at teacher in-service sessions. Most other professional development activities for teachers, like in-service days, teacher incentive pay, and Career Ladder levels, are all state-supported/mandated programs.

So, too, professional development efforts in the central office also appear dictated by the availability of state and/or federal support. For example, the two directors of special programs (funded by outside dollars) for drop-out prevention, sex-equity, Chapter 1, and so on, both appeared quite able, yet most of the efforts of these directors during our visits to the county appeared to involve constant proposal writing and submission. Many classroom teachers in the system were aware that these employees do grant-writing, yet several expressed confusion about what happens in the schools as a result of attained grants (except for random in-service programs sponsored by successfully obtained external funding).

One interpretation of these observations might be that continued grant seeking of central office employees in the county occupies most staff energies, while enthusiastically putting programs into place generates less interest. Alternatively, it certainly appears to be the case that communication within the system is poor, and only those personally in contact with the central office on a day-to-day basis have much idea of what transpires in the larger system. In either event, never were evaluation staff "sat down" by educators in Clinch County and lectured to by school officials or teachers regarding all the positive things going on in their system, which routinely happened in each of the other systems of this report.

Rather than trying to run innovative programs for particular children on resources already available (which may in fact be impossible), many Clinch County efforts appear to be directed at finding existing or proposed grant opportunities in state or federal funding announcements, and then using such funds to create new employment opportunities or to sustain already employed personnel in the school system. It may be the case that the constant grant-writing efforts and seeking of external funding we found in Clinch County is typical of many small and underfunded rural school systems. Yet we found nothing quite like these efforts in the first two districts studied; for in each of them, grant-writing activities appeared to seek monies for programs already being attempted or desired. Only in Clinch County did external funds for the sake of external funds appear to be a compelling reason for grantsmanship.

MONEY AND POWER IN CLINCH COUNTY

The implicit message of much of the preceding is that educational processes and outcomes deemed essential in the other three districts of this report are less enthusiastically pursued in Clinch County. Lack of funds, and (ostensibly) lack of parent commitment to schooling, both appear related to this observation. For example, while all four superintendents interviewed for purposes of this report verbally recognized that some of the rural poor students (and their parents) place little value on formal schooling, the Clinch County superintendent was the only one who suggested that such a fact overwhelmed many teacher efforts to improve the local school system. According to him, many county parents viewed schooling as of only marginal importance:

> [Many] folks here are poor but comfortable. They inherit farms from their folks that are paid for, and they raise a little tobacco and tend their gardens. This gives them cash in their pockets, and they aren't interested in raising taxes for schooling kids that [often] aren't even theirs.

On the one hand, this is probably true. Yet none of the other superintendents interviewed for the AEL study so quickly downplayed the remedial or change-oriented possibilities of formal schooling for the rural poor in their districts.

However, others contend that deep-seated factional politics and issues of control of the school system in Clinch County are also important factors related to its educational dynamics and are, potentially at least, as central to discussions about its claimed deficiencies than either lack of money or lack of parent interest. Furthermore, parent support for sports and fundraisers is quite high in all schools, and was particularly noteworthy at three of the five elementary schools. Yet some claim that many taxpayers don't support the academic programs or budgets of the school system because they don't trust the motives of the people who run them.

Discussions of local politics of education as they affect school programs is a touchy subject in an ethnographic evaluation like this one. On the one hand, several informants interviewed for this report view school leaders in the central office as much improved over those who occupied similar positions in years past. Also, the lack of economic resources and economic development in the county probably "explains" important aspects of the county's current political situation. Given the possibility that blaming the current victims of county "underdevelopment" would be unfair, much of the following discussion will be cast with reference to **past** interpretations of the political nature of decision making in Clinch County, since the nature of current patronage dynamics is sensitive, potentially harmful to some of our informants, and arguably improved under the current school superintendent.

Written reference to the patronage system in Clinch County goes back over 60 years. In an autobiographical account of his professional education career, one well-respected educator made mention of the early politicized nature of schooling there, as well as the dearth of students completing high school in the mid 1920s:

> From [the] only one telephone located in Sealsville, Tennessee, _____ called me in the spring of 1923 to ask if I would be interested in becoming principal of Clinch County High School. Clinch County was very backward at that time. There was not a foot of paved road or railroad in the county. Sealsville was the only town in the county and it was not incorporated. The population of the town area consisted of about two hundred people. The school system was poor and it was badly affected by county political factions. . . . The school building was a big two- story structure located on a hill that overlooked the town and the valley through which flowed the Clinch River. Without previous experience in teaching and courses in student teaching as required today, the position was a big challenge. The school consisted of twelve grades. The faculty was employed by the Superintendent and the Board of Education. It was a rather congenial and co- operative faculty. There were many ups and downs during this first year and at the spring commencement only three graduated from high school.

Some 40 years later, county politics and its relationship to local economic development was a focal concern of various researchers. In an extensive analysis of the problems of economic development in Clinch County (circa 1966–1967), a number of local students attending a regional Baptist college and serving as research assistants on a TVA-funded study reported on the political "situation" in Clinch County. Importantly, the discussion of this political situation frequently involved its relationship with the county's educational dynamics and school policies.

One project author was the granddaughter of a one time county judge, who several years after writing her analysis of "the political situation in Clinch County" became a teacher there. She also became a casualty of that political system several years later, when she was fired for "political reasons."

Several passages of her document suggest the politicized tradition of Clinch County two decades ago, if not currently.

> In Clinch county, as in most other Tennessee Counties, there is no responsible head of government. The county does not have an executive or manager who appoints different directors as in some of the more progressive governmental systems. Almost all of the officials in Clinch County are elected by the people. The voters elect the following office holders: county judge, justice of the peace, constables, superintendent of education, school board members, county court clerk, circuit court clerk, trustee, tax assessor, sheriff, register, and superintendent of roads. . . . The majority of the people are Republicans. The county would have almost a one- party system were it not for the factions in the Republican Party. . . . (But) in the writer's opinion, this factional system is carried to the extreme and acts as a parasite which clings to the roots, trunk, and limbs of Clinch County government.

While the author discussed in some detail the origins and composition of Republican factions in Clinch County, she went into particular detail regarding how schools until at least the late 1960s were used by these factions for political advantage:

> The educational system is an important source of power to the factions. Both factions want to have their man as superintendent, and both want to have the majority of the school board. . . . In Clinch County the effectiveness of the school board generally depends on with which faction the superintendent is aligned. If, for instance, four of the seven board members belong to faction A and the superintendent also belongs to faction A, the teachers nominated by the superintendent are hired, and the buildings he wants are built. . . . If, on the other hand, four or more of the board members belong to faction A and the superintendent belongs to faction B, the superintendent is not in a position to accomplish that which he wants. Here it seems one faction fights the other and there is a constant fear that one faction will get more credit for progress than the other.

According to the above-quoted author (and others interviewed for our study), the hiring of teachers and noncertified personnel has historically been of particular concern in the dynamics of school board operation:

One of the main powers that a faction exercises is the hiring of teachers. It is believed that this is one of the areas of political manipulation that has tended to hurt the quality of education in Clinch County. The faction in power gives the teaching jobs to the teachers it feels have pledged allegiance to it.

Formerly, many noncertified teachers were required in Clinch County, as not enough certified teachers were available. These noncertified and nontenured "permit" teachers were particularly vulnerable to the political whims of the school board, and wholesale firings and new hirings of permit teachers frequently occurred in the county when one faction was voted out and the other in. Yet, even when the percentage of certified and tenured teachers who ostensibly were protected from political machinations, increased in the county, other ways of instilling political loyalty among teachers were used.

(by state law) the board must hire certified teachers before offering the job to a permit teacher, but a method has been used at times to get around this law. There are a number of schools whose names invoke a knowing smile on the faces of Clinch Countians. These are Prospect, Elm Springs, Ramsey's, and formerly Paw Paw, to name a few. Prospect, for example, is located on top of Fleenors Ridge. The area is one of the more isolated in the county. The road is narrow and steep and not very well cared for. In winter it is almost impossible to reach the school. Prospect is a one-room school. These are not conditions which draw most teachers, and therein lies the basis of the strategy used by the school board. It has not been uncommon for a certified teacher who is thought to be on the wrong side to be placed in one of these out-of-the-way places. In some cases they go ahead and teach, but many times they just give up and move out of the county.

Earlier we suggested that school policy has historically been adversely affected by politics in Clinch County. For that matter, the Clinch County school system actually has no policy "handbook," to the best of our knowledge. Except for state guidelines, nowhere is there a set of readily available locally developed instructional, attendance, teacher assignment, or personnel evaluation policies as exist in all of the other counties of this study. Occasionally, we were told, minutes of previous meetings are referred to in order to discover past policy on particular matters. Yet even these documents do not appear to be readily available for inspection by board members.

Board decisions on hiring, purchasing, evaluation, placement, etc. appeared in our visits to board meetings to be decided on a case-by-case basis. Typically, the superintendent explained possible actions and made recommendations. Sometimes one of the superintendent's strongest allies on the board (who was one of the only two college-educated members among the seven on the school board in 1988 and 1989) explained state law or outlined efficient business practice in cases where purchases/ budgets were discussed.

The chairman of the board during the second year of our study typically "took his cues" from either the superintendent or Mr. J (mentioned above), whose principal occupation is a car dealership he owns in a neighboring Virginia town. For the most part, the rest of the school board was reduced verbally in public sessions to voting on specific policy decisions. As mentioned earlier, under the previous school board (in 1988) the superintendent's recommendations were typically ignored. As the board composition changed to one more favorable to him in the spring of 1989, his recommendations appeared to carry more weight, and the school board operated as a more unified unit in funding battles with the County Commission.

POLITICS AND PROFESSIONALISM IN CLINCH COUNTY

It is quite likely that a number of very good classroom teachers and teacher/ principals exist in Clinch County. Not having systematically viewed a large sample of classroom dynamics there, however, we have little evidence about the overall quality of teaching and learning. Official state-collected and -distributed performance indicators (see Table TN-5) suggest that county students perform at or just below most state averages.

Yet however well school personnel perform their jobs in Clinch County schools, it seems quite likely that most educators there could do an even better job, were there a reward and/or professional development structure which supported good teaching. Such procedures were relatively routine in each of the other systems we studied in 1988 and 1989, yet we were unaware of any systematic professional development/improvement efforts in Clinch County similar to those of the other three systems researched for this report (particularly Braxton County and Charlotte County). School improvement efforts in Clinch County, if and when they do exist, appear to be accomplished primarily as the result of individual teacher interests, or as a consequence of state initiatives.

To some extent, every educator in Clinch County is also a politician; and, come election time, every teacher (particularly untenured ones), principal, and school board member is expected to declare whose side he or she is on in whatever county office is being contested. Furthermore, much energy among school leadership in Clinch County is placed on being identified with positive community events. For example, every school board member takes up advertising space in the high school yearbook and states which district he (they are all men) represents. In the high school gymnasium, where basketball is king, a huge sign listing all contributors to the program is attached next to the scoreboard. Significantly, every board member's name, as well as those of the superintendent and the principal of the high school, appear.

Such indicators, in and of themselves, do not impugn the educational intentions or skills of school personnel. Yet the political spoils system that

Table TN-5. Tennessee, like each state discussed in this book, publishes various statistics on each school district. Here are approximate "system" and "testing" indicators released for Clinch County in 1988. Note officially improved test scores between 1985-86 and 1986-87. Also note percentages of students in vocational programs and those in special education.

System Information	Grade Level	1984-85	1985-86	1986-87	State Average
Number of Schools	K-12	6	6	6	12
Average Daily Membership	K-12	1,420	1,424	1,350	5,811
% Student Attendance	K-12	97.3	96.3	97.0	94.2
% Enrollment Change	9-12	−25.9	−31.2	−30.3	−25.1
% Oversized Classes	K-12	*	11.7	7.3	4.1
% of Students Free or Reduced Price Lunch	K-12	*	89	88	43
Expenditures per Pupil (approximate)	K-12	$1,772	$1,940	$2,130	$2,560
County Per Capita Income (1984)	K-12	*	*	$5,296	$10,400
% Elementary School Accredited by SACS	K-8	**			24.3
% Secondary Schools Accredited by SACS	7-12	**			57.4
% Students in Vocational Education Courses	7-12	*	64.7	76.1	51.0
% Students in Special Education	K-12	*	**	23.6	13.9
% Chapter 1 Students	K-12	*	49.6	3.7	11.7

Testing Information		Grade Level	1985-86	1986-87	State Average
	Reading	3	74	83	79
Basic Skills First		6	60	68	76
Achievement Test		8	75	81	82
(percent score)		3	78	89	80
	Math	6	64	67	66
		8	70	76	72
	Reading	2	7	9	6
		5	3	4	5
		7	5	7	5
	Math	2	9	9	7
Stanford		5	4	6	6
Achievement		7	3	6	6
Test	Spelling	2	7	8	7
	Language	5	4	6	6
(Stanine score)		7	4	5	6
	Environment	2	9	9	6
7-9 = High	Science	5	3	6	6
4-6 = Average		7	3	4	5
1-3 = Low	Listening	2	9	9	6
		5	2	4	5
		7	7	6	5
	Social Science	5	2	5	5
		7	4	7	6
	Reading	9	4	5	5
Stanford Test of		12	4	4	6
Academic Skills	Math	9	2	5	5
(Task 2)		12	3	4	5
(Stanine score)	English	9	4	5	6
		12	5	5	6
	Science	9	4	4	5
7-9 = High		12	3	4	5
4-6 = Average	Social	9	4	6	5
1-3 = Low	Science	12	3	4	5
	Language	9	52	80	78
Tennessee Proficiency Test	Math	9	73	96	90
(% Students Passing)	Both	9	49	80	76

historically (if not currently) has centered on the schools in Clinch County appears to have led (or leads) to a variety of noneducational pressures of little utility for educational success. Not surprisingly, a variety of unethical election efforts (like the buying of votes) have frequently been identified in Clinch County School Board and Superintendent races. One of our interviewees reports having been asked in the early 1980s to run for the position of school superintendent. She reports declining the political sponsorship then offered, saying that $20,000 would be required to run, and that too many political favors would have to be paid back to make the job worthwhile. Cynthia Duncan, in her analysis of the implications of vote-buying and patronage practices in several nearby Eastern Kentucky school systems, explains the impact of such dynamics on school quality thusly:

> Buying elections not only fills local institutions with corruption that puts loyalties over school quality. It also absorbs the energy of those in the system who would prefer to work on the content of their job. Teachers told us that even the well-meaning school administrators had to devote all their energy to surviving, and had none left for educational leadership. People say they cannot come in "and relax, and pay attention" to their jobs. They have to be alert to how the political winds blow, how they are changing, who's in and who's out. (Duncan, 1986, p. 29)

Importantly, issues of effective teaching and school leadership in Clinch County may best suggest the current structural and political inadequacies of education there. As earlier suggested, teacher placement in Clinch County has historically been used to send those in favor to consolidated (and reputedly better) schools, and those out of favor to more remote ones. While the threat of assignment to isolated schools has been diminished somewhat in the county with continued teacher certification policies and school consolidation, there clearly seem to be preferred Clinch County schools for teaching in, even today: most teachers prefer to teach in the graded schools in the county seat; few wish to teach in the multigrade schools in the outlying areas. Yet, while state law guarantees tenured teachers a job in their local system, actual school assignments in Clinch County are never announced until the spring of each year, probably in the hope that teachers will politically back the local board member from his or her district as long as possible.

A relatively recent inmigrant to the county was appalled by its teacher assignment policies. Her children's earliest educational experiences at Flat Gap, she claimed, were less than adequate. And she decided to send her kids into Clinch Central. She described the situation at the local school thusly:

> The whole system is wild. I've never been exposed to such wildness. There is absolutely no communication with the school. Our friends and I worked an ice cream supper (a major fund raising effort done at every county school). We had no

idea what the whole thing was about. You don't even know when school is going to start in the fall. You hear by word of mouth.

This same mother claimed that many, if not most, parents with high expectations for their children bypassed the local school:

There are about 28 families who pass up Flat Gap. My son's teacher (before she transferred him to Central) was intelligent (but) lazy. He got the older girls to write on the blackboard (and) sent home work that wasn't being taught (in class). It seems (whichever teacher) is not wanted at Central is shipped out. If some of the good ones from Sealsville were transferred in, we'd send our (children) back.

The assignment of building principals in Clinch County for the 1988 school year was perhaps even more illustrative of how politics can compromise effective schooling practices. Only three of the county's six principals that year had administrative experience. Furthermore, only one of these three remained as principal of the same school he had had the year before. This was the high school principal.

The other two experienced principals also taught regular (split) classrooms, yet at different schools than the year before. One had asked for and been reassigned to a different school. The other had been reassigned against his will from Clinch Central to an outlying small elementary, ostensibly because he had backed the eventual loser in the county race for school superintendent in 1988.

Three other principals were new to the principalship. Two were newly credentialed teachers assigned to lead schools full of already experienced teachers. The other new principal had retired from the Tennessee Farmers Cooperative to Clinch County, where he expected to help run the farm of his elderly parents. According to him, the superintendent had called him up one day quite unexpectantly and offered him the vacant principalship. Of course, how this principalship became vacant is explained differently, according to who is asked about it (see above).

Not surprisingly, different sources claim that the principalship of Clinch Central in 1988 was actively sought by the man who later got it. In point of fact, the new principal was known to be a "drinking buddy" and political ally of the superintendent. His son also happens to be the chairman of the county Democratic party. To make a long story short, no one we talked to about the principal rearrangement at Clinch Central for the 1988–1989 school year was very surprised. As in many other cases, explanations for why this reassignment was made were typically "it's political." And the reassigned principal apparently accepted the fact, for, after explaining the course of events to us, he pleaded that we not use his name for the sake of his children's future in the school system. He also never appealed his treatment by the board, treatment that had no equal in the other systems we studied in 1988 and 1989.

Another example of how political motives can potentially get in the way of school improvement efforts we judged was visible in the way Clinch County used (or didn't use) the Clinch-Boone Educational Cooperative located in an adjacent county. We spoke earlier about the lack of outreach and/or professional development opportunities in Clinch County as made available through regional colleges. Another relatively unutilized resource for collaborative and region-wide improvement efforts by Clinch County is this Co-op, which coincidentally was itself initially instituted with the help of AEL in the 1970s.

The current director of the Clinch-Boone Cooperative lives in Clinch County and was previously the school superintendent there. He stepped down in 1982 to become the head of the Co-op, yet he backed a political ally of his for the superintendency, and opposed to the current one. Since he belonged to a different political faction from Mr. A, "bad blood" existed between them until quite recently. In fact, one of the current superintendent's 1988 campaign planks was to withdraw Clinch County from the Co-op, a move which would also cast some doubt on the long-term future of his political enemy's relatively stable job, and the source of his continuing political influence in Clinch County.

So too, some school programs initiated by, and identified with, previous school administrations appear to routinely be discontinued by newly elected superintendents from opposing factions. For example, in the early 1980s Clinch County ran a program for dislocated workers which won a state award as a model program. The program was externally funded through the initiative of the former superintendent who now heads the Clinch Boone Co-op, and headed by a former school teacher seeking 2 additional years of administrative experience. Such experience would have made this individual eligible for school superintendency under Tennessee law. Yet, even though (according to our interviews) the program was very successful, brought in thousands of dollars to the school system, and ostensibly would have been funded almost automatically by the state, Clinch County never applied for its continuance. And, in fact, the current superintendent never even discussed with the board (in open session) the possibility of so doing. Again, observers of the political dynamics of Clinch County did not see this as idiosyncratic or mindless: rather, it was viewed as the natural distancing of the current superintendent from a program credited to a political enemy, as well as an effort to head off the political future of an up-and-coming county figure who might one day be interested in running against the incumbent superintendent.

Yet it isn't only the internal lack of attention to professional educational issues and innovations which may harm schooling practices in Clinch County. Rather, competition for scarce resources at the county level also appears to take up much needed time from the working agenda of school personnel. An excellent example of this is the additional duties of each school principal in Clinch County as a school fund raiser.

Other than heating, electricity, and janitor expenses, the county school system pays for almost no other material or service cost. Rather, various fundraisers are held throughout the year to purchase varnish for the floors, curtains for the windows, books for the library, and toilet paper for the bathrooms. Paranthetically, one of the strangest scenes we have witnessed in most Clinch County schools is the chaining of toilet paper rolls to the walls with a padlock. As school supplies like these appear in short supply, and perhaps because toilet paper rolls have been known to occasionally plug up the commodes, "defensive" bathroom strategies may be understandable administratively. However, no practices of this sort were quite so apparent in the other schools of this study.

And it is literally the case in Clinch County that each building principal has to have some reserve from the previous year's fund raisers in order for children to use the bathroom when school starts in August. It is expected that each principal will personally see to the material condition of his school (particularly in the outlying schools) as part of the job of being principal, and personally pay for whatever is needed to open up in the fall if necessary.

Translated into action, what all of the above means in Clinch County is that huge fundraisers are held throughout the year in the county so that parents and others in the community have an "opportunity" to contribute to the material needs of each school. For example, in Hickory Gap, the Fall 1988 kicked off with an Ice Cream Supper and concluded with a Ham Supper. In between, revenues from (elementary) interscholastic basketball competitions and candy/soft drink sales to students helped purchase necessary supplies for the year. And make no mistake about it–the fundraisers are very successful. The 1988 Hickory Gap Ice Cream Supper generated in excess of $2,000 dollars for the school. And fundraisers at Clinch Central and Clinch County High raised even more. The Ice Cream Supper activities at Clinch County High generated over $18,000 in September 1988.

These fundraisers, importantly, are not under the control of the school board or the superintendent. Rather, they are "staffed" with the volunteer labor of students and local PTO members and are managed by each building principal (who, remember, also teaches regular split classes in four of the six schools). Also, in the case of each of the four outlying schools, the building principal also (typically) coaches several basketball teams, drives these teams to other schools for games, is in charge of candy and soft drink sales, and controls all funds raised by the local school. Since the typical building principal in Clinch County must work 10 to 12 hours to day just to enable the school to keep its doors open and teach its classes, it is probably no wonder none of the principals can think systematically about becoming an effective "instructional leader."

Importantly, with the exception of the high school, there are no administrative personnel in any county schools. Even Clinch Central, with over 500 students and 35 teachers, has no secretarial help for the principal. A part-time aide, paid at minimum wage, is his only source of assistance. Which may be one important reason why he spends most of his time coordinating buses, helping out in the lunchroom, and making announcements over the school public address system, rather than developing and/or leading instructional programs.

Perhaps the only school administrator in Clinch County who has a vision regarding the way his school ought to be run and the time to devote to this task (there are no female building administrators currently) is the principal of Clinch County High School. Yet his vision is quite a stern one compared to other administrators in this study. Academic excellence, school discipline, and athletic pride appear to be his primary concerns. In the multiple situations in which we have observed this individual, either he was asking (the school board) for permission to suspend/expel one or more students for disciplinary reasons, extolling the virtues of hard work and dedication to academic coursework, lecturing students about their behavior/dress in the hallway, or establishing academic/athletic awards ceremonies for students.

None of the above is necessarily meant as any criticism: if one assumed that strong and disciplined leadership was a prerequisite for effective high school leadership, Mr. J might well serve as a model for any high school principal. Yet we sensed little interest in broad-based (or based on R&D strategies) notions of "school improvement" in this building leader, and little interest whatsoever in the utility of outside expertise for informing and addressing educational practice at his school. Never, for example, did Mr. J appear at any AEL sponsored activities, and never did he go out of his way to ask evaluation staff questions about their interests or perceptions on school policy in the county. Yet Mr. J knew about the RSS project, both because he was present when it was first discussed, and because one of his teachers was chosen to head the steering committee and run the county-wide school improvement project, which was also to be housed at Clinch County High.

To be perfectly fair, however, it must be pointed out that almost all facilities (with the possible exception of the gym) at Clinch County High pale in comparison with those of the other three high schools visited as part of this study. The only organized sports programs at the school are boys and girls basketball and boys baseball. Clinch County has no high school football team, no outside track, no band, no forensic teams, or any other program or facility which is not mandated by the state and would cost additional local dollars to support. If and when intensive school improvement programs were to be desired in the county, it is difficult to imagine where funds to provide them would come from, which may possibly be related to why they aren't aggressively pursued.

As suggested earlier, dealing with professional development matters likewise never appeared a preoccupation of the county school superintendent. Rather, struggling to raise enough money to keep the school doors open appeared to be his major role, and he talked almost wistfully about a more "golden era" decades ago when federal dollars were readily available. And 1988–1989 may have been the most difficult financial year for the system since state aid first came to Clinch County.

Throughout the 24-month course of our research in Clinch County, the school superintendent has had a running battle with the County Commission, which provides local funds for school operation. In particular, the County Executive, who technically is supposed to work for the County Commission, was at odds with the school system over the school budget. Much of the County Executive's overt hostility toward the superintendent appears to have begun when Mr. A did not rehire the other's son-in-law to teach several years ago.

All during the 1988 year, charges and countercharges about misspending of funds and inappropriate record keeping by the school system have filled the pages of the major regional (not county) newspaper. Even the (only) weekly county publication, the *Sealsville Shopper*, began to run stories about financial difficulties of the local schools, along with its regular shopping advertisements (the county's only real *news*paper went out of business in the 1970s).

While the state of Tennessee actually funds most of the school operating costs for Clinch County schools, the county still must come up with a minimum appropriation to qualify for state supplements. For example, in 1988, the state of Tennessee supplied 73% of the operating costs of Clinch County schools, compared to a federal contribution of 14% and a local contribution of only 12%. Yet local dollars are not delivered as a lump sum in the beginning of the year and instead are forwarded to the school system at various times as tax receipts are collected and the County Executive sees fit to send monies forward.

During 1988, the County Executive (who belongs to a Republican faction other than the superintendent's) continually claimed that county tax receipts were behind projections, and he rarely forwarded promised funds to the school system on time. Likewise, Mr. R (the County Executive) continually claimed that the schools were mismanaged and that they really didn't need money immediately anyway. The County Executive reputedly even called the state auditor to come and inspect the school system's books in the spring of 1989. Mr. R was particularly fond of pointing out that the school system's central office employed two individuals with high salaries who he claimed had very nebulous job descriptions. And one of them was the superintendent's wife.

In response, Mr. A argued that his budget had been approved by the County Commission and was open for inspection by anyone wanting to see it. He also argued that the several salaried workers in his office who were the target of Mr. R were being paid out of federal funds tied to specific projects they administered (like JTPA and an the ARC dropout prevention program mentioned earlier). Thus, this criticism had no bearing at all on the financial obligations of the county to fund local appropriations. Furthermore, Mr. A argued that continued stalling on the part of the County Commission to provide local school funds would jeopardize payments from the state.

By January of 1989, charges and countercharges by the two political enemies had escalated to the point that Mr. A discontinued transportation services throughout the district, telling local bus drivers to complain to the County Commission, which they did. Very quickly, the County Commission found enough money to pay the bus drivers, and school went on as usual for the remainder of the year.

Yet Clinch County ended the year financially in the red, and money held in escrow for teacher salaries (paid over a 12-month period instead of during the school year) was used to pay other school expenses. Thus, Clinch County Teachers were not paid in June and July for work they had already completed. Not surprisingly, teachers refused to return for work in August until they had received back pay.

FUNDING THE SCHOOL SYSTEM WITH MONEY FROM THE JAIL

Earlier we discussed the fact that the County Commission had agreed to house state prisoners in order to generate more local funds for the operation of county government. In 1988, 33% of the County's expenditures went toward funding the local schools, 60% of the County's income went towards the general fund, and 7% went toward payments on outstanding debts. Except for money spent by the school system, in other words, the County Executive controlled almost all expenditures in Clinch County. And when pushed to redistribute total county funds as a consequence of shortfalls in local tax receipts, he was not ready to reallocate some of his budget to the school system under control of a political enemy.

Therefore, the years 1988 and 1989 saw a tremendous push by the County Executive and the County Commission to find new ways to raise tax dollars. And Mr. R spent quite a bit of energy attempting to convince the public that new taxes to be raised would primarily be used to subsidize the school rather than to be spread across all county services. In other words, the general emergency status of tax talk in Clinch County in 1988 and 1989 was laid at the feet of the school system and its superintendent.

Rather quickly, the possibilities of increasing the number of state prisoners was accepted as a way to increase local revenues. The county had already built a jail for such purposes the year before and was able in this way to generate over $100,000 for local purposes in 1988. Recognizing a "good" thing when they saw it, the County Commission (through its executive) entered into an agreement with the District of Columbia to house hundreds of D.C. prisoners in a proposed new wing of the county jail that would be built for just this purpose. While costs per prisoner were calculated at less than $10 per day, the contract drawn up between Clinch County and Washington, D.C. would compensate the county at $45 per day. Such an agreement would bring to the county literally millions of dollars per year and, according to the County Executive, solve all of the county's financial problems.

Yet many county citizens became outraged about housing these prisoners in an addition to the county jail (which is just off the main street in downtown Sealsville) and effectively blocked talk of expanding the already new county jail beyond its capacity of 67 beds. Of course, by this time the county government and the school system were equally the target of much public hostility and anger. The County Executive had claimed that, because the school system couldn't responsibly budget its money, he had had to negotiate a jail contract in order to bail out the superintendent (who remains an important political enemy). Meanwhile, the superintendent claimed that he had been warning the County Commission for over a year that they were not allocating enough money to cover local operating costs as mandated by the state. And according to Mr. A, Mr. R's political career was "probably over" following the public outcry against the jail contract he had tried to sign with the District of Columbia.

Yet matters continued to worsen in Clinch County's financial situation into Spring/Summer 1989. As allegations of impropriety and mismanagement continued to intensify, Mr. A contracted a strange pulmonary disease (blastomycosis), which hospitalized him off and on for several months. And August 1989, he ruptured a disc in his back which required surgery.

Meanwhile, monies earned from the housing of state prisoners were being channeled into the school system to alleviate the 1988 shortfalls previously discussed. Furthermore, as such monies looked like the only way of increasing local funding possibilities in a county with a long history of keeping taxes low (which is a major campaign theme of most county commissioners), Clinch County built into its proposed school funding budget (for 1989–1990) a portion of such future revenues. And the county entered into a contract with the private D.C. firm for housing a reduced number of their prisoners, who could be accommodated in their existing facility.

Unfortunately for the county, the state department of education had to approve the local budget and its funding sources prior to forwarding state funds for the beginning of the 1989 school year. And these funds were required by the local schools in order to make back payments to teachers for them to return to work. Yet, according to state guidelines, there are only several acceptable financial sources for funding local school appropriations, and housing out-of-state prisoners is technically not one of them. (We assume this is based on the lack of predictability of such funds, rather than upon moral grounds.) To compound matters, while the Clinch County jail is only certified to hold 67 prisoners, on August 28, 1989, it held 12 county prisoners/detainees, 29 state prisoners, and 70 D.C prisoners. And the County Commission was warned by state correctional officials that continued housing of prisoners beyond its capacity might cost the county its state contract.

Therefore, schools did not open as planned in late August 1989, as the state had to consider whether jail funds could be used in the manner proposed by Clinch County. Finally, in the third week of August, the State Department of Education agreed to make the first installment of its payments to the local school system contingent upon a first payment from the District of Columbia to the County Commission for the housing of their prisoners.

With great fanfare, a check was sent to the County Commission by the District of Columbia for $100,000, and Mr. R went to some lengths to convince Clinch Countians that his political influence with Tennessee's Senator Sasser in Washington had helped expedite this payment. Subsequently, a check from the County Commission to the School Board for $35,000 enabled the county to show the state (on paper, at least) that enough local funds were on hand to then qualify for state education supplements.

At a special School Board Meeting on August 29, teachers were promised that, if they came for a half-day in-service on September 1, they would receive back pay due them for the month of July, and that, from then on, salaries should be paid regularly for the 1989–1990 school year. Yet, in order to underscore the lack of trust and political discord between the School Board and the County Commission, the board went on record (unanimously) that schools in 1989-90 would immediately close upon the first occasion when the County Commission failed to forward a promised monthly payment to the school system.

All of this had transpired, in the meantime, while the superintendent was in the hospital with the two serious ailments previously mentioned. And rumors were flying among his political opponents that, soon, they would be able to put one of their own back in the superintendency, as Mr A would have to resign in the face of continued pressures on his job. Yet, while objectively it seems odd that either Mr A or his rival could survive the roller-coaster years both had in 1988 and 1989, the history of the county's leading political figures suggest that adversity and embarrassment have been cornerstones of elected leadership. As the former teacher cited earlier describes the process of being elected to positions of importance in Clinch County, previous job performance and/or experience appear of little importance. And being seen as a competent professional educator still may not carry enough political weight in Clinch County today. According to her, a different set of "competancies" is required of county political officers:

> A few weeks before election day, (candidates) begin their electioneering. They
> themselves, or a relation, go from house to house in a particular community. . . .
> Many of the candidates lack educational qualifications, have little insight into the

problems of the county, and do not understand the real duties of the offices (they are running for). Many times they run on the basis of need. It is often the person who can tell the saddest story that is elected to office. One gentleman ran on the basis that he had a sick wife with whom he had to stay almost constantly. As a result he couldn't do much work outside of the house, so he needed the job for a living. Even though the job pays nothing, he was elected school board member. He had less than a fifth-grade education. The man who ran for tax assessor campaigned on crutches. A short while after his election, he was getting around fine without them.

REFERENCES

Allison, C. (1983). Training Dixie's teachers: The University of Tennessee's summer normal institutes. *Journal of Thought, 18*(3), 27-36.

Duncan, C. (1986). Myths and realities of Appalachian poverty: Public policy for good people surrounded by a bad economy and bad politics. In R. Eller (Ed.), *The land and economy of Appalachia: Proceedings from the 1986 Conference on Appalachia.* Lexington, KY: The Appalachian Center.

Eller, R. D. (1982). *Miners, millhands and mountaineers: Industrialization of the Appalachian South, 1880-1930.* Knoxville, TN: University of Tennessee Press.

Folmsbee, S. J., Corlew, R., & Mitchell, E. (1960). *History of Tennessee.* New York: Lewis Historical Publishing Company.

Foster, A. P. (1923). *Counties of Tennessee.* Nashville, TN:Department of Education, Division of History, State of Tennessee.

Fowler, F. (1988). The politics of school reform in Tennessee: A view from the classroom. In W. Boyd & C. Kercher (Eds.), *The politics of excellence and choice in education* (pp. 183-197).

National Governors' Association. (1986). *Time for results: The Governors' 1991 report on education.* Washington, DC: National Governors' Association Center for Policy Research and Analysis.

Perkinson, H. (1976). *The imperfect panacea.* New York: Random House.

Smith, D. T. (1988). *Appalachia's last one-room school.* Unpublished doctoral thesis, University of Kentucky.

State Research Associates. (1988). *Education reform in rural Appalachia: 1982-1987.* Washington, DC: Appalachian Regional Commission.

Stuart, J. (1965). *Daughter of the legend.* New York: McGraw-Hill.

Tennessee Department of Education. (1988). *Annual statistical report of the Department of Education.* Nashville, TN:

Whisnant, D. (1980). *Modernizing the mountaineer.* Boone, NC: Appalachian Consortium Press.

Works Progress Administration. (1986). *The WPA guide to Tennessee.* Knoxville TN: University of Tennessee Press.

5
Cave County, Kentucky

Cave County was the second site volunteering to become affiliated with AEL in several of its rural programs, and it specifically agreed to become a school/community demonstration site in the fall of 1987. Also, technically speaking, Cave County completed its formal school improvement project with the RSS program within a year of its initial commitment. And it was one of only two completed projects falling within the time frame laid out by the Lab in its original technical proposal.

In our evaluation report, Cave County's case study and project evaluation came last, for reasons to be mentioned shortly. Yet our choice of where and when to focus on Cave County was fortuitus, because only in Cave County did we have anything to say about the **continuing** impact (or lack of same) of a school improvement project put into place there as a result or early RSS activities.

In essence, the long term utility of the school/community improvement project undertaken in Cave County was severely compromised by a number of local political events, in combination with a school facilities report of the state department of education. Details of these developments will remain until later in this chapter. We mention these topics here primarily because the character of the Cave County "story," with regard to aims of the AEL project, will have a slightly different look than earlier ones: that is, much of the analysis to be presented later in this chapter deals with school/community interactions which occurred *after* AEL completed its project and left the county.

The fact that (in our view) the post-RSS school improvement dynamics proved more interesting than those of the three other sites is not the main reason we did not investigate this system sooner. Rather, because the Kentucky site was closer to the University of Kentucky (our "home base") than the others, and because we were involved to some degree in following developments in all four demonstration sites by the fall of 1988, we chose to perform more extensive field work in each of the comparatively far flung school districts during 1988 rather than in Cave County.

We assumed that, since Cave County was in our state, we could keep abreast of many contemporary developments there from a distance, and that we could probably reproduce important aspects of state historical issues related to education from earlier works completed by the principle investigator and his colleagues (e.g., DeYoung, 1983; DeYoung & Boyd, 1986; DeYoung, Vaught, & O'Brien, 1981). Besides, our first site experiences in Braxton County, West Virginia, suggested that selection and implementation of a school improvement project would be a long-term operation, and that project evaluation staff would be able to return almost anytime during the 1988–1989 school year to catch up on whatever slowly emerging school improvement activities were currently underway.

Yet, in many ways, the above assumptions/expectations proved untrue. I have already mentioned that the school improvement project chosen (increasing parent involvement in the schools) was implemented relatively quickly in Cave County, and due to the nature of the project(s) undertaken (see Chapter 6), we were unable to be available for several specific (classroom and school) projects funded by the Lab. Furthermore, obtaining "objective" accounts of school improvement activities (and issues) in Cave County was more difficult than first expected.

For example, we assumed that, since two newspapers covered many school events there, readings in these papers about local educational activities would frequently be issue directed and would expose district "warts" as well as district "success." After all, in each of our other three districts, local reporters and/or newspaper editors either presented controversial images of the local schools in their pages or were actual antagonists of school officials in each county. Yet, perhaps because the primary reporter covering the school "beat" in Cave County was also on the staff of the school system (and was frequently the recipient of school board and superintendent praise for various programs he administered there), very little of the problematic and/or negative contemporary commentary available in Cave County ever surfaced in either of the county papers (until late in our fieldwork). So, too, the two county papers were actually one: same publisher, same news, same columns, and similiar editorials, but one edition was targeted at the Bear Cave (south) end of the county, the other toward residents of Craddockville on the north side of the Ralston River. And during the course of our fieldwork they were merged into one county-wide publication.

Obtaining school leadership information from key informants inside the system also proved more difficult in Cave County than it had been for any of the other districts in this study. As had been the case in Clinch County, finding persons critical of various aspects of the schools' operations there was not difficult. And to be fair, finding enthusiastic supporters of recent school programs in Cave County was also relatively easy. Yet locating persons inside the system who both remained there and appeared comfortable talking about *both* the positive *and* negative aspects of Cave County schools was comparatively difficult.

One of our early observations related to the above theme centered on how principals, central office staff, and the school superintendent of Cave County during the course of our study frequently congregated together in public as a very tight-knit group. That is, at most school board meetings and school-sponsored functions we attended, many if not most building principals (in 1988) were present and set themselves physically apart from others in attendance. And we were informed by several critics of the superintendent of Cave County schools "that he tells all his principals what they are allowed to say and what they are allowed to do" with regard to school issues in the county.

Furthermore, among the several then-school principals we surveyed, both high respect for the school superintendent and an unwillingness to criticize or second guess most of his actions was in evidence (even in private), although more than a few private citizens of the county were quite willing to provide negative impressions of various policy decisions. Among school personnel who might have had negative insight into system dynamics, the concept of "loyalty" was often mentioned. In essence, many teachers, principals, and central office staff felt intensely loyal to the superintendent for their positions in the system, and volunteered that, as long as he and they worked in the Cave County schools, they felt obliged not to inform outsiders about inner workings of the system. One particularly well-located official underscored this possibility when he invited the principal investigator to "come back and ask me some of these questions again in 5 or 6 years" (after his retirement).

On the other hand, it is quite possible that evaluation staff had comparative difficulty "penetrating" the "inner circle" of Cave County school administrators because they were typically very task oriented and only marginally interested in the nature of our work. Having visiting educators and/or professors of some sort or another is probably not uncommon in Cave County, for the system is hard driven by school improvement concerns (as directed by the superintendent). So, too, in Kentucky there is a moderate rivalry between regional universities and the University of Kentucky. Inasmuch as many or most teachers and school administrators in the county either graduated from or have completed in-service training under the auspices of Western Kentucky University (including the superintendent), having evaluation staff from the University of Kentucky was probably viewed by some school leaders there either as irrelevant to their jobs or actually an intrusion by representatives from a rival college of education. Related to this theme, there has historically existed some antagonism between Lexington and most of rural Kentucky (a theme developed later in this discussion) which may have influenced the comparative antipathy we received in Cave County.

CHOOSING A KENTUCKY SITE

In Cave County, the RSS school/improvement demonstration went almost picture perfect by standards outlined in the AEL technical proposal. Yet, as we will suggest shortly, the actual utility of the project and its long term benefits probably had little lasting impact, for reasons which will be suggested later. On the other hand, increasing parent involvement in the school system (the chosen improvement project) may become a key story in Cave County by the mid-1990s, a story line which will have to wait for elaboration in the final chapter of this book.

Inasmuch as descriptions of site selection processes in two earlier states of the RSS demonstrations were relatively extensive, details of the Kentucky deliberations on this matter won't be provided. Technically speaking, Kentucky Advisory Group deliberations went pretty much according to how they were supposed to as outlined in proposal documents.

As mentioned in Chapter 1, Kentucky has 120 county school systems and approximately 58 independent districts. The few independent districts which remain in the state are holdovers from an earlier era when many towns and small cities had their own districts. Yet, with continued state economic and population decline in many rural areas, many former independent districts have merged with surrounding county districts during the past three decades (with the active support of the state legislature). Interestingly, Cave County has two separate school systems (Cave County and Penneyrile Independent), which appears at various times to have engendered a sense of competition between them. Yet evaluation staff never sensed in our fieldwork any undercurrent of animosity, even though we expected to find some.

At the Kentucky Advisory Group meeting (held in the state capital), several county school systems eligible for invitation/participation as an RSS demonstration site were discussed. As opposed to site selection discussions held in Virginia and Tennessee, it appeared from our vantage point that two of the four "advisors" had some personal knowledge regarding most systems in question and the leadership there. This may have been the case because of rather intense school reform/improvement efforts in the state during the leadership of State Education Superintendent Alice McDonald, for the two dominant discussion leaders at the meeting were reputed to be among the "inner circle" in the state department. Of course, it could be argued that, since many of the most needy rural and poor districts lay in the "excluded" fifth congressional district (see Chapter 1), picking a target district would have been more difficult had all theoretically eligible counties and independent systems been contenders for an AEL invitation.

In any event, the top two "finishers" in the Kentucky selection process were Bath and Cave Counties, respectively. Importantly, even though balanced discussion and close votes were recorded regarding each of the two identified schools, both Bath and Cave County superintendents were well known by at least one of the advisory group (AG) members. One AG member (an assistant superintendent from a Western Kentucky county) identified herself (particularly in a later interview) as a good friend of the Cave County Superintendent;

meanwhile the AG representative from the Kentucky Farm Bureau (whose home office was in Bath County) knew that superintendent quite well.

Several weeks later, the Bath County Superintendent and another central office administrator were invited to Charleston to hear about the RSS program and the school/community demonstration project. After several hours of presentation and discussion, the Bath County representatives appeared to remain somewhat unclear about the nature of RSS objectives. One concern they had was that government funding for school improvement projects they had written grants for earlier had rarely materialized, and that lots of valuable time had been spent on the writing of documents which later proved unsuccessful. In other words, they seemed to think lots of time and energy could be invested in the Lab project without immediate payback. And perhaps because the Bath County Superintendent was near retirement, he seemed reluctant to take on yet another project. Besides, he explained, a major school building project was currently underway in Bath County, and the RSS demonstration project would probably just add to what promised to be an already confusing year in his district.

In any event, Bath County representatives decided in the week following the RSS presentation to decline the invitation to participate in the demonstration project. Accordingly, Cave County, Kentucky, was approached and apparently agreed relatively quickly to participate. As it turned out, the Western Kentucky assistant superintendent had already mentioned the possibility of the AEL project to her colleague in Cave County and encouraged him to participate if invited. Which he appeared to do.

EARLY KENTUCKY SETTLEMENT PATTERNS AND EDUCATIONAL ISSUES

As an original county of Virginia and contiguous to the states of Tennessee and (later) West Virginia, Kentucky's early educational history approximates in a number of ways those of each of these previously discussed states (particularly that of Tennessee), which is one reason why extensive discussion of Kentucky's early economic, political, and educational history is relatively truncated here.

Reminiscent of our earlier discourse, a number of historians suggest that struggles over land titles on the frontier between elites and squatters were a predominant theme of late 18th- and early 19th-century Kentucky history. As in Tennessee, representatives from many wealthy families supposedly were able to acquire from the Virginia legislature titles to large tracts of land in the west. Apparently, surveyors were frequently sent ahead to advise potential wealthy immigrants about the best lands in Kentucky. Thus, as was the case with Tennessee, the more agriculturally desirable lands of Central Kentucky (the Bluegrass region) were settled by more prosperous newcomers, and later-arriving (and less well-connected) settlers attempted to lay claim to more marginal lands in the east and west.

Apparently, much of the early history of land settlement in Kentucky had serious legal and political overtones.

> the pioneers who began to pour into the Virginia territory of Kentucky County were land hungry. They wanted good land and plenty of it; and what is more, they intended to find a place in which to live and to bring up their families. . . . The population of Kentucky came from several strata of society; it was recruited from tenants and farmers from Ireland and England, who, after migrating from the motherland to Pennsylvania, Maryland and Virginia colonies traveled over the long roads into Kentucky. . . . A roster of the leaders of Kentucky of that day contains the names of the employers of the surveyors and explorers who soon followed their advance agents to the lands that had been prospected and claimed. They were speculators in land either on their own account or as representatives of large holders of Kentucky land who had acquired extensive acreage through congressional grants. (McVey, 1949, pp. 4-5)

The virtual "stampede" into Kentucky through different routes and by people from various socioeconomic backgrounds (the state's population almost tripled from 70,000 to 200,000 between 1790 and 1800) led to heated land title disputes which would (as was the case in Tennessee) eventually negatively affect 19th-century public education efforts.

> Almost before the settlers had begun to arrive in the Bluegrass section, the lands had been taken up and titles obtained. In many instances, not only one title but many brought complications into the ownership of land which made for insecurity and often created hard feelings, since a settler might be ousted as a squatter from land he had regarded as his own. (McVey, 1949, pp. 5-6)

Given that the wealthier and more politically powerful settlers in the Bluegrass were also better educated and organized, they reputedly managed to dominate the new state legislature and to put into place a state constitution in 1798 which guaranteed their property rights and a more conservative political apparatus than populist forces favored (Hackensmith, 1970). Therefore, from the early 19th century considerable animosity grew between more elite forces centered in the Lexington area and those of other, more distant, and less agriculturally desirable state locales.

For example, in West Central Kentucky (where Cave County lies) fewer wealthy planters and horse breeders located.

> Much of the area in the western portion of the state, especially that south of the Green and Cumberland Rivers, was settled by people who had bought their land from the state on credit. With cash hard to obtain, many of the settlers quickly

became delinquent in their payments. Opposition to the state's attempt to collect the money soon began to be felt in politics. The result was the abolition of the quarter-session courts inherited from Virginia and the substitution of local county courts presided over by the debtor's friend and neighbor. This pressure by the debtor class divided the people and caused a choosing up of sides when almost any political issue came up for decision. The conservatives of the day were those in possession of good land, who controlled politics, and held significant offices. Their strength was centered in the Bluegrass with Lexington as their capital. The radicals were the "red necks," squatters, tenants, debtors, and small farmers. (Hackensmith, 1970, p. 7)

In any event, little sentiment towards the building or maintenance of public schools was visible in Kentucky during the first several decades of its statehood (Clark, 1985). Wealthy landholders would provide tutors for their children, and small-scale farmers saw little value in schooling when all family members were required to help establish new households in the wilderness. Besides, since most state citizens with taxable wealth were already educating their own children, they could not envision paying to educate those of "radicals" with whom there remained significant class differences.

The conservatives felt that in the free society in which they lived, the radicals were in their financial condition due to their lack of initiative and industry. To them, an educational system based on property tax would be nothing more than sheer charity to the children of those unwilling to help themselves. A system of state-supported schools would require a far heavier tax burden than the landed class cared to bear. Besides, the ideas for such a system were quite vague and there was no one with enough status in the existing socio-political structure to take the initiative. (Hackensmith, 1970, p. 8)

Furthermore, even the revival movement which swept Kentucky (and much of the South) in the first several decades of the 19th century laid little emphasis on schooling. The hearts and souls competed for by rival Baptist and Methodist churches in rural Kentucky were typically led by lay preachers, themselves of humble origin and not formally trained. Apparently, the pentecostal zeal with which they preached salvation did not include in the early years any formal instruction, especially instruction which public schools might give.

SCHOOLS IN ANTEBELLUM KENTUCKY

All of the above notwithstanding, there were various schooling opportunities available to small groups of children in Kentucky by the early 19th century. As in Virginia and Tennessee, the limited types of formal education available during this period consisted of many tuition academies for the wealthy, some (typically church-run) charity schools for the poor, a few "old field schools" for children of some farm families, and apprenticeship for most children trained outside of the household.

Old field schools, which also existed in Virginia, West Virginia, and Tennessee during the 19th century, were frequently to be found in many rural locales of the Southeast and the mountains. In essence, these were poorly funded academies or subscription schools and literally were held in small cabins constructed in farmed-out old fields not then in production. In these schools, whatever books and materials at hand were frequently deemed acceptable for "classroom" use, and virtually anyone available for two or three months of instruction might be invited to "teach."

> The old field schools were taught by men possessing some special qualification which made them the "observed of all observers" in the community. Sometimes the teacher was a surveyor who, after completing his work of surveying, would be induced to stay and teach a subscription school; sometimes a traveling Irishman, English- man or Yankee would pass through the county on pleasure bent and be persuaded to stop over long enough to teach a three months' school. (Sewell, 1919, p. 95)

As was the case in Virginia and Tennessee, the only seriously pursued education institutions of elite and/or denominational groups were "private" academies primarily attended by those who could afford to go. And, as in Tennessee, early attempts to establish public *county* academies ran afoul of legal issues over land ownership and taxes required to fund such academies.

> To the north of Kentucky, under the provisions of the Land Ordinance of 1785, a section of land in each township was specifically designated for the maintenance of public schools; and seventy-two sections in each of the states formed from the Northwest Territory were retained for the establishment of an institution of higher learning. The states, as they were admitted to the Union, could not depart from the plan established in the territorial act, and thus came into possession of definite amounts of land which were sold, and the proceeds of the sale were used as state funds for a public system of education. The Kentucky system of land titles and holdings on the contrary made it impossible to designate specific plats of land for public purposes. (McVey, 1949, p. 41)

Accordingly, many rural counties uninterested in building county academies, having been deeded unsalable acreage and/or unable to disentangle ownership claims of lands designated by the state legislature for schooling purposes, frequently appealed to the state for alternative land uses, or did nothing at all.

> Often there were conflicting claims, as in the case of Cumberland County. In other instances no charters were issued, but the lands designated for the county were

turned over to the common school commissioners. Now and then the county received the land but no school building was erected. In Morgan County, the county court appointed one Peter. a surveyor, to locate the seminary lands. Peter agreed to do this for as much as the land would allow. The trustees did not think much of the land; certainly they were not of the opinion that the proceeds would erect a seminary building. So they applied to the legislature for relief, and that body showed its attitude by declaring in the act "that the said lands are mostly of an inferior quality, worth but little and greatly inadequate for the purpose of erecting a suitable building as a Seminary; and that if said lands are permitted to be sold by said trustees, and the proceeds vested in the completion of the court-house of said county, the result will prove more beneficial to the inhabitants of said county, and the benevolent intentions of the law in relation thereto, more completely carried into effect. (McVey, 1949, p. 41)

As the 19th century progressed, public clamor for the adequate funding of public schooling began to grow. Reminiscent of earlier Virginia efforts, the Kentucky legislature established a Literary Fund in 1821 to help support public education, but its resources were apparently insufficient to have a great impact on most rural and poor academies/seminaries. So, too, legislation passed in 1830 formally allowed counties to establish schools if they wished, but did not compel them to do so; nor did they provide any specific monies for their establishment.

Complicating concerns for enhancing public schooling were other pressing needs perceived by citizens of the Commonwealth and the Kentucky legislature requiring attention. In other words, as the notion that state taxes would be required to establish important services, other services than schooling were typically argued as being more important. For example, Kentucky "inherited" from the U.S. Congress over $1 million in 1836, and the state legislature decided to create a "School Fund" with a large percentage of this money. Yet, by the time legislation chartering official use of such monies was put into effect, many of these dollars had already been borrowed for other purposes:

The pruning of the new School Fund opened a new chapter in the old struggle between education and internal improvements for funds in Kentucky (sic). It is not surprising that citizens of the state were interested in roads,bridges, canals, and other means of transportation. Kentucky was cut off from the east by the Appalachians and it was a long journey to the prime New Orleans market. It was unreasonable to expect either the average voter, or his leader in politics, to disdain the implications to be found in internal improvements. Kentucky was already in the throes of an economic panic. It was obvious that her leaders would cast covetous eyes at the handy School Fund. (Hackensmith, 1970, p. 68)

For all intent and purposes then, it wasn't until after 1838 that educational historians begin to talk about a real system of public education in Kentucky. As in the other states discussed, the Kentucky legislature was beginning to focus on enhancing public school facilities in the decades just before the Civil War, and in 1849 and 1855, Kentucky citizens approved tax levies for public school support.

Much of the growing sentiment in favor of making education more readily available in the commonwealth was associated with the state superintendent of education in Kentucky, who served in that post from 1847 to 1853. This was Robert J. Breckinridge, dubbed later as the "father" of Kentucky's system of public instruction. Breckinridge was a Presbyterian minister, a (Lexington) lawyer, and served at one time in the Kentucky legislature. Like many early 19th-century Kentucky leaders, Breckinridge appears to have had "Northern" connections as well as Virginia ones. Positive transformations in education that occurred during his administration as state superintendent are suggested by the claim that "in 1847 [when he became superintendent] only one in ten Kentucky children went to school; by 1850, only one in ten did not attend" (Doyle, Layson, & Thompson, 1987, p. 84).

Upon Breckinridge's leaving of the state superintendent's post, he issued a "farewell report" worthy of some quotation. For example, contrary to later conventional wisdom (a wisdom which had arguably severe implications for most rural school districts), Breckinridge claimed that smaller school districts were better districts, as they better involved parents and townspeople in schooling matters. Importantly, he also argued that educational issues and progress ought to be considered separately from other local political and economic matters, keeping the governance of education out of the county courthouse and made directly accountable to the state superintendent (a practice later adopted in Kentucky but still practiced in much of Virginia and Tennessee). These positions were put in the form of two recommendations to the legislature in his 1853 annual report:

> (1) that no district ought to be allowed to contain more than about 50 children; and (2) that all towns having a separate school system of their own ought to be permitted to report directly to the superintendent instead of circuitously through the county commissioner, as if the whole town were a single district.

> The former change would probably greatly increase the number of pupils who actually attend school, as it would necessarily greatly multiply the schools themselves . . . the latter change would relieve the schools in the towns of a great deal of wholly needless trouble and embarrassment and put them on a footing to make greater efforts to enlarge and perfect themselves. (Breckinridge, in Doyle et al. 1987, pp. 85-86)

THE CIVIL WAR IN KENTUCKY AND ITS EDUCATIONAL CONSEQUENCES

Antebellum economic and educational dynamics in Kentucky approximated those of Tennessee to a great extent, and to some degree those in Virginia. Yet, while Kentucky struggled with the race issue in its late 19th- and early 20th-century history, some of the most negative political consequences of the war seen in Virginia and Tennessee appear not to have undermined all of the schooling advances seen during the antebellum period.

In particular, while Kentucky was split on the issue of secession from the Union, and while various counties and regions of the state identified with one side or another, the state never formally withdrew from the Union, and thus was not forced later to replace its state elected leaders with a reconstruction government. Therefore, lack of money caused by the physical destruction of the war and continued internal political fights (inherited from before) were the primary roadblocks to educational gains made in the 1840s and 1850s.

> The condition of the common schools in 1867, when Superintendent of Public Instruction Zachariah Smith took office, had been critical, because of the war and the lack of funds. The tax of five cents per one hundred dollars of property was producing only $185, 000 annually. Smith insisted that the assessment should be increased to around $740,000 annually, an amount calculated to keep the schools open for five months during the year. This would allow teachers from nineteen dollars to twenty-five dollars per month in pay. It was estimated that the sum would mean an annual pupil expenditure of $2.37. (Tapp & Klotter, 1977, pp. 105-106)

Importantly, the histories of education in late 19th-century Kentucky sound somewhat different than those of Virginia or Tennessee. As suggested earlier, state educational historians tell us there that rejection of reconstruction governments also implied rejection of most schooling reforms. In Kentucky, however, there seems to be no real break in the "evolutionary" progress of school developments, for educational histories continue to talk of substantive governance and economic "improvements" in the 1870s, 1880s, and 1890s. That is, while some trends seen in Virginia and Tennessee (like increased enrollments in White academies, philanthropically financed Negro industrial schools, etc.) all occur in Kentucky, histories of education in the latter appear to document somewhat more internal debates between governors, the legislature, state and county superintendents, and citizens over the direction and control of public schools, rather than complete rejection of any reconstruction government's agendas for school reform. For example, many well respected state leaders, including former Confederate sympathizers, appeared on the inside of discussions of school reform in the decades right after the Civil War:

> The General Assembly failed in 1880 to pass a comprehensive bill to reorganize the state's common school system. Many prominent friends of education consequently began to agitate the question to arouse public interest. A state central committee of prominent men was appointed to outline a program looking for legislative action (to) "devise a plan for a complete educational organization throughout the state."

The committee presented its report to Gov. James P. Knott, who in turn referred it to the General Assembly, which enacted a good portion of it into the Common School Law of May 10, 1884.

The new law set up a general plan of school organization on the state, county, and district levels. It provided a uniform system. The measure defined the length of the school year, duties of state and county boards of education, and duties of the trustees. It forbade sectarianism in the public schools, outlined the duties and liabilities of examining boards, and explained the method of tax collection. The law also regulated the course of study, provided free textbooks for indigent children, and required local reports. It authorized for the first time a state teachers' association. (Tapp & Klotter, 1977, p. 112)

EDUCATION IN THE EARLY
20TH CENTURY

While Kentucky school codes and guidelines on paper appear to have changed dramatically during the last three decades of the 19th century, it still appears to be the case that (White) academies throughout the state were a major force in schooling there, as were the numerous small colleges and universities. Perhaps only in the cities of Lexington, Maysville, and (especially) Louisville were public elementary and secondary schools systematically operating as aggressive public school advocates had hoped, although the history of rural public institutions is probably less well understood than those in Kentucky's cities.

Negro children, in particular, do not appear to have greatly benefitted by advances in Kentucky public education during the late 19th century. One major "Yankee" innovation/imposition on the state was the Freedman's Bureau which came into former border states as well as defeated Confederate states to help uplift all freed slaves. And even though Kentucky's Negro population was much less than that of either Virginia or Tennessee, many Freedman's Bureau schools (approximately 400) were set up there. Apparently, however, the violent opposition among the White population seen in Kentucky to such schools discouraged many civic and church groups from further aiding in this cause in Kentucky (Tapp & Klotter, 1977).

Yet, according to most observers, some educational progress had been made in Kentucky public schools during the 19th century, and when figures like school attendance and literacy rates were compared among the Southern states, Kentucky usually fared rather well, in some categories, almost as well as the national average (Tapp & Klotter, 1977). However, by contemporary standards it wasn't until 1908 that Kentucky's system of public instruction began to resemble what exists today.

Under the impetus of the aroused (public) interest in education, the General Assembly of 1908 abolished the local district as the unit of school administration and set up the county as the unit of administration. . . . This act brought about three outstanding fundamental changes in the administration of rural schools. The district as a unit of administration was abolished and the county made the unit. Local taxation for the support of schools was made compulsory. After the passage of that act local taxes for the support of schools were increased from time to time until the major portion of the revenue came from local taxes. The act made it compulsory upon the county board of education to establish one or more county high schools for the benefit of the children of the rural districts. Thus, after a struggle of seventy years since the establishment of the public school system, the state acknowledged its obligation to the rural children in the field of secondary education. (Hackensmith, 1970, p. 93)

As in each of the states discussed so far, other significant educational issues and battles emerged in Kentucky before World War II. Teacher certification requirements, for example, were changed several times during this period, and normal schools for the training of teachers became a prominent addition to the higher education scene in the state. So, too, further consideration of the roles and responsibilities of county superintendents and school boards appears to have preoccupied the state department of education and the General Assembly.

A number of what we might now term *equality of educational opportunity* developments also occurred in Kentucky in the first decades of the 20th century. On the "positive" side, public high schools for Negroes increased dramatically after the legislation of 1908 mentioned above, although it is unclear that the General Assembly was initially concerned when it passed this legislation about the plight of Negro students. Of course, provision of transportation to county Negro secondary schools was probably never provided by individual counties, and an essentially industrial arts curriculum was probably the norm. So too, the passage of the Day Act in 1904 specifically prohibited the presence of Negro students in schools for Whites. Such legislation set back the process of voluntary integration efforts in schools like Berea College, which had an integrated program in effect long before the state ruled it illegal to do so.

A short-lived but probably quite effective educational innovation in (rural) Kentucky was the "moonlight school" movement championed by Rowan County Superintendent Cora Wilson Stuart. Responding to national illiteracy data (which portrayed Kentucky adults as having greater than average rates of adult illiteracy), various philanthropic organizations and the state department of education helped finance a massive adult education program, which typically operated out of rural school buildings and relied on voluntary efforts of county school teachers between 1911 and 1920 (Estes, 1988).

Another "progressive" development in Kentucky in the 1930s (and subsequently) focused on the perceived inequities between county and independent school districts in terms of per-pupil expenditures. In 1930 the General Assembly passed legislation earmarked to supplement teacher salaries in the poorest of school districts, but this law was soon judged unconstitutional by the state court of appeals. Therefore, a constitutional amendment was passed just before World War II which allowed the state board to differentially supplement school district budgets in districts with lowest property values (the taxes upon which were a primary source of local school revenues).

Furthermore, school consolidation and "appropriate" school size and governance patterns has concerned Kentucky state legislatures and the state boards of education in every decade of the 20th century, as appears to have been the case in each of the other states of this report. In Frank McVey's analysis of educational progress in the state, the movement towards larger, more efficient, and more professionally administered school districts is suggested by his analysis of political debates in the 1920s, 1930s, and 1940s. McVey's position on the duties and selection of county school officers is not hard to interpret:

> Considerable advancement can be seen during the past thirty years in the development of a better school administration. The district system hung on long after the county had become a unit for taxation, legal procedure, administration of justice, and the execution of the law. . . . The whittling down of school districts went on until the legislature, in 1920, created a county school board of five members elected by the people from the county at large. Nominations were made by petition, and the county superintendent was selected by the board; more important still, the teachers were nominated by the county superintendent and elected by the county board.
>
> The enemies of the new law were able to secure modification in 1922; after amendment in that year, the county was divided into five districts with one member elected from a district every five years. Again, two years later, the power of nominating and of placing teachers was taken from the county superintendent and given to the district trustees. (McVey, 1949, p. 241)

Nor are McVey's opinions on school district consolidation.:

> In the law existing before 1933, there were three types of school districts - county, independent, and city districts which were organized in the first, second, third and fourth class cities. Only two types of districts have been recognized since the code was adopted by the legislature. In cases where the independent graded districts are continued, they must have at least 250 children of school age in the district according to the school census. The purpose of the law is to draw into the county unit all independent graded districts as rapidly as possible That this process is going on is (shown by the drop in the number of school districts). The change in four years indicates a contrast of 305 districts in 1935 against 262 existing in 1939 and 256 in 1941. (McVey, 1949, p. 242)

McVey, who was himself an important state education reform leader and a president of the University of Kentucky, also talked about the beneficial progression of school consolidation within county systems, and especially noted the positive influence of (first) WPA projects (and later) improved highway systems in helping to facilitate this movement during the depression era and in the decades that followed. In particular, he noted with satisfaction the decline of rural one-room schools from over 5,000 in 1936 to 4,383 as early as 1939; and he credited state and federal school- and road-building efforts of the 1930s and 1940s with revolutionizing the possibilities for secondary education in the state. School consolidation themes, of course, have played heavily in each of our earlier case studies; and the direct impact of the WPA on school attendance areas was discussed at length in our look at Clinch County, Tennessee. In the case of Kentucky, McVey had this to say:

> Time has been a factor in the development of the Kentucky educational system as it now stands, for an individualistic people were not to be easily deprived of the district, one-teacher, one-room school. The politicians were not particularly keen about a consolidated system, and those who trafficked in teacher placement were even less pleased. New expense would be incurred for the added buildings, and the bus operation required by any consolidation plan would increase the cost of common schooling. Although at first the consolidated school idea moved slowly, in the last ten years it has gained ground rapidly. One reason for this change has been the help given by the Federal government to school building projects by the WPA and the PWA.. . . In the period 1930-1939, there were 1,758 school projects undertaken in Kentucky, which cost $24,708,627; of this sum, the Federal government contributed $9,708,921.

Yet the location of new and consolidated schools in Kentucky, as in each of the other states discussed earlier, posed special problems:

> The State Department of Education rejoiced, as did the people, in the advance-ment of the school system; but an orderly and wise development of consolidated schools was not always possible. School boards wanted school buildings located on main highways without regard to centers of population. . . . [Yet], as roads have improved, the location of school buildings has been become a matter not merely of paved highways but of educational purpose based on the needs of communities served by the schools. Sometimes the location of a school building has been decided on by the ownership of real estate; but as a professional view of education comes to dominate, these problems are determined more and more on their merits. (McVey, 1949, pp. 243-244)

SCHOOL REFORMS IN THE MODERN ERA

Observers of school improvement and reform in Kentucky suggest that, right up until World War II, positive things were occurring in the state with regard to remediating educational inadequacies and inequities around it. Unfortunately, the war appears to have deprived school reform advocates/legislators of both teachers and school transportation equipment necessary for continued upgrading and consolidating the state's schools. Published sources (like McVey) argue that many teachers either joined the armed services or obtained better paying jobs in war-related industries. Meanwhile, expenses for school transportation increased exponentially, as school districts were in direct competition for transportation resources (e.g., tires and fuels) with the U.S. Armed Forces.

In the period after the war, several extensive studies of the problems of Kentucky schools led to yet new rounds of legislation in support of educational reform. In fact, according to former Dean of the College of Education at the University of Kentucky (and later State Superintendent of Public Instruction) Lyman Ginger, the problems of public education in the state have been studied to the point of exhaustion:

> Education in Kentucky has been studied so many times by so many citizens, teachers, legislators, and foundations that mention of another study brings forth hoots of derision and the raised eyebrows of skepticism. "Study it to death" and "gathering dust on the shelves" are but two of the phrases associated with studies of education and its problems. (Ginger, 1987, p. 313)

As a result of national trends (like school integration) and various state education self studies, school reform legislation has occurred throughout the period from 1950 to the present day. Inequities between systems led in the 1920s to state supplements for poorer school districts, and in 1954 the Minimum Foundation Program was introduced in Kentucky, which substantially altered local vs. state funding formulas for Kentucky schools. While each of the county systems discussed in this report relies heavily on state supplements to local tax dollars, Kentucky as a state ranks among the nation's leaders in funding equalization monies to poorer districts. And Kentucky was among the first in the Southeast to institutionalize such a program.

However, a study completed in 1960 for the state legislature found that patronage and inefficiency were significant factors in many rural school districts, and proposed reforms which were targeted at making schools more academically and administratively accountable. Eastern Kentucky lawyer and famed Appalachian author Harry Caudill chaired the review committee and urged numerous recommendations, some of which found their way into state law.

> Caudill's committee made twenty specific recommendations. Some of these recommendations, such as empowering the attorney general "to proceed in Franklin Circuit Court (where the state capital lies) against local school board members and superintendents who misuse public funds or otherwise violate the law," conducting annual audits of school accounts, and raising the qualifications of candidates for the office of school board member, were eventually adopted.

A recommendation that the foundation program law "be amended to define clearly and specifically the content of educational services which the General Assembly wishes to guarantee in every district" was not addressed until the School Improvement Act was passed in 1978. It was refined and strengthened in the essential skills and academic bankruptcy programs enacted in 1984. (Ginger, 1987, p. 322)

According to Ginger and a number of other school reform advocates, the variously directed school improvement initiatives of 1954, 1978, and 1984 gave new direction and guidelines for all Kentucky's school systems. And as we shall soon see, operating within these guidelines appears to be an important concern of Cave County schools, for their system is very conscious of external review and performing to the letter of these various laws.

With the enactment of the School Improvement Act of 1978, the three components of a foundation for academic excellence were in place in Kentucky. The money was allocated through the Minimum Foundation Program. The academic programs were determined by the School Improvement Act. Academic performance, the outcome component of the two "input" components, was also addressed in the 1978 legislation.

For the first time in Kentucky, a statewide testing program was ordered by state law in grades three, five, seven, and ten. The act also ordered that national norms be used to compare the performance of Kentucky's students with that of students in other states. Through the testing program, Kentucky's educators finally had the information they needed to make sound decisions on instruction. (Ginger, 1987, pp. 329-330)

Yet the 1988 and 1989 school years found "sound educational decisions" apparently not occuring in at least two of Eastern Kentucky's county school systems. In one of these cases, the state board of education declared the district academically "bankrupt," based on achievement test scores and dropout rates. In the second case, state-run audits discovered (apparently) that foundation money was not being spent in accord with guidelines previously mentioned. In each of these two districts the state department of education was "providing assistance" to local boards in efforts to remedy inadequacies during our fieldwork in Cave County.

Another early 1980s development that suggested the jaundiced view many rural Kentuckians appear to have on increasing local contributions to schooling was the passage of Senate Bill 44. This legislation placed a mandatory 4% cap on increased (local) educational spending within each school district. In other words, school systems in the state (before 1990) could increase a local school budget (as set by local boards of education) by no more than 4% per year without a popular vote on increasing local taxes. Given that the source of most local income for school funding is local property taxes, and given that property values in Kentucky generally rise somewhat each year, SB 44 had the net effect of actually lowering tax assessments in many school districts each year, for maintaining a previous year's tax rate would frequently elevate a local districts current budget based merely on the rise in real estate values.

To illustrate, the Cave County Board of Education actually lowered its 1989 tax rate from that it assessed in 1988 in order to keep within state guidelines. According to the superintendent, of Cave County's 1989–1990 school budget of $7,243,000, only 4.75% came from local taxes. Most of the district's expenditures come from state sources (72.2%), with federal sources accounting for approximately 12.6%, and interest, building rentals, etc. generating the remaining dollars.

As in each of the other districts covered in this report, winners of Cave County Board of Education elections have typically run on a no-tax-increase platform. And lowering of tax rates made possible by SB44 enabled all incumbent board members to live up to campaign promises. Importantly, the 1989 decision to lower tax rates was all the more interesting given that, in 1988, a decision was made to build an expensive sports complex by the school system, which was to cost $1.7 million.

Quite recently, however, the Minimum Foundation Program (earlier discussed) was found unconstitutional, as a legal challenge to the "efficient" funding of state school districts was ruled upon favorably by a state court in Summer 1989. As had been the case in each of the other rural and poor school systems discussed, Cave County schools were involved in educational equity activities during the course of our fieldwork. And in Summer 1989, the Kentucky court(s) ruled in favor of 66 county systems (including Cave County): that educational opportunities were unequal in the state and would require a complete restructuring, not just a reworking of the state equalization funding formulas. Rather, the court mandated that it was the responsibility of the state legislature to completely revamp the state's educational system. The results of this mandate, and their potential impact on Cave County schools, are the focus of some discussion in Chapter 6 of this book, as this court decision occurred after our initial fieldwork in Cave County.

CAVE COUNTY, KENTUCKY: ITS ECONOMIC AND SOCIAL DEVELOPMENT

Cave County is a rural county in a relatively sparsely populated area in the south central portion Kentucky. Its current population (15,402 in 1980) is also fairly homogeneous, being approximately 92% White and 8% Black. Historically, Cave County has been an agriculturally dependent county, and over half of all current residents are still involved to some degree in farming, principally dairying and burley tobacco production.

Geographically, Cave County lies several counties over from what many consider to be the most agriculturally advantageous Bluegrass area of the state, and in the Pennyrile region:

> The large area lying at the south end of the central plain, of which the Bluegrass region is the northern section, is known as the Pennyrile. . . . The eastern portions of the region rise 600 and 700 feet above sea level, but they drop gradually on the west to about 400 or 500 feet, as they approach the Purchase in the southwest and the western coal fields along the Ohio. The streams cut broad valleys except in the karst or sinkhole areas, where only larger streams flow on the surface. . . . Waters, either surface or underground, are abundant. In the underground drainage courses are thousands of miles of subterranean passages. (WPA, 1947, pp. 11-12)

Now officially located in the Nolin River Development District, the county covers a land area of over 400 square miles. The terrain is gently rolling, with some rough and hilly portions with "mostly productive soil." It is also geographically located in what is known as the Central Kentucky Karst, a limestone belt of underground passages and crystalline formations. Of major geographic and economic importance is the fact that a famous national park is (partially) located in Southwest Cave County; this park contains one of the world's largest cave systems, which has historically been a major national tourist attraction.

Paradoxically, Cave County seems to be a place with much concern for its history and has an active county historical society. Yet no comprehensive county history exists, and much of the activity of the Cave County Historical Society seems given over to collecting anecdotal accounts and oral histories of earlier times, and to comprehensive compilations of genealogical origins of county residents since the early 19th century. So, too, as was the case in two of three other sites visited for this report, most of Cave County's official records of its early history were destroyed in the courthouse fire in the late 1920s. Yet one local "lay" historian spent much of his twentieth century life attempting to piece together histories of the county in the 19th and early 20th centuries.

Unfortunately, there is also no comprehensive history of Cave County schools even as adequate as the histories overviewed in previous chapters of this document. On the other hand, there are numerous personal descriptions of early one- and two-room school experiences included in the archives of the Cave County Historical Society, one relatively brief overview of the county's educational history prepared by a former Cave County educator, and one detailed history of Memorial Consolidated High School. The latter two documents figure prominently in later school-related discussions.

While settlement in the county first occurred in the very late 18th century, Cave County was politically formed in 1819 from parts of two other counties. The caves, which have historically and currently influenced the county's development for almost 200 years, were first discovered by Europeans in the early 1800s. In terms of early nonagricultural "economic development," Bear Wallow in the southeastern portion of the county, and Deer Run in the western portion, appear to have served as a early "resorts" or campsites for central Kentucky bear/game hunters in the first several decades of the 19th century. Also, mineral deposits discovered in several underground and creek locations supplied powder-mills used for munitions works during the war of 1812. As well, iron ore deposits discovered in several county sites enabled the construction of several short-lived iron furnace operations. Agriculturally speaking, we are told that the northern half of the county was the first to be settled and cultivated, as the southern portion of the county (below the Ralston River) was reputed initially to be strongly defended Indian territory.

While Cave County is rural, it is probably the least "remote" of the four discussed in this book. Historically, several Cave County towns appear always to have fallen on several north/south or east/west highways. As Louisville, Kentucky, and Nashville, Tennessee, were two of the largest 19th-century cities on the western frontier in their respective states, a great deal of commercial and personal travel between them (and points further north and south) has occurred during the past two centuries, and towns and cities serving as way-stations between them, including several in Cave County, probably owe much of their early (and continued) existence to this traffic.

For example, in the early 19th century a major mode of travel on the western frontier was by stagecoach. And the stage line ran through the old Louisville-Nashville "trace" in Cave County. The towns of Wayland and Rogersville both probably owe much of their 19th century development to their strategic north–south travel location, in addition to development associated with their agricultural marketing importance. Later, rail travel was an important link between cities on the main river arteries. For example, Louisville was a major commercial hub on the Ohio River throughout the 19th century, and connections to points south were an important aspect of its regional development. Importantly, one of America's major rail lines connected Louisville and Nashville via Bowling Green: the famous L(ouisville) and N(ashville) railroad. And, the (then) small agricultural towns of Craddockville, Buckners (Station) and Marion were really "put on the map" as important stops on the L&N line following the Civil War.

North/south travel by the early 20th century also increasingly involved the automobile and an emerging highway system. And once again, major north–south arteries connecting Louisville and Nashville via Elizabethtown (to the north) and Bowling Green (to the south) ran through Cave County. Importantly, not one but two separate major north/south routes were built there before World War II. These are 17E, which passes through the towns of Linwood, Wayland, and Rogersville; and 17W, which passes through the towns of Marion, Craddockville, and Bear Cave. Later, when the interstate highway (I67) was built through Cave County in the 1960s, its route paralleled 17W and provided easy access to Marion, Craddockville and Bear Cave. And as agriculture went into decline by the mid-20th century, almost all new nonagricultural economic development initiatives occurred in these three towns.

Meanwhile, the three earlier prominent towns along 17E and the other state highways have slowly declined during the 20th century. Even the numerous "mom and pop" tourist-related industries (i.e., motels, restaurants, souvenir stands, etc.) on 17W (as one approaches the national park) have gone into decline. The interstate exits at Bear Cave and Cave City (in the next county south) appear to have redirected all tourist traffic into developments right at those exits, and major restaurant and motel chains have seemingly taken over the lion's share of local tourism.

Much of the north–south story of Cave County remains historically and ethnographically focused around the Ralston River, which is an important dividing line in Cave County. Like most rivers in the state, Ralston originates somewhere in the eastern (mountainous) region of Kentucky and finds its way eventually into the Ohio River to the west. Furthermore, as the Ralston River approaches the Ohio through Western Kentucky, it becomes increasingly navigable, and was once a waterway of some commercial significance in the western part of the state.

In Cave County, however, river commerce appears to have been only marginal in the mid-19th century. To be sure, some agriculture and/or timber markets to the west/south must have been reached via the river in the first half of the 19th century, but the north–south rail connection appears to have overshadowed river traffic in Cave County relatively early. Instead, the Ralston River appears to have been almost as important regionally because it was an *obstacle* during the mid- and late 19th century to north–south travel, rather than because facilitated movement to the west.

CAVE COUNTY AND THE CIVIL WAR

The Civil War was a dramatic event in Cave County although perhaps not as forcefully remembered as it appears to be in Charlotte County, Virginia. On the other hand, continued contemporary antagonism between several communities in the county probably originated during the Civil War and Reconstruction eras, when being from either the north or south side of the river had deep symbolic consequences.

As mentioned earlier, Kentucky was a border state in the Civil War and did not secede from the Union. Yet the reason the state did not secede appears due to the vast split on such a course of action. For example, the 1860s governor of the state was avowedly in favor of joining the Confederacy, while the state legislature appears to have been "more cautious" (Cave County Historical Society, 1984). Thus, the state chose to remain "neutral" during the war, yet with large volunteer armies from different regions of Kentucky fighting on different sides.

Importantly, one of Cave County's most prominent citizens was a plantation owner and, first, a prominent leader in the pro-Cconfederacy forces at the state level, then a general in the Confederate Army, a governor of the state of Kentucky at the end of the 19th century, and finally a Democratic vice-presidential nominee. In all of these many endeavors, he clearly identified himself with the cause of the Confederacy and state's rights, even during his last days as a political leader in the 1890s.

As an armed but neutral state, military forces from both sides in the Civil War located armies just outside of Kentucky for most of 1861, seemingly looking for some transgression by the other side as an opportunity to secure the state from the opposition. And even within the state, quasiofficial standing armies were sponsored by sympathizers of one (external) side or the other in state government.

With regard to the Cave County, the north–south connection between Louisville and Nashville was deemed strategically important, particularly with the newly established rail system. Both sides, in other words, viewed inroads either north or south as dependent on supply lines. And control of the rail link through Central Kentucky was apparently viewed as crucial by each of them.

Accordingly, a Confederate advance into Kentucky in late 1861 led the state legislature to request federal assistance in the fall of that year, thus formally linking Kentucky to the Union side for the first time.

> The struggle for the possession of Kentucky was thus commenced. By November 1st, 1861, approximately one-third of the State was in possession of the Confederacy which had established a provisional State capital at Russellville; the Secessionists of the state having refused to recognize he act which had committed Kentucky to the Union. They maintained that the same was an unfair political coup in no way indicative of the true sentiments of the inhabitants at large. The Confederate lines extended from Columbus through Craddockville to Cumberland Gap. The Confederate Army headquarters were at Bowling Green. (CCHS, 1984, pp. 2-3)

To briefly review the Civil War story of Cave County, Confederate forces interested in expanding their hold in the state were located south of Cave County in Russellville and sought to move against the Union forces headquartered in Louisville. Meanwhile, the Union forces located north of Cave County in Louisville (the division army headquarters for four states) were interested in running the Confederate forces out. Ostensibly, army headquarters were located in both of these towns/cities because of the L&N railroad and its potential to serve as a supply line for advances into the other's territory.

Control of the bridges lying on the L&N (and other roads) were deemed essential to both sides, and the (just built) bridge over the Ralston River at Craddockville was one of these. Craddockville up until that time was a small village in the center of the County, with a population of fewer than 300. Initially, Confederate forces occupied Craddockville, but the Union army rapidly organized to counter the Confederate threat, and a force was sent against them to gain control of the bridge.

In their retreat across the river, the Confederates attempted to blow up the Craddockville bridge, but only damaged it. Thereupon, Union forces securing the rail line and the bridge set up camp on the south side of the river at Rowlett's Station, and a Union Army construction crew began to repair the damage, the expectation being that a general advance by the main Union army would occur shortly.

Unhappy with their loss of the bridge, Confederate troops staged an attack on the defending Union soldiers in mid-December 1861, and while they were temporarily victorious, they were eventually run off by superior federal forces. By early 1862, the Union Army had control of Craddockville and the partially repaired rail bridge across the Ralston River. And, judging by the temporary fortifications and numbers of troops assigned to defend the bridge, it appears as though the Union General wanted to maximize his strategic advantage at Craddockville. *Harper's Magazine* described the situation thusly:

> The wooden substitute for the central portion of the iron railroad bridge over the Ralston river, destroyed by rebels, was at last finished on Tuesday, and the evening before last, a locomotive made an experimental trip to the south bank. . . . Railway facilities to the south bank were a conditio sine qua non of a successful campaign in the southern part of the state, and an advance of our troops could not be thought of without them, in view of the general spoilation of the counties now under rebel control of everything in the shape of food for man or beast, and the indispensable necessity of ready means of supplying the immense columns about moving on the enemy. (CCHS, 1984, p. 5)

In the weeks and months following the battle at Buckner's Station, the Union Army drove deep into southern Kentucky, and forced Confederate troops out of the state. Meanwhile, federal forces further solidified their fortification of the Ralston River bridge at Craddockville in attempts to insure their pipeline for supplies, materials, and information behind their advancing armies.

By Fall 1862, Union forces were deep into Tennessee and moving to the east, having won several pitched battles (including the battle of Shiloh). According to the Cave County Historical Society, a major reason why the federal forces had been able to strike so surely and swiftly in Central Tennessee was their control of the L&N railroad lines. Apparently, however, seeing how far overextended the Union Army was in the south, the Confederate leader and his army (along with other famous generals like John Hunt Morgan) undertook a northern campaign to occupy Kentucky and capture the Union army headquarters in Louisville.

Part of the confederate strategy, it appears, was to cut the Union Army's supply line to the south enroute to Louisville, and retaking (or destroying) the Ralston River bridge at Craddockville was part of this agenda. As the Confederate force approached the bridge in mid-September, the garrison defending it appealed to Louisville (approximately 70 miles north) for reinforcements, which arrived just in time for the first round of the Battle of Craddockville. In the meantime, however, Confederate forces had come in from the north and destroyed much of the rail between Craddockville, Elizabethtown, and Louisville.

In the final analysis, the battle at Craddockville for control of the Ralston River bridge lasted several days and ended with the surrender of the Union garrison stationed there. Apparently, the Union position was also compromised because the strategic northern side of the river was held by the Confederates, as advised/supervised by the native Cave County general earlier mentioned.

All told, there were over 350 soldiers from both sides either killed or wounded in defense of the Craddockville bridge in mid-September 1862. Yet Confederate encampment at Craddockville after their success did not last long; for before the Confederates could continue their advance upon Louisville from Craddockville, the Union Army returned via Bowling Green to confront the rebel forces. Two weeks later, one of the largest pitched battles seen in Kentucky between the North and South was fought between these armies approximately 50 miles east of Craddockville. In this confrontation, thousands of men on both sides were killed or wounded, and Confederate hopes for gaining Kentucky all but abandoned.

20TH-CENTURY ECONOMIC AND DEMOGRAPHIC DEVELOPMENTS

A number of large estates, but primarily small farms, existed in Cave County up until the period of the Civil War. According to historical documents earlier cited, most slave holders (and later, Confederate sympathizers) were located south of the Ralston River, while landowners in the slightly more rugged northern portion of the county appear to have had smaller farms and were more oriented to small-scale farming and several industrial pursuits (like iron smelting).

Yet whatever agriculture patterns existed before the war appear to have been undermined by the siege of the County during 1861 and 1862, with opposing forces appropriating most livestock and burning fences and outbuildings for survival; enlistment of many men in the various Kentucky volunteer divisions; and the emancipation of slaves in the County before the war's end. So too, the legacy of property and life loss appears to have led to bitter resentment among the County's people: and it was localized at the Ralston River. That is, to this day (we are told), families north of the river actively dislike families south of the river as at least partly an aftermath of the Civil War. And, we have been told, most Cave Countians north of the river still identify, shop, and recreate in and around the Louisville area, while residents south of the river are oriented towards Bowling Green and Nashville. As one County resident phrased it, "the Iron Curtain can't hold a candle to the division in Cave County which exists north and south of the Ralston River." Others refer to the county-wide schism by suggesting that the Ralston River represents the Cave County equivalent of the "Great Wall of China," where parents admonish their children not even to associate with those from the wrong side of the river if at all possible.

Returning to early 20th-century economic developments, while we have uncovered no direct account of daily life in Cave County just before the turn of the century (or details of how the north–south split was "institutionalized" during this period), it seems logical to assume that the County's reemerging and increasingly prominent rail and highway transportation systems (by the end of the 19th century) supported relatively stable agricultural developments, as judged by the statistics in Tables KY-1–4. So too, since a "favorite son" of the County was governor of the state late in the 19th century, we surmise that the County was well treated by the state government during the years he was in power.

Symbolic, perhaps, of the emergence of Cave County as a viable turn-of-the-century agricultural marketplace was the transformation (visible in photo collections) of small pre-Civil-War villages like Wayland, Craddockville, and Rogersville into recognizable towns with wide main streets (i.e., what would become 17E and 17W) and two story brick public and private buildings.

Furthermore, many one- and two-room schools were built in the county in the early decades of the 20th century, which suggests some emerging prosperity

KY-1. EMPLOYMENT INDUSTRIES.

	YEAR					
	1930	1940	1950	1960	1970	1980
Total persons employed 14 or 16 years old.	5,401	4,399	5,209	4,504	4,679	5,070
% in AG.	76	75.6	64.4	47.3	26.5	22.0
% in Mining	–	.74	.6	–	.85	1.0
% in MANFG	4.6	2.0	2.9	22.0	21.0	23.0
% in TRANS/COMM	2.6	1.5	1.8	2.3	2.7	6.0
% in RETAIL	4.8	6.0	17.5	11.0	7.5	13.0
% in FIN/INS	.5	.5	.72	.82	.57	1.5
% in SERVICES	8.2	9.2	15.0	11.2	17.2	17.8

KY-2. INCOME CHARACTERISTICS.

	YEAR					
CHARACTERISTICS:	1930	1940	1950	1960	1970	1980
Median income of:						
All families	–	–	1,221	2,436	5,957	11,509
All households	–	–	–	–	–	9,672
Families with own-children 18 years						
Married couples	–	–	3,600	–	–	13,201
Female householder (no husband)	–	–	–	–	–	6,528

KY-3. POPULATION CHARACTERISTICS.

	YEAR								
	1900	1910	1920	1930	1940	1950	1960	1970	1980
Total Popln	18,390	18,173	18,544	16,169	17,239	15,321	14,119	13,980	15,402
Male	–	–	9,501	8,356	8,964	7,883	–	–	7,567
Female	–	–	9,043	7,813	8,275	7,438	–	–	7,835
White	16,170	16,161	16,828	14,751	15,637	13,866	12,542	14,173	
Black	2,220	1,991	1,706	1,403	1,620	1,455	1,512	1,365	1,211

similar to that earlier discussed in Charlotte County, Virginia. In particular, there had emerged no fewer than seven small towns in Cave County by the 1930s with either their own "graded" schools and/or their own town high schools; and in each of the other counties so far discussed, aggressive school construction/consolidation programs were clearly associated with economic growth in the days before state equalization funds made many educational programs possible.

CAVE COUNTY SCHOOLS: SOME EARLY HISTORY

The first grammar schools in Cave County appear to have approximated those earlier profiled in Charlotte County, Virginia. Itinerant teachers would enter a community unannounced "and make the rounds with a written contract binding each subscriber to pay a stipulated sum per pupil, for a term, usually three months." In 1822, under state mandates discussed earlier, the county commissioners created 16 districts in an ostensible effort to encourage communities to establish schools.

KY-4. LABOR CHARACTERISITICS.

	YEAR				
	1940	1950	1960	1970	1980
Labor Force.					
Persons 16 yrs and older	12,273	10,375	10,907	9,709	11,475
Male 16 yrs and older	6,409	5,143	5,642	4,661	5,542
% in labor Force	83.6	80.0	80.6	71.0	57.2
Females 16 yrs and older	5,864	5,232	5,256	5,048	5,933
% in labor force	7.7	17.4	14.2	32.0	35.0
Females 16 yrs/older (with children 18 yrs)	–	–	–	1,058	1,273
% in labor force	–	–	–	42.0	50.2

Overall, however, the on-again–off-again pattern of educational acceptance among rural residents seen in the state appears to have had its counterpart in the attitudes of Cave Countians toward public schools. State historian Thomas Clark maintains that an "agrarian ideology" diminished the emphasis on schools in Kentucky, coupled with the fact that much of the wealth from natural resources and staple crops historically left the state and thus had no local "multiplier effects" (Clark, 1985, p. 188). Later, additional problems arose over time with the issues of desegregation and consolidation (to be discussed shortly).

Following the 1822 division of the county into 16 school districts, the year 1838 saw for the first time some very limited state funding for actual school facilities ($850 per county), and the state guaranteed provision that individual districts could tax their residents (subject to their vote) for education. Yet only a few of Cave County's districts in fact established schools, while wealthy families continued the Virginia practice of eschewing public institutions in favor of private seminaries/academies.

Before the Civil War, a number of local academies did in fact educate the children of wealthy Cave Countians, as well as some from nearby communities:

One of the oldest Cave County academies whose origin probably dates to pre-civil war days was the   Institute located north of Wayland at the site now known as   Church. It is now known that this old church building and the hall above was used for classrooms at least during part of the history of the school. Closely associated with   was   Seminary for girls located north of   on the west of what is now 17E.   , established in 1892, was probably a type of finishing school for girls.

And there were several other private tuition schools in and around Cave County. Importantly, as the above suggests, various such private schools in the county and in those contiguous to it were the only secondary schools available for Cave County children until after 1908. Most probably, such schools were liberal arts oriented and viewed as preparatory for college (at least for boys).

As well, there existed an institute in Craddockville whose evolution appears somewhat similar to that of the one earlier discussed in Clinch County, Tennessee; that is, an institute which was privately operated until it was taken over and operated as a public secondary school:

> During [the late 1800s] Ralston River Institute at Craddockville, was a two-room school. [Later, the] Ralston River Collegiate Institute was a two room frame structure which stood on the grounds where the old Craddockville High School now stands. This school of about three main rooms was called a college, offering four-year courses in English, science, mathematics, history, and Latin. Bachelor of Arts or Bachelor of Science degrees were issued to graduates. Tuition for a 19-week term was from $15 to $20.00. Board was offered in homes at $2.25 per week, excluding laundry.. . . The school ceased to be, with the establishment of the Craddockville Grade and High School in 1912.

As in the cases of Virginia and Tennessee, part of the reason why tuition academies continued to exist in Cave County was that wealthy landowners did not want to pay to educate poor children, and that poor parents resisted notions that more than rudimentary literacy skills were required to live an agrarian lifestyle. So, too, fear of racial integration appears in late 19th-century opposition to the provision of public schools for Cave County children. In point of fact, the initial flowering of pro-public school sentiments in Kentucky was argued to be a direct casualty of the war between the states.

Importantly, sentiments expressed in a series of editorials published in the *Cave County News* (in 1886) seem to substantiate such an interpretation of this dynamic among many rural Kentucky counties in the late 19th century. One of these editorials lambasted the Republican candidate for state congress, and his support for a major federal education reform bill then under consideration. This bill "provided for the annual distribution of certain sums to States and Territories in proportion to their illiterates over ten years of age, as determined by the Secretary of the Interior." It also required the teaching of certain subjects, and that there be no discrimination on the basis of race as far as the distribution of funds. However, the October 13, 1886 *Cave County News* argued:

> Once allow the Federal Government control in the common schools of the country and they cease to be a blessing to the people of the South. Such an event would be the sure precursor of mixed schools, though it would not affect those sections where the Negro does not reside.

The next year (January 5) the *News* editor described with apparent disdain a congregation of several "Colored" men who had come to the courthouse to meet with White trustees in order to have their children's right to an equal education met. Yet, as the 19th century progressed, there appeared both a decreasing reluctance in the *Cave County News* towards accepting the possibilities of public schooling, yet continuously expressed concerns over increasing taxation and the need for federal aid.

One long-time county educator may have summarized general county sentiments on such issues as he remembered early educational dynamics in Cave County:

> For some time after the war, negro schools were supported by taxing of the property of negroes. White property taxes could only be spent on white schools. Each district levy was by vote of the people. Some districts were reluctant to support free schools, often going without schools rather than pay the price. When the state money ran out, the term was shortened. Often the progressive-minded people made up, by subscription, enough to complete a term of six months. . . .

> About the turn of the century it became the ambition of the County (Superintendent) to build a school within walking distance of each child. A farmer would donate a plot of land usually near a spring of water and the Board of Education would split a district, appoint a trustee, and erect a building. This was considered a progressive era. By the mid-twenties the number of schools reached approximately 75. A community was identified by the name of its school. Names usually originated as the result of the nearness of some physical feature, for example, Rocky Hill, High Hickory, Chestnut Grove.

This aforementioned history of Cave County Schools also introduced the suggestion of corruption and patronage there earlier this century. It talked of bribing trustees for jobs and a failure to take a proper census, the census of course being the mechanism by which the state partially reimbursed local districts for educational costs. As suggested earlier, the possibility of "padding" the number of children potentially available for public schooling submitted to state officials may have been quite widespread in Kentucky (and in Tennessee).

> Even with the county as the administrative and taxing unit, the schools remained in the control of the district trustee. He selected the teacher of his choice, many times a member of his family or kinfolks, and bribery by the teacher for choice jobs was not uncommon. . . . Each year it was (also) his duty to make a house to house canvas of his district to get a census of all people of school age. This census was the basis on which state funds were distributed to the counties.

STATE EDUCATIONAL REFORM MOVEMENTS

As was also the case of Virginia (and no doubt a contributing factor in the moonlight school crusade of Cora Wilson Stuart), a number of important state educational reform efforts were led in the early 1900s by the Kentucky Federation of Women's Clubs. They pushed for public education and literacy, linking the lack of same to crime and other social problems. They were supported by State Superintendent of Public Instruction, John Grant Crabbe, who was elected in 1908. "The 1908 General Assembly, described as the education legislature, marked a turning point for education reform in Kentucky." And, as suggested in each of the previously discussed states, other outside philanthropic efforts were seen in Kentucky school reform developments (see also Silver & DeYoung, 1986).

Under Crabbe's administration the school system became a County system instead of one organized into separate districts. This helped get local financial support for expenditures beyond teachers' salaries (Kentucky Department of Education, 1914, p. 3). Under Barksdale Hamlett's administration in 1912 a merit-system of paying teachers (based on training) was begun (Kentucky Department of Education, 1914, p. 4).

Other changes in Kentucky's education were the new school code of 1934 and the foundation program previously discussed. The new school code replaced the state board of education with seven lay members. It gave more authority to the state superintendent of public instruction and redefined school districts into county and independent districts. County superintendents were to be employed by the county board instead of elected (Kentucky Department of Education, 1963, p. 13). These measures were complied with in Cave County. The *Cave County News* (July 19, 1934, p. 1) recorded a teachers' meeting to discuss, among other, things "The New School Laws and Code." The county superintendent discussed redistricting of schools at that meeting (*Cave County News*, July 19, 1934, p. 1). He was replaced in accordance to the new law, by a board-appointed superintendent a few months later (*Cave County News*, April 5, 1934, p. 1).

As discussed previously, money has always been a problem for Kentucky's schools, and the changing demographics (disparities between wealthy and poorer districts) of the state appeared to exacerbate the problem. The legislature enacted the Foundation Program Law to allow the government to tax where the wealth is and spend where the children are (Kentucky Department of Education, 1963, p. 13). Another effect of the population shifts and the need for financial efficiency was the push for the centralization of schools.

As in the other districts covered in this report, school consolidation in Cave County has been extensive during the past 50 years. And as I will soon discuss, its perceived threat to local communities still exists and plays a part in local interactions with the school and school board in Cave County. The idea of transporting children to ever-larger consolidated schools appears to have been on the minds Kentucky school reformers since about 1914–1915 (Kentucky Department of Education, 1939, p. 8). In Cave County, several small rural schools appear to have been replaced with larger "graded" structures in cases where former "crossroads" evolved into legitimate small towns (for example, at Deer Run, Marion, Rogersville, Wayland, Craddockville, Grandeville, and Bear

Cave). Later, economic stagnation, coupled with ever improving transportation systems (particularly following World War II) and state consolidation thrusts, "enabled" the county to consolidate the smaller one- and two-room schools into the larger town schools just mentioned. And a real push for the abandonment of remaining small and "scattered" school buildings took place in the late 1940s.

A number of former schoolteachers and/or students recalled for the Cave County Historical Society the implications of consolidation for the small and rural schools which they once lived and worked in. One told of the reasons for closing the old Dog Creek School, and its eventual destiny:

> By the forties it was apparent that our school was dying for lack of children. All the farms here were small. We had no renters, and had grown to be a middle-aged community. . . . [the] property on which the old frame building stood was returned to the Tom Thompson farm and the school fell down.

Of course, not all outlying one-room schools "fell down" so quickly. Many such schools, to be sure, were returned to the farms on which they were erected and probably became storage sheds for farm equipment, or dry spaces to keep hay. Others, we are told, became churches or community buildings, as frequently, the families around the old schools had become greatly attached to them.

Discussions of school consolidation in Cave County appear to have mirrored the state-wide debate over such developments, as we have suggested they did in each of the other counties previously considered. James Pack studied the impact of school district consolidation throughout Kentucky during the 20th century. And he too suggests that school/community turmoil appeared/appears to increase during times of probable closure of small and rural schools, which seems to have had the same effect historically in Cave County. As he put it:

> The ideas of reorganization and centralization often bring out the issue of local control and forces a closer examination of the role of the local school as it relates to the community. (Pack, 197, p. 24)

THE POLITICS OF SCHOOL CONSOLIDATION IN CAVE COUNTY

Immediately following the completion of the AEL school improvement project for Cave County, major controversies emerged there with regard to potential school consolidation, student redistricting, and hiring policies in the district. As we will soon suggest, these issues may limit the faith and trust in current school leadership practices required to promote parent involvement in the school system (which ended up being the object of AEL school improvement activities).

Furthermore, current controversies in Cave County have a very real historical dimension which perhaps underlines why keeping communities integrally involved with the changing nature of rural schools is problematic. Therefore, before moving on to other significant local economic and school based issues (like the proposed middle school consolidation), I have chosen to "recap" the high school consolidation controversies/issues which took place there 20 years ago as a (somewhat lengthy) prelude to contemporary dynamics.

Cave County High School was formed in 1969 by consolidating the ninth, tenth, eleventh, and twelfth grades from the schools of Deer Run, Craddockville, and Memorial into a central unit in the county seat. Even before this time, we should mention, the two towns of Bear Cave and Cave City (in a neighboring county) formed an Independent System, which encompasses much of the rural area in southern Cave County. Not only is this a rare situation in Kentucky (an Independent district involving two towns in different counties with a large rural attendance area), but it is arguable that the better economic conditions surrounding Penneyrile Independent have historically benefitted its schools in comparison to Cave County schools.

In any event, school consolidation in the state and in Cave County have had an interesting history. Of course, our earlier description of Braxton County high school consolidation concerns, and available literature on this topic (e.g., Peshkin, 1982), suggests that such dynamics are often controversial and emotional even under the best of circumstances. Unfortunately, while a broadening of the curriculum appears to have been made possible with such a consolidation in Cave County, the perceived arbitrariness and contentiousness with which the move was made by the then Cave County School Board has seemingly had long lasting negative consequences on the system as a whole.

As Tables KY-1, -2 and -3 suggest, the agricultural economy of Cave County appeared to weaken significantly sometime following World War II. So, too, school budgets appear to have remained increasingly tight since the 1960s. And since general population decline in the county was approximately 3,000 (17,239 in 1940 vs. 14,119 in 1960), we must assume that school enrollments (and state contributions to the county based on student membership) were also dwindling. Financial problems of the mid- to late 1950s may have been particularly severe and led to the shortening of some school calendars in 1953 (and probably in several subsequent years).

Furthermore, the state of Kentucky made a program and facilities review of all three Cave County high schools around 1960 related to accreditation, and appears to have found some problems at Deer Run and significant weaknesses at Craddockville High School. Informants we have talked to in the county more succinctly suggest that "Craddockville was literally falling down." Thereupon, the Cave County Board of Education appears to have decided to pursue the building of a consolidated county high school rather than (substantially) remodeling buildings and upgrading course offerings at the three existing high schools.

According to lifelong resident of Cave County, and a former teacher at Memorial Consolidated High School, most deliberations of the school board, as well as their policy decisions, involved little or no public discussion or input. And even when many county residents sought to legally restrict the issuing of bonds for the new high school construction, the board continued to press for consolidation over heated objections of residents in both the Memorial and Deer Run school attendance areas.

Significantly, parent involvement in both the Deer Run and Memorial Schools appears to have been quite high in the days before high school consolidation with Craddockville. And many residents of the towns which comprised the attendance areas of these two schools still argue that county-wide consolidation harmed their children and their communities.

An interesting account of the history of Memorial High School was written by the previously cited individual, who originally lived near Rogersville, went to school, and taught at Craddockville before consolidation (1969). Her book, *The Legend of Memorial*, interweaves personal narrative, newspaper accounts and interviews with former students and staff at the school covering the years from 1919 to 1969. As an institutional history written by an admitted amateur historian, the work clearly underestimates the extraschool dynamics which influenced the school's birth, growth, decline, and death. For example, even a cursory content analysis of the book would no doubt uncover that between 40 and 50 percent of the text is devoted to yearly description and analysis of boy's sports activities (mostly boy's basketball), and the impression is clearly given (without ever any detailed discussion of the assumption) that good years vs. marginal years at the school were directly related to how well the school fared in district basketball play. So, too, we have come to learn in several interviews that interschool factionalism and controversy was not uncommon at Memorial. Yet *The Legend of Memorial* never suggests such dynamics; rather, in the pages of this book only harmony and common pursuit are detailed. Thus, there are important omissions in this work which cast some doubt upon some aspects of its adequacy and accuracy.

On the other hand, approximately 200 pages of text and literally hundreds of quotes found throughout the book address themes relevant to the types of concerns this book has targeted, and later commentary in *The Legend of Memorial* centers on perceived betrayal and unethical leadership practices at the county level.

One important early topic of discussion presented in this book concerns parent and community involvement throughout the history of the school (which again was the weakness of the school system when AEL assessed the district in 1988). Even though rural Kentucky has rarely been credited with aggressively pursuing formal schooling, the author argues that Memorial Consolidated School was either the second or third consolidated high school in the Commonwealth. And was built primarily with funds donated/collected from parents and businesses in the Wayland and Rogersville communities. In 1919, the possibility of building a new consolidated school on the road between Wayland and Rogersville was proposed and acted upon by local citizens:

> Although the Board of Education supported consolidation and had made a financial commitment, the final decision, rightly so, was to be made by the people involved. A special election was held, and at least one [community] made a celebration out of it. . . . [the] overall decision was that the independent districts of Rogersville and Canmer and the rural school districts of Stringtown, Sunshine, and Burk voted to become one consolidated school, and most importantly, the PEOPLE—not a local or state board–had spoken.

Once the consolidation decision had been voted in by the people, it was time to collect the money to build the new school. And given that there were few wealthy residents in the new Memorial attendance area, this was not expected to be easy. But such expectations proved incorrect:

> Then came the house-to-house canvassing, the task of seeing every person and obtaining pledges of contribution. Even though the vote had been close and many were opposed, the people of the community came through. . . . [The] manifestation of cooperation, confidence, and desire cannot be overemphasized and cannot be adquately appreciated. The people of this community, most of whom were farmers, laborers, and small business men dug down into their pockets and paid, through donations, [more than half] the cost of the construction of Memorial School.

As mentioned earlier, most of *The Legend of Memorial* deals with high school student and teacher life, and with social events centering on boys' basketball. Yet throughout the book, the author details how the school and its academic, social, and athletic events appeared to become a community focus, not just an academic one. For example, in 1957 the boy's basketball team (there were no girl's athletic teams between 1940 and 1975) won the regional title and a chance to play for the state championship in Louisville. If accounts gleaned from local papers were right, this event probably completely drained the countryside around Memorial School for several days. According to the *Cave County News* in the spring of 1957:

> It was probably true that it would have been hard to have "put out a fire" in most parts of Cave County last night, especially in the Wayland–Rogersville–U.S. 17E section, for by mid-afternoon, a Great Exodus had greatly depleted the manpower

(and womanpower too) in Cave County. Objective: Freedom Hall and the State Basketball Tourney.

The atmosphere was charged everywhere all week and it was much easier to say, "Wouldn't miss it for anything," to the dozens of questions asked, ("Going to the tournament?") than to admit that a little item like "work" precluded your going. But plenty were able to take off—it was reported that between eight hundred and one thousand had tickets for Wednesday night's opening game at Freedom Hall.

Parent involvement in the life of Memorial Consolidated High School (later to become Cave Memorial High School) appears to have involved more than just appreciation of its athletic teams. As was probably the case with some other rural schools previously described, the Parent—Teacher Association at Memorial was a primary contributor to equipment and supply needs there. The involvement and prominence of the this organization for school support thusly:

[The] early Memorial Parent–Teacher Association belonged to the State and National organizations, paying dues to both; it was one of the first P.T.A's in Kentucky. This organization was to be the bulwark of Memorial for years to come. The work of this association would be a volume within itself, and . . . [would] reveal an almost unbelievable record of accomplishment. . . . [it] is imposible to express adequately how much this group meant to the school and to the community.

Interestingly, the author also commented on how far things have changed with regard to professional control of schools since the 1940s:

An organization that functioned today as the Memorial Parent–Teachers Association did in the twenties and thirties would be "Meddling—trying to run the school." In a way maybe the P.T.A. then did help to run the school but not as a meddler. In fact, there is much to be said for the school organization as it existed then. Directly over the students were the teachers, supervised by a principal and school superintendent; over these two individuals were the local trustees; all these individuals were assisted, supported, and encouraged by the local P.T.A. . . . In a sense, the Memorial P.T.A. **was** Memorial School, and it is possible, even probable, that Memorial would not have endured, at least as successfully, without the loyalty of its oldest and best friend, the Memorial Parent–Teachers Association.

Many if not most of the activities of the Memorial PTA appear to have benefitted both the school and the community, that is, provided ways and means for parents and other community adults to view and/or participate in the life of the school. Two good examples of the "open-door" between Memorial and the outside world are reflected in the response of the school to state and national crises completely unrelated to instruction. In 1937, for example, Memorial served as a refugee center to hundreds of families flooded out of their homes in Louisville and Jefferson County by the Ohio River. Later, during World War II, local agricultural communities were encouraged to grow, can, and distribute their own produce in order to aid the war effort. Responding to this call, the parents, teachers, and children of Memorial School went into the canning "business."

> For a number of years the cannery was a very popular and busy place. Not only were the facilities used by the patrons of the community in preservation of food for family use, but every opportunity was utilized to can foods for the school lunchroom. Many parents, teachers, and students spent many hours peeling apples and breaking beans. One teacher remembers that frequently in their weariness after breaking beans for a long time, workers would get careless and allow as many strings as beans in the kettle. They paid for their carelessness, however, in having to eat stringy green beans the next year in the cafeteria.

Fund raisers run by the PTA. (which also apparently decided what raised funds would be spent on) typically generated hundreds and/or thousands of dollars, which was no mean feat in the 1930s and 1940s. Proceeds from the 1950 Homecoming Fair were spent as follows, according to *The Legend of Memorial*:

> The Homecoming Fair netted $1385.42 for the P.T.A. which was spent for many needed items at the school, some of which were as follows: metal basketball lockers, hall lockers, installation of outside lights for the Vocational Building, gravel for driveway, footlights for stage, final payment on a baby grand piano, equipment for all grade rooms and four highschool departments, assistance in lowering bleachers in the gym, adding partition on the stage, contribution toward school's purchase of 16-millimeter projector, and other smaller improvements.

> In addition, the P.T.A. established quite a reputation in the district and state by winning the Gold Seal Award at the Fall Conference, Open House was sponsored in November, and in February an impressive celebration of Founders' Day was observed with a pageant, "Deep Are the Roots," with teachers, parents, and students participating. This dramatic production contrasted 19th and 20th century educational methods and organization.

Other passages in *The Legend of Memorial* document later accomplishments, involvements and awards of the Memorial PTA; significantly, this organization appeared impressively accomplished and involved with all aspects of school life at Memorial in the years just before the school board voted to consolidate all county high schools:

> Memorial was host to the Fourth District Fall Conference of P.T.A. in October [1958] with one of Memorial's own [parents] presiding at the meeting. This was the first time Memorial had been honored by hosting the District Association and the

first time to be honored with one of its own members being President. The second Vice-President, was also a Memorial member. At this conference the unit received the Extra Superior rating, the Acorn Award, the Health Award, National P.T.A. Magazine Award, Kentucky P.T.A. Magazine Award for 255 Club, and Kentucky P.T.A. Magazine Award for 100% Executive Board. With Mrs.   as President and   as Secretary and Treasurer, the annual Fair was conducted on September 26 [1958] and profited $1485.95. This money was used for various needs at the school, including another water cooler and some new folding chairs.

Not surprisingly, given the longevity of Memorial as a school facility, some of its graduates ended up being prominent figures in education, including one member of the State Board of Education. On the other hand, ostensible pride and success in Cave County educational circles appears to have earned Memorial some jealousy: and we have been told in other circles as well that open hostility between the towns of Rogersville and Wayland (south of the Ralston River) and Craddockville (just north of river) frequently existed. And, as was suggested to be the case in Clinch County, identifying and obtaining external funding for school programs appears not always to have been viewed favorably by the Cave County Board of Education, at least in the days before such efforts were controlled at the superintendent's office:

In the late thirties there was countywide controversy over the schools, caused by a number of factors, some of which were partially political, dealing more with personalities, beliefs, and whims than with the needs of boys and girls in Cave County. Some of these conflicts centered around Memorial, with various charges being made not only against the school but against some of its personnel and community members. One was that Memorial received more than its share of the money available for education, ignoring the fact that Memorial had voted on itself and had for some time paid an additional tax. Another accusation was made that Memorial's principal made more than certain other county principals. This led to controversy on the Board regarding the rehiring of Memorial's principal [for the 1939-40 school year] and the question as to the legality of the County Super-intendent's recommendation. The matter became so 'sticky' it was referred to the State Board of Education [which ruled in favor of Memorial]. . . . Memorial was then accused of controlling the State Board of Education because a member of that commission,   , lived in Wayland.

Instead of fellow Cave Countians being proud of having one of its citizens in this high position, further resentment against Memorial arose.

[Later] there was an [other] attack against the principal's salary which was indeed higher than that of some other principals; this was because Memorial was under the Smith-Hughes Act, having qualified for this program back in the early twenties due to the efforts of an early Memorial edcator and friend, Mr.   . Under this program the Federal Government allocated funds to the schools, a large portion of it to supplement the salaries of the agriculture instructors.

Unfortunately, the school board budget approved in Spring 1939 did not include making any application for Smith-Hughes funding for the following year, even though a petition was subsequently submitted to the board (signed by over 500 citizens from the Memorial community) requesting them to reverse their earlier decision. And in the following year there was no Vo-Ag program at Memorial High School.

THE WINDS OF HIGH SCHOOL CONSOLIDATION

Tragically, as viewed from the perspective of the author of *The Legend of Memorial*, even though the facilities and academic programs at Memorial appear to have been among the best in the county, state-wide consolidation/ centralization forces were interpreted by the Cave County school board as calling for the building of one central high school facility. Craddockville, lying in the center of the county, and perhaps being the most accessible town there, certainly must have been a best compromise choice for a new consolidated high school. Yet it appears that the decisions to consolidate county high schools, as well as to select a site for the new school, were carried on behind closed doors.

It is ironic that forces were already at work which would result in Memorial, as a highschool, soon becoming non-existent. By the fall of 1960, there were disturbing undercurrents in regard to the school organization in Cave County as in the race for county board member there were phrases like "strong supporter of Memorial School," "fight for its present existence and location and its growth," "meeting needs of all county schools," etc. A Superintendent's Progress Report in the December 15, 1960 issue of *The News* includes a sentence, 'I assumed that the people of Cave County wanted a progressive program of education for their children. I have been convinced recently that they do not.' Exactly what or who is meant is not clear to the author, but it is clear there was unrest and disturbances of some kind. In the July 18, 1963 issue of the same paper occurs a discussion of education in the county with a listing of the curriculum areas in the three county high schools. In the twelve curriculum offerings listed, Memorial surpassed other schools in four, tied with one or another of the schools in five areas, and was deficient to one or both in three categories. The same article stated Memorial as having a standard rating whereas the others were provisional. All schools were deficient in laboratory facilities. The report stated, 'In planning an educational program and adequate facilities,. . . it is evident in long range consideration that the question of how many high schools are needed must be decided first.'

In a subsequent passage, the author noted:

While the [basketball team was] mapping out plans and strategies on the hardwood, others were mapping out plans and strategies along other lines. The December 5, 1963 issue of *The Cave County News* announced a county-wide meeting in December in regard to a centrally located high school in the county. The January 6 issue of the same paper announced a 'meeting in regard to consolidation of schools in Cave' at Memorial January 30.

Much to the concern of Memorial, and apparently Deer Run Schools, the board passed in 1963 a motion to consolidate all county high schools, and several accounts suggest that it was the poor condition of the Craddockville School that made this even a possibility. According to our later interviews with the current superintendent, three members brought the motion up under the "miscellaneous business" category at a routine board meeting, and it was passed. There was never an open forum related to this topic on the board agenda, we have been told, before the vote was taken. As the current superintendent further recalls, many citizens of the county protested that the other two high schools were in good condition, and that many children would now have to be bussed 50 miles round trip. Parenthetically, we might add, regional factionalism probably played some role in the serious opposition to consolidation once announced. Several of our informants suggested that many parents in the Deer Run area bitterly opposed consolidation (among other reasons) on racial grounds, as no Blacks lived or went to school at Deer Run.

The Legend of Memorial tells the tale thusly:

Basketball players had racked up victories; baseball, tennis, and track teams had upheld the honor of Memorial; speech, debate, and music students had brought home high ratings and had excelled in performances; Junior and Senior classes had furnished dramatic entertainment; honor students had maintained top grades; and seniors had graduated and enjoyed a fantastic trip. School had gone on - successfully and creditably—for all at Memorial—but—work had gone on in another area also. The consolidation issue was really at a high fever by this time with the Fiscal Court having become involved in August of 1963; this body rejected the School Board's request for building bonds by a vote of 3-2, and favored placing the issue on the November ballot: Those opposing the measure held that the people of the county should be given the opportunity to decide for themselves, by ballot, whether or not they favor the consolidation and building construction.

It is to note at this point that is how it had been done when Memorial was first consolidated in 1919—the people voted! It was a close vote—but democracy was at work in that **the people involved voted on the issue.** Almost immediately after the Fiscal Court's vote, according to the August 27 *News*, the County School Board took steps to reverse Fiscal Court action, seeking to have the way cleared for the Board of Education to proceed with the school building program. In September (according to September 24 issue of the same paper) suit was filed to force the Fiscal Court to advertise the sale of bonds for a proposed centrally located high school for Cave County. It was noted that the Fiscal Court had twice rejected a proposal to advertise the bonds.

In the final analysis, Cave County High was built, and the other three county high schools consolidated (leaving elementary school classes behind in the three former buildings). However, efforts to defuse the unhappiness over the school consolidation issue in the county apparently continued to be of little importance to the school board. Even such simple matters as allowing parents and students some voice in (nick)naming the new school mascot appears not to have been proposed by the board. The headline on the front page of the *Cave County News* on April 18, 1968 read: **Cave County School Nickname Rucus** [sic] **Grows; Students Protest.**

As in the earlier instance when the school board basically announced its decision to consolidate high schools, so too the board had chosen and announced the school nickname and school colors. Students protested not being allowed in the decision making, since it was to be their school. And while the controversy was eventually resolved, local residents still talk of the hard feelings which remain from this incident.

THE CAVE COUNTY ECONOMY TODAY

School consolidation issues reemerged in Cave County in the late 1980s. Yet, before describing this phenomenon, some current economic and demographic conditions of the county will be highlighted—and these conditions are also part of the story of current school controversies.

Tobacco and dairy farming are the principal agricultural commodities and activities currently pursued in Cave County, and in fact, Cave County is among the three largest producers of dairy products (among 120 counties) in the state. So, too, tobacco is grown on over 80% of all Cave County farms. Yet industrial development in the county has not replaced declining agriculture, as some had hoped:

> Industry in Cave County has not been able to move beyond the middle stage of development. Agriculture developed quite rapidly in Cave County's early days. Then, agriculture-related industries developed; but development virtually stalled at that point. Cave County has only attracted a small number of industries not involved in agriculture.

In the wake of generally falling agricultural prices, researchers and USDA extension agents in the area during this decade have encouraged the growing of hay (mostly alfalfa) and some produce as farm product alternatives. Also, there continues to be some encouragement to expand dairy and beef production.

Traditionally, Cave County has had a large number of tenant farmers who work for larger landowners and/or rent available land to grow tobacco on. About half of all Cave County farmers are "part-time" farmers with at least one family member working in the wage labor force. Per capita income ($7,200 in 1984) is low relative to state and national averages, and unemployment is still fairly high (13.4% in 1984). For the most part, workers who have outside jobs are employed in low- to moderate-wage manufacturing plants/retail outlets either in Bear Cave or Craddockville. In addition, a number of county residents commute to some better paying jobs in larger towns to the south, or in several others (like Louisville) to the north.

With the general decline in agriculture during the 1950s and 1960s, an early push to industrialize the county became formalized with the creation of the Craddockville Industrial Foundation in 1962. The Kentucky Department of Commerce, in cooperation with the Bear Cave and Craddockville Chambers of Commerce, published an economic report in 1971. This publication outlined the potential for industrial growth in the county because of its location, labor pool, livability, and so on.

Major obstacles to (industrial) economic development in the county are geographical characteristics which limit almost any development dependent on an extensive sewerage system. As discussed earlier, Cave County is located on what geologists have called the Central Kentucky Karst, a limestone belt of underground passages and crystalline formations. In fact, this area, which includes several other counties, boasts 294 miles of subterranean passageways, making it one of the world's largest cave systems. While this geologic fact has attracted tourists to the region, it has created such a strong potential for underground water pollution that it has made the possibility of hard core industrial development virtually unthinkable. Throughout the years, many tests have found that groundwater flowing into the caves and the Ralston River has been contaminated by raw sewage. Historically, there have been poor sewage treatment facilities in the many towns that dump upstream (and downstream) into the Ralston River; and even some of the tourist trade in and around Cave County has been adversely affected by (temporary) closing of caves for sanitary reasons during the past 20 years.

> Tests in recent years have confirmed that much of the ground water that flows into River Cave and ultimately to Ralston River is contaminated by raw sewage and industrial wastes that are not adequately treated by aging sewer systems in Bear Cave and nearby Cave City.

Recently, a proposed upgrading of the county's sewer system has been put forth in an effort to prevent the pollution from spreading to other caves and to drinking wells. Furthermore, recognition of the fact that water/sewage quality problems may continually plague the region appears to have been a factor of considerable weight in the recently formed County Chamber of Commerce's decision to attempt to make Cave County a distributing and warehousing center rather than a center for industries which could produce chemical waste. Taking advantage of Cave County's central state and regional location (half-way between Louisville and Nashville) and its easy access to I-67, some civic leaders have voiced hopes of serving the growing auto industry in this distributive capacity.

Yet others appear less concerned with local Chamber efforts at presenting a "clean image" to prospective industries. Most recently (1989), a fight erupted concerning the location of a new county landfill. In the dispute, a private company wanted to build this landfill in the eastern part of the county near the Ralston River. However, community leaders feared (and continue to fear) that such an operation might lead to even more river pollution. State landfill permit regulations in 1988 and 1989 were a hot political topic, as environmental groups contended that state laws did not protect enough against long-term leakage possibilities. Inasmuch as the proposed landfill in Cave County could potentially leak into the river County officials were trying to clean up, legal proceedings were underway during our late fieldwork stages relevant to blocking the landfill. In point of fact, the Cave County school superintendent and one school board member appeared at a public meeting in September 1989 to protest against this landfill, abbreviating a heated discussion of the renewal of the superintendent's contract on that day.

OTHER ECONOMIC DEVELOPMENT INDICATORS

Data compiled by two rural sociologists at the University of Kentucky for 1986 showed 699 manufacturing jobs in Cave County, 651 people employed in wholesale and resale trade, and 276 in services. Furthermore, approximately 500 county residents were employed by state and local governments. The largest employers in Cave County during our visits there were a container corporation (makers of plastic food containers and lids), which employed approximately 350 full-time workers; a metal fabrication and plating operation, which employed approximately 110 workers; and a bedding company (mattress and protector pad makers), which employed just over 200 people.

Needless to say, all of the above referenced businesses rely heavily on product transportation out of Cave County made possible how by CSX railroad and I-55. Also, unfortunately, much of this employment was located in Bear Cave, and taxable income from most of this development did not have an impact on county revenues available for the county school system. Even more unfortunately, while the bedding company was increasing its investment in Cave

County (near Craddockville), a satellite dish construction company (Marion's only major employer) went out of business in 1988.

The two other employment industries in the county are also located primarily in either Bear Cave or Craddockville: tourism (near the caves), closest to the former, and county government in the latter. Interestingly, there is also a local repertory theater in Bear Cave (which opened in 1977) that has added to the cultural attractiveness of the area, as summer performances draw crowds from all over the state. Raising its $200,000 annual budget through community fund drives, the theater "has established itself as a valuable showcase for Kentucky art and artists."

In general, the attractiveness of Cave County as a potential site for development led the state to forecast increasing population growth there in the coming decades. That is, while the 1980 census reported a population of just over 15.400 persons, state projections forecast that about 17,000 would reside in the county by 1990. Yet so far such projections do not appear quite accurate, although it is clearly the case that the county has recovered from the pattern of population decline earlier this century. The Bureau of the Census reported over 18,000 people in the decades of 1900, 1910, and 1920, with a drop to just over 16,000 in 1930.

Meanwhile, minority population in the county has decreased compared to the white population since the turn of the century. Approximately 8.1% of the population was non-White in 1980, whereas in 1900 over 12% of the population was non-White. Related to this theme, sporadic hostility towards Blacks has been reported in Cave County and in Cave County schools, although none (officially) recently. And while the word around the county is that some (at least one) communities are not welcome places for blacks, there are no recent published accounts of overt racism being practiced this decade.

In recent years, Cave County has been touted by at least one metropolitan newspaper as an ideal place to live. In 1979, results of a state-wide survey showed Cave County to have a higher level of lifestyle "satisfaction" (97%) among its residents than any other rural Kentucky county. Yet concern has been voiced over the loss of young people from the area. Given limited economic opportunities, outmigration of young people seeking jobs in other industrial centers was fairly steady up until recently.

In response to this drain of human resources, a Craddockville attorney and his father campaigned to encourage college graduates in the "back to the nature movement" to consider inexpensive land in Cave County for settlement some years back, and placed ads in four Midwest and Southern college campus newspapers. As a result, between 20 and 30 families are estimated to have come to the county for homesteading during the 1970s, and many of these remained and became actively involved in state and local conservation issues. Those who still remain in the county have organized a local food cooperative and become involved in recent battles to clean up the Ralston River, and one family has the first and only (1989) "certified" organic farm in the state. So too, we have been told, many organically minded inmigrants from previous decades remain actively opposed to industrial development in the county. Even more recently, an Amish Community seeking productive but affordable agricultural lands has moved into Western Cave County near Deer Run.

Yet the only economically and culturally viable "towns" remaining in Cave County (by contemporary standards) are Bear Cave and Craddockville, where almost one-third of all county residents now live. And, as stated before, much of the taxable income collected in Bear Cave goes to support its separate city government and the independent school system there, rather than into the general County or Cave County School system coffers.

CAVE COUNTY SCHOOLS SINCE 1968

From interviews collected in our fieldwork, few memorable school issues appear to have dominated attention in Cave County during the 1970s. Mention was made of problems related to the school consolidation issue and the starting up of the new high school, and general problems related to low funding levels drained much time and energy. Furthermore, Cave County High athletic teams rarely achieved hoped-for prominence in the decade after consolidation, and the diminished status of the three older high schools (now elementary schools) seems to have set some tone of malaise in the Deer Run and Memorial communities by the late 1970s. Few people we have talked to, in other words, have had much (positive) to say about Cave County Schools before the current era. On the other hand, **lots** of people have talked about Cave County schools in the current era. And much of what they say is quite positive.

What we refer to as the "current era" in the county originated with the appointment of the present superintendent, Mr. S., in 1982. Several primary factors appear relevant to reasons why Mr. S. was selected as the new superintendent, some undoubtedly commendable, others perhaps less so. Ostensibly, the previous superintendent appointed by the board was terminated from his position for allowing the schools to physically and curricularly deteriorate. For example, almost everyone we talked to about earlier problems in the schools (in the late seventies) talked about poor building maintenance, lax or nonexistent teaching standards, little or no school building leadership, and "dirty," unkempt classrooms and hallways at almost every school. So too, we have been told, the high school dropout rate (from a school comparatively few community members identified with anyway) was extremely high: approaching "65%."

The "official" version of the hiring of the new superintendent was that the position was advertised for and filled in order (almost literally) to clean up and improve the Cave County school system. Yet other factors were rumored to surround both the firing of the previous superintendent and the hiring of Mr. S.

To put it bluntly but perhaps most succinctly, Cave County schools (for all of their currently positive virtues, which will be elaborated upon shortly) are "politically" run. To be fair, the political problems cited earlier in the case of Clinch County are not of the same magnitude in Cave County, and most current County residents claim things are better now than they used to be; but according to many of our informants (which include a variety of well-placed current and previous school officials), they are there.

Cave County schools operate under the direction of what some (then) Kentucky school reform advocates refered to as a "3–2 board." That is, many important school policy decisions are split decisions, with both the majority and the minority in these decisions typically being the same three board members voting one way, and the other two voting a different way. There are several important differences between the splits evident in the Cave County case, as compared to the case of Clinch County. In Clinch County, it will be recalled, there were seven elected board members and one elected superintendent. Thus, even a superintendent out of favor there would remain part of the decision making process because he or she was an elected official. Furthermore, in Clinch County recognizable political factions existing outside of the schools were reported behind the school board decision making process.

In Kentucky, however, school boards are constituted of five elected board members and a superintendent hired by the school board. And if and when a board tires of an appointed superintendent, it can replace him or her either at the end of the contract period, or even before in "malfeasance in office" cases. And except for perhaps an informal "old boy" network in Cave County, there do not appear to be political factions operating behind the (school) scenes.

In addition to the number of board members and the different constitutional locations of superintendents in the Kentucky and Tennessee cases, schools in Cave County (at least) have strictly enforced attendance area policies, and board members are elected by district. Translated into (informal) "policy" in Cave County, this means that each of the five elementary schools in the county is represented by a school board member; and it appears almost common knowledge that board members intercede directly in many school-based decisions within "their" schools, subject (at least technically) to the superintendent's approval.

In the case of "3–2 boards," our informants argue, the ability of board members to "suggest" individual school policy is much enhanced by being one of the three rather than one of the two. Put another way, forming or being part of the majority group on important policy issues appears historically to have guaranteed better attention to facilities needs or staffing issues at a board member's (own) school by the superintendent in Cave County. And, historically, school superintendents in Cave County have allegedly used the threat of withheld resources to bargain with individual school board members for their support on policy issue held dear by the superintendent. Such dynamics, while not fully explored in the earlier case of the formation of Cave County High, suggest that "behind the scenes" political decisions (like consolidating three former high schools into one) have almost been routine in Cave County.

The political machinations historically present in the Cave County school system were summed up succinctly in an interview conducted by the rural sociologists earlier mentioned with a local farmer who once taught and had been a building principal there. As a lifelong resident formerly employed by the school system, he confided that farm income remained an important source of revenue security for many teachers, when even the best professional educator could be teaching one day but gone the next:

> Well, I guess really the backbone of it is that there are a lot of political things involved in schools. The job security is not all that great, especially in some counties. This is one of them. You've got to have some base and some security. A piece of property is it. If you've got it you've got it. There is a little more security. It may be rougher in farming than a job in public education. The boards of education change. Just like that, they can meet one night and you are gone. It just takes three out of five people to do it. It happens all of the time.

Critics of the current administration in the county furthermore argue that political factors and "behind the scenes" activities also explain how the current Cave County Superintendent was hired, and explain his ability to affect (in many ways exemplary) school policy there. One alleged "behind the scenes" factor related to the hiring of Mr. S. involved the election of a new school board member who (for whatever reason) disliked one probationary teacher in "his" school. Under state policy, it is the superintendent's obligation to recommend teachers for hiring, and the responsibility of the board members to actually hire (or refuse to hire) those recommended. In addition to supposedly running a relatively "loose" school "ship," the previous school superintendent was in favor of retaining the teacher not liked by the incoming board member.

According to our sources, the election of a hostile (to the previous superintendent) new school board member altered the balance of power on the board, so that an even split emerged regarding support for the former superintendent. The "swing" vote on the board for firing this superintendent (thus also indirectly getting rid of the abovementioned teacher) supposedly held out for a particular candidate whom he favored as the new superintendent. Otherwise, he was happy with the status quo.

The candidate in mind was the son-in-law of the Deer Run district board member, who had earlier been a principal at Deer Run and was currently superintendent (under some pressure to resign) in a wealthier northern Kentucky school district. Supposedly, the "swing vote" board member was assured that his son-in-law would be offered the job, if he would vote to fire the then superintendent, which he (and the new board majority) did.

Subsequently, an official advertised search for a new superintendent was made, although only a 1-year contract was allegedly promised to any new superintendent. Speculation is that the reason relatively few eligible superintendents applied for the job was that no career-oriented professional would abandon other job possibilities for a 1-year appointment in a poor county with a politically oriented school board. One did apply, however, who was given the job – the Deer Run board member's son-in-law.

THE ERA OF MR. G

Attempts at setting the behind-the-scenes stage in Cave County, as we have just done, will serve for (partial) later analyses of how and why parent involvement in the county remained marginal even after AEL had completed its local school/community parnership demonstration. However, this "stage setting" actually does some disservice to the many quite positive accomplishments of the current school superintendent and his comparatively progressive school system. Before returning to what I (and many local citizens and school personnel) view as the problematic themes just hinted at, we would like to profile some of the many noteworthy school improvement efforts of the Cave County school system under its current leadership.

As Mr. G tells it, he was hired by the Cave County Board of Education to accomplish four objectives: "improve the curriculum, clean up and improve physical facilities, improve student achievement levels, and lower the dropout rate." And, to the best of our judgment, he has done just that. And more.

School physical appearance in Cave County is quite good, compared with any of the other three districts in our study (except, perhaps, the Eureka School in Charlotte County). While complaints about some major mechanical components in some schools surfaced in our interviews, walks through any building in the system typically suggested better than average care. All buildings were neat and clean, lighting was good, lunchrooms and kitchens were spotless, hallways were freshly painted and decorated with children's work, no broken furniture was visible, etc.

Yet, while physical facilities appear more than adequate (even if some buildings are reputed to be cared for better than others), it is perhaps in the academic programs available in rural and poor districts that the Cave County system appears most advantageous. And, as the mastermind behind such programs, the current superintendent would appear to be the model school superintendent, one whom any state department of education would want to showcase for public inspection. As numerous county residents (both critics and admirerers) have commented, "[Mr. G] lives, eats, and breathes education."

Curricularly speaking, Cave County schools have enrichment programs, programs for adult learners, programs for impoverished children and their mothers, after school tutorial programs, advanced placement programs, dropout prevention programs, and almost any other program available to school districts that carefully budget their monies and go the extra mile in seeking external dollars, both of which Cave County does very well.

According to Mr. G, much of his long professional career as a principal and superintendent (even before becoming the superintendent in Cave County) was dedicated to seeking out, viewing, and borrowing/adapting good school programs from other places for eventual use in his own system. And, as Mr. S. put it, he always had in the back of his mind that someday he might get to put the innovative programs he found in other places into effect in the county where he himself was educated (at least as a high school student). Parenthetically, he claims now to frequently use his central office staff and building principals to "scout out" other innovative programs for possible use in Cave County.

The possibility that Mr. G was hoping/expecting to get back to Cave County to put into practice the many educational programs he thought worthwhile was also sounded by the AEL advisory group member earlier mentioned in an interview we had with her following Cave County's agreement to become a demonstration site. The AG member had nothing but praise for Mr. G. in this interview, noting his enthusiasm for improving education in his county, his conviction that the system could be turned around under his leadership, and his well-established reputation as an excellent superintendent among those in the State Department of Education. Confirmation of his reputation and close ties in the state capital was demonstrated in 1984, when he was invited by the then Kentucky Governor to chair a 25 member commission aimed at reducing Kentucky's dropout rate.

In our earlier mentioned interview with AEL advisory group member Ms. K, she noted that the school situation Mr. G would find himself in was not unlike that of many other rural school systems in the state: one with a previous tradition of nepotism and political gamesmanship at the expense of sound educational practice. Just as importantly, she suggested, previous superintendents in Cave County had very poor management styles to go along with their political motivations for being in the school system to begin with.

With regard to school leadership issues, Ms. K (now a superintendent herself in a neighboring county) elaborated a bit on how Mr. G went about the business of reforming the Cave County system. One component of Mr. G's approach involved putting together a sound "management team" in the central office to help implement new academic programs and to help coordinate such activities through the building principals. And one particularly "tough" agenda item of his, she claimed, was to "personally" help "upgrade the teaching staff" in the county.

On paper, and in practice, the Cave County system of five elementary schools and one consolidated high school has come a long way in the past 8 years. Outside commentators (like the earlier-quoted journalist who wrote the complimentary county story for a major metropolitan newspaper) marveled at the turnaround in the system several years after the new superintendent came in. Speaking in school performance terms, a major statistical transformation in the system involved the changing dropout rate: going from over 60% in the late 1970s to below 10% by 1988.

Most of the credit for this change has been directly attributed to the superintendent's performance. He is creditied with:

> [finding] money for tutoring programs, job training and work experience to help rural youngsters prepare for non-agricultural jobs. . . . He also started accelerated studies, seen to it that there were plenty of computers in the system, and revived the Cave County (high school) Band.

Most recently, and the academic activities that in our visits to Cave County, have seemingly drawn most of the superintendent's praise, are the academic competitions hosted and/or participated in by the high-school- and middle-school-age students each year. As is probably the case in many states, athletic tournaments in several sports are held at the end of each season (in Cave County, as in Clinch County, basketball appears the most popular: see our earlier discussion of Memorial). And the Cave County Raiders were district basketball representatives in the 1989 boys' championship the year we were doing our fieldwork.

Yet Cave County also originated and hosts a state-wide academic competition along the lines of the state basketball tournament; and, while other school districts (and the state department of education) now also host such competitions, perhaps no small, rural, and poor district in the state has been able to locally develop and operate such a contest as well as Cave County has.

As state academic tournaments have grown in popularity (now including elementary, middle, and high schools), Cave County has also vigorously competed in them as well. In February 1988, Memorial Elementary (formerly Memorial High School) hosted the Governor's Cup competition for the district and was the overall district winner. They went on to win in some categories at the regional level and compete at the state level. And Mr. G (through his building principals) is credited by all observers to have made most of these academic events both possible and noteworthy.

Other important turnarounds have also been accomplished in Cave County in the past few years. The superintendent's quest to upgrade academic course offerings at the high school, in conjunction with the high school principal, has led to the introduction of many advanced placement courses, which enables Cave County High to grant the "Commonwealth Diploma." And Cave County is one of the only rural systems in the state to be in a position to offer all three types of Kentucky high school diplomas (Standard, Academic, and Commonwealth).

As well, Cave County has created an interesting half-day program for all county eighth graders, who are bussed to the high school in the afternoon for classes not available separately at each of the elementary schools. At first, the intention was that the half day program would facilitate advanced math for eighth graders; but, according to Mr. G, attending the high school for a half-day was increasingly requested by many parents and other students in the elementary schools, so their wishes were granted.

Standardized test scores have also been a target of improvement in Cave County, and special emphasis on test-taking skills and matching school curricula to these tests ostensibly resulted in an impressive district performance in 1987. The last year that the former state-developed tests were administered in Cave County, the district ended up ranking among the state's top 25 (of 178 school districts). Even more recently, the significance and variety of academic programs available in the county garnered one of five special recognition awards for program excellence by the National Rural Education Association, which was made aware of Cave County's progressive programs by AEL.

SCHOOL IMPROVEMENT AND PUBLIC RELATIONS
IN CAVE COUNTY

Most of the last half-dozen pages have been compilations of facts and descriptions of ongoing programs; and, were the task of this chapter to profile "promising practices" (which was another RSS agenda discussed in Chapter 1), we could probably end this essay by elaborating on how these programs actually (and admirably) worked in Cave County while we were there. Another piece of evidence to corroborate the academic strength and successes of the Cave County system, as currently led was evidenced in the AEL Profile of School Excellence, where no "strong evidence of need" was detected at any system wide level. And to the best of our knowledge, the Cave County system as a whole fared better on the Pro S/E than any of the other three systems which were part of the RSS demonstrations (all of which were reputed to be among the best small and rural school systems in their respective states). The only (albeit important) area of some system-wide weakness in Cave County on the Pro S/E related to correlations between test scores and pupil SES at several district schools.

However, the key purpose of our investigation (as in each of the other RSS sites) was not to systematically document all, most, of even some of the "strengths" of the Cave County school system. Rather, our interest was to sketch the contextual factors in Cave County, particularly as they related to the short- and long-term prospects of school improvement activities sponsored by AEL. Rather, our study was to investigate school district problems and issues in Cave County which related to the possibilities of RSS success. And in order to accomplish this objective, we return now to some of the contemporary problematic local and state events related to AEL's impact there. As will soon become obvious, these issues have histories of their own in the County.

As one of the evaluation staff members who summarized the Cave County situation early in this study commented (before she left to teach at another institution):

> It would appear that community involvement in its school system has been an issue for Cave County for some time. With the consolidation of the high school and the existance of the Penneyrile Independent School District within its borders, district cohesiveness would appear even on the surface to be currently problematic. Furthermore, similar forces appear to have been at work almost from the beginning of the county's history, and encompass larger factors such as war, desegregation, economic feasibility, and geography. And, of course, all of these factors are interrelated.

The RSS school and community studies' results suggested that parent involvement in Cave County schools appeared to remain less impressive than other important aspects of local schooling. While this "finding" was partially suggested by AEL's conception of factors relevent to school improvement (see Chapter 1), community groups we participated in also seemed to agree that parent involvement and communication were concerns, especially with regard to parents of lower achieving students in the system. On the other hand, parents whose children were in advanced academic programs were reputed to have good communications/relations with the Cave County central office.

Importantly, we should note that, in the community needs assessment completed by the AEL, the parent/community involvement theme was not among those scoring highest in priority. Rather, financing issues and their symptoms (classroom overcrowding, combined rooms, etc.) were the problems cited most often by parents, teachers, and community members. Yet, because the RSS demonstration project could not (according to AEL) address funding problems, and because the superintendent could not foresee the feasibility of increased local school financing, "needs" specifically related to more local school dollars were not chosen for improvement via the RSS model. Rather, improving parent involvement (which may itself be greatly affected by declining school revenues) became the focal point of school improvement activities in Cave County.

Of some note, it was suggested by several observers that the needs sensing group assembled by the superintendent in Cave County was comprised of many individuals already involved with the school system in other capacities. And while the racial and gender characteristics of this group appeared to reflect county demographic characteristics, we noted that most RSS participants were employed, well educated, and listed postal addresses either from the county seat or Bear Cave, which lies in the Penneyrile District. Thus, we suspect that some bias in favor of professional/academic outlook among community needs-sensing participants may have influenced perceived needs of the district.

Another observation noted in our evaluation report focused on the positive relationships between the school district and the local business community, a fact suggested as potentially problematic in AEL's earlier formulation of rural school/community problems. This was not a problem in Cave County (nor had it been in Charlotte County). For example, the "community needs-sensing" group assembled for the RSS project was full of county banking and business leaders, and included the county judge executive (previously a teacher himself, who allegedly was forced out of the system by an unhappy school board member). And the eventual steering committee chairman was the (Louisville-born and private-school-educated) wife of a wealthy businessman who is very active in local economic development efforts.

Furthermore, Mr. G has himself been quite proactive in appearing before business groups and encouraging economic growth in Cave County. In the quest for economic development, the former Cave County Chamber of Commerce president credited Mr. S with "making a significant difference." According to him, Mr. G in fact helped to put together the new County Chamber of Commerce (where previously Craddockville and Bear Cave had the only ones); and under his tutelage, the Cave County School system "has improved tri-fold in 4 or 5 years." The former Chamber of Commerce president believed that the quality of schools is essential to development, and that industry regularly makes decisions on the basis of a well-trained, "up-to-date" labor force. In this vein, he cited Mr. G's aggressiveness in helping to institute or promote projects relevent to local job possibilities by expanding vocational education programs in auto mechanics and diesel engine training.

Yet, returning to specific themes of the Cave County RSS demonstration, while strong academic leadership and close working relationships with local economic development groups are both characteristics of the Cave County situation, we judged that building bridges between parents, teachers, and school administrators was in fact not as much a priority there as it was in other systems of this study (particularly, for example, Charlotte County). Rather, public involvement in the schools appears in Cave County (based on our observations) to be very much a matter of public relations.

Put another way, the Cave County superintendent and some of his building principals surely wanted all parents to know about the good things the schools were doing, and they appeared to have no aversion to using parents to help attain instructional goals of the system (like reading questions and helping to keep score in annual academic competitions, or aiding children with their homework). But we sensed in our visits to Cave County no open door policy on the part of the school system to seek the advice or counsel of interested parent groups in formulating new directions in school improvement, particularly at the building level.

To be sure, informal surveys of parents and community members did and do take place in Cave County, with regard to new programs (for example, in potentially attractive adult eduction offerings). Yet, once again, such offerings are system-wide efforts instigated by the central office, and appeared to us as a qualitatively different phenomenon than (for example) enabling/encouraging individual principals to form school-based (as opposed to district-based) school improvement teams.

The bottom line, in our opinion, was that the Cave County system is highly centralized, and that most innovation there is coordinated by the superintendent. If Mr. G hasn't seen a program or doesn't like one, it won't get into the system. And because the superintendent is quite active professionally, he appears to have seen and (pre)judged many available school-based programs before they find their way to the county.

Another way to illustrate this interpretation was available to us in observing several public meetings involving the superintendent (and sometimes building principals). On none of these occasions (including one where his defined role was ostensibly to be "advised" by teachers and school staff) were we privy to a situation where Mr. G actively listened to parent (or teacher) concerns, as was the case in all three of our other sites. Rather, when Mr. G was in a school-based environment, he was always **the** (or in the case of school board meetings, one) dominant player. Meanwhile, in a number of public situations where both the superintendent and building principals were present, principals spoke only when spoken to.

With regard to the "public relations" theme earlier suggested, Cave County schools are big on portraying in multiple ways the successes of its programs and its students. For example, student awards for academic, vocational, and athletic achievements are routinely made in public places in the county, including school board meetings and at student assemblies. So, too, official pictures are staged where recipients are seen shaking hands with either the superintendent and/or directly involved building principals.

As mentioned earlier, most award pictures are taken by the district public relations central office (half-time) staff member. Suggestively, only Cave County appears to have had the luxury (among our four districts) of having a public relations staff member in the central office who also happens to be formally connected to the county newspaper.

Good public relations appears to be striven for by the district superintendent in other ways as well. For example, the comparatively high state test scores earned by the school system in 1987 are hard for any parent to miss: for they are (still) prominently displayed at the entrance of every district school and the central office in the form of a color-coded map with high- vs. low-scoring districts. On the other hand, the comparatively marginal test scores Cave County schools received on most recently completed CTBS tests (from 1988) have yet to be "enshrined" on the walls of any school buildings, although they were presented in the county newspaper. Concerned that such dynamics not occur again, the district curriculum supervisor was assigned to visit the State Department of Education numerous times in the fall of 1989 to become more familiar with new CTBS protocols and test materials, so that he could work with teachers in each subject area before the next round of state testing. And he essentially spent several weeks in Frankfort so doing in Winter 1989.

One final example illustrating the "positive image" concerns of the superintendent was also available in the first steering committee discussions of the RSS project. At this meeting (as Lab documents outline), both Pro S/E and Community Needs Sensing "findings" were presented to the steering committee, whose job it was to select from among several profiled "needs" in order to establish a school improvement project. In the first place, the Cave County superintendent was one of only two district superintendents who attended both the needs assessment process and the feedback of the results to the later steering committee. (In the other district, we assume this occurred because the superintendent there did not even know most members of the group he was advised to choose.) Furthermore, only in Cave County did the superintendent hand out facts and figures on the school system to those in attendance, as if the assembled participants were new to the area. Finally, Mr. G was quick to publicly announce to the steering committee that none of the four complaints about the school system which existed before he came in were on the list of AEL's reported needs.

LEADERSHIP STYLE, POLITICS, AND PARENT INVOLVEMENT

While aspects of the above might be construed as some sort of criticism of the central office, the arguably successful top-down management style witnessed there, in and of itself, may not deserve an overly negative reading. It is possible, for example, that the dramatic academic turnaround seen in the county during the past 8 years might only have been possible (in such a politically charged and low-budget environment) with exactly the type of forceful and innovative leadership provided by Mr. G.

According to our interpretation, for example, building principals in Cave County are not nearly as autonomous as they are in (for example) Braxton County. The tradition there has been that board representatives (frequently without advanced education themselves) have direct say in building dynamics (like who gets hired). Thus, a number of what we considered to be potentially effective building principals have complained about their lack of control over important aspects of decision making in their own schools. And it appears that moving into the central office has been the best way to actually become more effective professionally in the larger system, at least for those who have been able to accept the current superintendent's management style.

Thus, we judge the relative success of the Cave County system to be built around top-down central office initiatives within an enveloping politicized system. Which, if my interpretation is correct, poses problems for meaningfully involving parents in future school improvement efforts. Related to this theme, significant amounts of distrust and animosity toward some school leaders in the Cave County system were voiced by numerous teachers, parents, and two school board members. Distrustful parents, combined with those parents claimed by many local teachers not to be interested anyway in their children's education, may greatly diminish the "pool" of community members eager and willing to involve themselves with school issues and problems in Cave County.

SCHOOL CONSOLIDATION ISSUES REEMERGE

Until 1990, the State of Kentucky required that permanent schools receiving state building improvement funds must have an enrollment (for elementary schools) of 350 students. In Fall 1988 (after AEL had come and gone), a state department accrediting team performed an extensive evaluation of Cave County schools and programs. Not surprisingly, virtually across the board the Cave County system sailed through this accountability process (after much work on the part of the system before the external team arrived). Yet, according to the state, the Cave County school population did not justify the existence of five elementary schools, one high school, and no middle schools. Rather, state monies for future building projects (i.e., low-interest loans) must be earmarked (according to the accreditation report) to repairing/adding some space to three permanent elementary school sites (with some improvements to be made at the high school), and toward the eventual construction of a county middle school.

To put it mildly, the release of the accreditation report sent shock waves through the county, especially when it was learned that only three of the five existing county schools were to become permanent elementary schools, and the other two were to become "interim" facilities. In essence, accepting the state accreditation report meant that two Cave County schools would eventually have to be closed, and all county elementary students (some distance in the future) would have to attend the three permanent schools (unless local communities want to raise taxes to maintain the two interim schools).

Thus, as has occurred in Cave County before, many parents there were concerned about the schools in their local community (two communities in particular). Parents of designated interim schools were so upset about the guidelines laid out by the state in Summer 1989 that the school board was virtually forced by public outcry to ask for reconsideration of the facilities portion of the accreditation document. Yet the letter sent to the state did not cite particular errors in the first assessment, nor did it itemize the nature of the local board's disagreement. Speculation is that, by not refuting the facilities portion of the report with contrary details for renewed consideration by the state department, this letter probably had little effect on the state department's accreditation team.

For such reasons, while it is possible that some parent involvement was facilitated by the Fall 1989 school improvement activities sponsored by the RSS program (mentioned above), it might well be argued that enhancing or maintaining active parent interest and support for the two schools currently targeted as "interim" schools by the state will have some difficulty in being achieved. Based on our observations there, parents are more anxious and angry in Marion and Grandeville (interim school sites for Cave County, according to the state) than they are interested in supporting parent involvement efforts by the district. In point of fact, in these two communities many parents are extremely frustrated and upset at the school system currently, and were quite vocal in Fall 1989 in opposition to Mr. G and the Cave County Board of Education. On the other hand, Mr. G suggested that the RSS project may have helped to instigate some of the public opposition to the accreditation study, which later became targeted at him personally.

THE POLITICAL CLIMATE OF CAVE COUNTY SCHOOLS, 1989-1990

School consolidation issues in rural school districts are probably as difficult as any community/educational issue in rural America; yet consolidation issues seen in a historically politicized system may be even more problematic. And if ever there were in Kentucky a prototypical politicized system (signified by a "3-2" school board), Cave County would certainly qualify as an example. While we were in the county, virtually every split policy decision there was on a 3-2 vote. Of course, we must qualify this by suggesting that virtually never were we actually witness to any split decisions regarding academic programs. For that matter, we rarely witnessed any discussion of academic programs at all, as such policies appeared to be decided upon by the superintendent (and his central office staff), who typically announced to the board the programs/policies which would be put into practice. Of course, this fact is probably not all that infrequent in most American schools, and a lack of sustained academic focus by school board members has been in evidence in most of the school board meetings we witnessed in each of the four districts under review here.

On the other hand, one Cave County board member was fairly prominent in the state-wide Prichard Committee for Academic Excellence, and had much to say about academic policies and concerns. However, as one of the board members who frequently was at odds with the superintendent, her academic questions and concerns rarely appeared to coincide with his.

On nonacademic matters, however, there were several serious discussions of hiring, building, and redistricting practices at the half-dozen or so Cave County board meetings we have attended in 1988 and 1989, typically ending with a 3-2 vote in favor of the superintendent's wishes. An excellent example of a hotly debated policy debate and split vote was to be seen in the board decision to build a new athletic facility next to the county high school in Winter 1988.

According to the superintendent, substandard football/baseball/track facilities in Cave County were detracting from the recognition that Cave County High sports teams need and deserve in the region. As well, since healing some of the old wounds related to high school consolidation and intercommunity enmity was a concern of his, he argued that the building of a grand new sports complex would build community cohesion **and** enhance regional respect for the "Raiders." The high school principal, too, was greatly impressed with a professional literature he identified as the high school "Renaissance Movement," a movement which ostensibly calls for enhancing the position of public high schools in the civic eye. So, Mr. G presented to the board a proposal for a new, large, and expensive high school sports complex (to be used by the community for other events as well), along with a funding plan (based on district bonding capacity) for building it. The initial cost of the complex was to be approximately $1 million. And the high school put together a track team for the 1989–1990 school year, once it became clear that a suitable surface would become available within the athletic complex.

While all five board members originally agreed to build the sports complex, only three board members continued in their support for the proposal as projected costs increased. As estimates began to grow, the two other board members objected that perhaps financially strapping the district for many years in order to fund such a nonacademic project was a bad idea. According to several community observers of these dynamics, the two board members, increasingly critical of either building the sports complex or borrowing the money to build it, were the same two board members typically on the losing side of split board decisions. Sure enough, final 3-2 votes on both the building and the financing of the sports complex was registered in Cave County in Winter 1988.

Furthermore, the accreditation report earlier alluded to appears to have set into motion a number of behind the scenes political maneuvering in Cave County along the lines just mentioned. And several predictable 3-2 votes were to be seen in these policy debates. Rather than report primarily interview data relevant to these discussions (which might compromise the anonymity of several informants), we return at this point to coverage of several school board meetings by the *Cave County News* in July and August 1989. Also note the similarity of numerous quotes in the following consolidation dispute to that expressed in the earlier work cited from *The Legend of Memorial*.

In order to comply with the abovementioned state accreditation guidelines, the schools of Grandeville and Marion would eventually have to close and their students sent to one of the other three "permanent" elementary sites. This eventuality led the school board members to release their own public statements (also given to the local paper and read over the local radio station) regarding this situation. Mr. B of Marion disagreed with the thrust of the report, suggesting that consolidating elementary schools would harm children. As he phrased it, "We can't streamline the school at the expense of the students." Mr. G of Grandeville, however, had a more elaborate response:

> I would like to ask (the State Department) to reconsider classifying Grandeville as an interim school. Existing as an interim school (carries) the risk of elimination and the loss of Grandeville School would be detrimental to the community. Over the years Grandeville has drawn an enormous amount of community involvement into the school system. The school system as a whole would suffer because of the inability of Grandeville School to grow. The community is proud of Grandeville School, the programs the schools have to offer, and the staff.

One of the most interesting themes to surface around the state accreditation report involved the expressed ignorance of its contents by board members who had the most to lose from its full implications. This "lack of information" or "lack of time to study implications" theme was expressed also in a board meeting set to approve the 1989–1990 annual budget.

Suggestive of the possible hasty and "behind the scenes" negotiations on policy issues in the county was an effort to redistrict schools in compliance with intentions of the state accreditation report before all board members had reportedly even seen the state document. At the end of a regular board meeting during the first week of July (before the state accreditation report had been made public), the newly elected board member from Deer Run introduced an elaborate and detailed resolution calling for the redistricting of 59 students from Marion and Craddockville into his school. Apparently, even though he was a novice at school board policy- and decision making procedures, the central office had supplied him with all the appropriate details, facts, and figures necessary to support his resolution (which went on to pass on a 3–2 vote).

However, the two board members who typically form the minority on controversial policy decisions in the county, reacted negatively to this resolution and were (predictably) the only two to vote against it on July 10. Coverage of the meeting by the *Cave County News* read thusly:

> Mr. B., whose Marion attendance area was the most affected seemed stunned by the resolution and stated, "you could have shown me the courtesy of showing it (the proposed resolution) to me."

> [the Deer Run board member] replied that he had been thinking about ways to solve the problems of bussing from one school to another, and asked the central office personnel to put together the figures which would accomplish that. He

emphasized that with the accreditation report released last week calling for Marion to be an interim school until a middle school could be built, no additions could be made to the Marion facility to relieve overcrowding. . . .

Mr. B. requested that the matter be tabled until a continued session in order to study it further: "I need more time to study it." Board member D. C. (Craddock-ville) pointed out that Grandeville received the same interim status in the accreditation report and perhaps the board needs to look at both Marion and Grandeville: "If its good for one [school area], its good for the other."

Board Chairman [from Memorial] L. R. called for a vote on the motion. It passed 3-2 with [Deer Run, Grandeville, and Memorial board members] voting "aye"; [Marion and Craddockville members] voting "nay."

To further underline the possibility that the central office was somehow involved in the redistricting process, the superintendent quickly proposed some immediate staffing changes between the three affected schools, most of which were also opposed by Mr. B and Mrs. C, but both of which passed on a 3–2 board motion anyway. Then, after the meeting, Mr. B issued the following statement to those in attendance and the press:

At the Cave County Board meeting July 10, [the] board member from Deer Run made the motion, seconded by [the Grandeville member], with board chairman L. R. [from Memorial] also voting "yes," to change the attendance boundary lines of the other two board members' [schools]. State statutes require that a school board district like Cave County have members duly elected by the people, each with a voice in implementing board policy. This is not always followed, for Mrs. C and myself were never informed although the boundary changes were in our districts only.

As well, the Craddockville board member, D. C., went on record opposing the redistricting decision:

At the July 10 school board meeting a resolution was passed that affects primarily Marion School District and to some extent, Craddockville School District. As you know, we're talking about people and children whenever redistricting takes place. It is a serious and important concern for all involved.

The vote to redistrict was 3–2 with [Mr. B] and me voting "no." We asked for a reasonable amount of time to consider the proposal and whom it would affect. We requested that we be given an opportunity to study the same information that Mr. G [from Deer Run] had been given by central office personnel. We were denied that opportunity.

It is discouraging when partisan considerations are considered more important than the lives of children in our school system. I support a strong educational system for Cave County and will discuss and look at any proposal which is a result of the **entire** board having input and where the welfare of our children is the main concern.

Significantly, a resounding public outcry against the board redistricting decision was heard several weeks later during a quickly arranged early afternoon meeting of the board. According to some, this special meeting was set up in hopes that few citizens would find out about the session, but minority board members are alleged to have raised the alarm on the meeting time and place. Subsequently, several hundred citizens are reported to have showed up "in an ugly mood" that August afternoon, and the redistricting decision was (at least temporarily) reversed.

A DEER RUN CONNECTION?

The mood in Cave County schools remained one of suspicion and distrust in Fall 1989. Although few doubted that the superintendent had done good academic things for the County, some of his quick decisions, top-down administrative style, and the backdrop of a politicized school board (amplified by the then-current school consolidation fears) appeared to have compromised some of the system's positive advances. As Mr. G put it, "I didn't write the Accreditation report; yet the fallout from this document has made this the most difficult year in all of my 21 years as a school superintendent."

Yet, since the school targeted by the state to eventually become a permanent elementary school (once a middle school is built) is the one he graduated from, the one where he began his professional career, and is home to school board member(s) who have always been on his side in 3–2 policy decisions, his claims of neutrality with regard to the state accreditation report rang hollow to many of the people we interviewed in Fall 1989.

Some county residents remain convinced, for example, that the superintendent's ability to "wheel and deal" in Cave County has always been based on both his local Deer Run "connection," and upon his "insider" status with the state department of education. I have already alluded to the father-in-law vote to remove the previous school superintendent (but who could not vote to hire Mr. G, as he was a relative). Later, critics point out, the first central office staff inherited/put together by the superintendent included seven members, five of whom were either from or had taught at Deer Run. And furthermore, we were told, only a combination of board pressure and some career decisions by prominent central office staff members to retire/leave the county compelled Mr. G to reconstitute the central office with an altered "management team."

Yet we are not sure this is entirely accurate. In point of fact, our earlier interpretation that the Cave County system is a top-down one rests partly on our observation that its central office staff (almost all of whom were earlier building principals) is comprised of the most innovative (male) educators in the system. Meanwhile, compared either to the Braxton County situation or even to Charlotte County, most current building principals in Cave County are either new to the principalship, comparatively less interested in school improvement, and/or under suspicion of not carefully enough following the superintendent's wishes in their respective schools. And more than one building principal refused to speak candidly over the phone regarding the contents of this essay for fear of being identified with this document.

Another observation underlying what appears to us to be an uneasy tension between "politics" and "professionalism" in Cave County involved the school board election in Spring 1989, when two of the three board members typically supporting the superintendent's policy decisions were replaced. Interestingly, in both cases board incumbents "retired" yet backed a local candidate for their district seats. And the election (which the superintendent revealed to us he was quite nervous about) was won in both cases by political newcomers backed by the previous board members. One from Deer Run, and one from Grandeville.

Critics of the superintendent and the alleged "behind the scenes" negotiating they accuse him of doing were perhaps disappointed but not surprised by the redistricting affair mentioned earlier, or by the somewhat curious state announcement that Deer Run should become a permanent elementary school and Marion closed at such time as a county middle school was built. After all, attendance figures would suggest the reverse, as, at the time of accreditation, Marion had the third highest enrollment among the county's five elementary schools. This fact, Marion parents contend, should have made it the logical third permanent elementary school site (rather than Deer Run) for the county. Also, some note, since the only foreseeable population growth in the west end of the county (near Deer Run) are the Amish (who have their own school), it would make sense on paper to continue the Marion school where some future growth would be possible (since this town lies on the interstate and 17W).

Critics of the superintendent's policies therefore contend that political rather than rational grounds were been behind the board decision to initially accept the facilities portion of the state accreditation report. Furthermore, critics of the superintendent argue that, as he is closely tied to the state department of education, has his staff routinely involved in accrediting teams for other school districts, and was the Cave County chairman for the recently elected State Superintendent of Public Instruction, he had some ability to "shape" the facilities portion of the state accreditation report before it was formally delivered to the county.

On the other hand, the official position of the central office was that transportation problems in the west end of the county made Deer Run a logical place to have a school, since bussing children from there would be more difficult than bussing them along the interstate from the Marion attendance area. Also, the superintendent claimed that history is on the side of Deer Run, which was one of the three high schools before the building of Cave County High, whereas Marion has always been an elementary feeder school to Craddockville.

Apparently, however, the superintendent felt it unnecessary to personally explain the accreditation report to outraged Marion parents, yet he found the time to do so for parents at Grandeville. This led (the same) critics of central office politics to believe he had made some sort of behind-the-scenes deal with the new Grandeville board member—Including many angered Marion parents who pushed for a confrontation with the school board and superintendent (with some success) at the board meetings in August and September 1989.

NEGOTIATING THE SUPERINTENDENT'S NEW CONTRACT

Hot on the heels of the county controversy of the accrediting report and redistricting decisions came a motion to renew Mr. G's contract. During our early interviews in Cave County, the superintendent had suggested that, within a year or two, he would be stepping down as superintendent to pursue other interests—perhaps even going south to take on other educational career possibilities. We were quite surprised, therefore, to find a year after our initial interview with him (then September 1989) that the school board was prepared to offer Mr. G a new 2-year contract. As it turns out, unofficial discussions behind closed doors are alleged to have featured debates over whether the superintendent's new contract would be for 4 years, 3 years, 2 years, or 1 year. Significantly, all but one board member agreed that, even given ongoing local controversies, some extension of Mr. G's contract was justified: critics of the superintendent allegedly favored a short extension, supporters a longer one.

Yet parents (primarily from Marion) attending the September board meeting virtually turned the unadvertised discussion of the superintendent's new contract into a shouting match. And they specifically came (according to those we interviewed in the parking lot while the board went into executive session) to complain about renewing the superintendent's contract during a time of confusion and concern over the state accreditation report.

Yet the board voted 3–2 to renew Mr. G's contract for 2 years (for 1990–1991 and 1991–1992), making their announcement even before all who had waited outside returned to the room to hear the results of the board vote. And, citing the importance of appearing at the landfill ordinance meeting (previously mentioned), the September meeting was adjourned right after the contract vote, at which time a concerned parent from Marion had to be restrained from attacking the board chairman.

THE STATUS OF TEACHERS IN CAVE COUNTY

From all outside appearances, the superintendent and the majority of board members in Cave County would appear to have decided that, as long as they have a policy-making majority in the county and "everything (curricularly speaking) looks good on paper," they don't have to bend toward, or appease, particular interest groups in the system.

So, too, it would appear, particular interests of the Cave County Education Association (which represents over 80% of the county teachers) are little recognized. In point of fact, at the September board meeting previously mentioned, the board chairman announced to the audience (and the President of the CCEA, who teaches at Grandeville) that the Cave County School Board does not formally recognize the CCEA, and that teachers wishing to speak at board meetings can be recognized as individuals, but not as representatives of "a teacher's union."

And the animosity between some teachers and the superintendent is also well documented in Cave County. According to the president of the local NEA affiliate (who is an outspoken critic of the superintendent), Mr. G had been requested by teachers in Fall 1988 to clarify/improve several relatively minor aspects of their employment.

For example, some teachers wanted the option of receiving all of their yearly salaries during their contract period, rather than having their 9-month salaries divided into 12-monthly installments. Of even lesser significance, some teachers in the system were concerned about the confidentiality of their salaries and requested the superintendent to have monthly paychecks individually addressed to them in sealed envelopes, rather than delivered collectively by representatives from the central office.

According to our early interviews with the CCEA President, requests like the above were entertained by the superintendent in 1988, but for some reason few CCEA requests had actually been acted upon during the 1988–1989 school year or in the first half of the 1989–1990 school year. According to Mrs. D., during the accreditation year the superintendent was looking for ways (briefly) to appease teachers who might be critical of the system. Yet once the "honeymoon" period was over, continued pressure on the superintendent and the school board to deliver on several requests acknowledged earlier led to verbal altercations between assertive teachers and the superintendent and board.

To counter this argument, the superintendent contended that the CCEA did not ideologically represent even one-fifth of the county's 162 teachers. And furthermore, he argued, there was no way that a poor school system could continue to meet all of the requests of teachers without raising local taxes, which would never be done by the school board. Other teachers queried about these issues revealed a true split in the county. Some felt that the lines of communication were poor in the system; others suggested that Mr. G was doing nothing out of line, and that the real reason most teachers even belong to the CCEA is for the right to participate in the state (KEA) liability insurance program.

The visible conflict between the official CCEA representative and the Cave County Board of Education led its president to became so frustrated by the whole process by Fall 1989 that she tried to resign from her office. Yet, since no other teacher (she argued) was willing to incur the continued wrath of the superintendent and board, she volunteered to return for another year of service. According to her, she had "already had her throat slit" and had little more to lose by remaining in her leadership role.

RELATIVES IN THE SYSTEM

A final point of issue in the Cave County system, which appeared to alienate some teachers, related to supposed special treatment of relatives of at least one board member and the superintendent. As may be the case in many school systems in which the district's school leaders/employers have relatives employed in or attending school in a district, gossip and innuendo appear to accompany such relatives particularly when relatives routinely move around within the system, and/or when their jobs fall outside of regular classroom teaching duties. Such an atmosphere pervaded sentiments in Clinch County, and they also did in Cave County.

Without going into details, there were several incidents in the Cave County system in 1988 and 1989 in which both children and spouses of the superintendent and at least one (majority) board member figured prominently. Whether accurate or not, the word around the system was that some teachers and principals had been severely chastised for not making special allowances in the academic/athletic advancement of children of these important school leaders. As well, "open" (i.e., advertised and well-defined) hiring policies for noninstructional school personnel were the crusade of some community members during these years, policies which were argued to be necessary, since relatives of school system leaders appeared to have been given well-paying jobs which were not subject to the same sorts of credentialling as classroom teachers.

So, too, a number of informants we spoke to were eager to point out several controversial decisions/confrontations between teachers, principals, and the superintendent and board members during 1988–1989. One was an (in)famous mid-year teacher reassignment scenario of Cave County in Fall 1988. According to the central office, the movement of "21," or "26," teachers (depending upon the source) to different classes/schools during mid-year was due to some necessary central office shifts—which of necessity involved new roles for all other district personnel (given certification concerns). Yet critics of the superintendent maintain that the entire incident was caused by a poor grade given his son in a math class at the high school, and that the abrupt teacher reassignment, which affected many, many students and teachers, was accomplished to move the "guilty" math teacher.

Another 1989 confrontation between the superintendent and a high school teacher, who was also an assistant football coach at CCHS (and husband of the president of the CCEA), seemingly fueled the fire of the superintendent's critics within the teaching ranks. The reported confrontation involved the (lack) of playing time for the superintendent's son in a junior varsity football game. Again, without going into any alleged details of this confrontation, a shouting/shoving match ensued between the superintendent and the abovementioned coach, witnessed by a number of students and at least one other teacher.

A CONCLUDING NOTE

While we have little hard "data" to support some of the earlier mentioned accusations, there definitely appears to be a basic lack of trust in the policy-making practices of the Cave County schools, as voiced by significant (though not all) numbers of county teachers and parents; and unfortunately, the superintendent's family eventually became some point of this contention. More importantly, the visible unhappiness of some county teachers, combined with published accounts of school board members who contend they are routinely excluded from the decision-making process in the County, probably does much to undermine central office efforts to enhance public confidence and parent involvement in the system. And, combined with the then current worries over school redistricting and consolidation, we suspected in Spring 1990 that it may be quite some time before serious bridges can be built between parents, communities, and the central office.

On the other hand, short-term and more modest parent involvement practices of an instrumental nature, we suggested, might have been possible in the system, once the school-closing issue died down. Little did we know at the time of the final evaluation report what the Kentucky School Reform Act of 1990 would portend for the state, or for Cave County. And significant portions of this act (see Chapter 6) directly bear on the political, leadership, and involvement dynamics/problems discussed in this chapter.

What we **did** end the evaluation report on was the following observation:

> According to one expert, "Most of the formats that are used to bring parents and teachers together are ritualized and ineffective; they prevent the building of adult relationships and obstruct the possibility of solving problems together" (Swap, 1987). If the latter is the case, Cave County schools may indeed be able to utilize some of the "ritualized" practices Swap describes. If more intensive parent involvement is to be achieved in the county, some of the political, management and demographic factors underlying its current situation may have to be resolved first.

REFERENCES

Bureau of the Census. (1900-1980). *U.S. Population.* Washington, DC: Department of Commerce.

Christenson, J. A., Warner, P. A., & Greer L. S. (1979). Quality of life in Kentucky counties. *Community Development Issues, 1*(1)

Clark, T. D. (1985). Kentucky education through two centuries of political and social change. *HSC, 83*(3), 173-201.

DeYoung, A. J. (1983). The status of education in Central Appalachia. *Appalachian Journal, 10*(4), 321-334.

DeYoung, A., & Boyd, T. (1986). Urban school reforms for a rural district: A case study of school/community relations in Jackson County, Kentucky. *Journal of Thought, 21*(4), 25-42.

DeYoung, A. J., Vaught, C., & O'brien, J. (1981). *Educational performance in Central Appalachia: Statistical profiles of Appalachian and non Appalachian school districts.* Lexington, KY: Appalachian Center, University of Kentucky.

Doyle, E., Layson, R., & Thompson, A. (1987). *From the fort to the future: Educating the children of Kentucky.* Lexington, KY: Kentucky Images.

Estes, F. (1988). *Cora Wilson Stewart and the Moonlight Schools of Kentucky, 1911–1920: A case study in the rhetorical uses of literacy.* Unpublished doctoral dissertation, University of Kentucky, Lexington.

Forderhause, N. K. (1985). "The clear call of thoroughbred women": The Kentucky Federation of Women's Clubs and the crusade for Educational Reform, 1903–1909. *HSC, 83*(1), 19-35.

Ginger, L. (1987). Some vital studies on education. In E. Doyle, R. Layson, & A. Thompson (Eds.), *From the fort to the future* (pp. 313-333). Lexington, KY: Kentucky Images.

Hackensmith, C. W. (1970). *Out of time and tide: The evolution of education in Kentucky.* Lexington, KY: Bureau of School Service, College of Education, University of Kentucky.

Kentucky Department of Economic Development. (1986). *Resources for economic development: Cave County, Kentucky.* Frankfort, KY: Kentucky Department of Economic Development.

Kentucky Department of Education. (1963). History of education in Kentucky, 1939–1964. *Commonwealth of Kentucky Educational Bulletin, 31*(11),

Kentucky Department of Education. (1939). History of education in Kentucky, 1915–1940. *Commonwealth of Kentucky Educational Bulletin, 13*(10),

Kentucky Department of Education. (1914). History of education in Kentucky. *Commonwealth of Kentucky Educational Bulletin, 7*(4),

McVey, F. (1949). *The gates open slowly: A history of education in Kentucky.* Lexington, KY: University of Kentucky Press.

Pack, J. E. (1976). *A history of school district consolidation in the state of Kentucky.* Unpublished thesis, Miami University.

Peshkin, A. (1982). *The imperfect union: School consolidation and community conflict.* Chicago: University of Chicago Press.

Robinson, D. M. (1932). Governor Robert L. Taylor and the Blair educational bill in Tennessee. *Tennessee Historical Magazine*, Series 11, *11*(1). Nashville: Vanderbilt University Press.

Sewell, M. (1919). The schools of the mountains. In E. Doyle, R. Layson, & A. Thompson (Eds.), *From the fort to the future* (pp. 93-103). Lexington, KY: Kentucky Images.

Silver, R., & DeYoung, A. (1986). The ideology of rural/Appalachian education, 1895-1935: The Appalachian education problem as part of the Appalachian life problem. *Educational Theory, 36*(1), 51-65.

Southern Historical Press. (1979). *History of Kentucky illustrated* (3rd ed.). Easley, SC: Southern Historical Press.

Swap, S. M. (1987). *Enhancing parent involvement in schools: A manual for parents and teachers.* New York: Teachers College Press.

Tapp, H., & Klotter, J. (1977). Educating the people in Kentucky. In E. Doyle, R. Layson, & A. Thompson (Eds.), *From the fort to the future* (pp. 105-121). Lexington, KY: Kentucky Images.

Works Projects Administration. (1947). *Kentucky, a guide to the Bluegrass State.* New York: Hastings House.

Old Charlotte Elementary School (for white children), for sale.

6

Struggling with their Histories

The issues, problems, and concerns experienced in the four county school systems that have been the focus of this book are in many ways quite different from those most frequently described and discussed in the professional education literature. Nowhere in our fieldwork or in these school districts have (for example) classroom overcrowding, (recent) overt racial conflict, life-threatening discipline problems, drug abuse, problems with educating a multicultural population, or children's safety been reviewed as locally problematic.

On the other hand, learning outcomes and ways to achieve them (though not the particular focus of this work) are and remain serious concerns of most of the schools we spent almost 3 years in and around. National educational aims and school improvement strategies, in other words, are for the most part the same aims of rural schools I have talked about; yet in significant ways, the contexts in which these aims are pursued are quite different.

The purpose of this book has been to serially investigate a variety of school and community contexts and issues in four rural Southeastern county systems; contexts and issues I have implicitly suggested have great but frequently unrecognized traditions, problems, and concerns. Most of the issues discussed here are well understood by rural education practiioners (at least the ones I have spent time with), yet professional educators and most scholars who write about public education in America seem unaware of much that I have tried to present in this manuscript.

The focus of this last chapter is threefold. On the one hand, I will attempt here to summarize the numerous mutually shared economic, political, social, and educational concerns from the four earlier-presented case studies, attempting to explicitly state what I perceived the shared rural and community problems are in these places. To underscore the aforementioned analytical effort, I will attempt to summarize points I believe are most cogent within four "postscripts" for each county and its school system. Each of these postscripts also update to Summer 1990 developments in each system relevant to themes discussed in the earlier case studies.

Before proceeding with final analyses and local updates, I will briefly present and discuss the four AEL school/community improvement projects undertaken in each school district. This will be attempted in order that those readers particularly interested in rural school innovation and change can glimpse what "worked" and what didn't "work" in this project, at least in the view of the evaluation team. So, too, since the AEL Rural/Small School program was the federally funded program which provided entrée to each system to begin with, it seems only fair to briefly review its impact for all readers.

Before I begin, I need once again to emphasize the limitations of the larger report and of this book. As a well-versed reader has had the opportunity to surmise, both the focus and the methodology used in developing the four previous case studies were influenced by larger qualitative evaluation concerns of a specific school innovation process. We were interested in school community dynamics and in school leadership issues related to community participation in the AEL project. As such, we observed, interviewed, and collected data relevant to school issues and problems as experienced at each county school system's central office, and the problematic educational concerns/schools where school improvement efforts were typically attempted. As well, since we quickly sensed a historical dimension relevant to school and community issues in each of the four places, we spent a moderate amount of energy on reading, analyzing, and interpreting local and state histories relevant to the earlier-mentioned themes of community and school leadership.

All of which is to say that, methodologically and academically speaking, much of the previous 240 pages might be considered less than adequate for themes and questions which we did *not* pursue. For example, readers interested either in classroom dynamics or community stratification patterns would likely obtain little from this manuscript, for we did not focus on such topics except as they related to the earlier themes suggested, and in fact neither of these pursuits (or many others which could have been targeted) is discussed in the previous pages. As one key informant who read my analysis of his county/school system phrased it, "This is very good, and it is amazingly accurate . . . but between every sentence there is another whole story."

The intent of our earlier evaluation study and of this manuscript was to describe and discuss school and community cultures in each of the four sites we were "assigned to" by the RSS School/Community project by AEL. And we were primarily focused on school leadership and the community contexts in which it operated. Accordingly, none of our case studies can be technically defined as an "ethnography."

Similarly, as we used a rather eclectic collection of collateral research methodologies to develop contextual discussion over and above observations and interviews, I cannot claim that this work contributes significantly to other scholarly traditions or literatures. For example, as I have primarily used local and secondary state historical sources (rather than archival material) to provide a historical backdrop on current dynamics, I cannot claim that the case studies presented are historically adequate from a scholarly perspective. So, too, I have spent many pages in this manuscript talking about economic change and decline in these four counties; but these factors are talked about typically in local terms and from descriptive accounts, rather than in econometric terms or statistical categories.

Finally, advocates of school reform and educational innovation in rural America and the Southeast would probably find little of instrumental use in the preceding pages. From my experience, professionals in these areas typically view description, discussed problems, and ironies of rural education in declining economic and/or community contexts as either inconsequential or too "academic." Rather, before lengthy discussion of local school contexts or community issues are even concluded, such educators want to know about "policy implications" of the research. Unfortunately, I remain convinced that many of the implications for improved education in each of the four counties discussed herein probably originate in extraschool community and economic changes, rather than the reverse. However, I certainly applaud the efforts of those within many of the schools earlier discussed in attempting to improve the educational and social conditions of their children within the limited span of control they have over such factors.

EDUCATIONAL CONTEXTS AND SCHOOL IMPROVEMENT PROJECTS

As discussed throughout this manuscript, the primary focus of this research was upon an evaluative study of four school/community improvement projects, projects which were intended to demonstrate a *process* for collaborative problem solving, followed initially by four specific school improvement strategies and projects. However, the main purpose of this book has not been on these processes/projects, but upon the community economic and social contexts within which they operated. Readers interested in particular dynamics of the AEL process and procedures used should contact the Lab directly for specifics of that research.

Related to the evaluation itself, evaluation staff abstracted from the RSS technical proposal (see Chapter 1) components of the school/community partnership model held as unique and important for success of the project(s) as outlined by AEL. Subsequently, we spent hundreds of hours interviewing, being observers and participant observers, collecting school-based documents, discussing change efforts with involved teachers and parents, and even constructing and using an "exit" survey for all primary participants in the four AEL sites. The following observations and interpretations are based on these multiple data sources.

General areas of questioning undertaken in our multiple evaluative strategies and documents were based on our interpretation of both the focus and hypothesized uniqueness of AEL's School/Community Partnership the Model.

That is, we asked questions about how both school and community participants viewed the desirability and promise of coming together to help improve local schools, and we asked questions about whether participants viewed ongoing and completed Lab activities (as well as relevant efforts of local school officials) favorably.

The first district chosen and volunteering to become an RSS demonstration site was Braxton County, West Virginia. To our surprise, we found school improvement efforts in that county to be very much in accord with the Effective Schools literature, a literature which also informed much of the school improvement interests of AEL (for example, the PRO-S/E). Importantly, while Braxton County had achieved measured success in improving academic instruction in its elementary and middle schools, high school dropout rates and teacher morale in the high school were a major concern of the district superintendent, and this concern was reflected in the views of many community leaders.

In accord with AEL's belief, the district superintendent was a big believer in "use of assessment" (to use Effective Schools terminology), in constant "monitoring," and in continuous and *long-term* school improvement and due process. So, too, the choice of the Braxton County steering committee (which sifted through the two RSS studies and came up with a school improvement plan) was targeted precisely at the concern of the superintendent: improving school climate (and student success) at the high school. Significantly, even though climate assessments and improvement committees were available at two of the middle schools (as a result of principal "conversions" to the Effective Schools literature at the West Virginia Principals' Academy), the superintendent urged inclusion of all three middle schools, as well as the high school, in climate assessments and improvements, believing that new and improved data upon which to base decisions are always desireable, and believing that (further) targeting/stigmatizing the high school as a problem institution might backfire in terms of school improvement efforts.

In order to assess and help improve school climate in the Braxton County middle and high schools, the steering committee decided to assess both total *school* and selected *classroom* climates. For the first objective, the Kettering School Climate Profile (SCP) was chosen (from among many), and for the second, a Classroom Climate scale developed by Barry Fraser was utilized.

Classroom climate assessments (which involved a pretest, directed classroom improvement strategies for half of the participating teachers, and a posttest) were completed in the county under the supervision of a locally based school climate consultant (then a county elementary principal, who later accepted a position as school superintendent in a neighboring county). Yet it took some months for the classroom climate project to get underway, as RSS staff took some time in locating and finding an acceptable local representative to supervise the process.

With regard to the second (and perhaps more importantly viewed) school (building) climate assessment, parents, teachers, students, and school administrators filled out and returned the school climate instruments via mail to AEL in Charleston during September and October 1988. Yet, because AEL had no previous experience in analyzing the elaborate climate surveys, and because scoring of each district proved a quite cumbersome process, school climate results were only slowly returned to the district, and no RSS representative ever returned to Braxton County to formally "debrief" principals or the superintendent regarding results by the project's official end.

However, this delayed last RSS phase did not negatively influence the Braxton County superintendent's view of the Lab or the program, even if some steering committee members were left ignorant of final project outcomes. Rather, since the high school principal appeared to have terminal cancer but would not resign (or could not financially afford to resign), redirecting the climate of the high school was judged to remain a future undertaking (according to the superintendent) until there was some resolution of the building leadership issue.

The second system discussed in the evaluation report, although technically not the second district to participate in the project, was Charlotte County, Virginia. Both the selection of the school division in Virginia, and the characteristics of the system and its leadership, were quite different from any of the others in the RSS demonstrations: teacher morale in the state and local division was comparatively high and remained so through 1989–1990, high school dropout rates remained below 10% (and never appeared a real issue), there was a large minority population in the county, the local communities traditionally (since the 1940s) appear to have supported and been involved in many aspects of school functioning, aggressive school improvement protocols had been put into place throughout the state under state mandates/incentives, an appointed rather than an elected school board ran the school division, and the superintendent was new (to the role, and to the county).

While Charlotte County appeared to us to have had a tradition of professional school interests and support, we found few overt "crusaders" in the division seeking to dramatically transform or reorient the entire system, as was arguably the case in the two most aggressive school improvement districts, Braxton and Cave Counties. Rather, what was of concern there were establishing and renewing channels of communication between the school division and the community, communications which had become brittle and weakened under the previous superintendent.

At the same time, school facilities were a major concern of many school and community people in Charlotte County. Randolph-Henry High School, and the new Eureka Elementary school, were both symbolic of community interests in education; but the county middle school continued to exist in virtual piecemeal fashion. The legacy of a dual Black and White educational system manifested itself in the county at the middle school level, as the former Black high school and former county seat elementary school (divided by the main road into Charlotte Court House) provided the buildings in which middle school classes were taught. Yet, as the school board in Charlotte County does not set its own budget but must work through the county Board of Supervisors, talk of major school building improvements or new building construction must be approved by the Board of Supervisors before bonds can be approved or state loans requested.

In order to assess the financial implications of building a new middle school without spending division money, the steering committee for the RSS demonstration project in Charlotte County chose to seek AEL funding for a middle school feasibility study. Steering committee members in Charlotte County seemed to agree with our assessment of the poor "stepchild" status of the county middle school. Importantly, the division school board approved of the feasibility study in the hope that, once a new building for the middle school became more than just an idle wish, the county Board of Supervisors would sit up and take notice of this grass roots school improvement effort (fueled by prominent citizens on the school board and on the steering committee). Hopeful speculation was that, if enough attention to the feasibility study was forthcoming, eventually such a building project (requiring the borrowing and repayment of low-interest loans available to the division from the state) would be approved by the Board of Supervisors.

The clear "outlier" among all four of the school systems identified by state advisory groups for inclusion in the RSS demonstrations was Clinch County, Tennessee. Although test scores and attendance rates in the district had ostensibly improved in this system during the past decade, we could find no particular reason for such improvements. As the district superintendency is an elected position in Clinch County, we were only mildly surprised to find out that the then-current superintendent there identified himself as a politician as much as an educator.

This was not to suggest that no qualified central office supervisors work in Clinch County, or that all practicing teachers were unqualified or lacked student respect. Rather, we found little *building* level emphasis on school improvement, use of data, monitoring of student progress, or other aggressive practices designed to lead classroom teachers to better performance (with the possible exception of some practices at the county high school). And even the district superintendent confided to us late in the RSS project that what the system needed was a true "instructional leader," one who understood newly proposed state accountability measures and how to incorporate them into Clinch County schools.

The Clinch County system was poorer and smaller than any of the others included in this study. Four of the small elementary schools had enrollments of fewer than 100 and were administered in each case by teaching principals. Only two district schools had regular building principals, and both were much involved with the types of bureaucratic details (like answering the telephones) not seen in any of the other systems. The lack of clerical staff in each school likewise appeared a fact of life in the central office, where most personnel were hard driven to find, implement, and document special state and federal programs. And all of these lack-of-resources dynamics were further confounded by a reported history of political intrigue, and a continuing battle between the district superintendent and a political enemy of his, the Executive of the Clinch County Commission, an official who has very real authority over some local school appropriations under Tennessee statutes.

Given all of the fiscal turmoil and political infighting in and around the school system, a severe illness of the superintendent, and an admitted lack of instructional leadership at most buildings, parent involvement was chosen (from among many) identified needs to be addressed by the Clinch County steering committee for the RSS demonstration project. More specifically, it was argued that minimal building leadership and a geography which oriented small communities away from the county seat helped to weaken parent involvement in schools. And even the posting of school information of potential interest to parents in a county paper was not an option, for there is no remaining county newspaper. Rather, news from out of the county (and out of the state) were primary information sources for many Clinch Countians. And neither the school system nor even the high school had a weekly or monthly paper, another fact separating the Clinch County system from others studied in this project.

Thus, the steering committee decided that instituting a school newsletter would be an excellent first step in better informing and involving parents in the day-to-day operations of the school system. Unfortunately, the chair of the Steering Committee, who also teaches English at the high school, was the only in-school volunteer deeply committed to the project. No building or central office administrator actively worked on the newsletter, with the exception of several (teaching) principals of more remote schools who donated copy. From the community, several interested county seat citizens donated time (and one an older model Apple computer). Yet little active administrative encouragement and/or resources were forthcoming in early project stages.

Likewise, several AEL developments, coupled with the superintendent's life-threatening illness during Winter 1988 and Spring 1989, stalled and/or minimized the implementation of the RSS demonstration project. On the one hand, the district superintendent seemingly became more interested in the possibility that AEL could help identify for his district additional sources of external monies than any other school improvement project they might facilitate. Yet, when it became clear to him that the Lab wanted Clinch County to work in conjunction the Clinch Valley Cooperative (an agency initially set in place with the help of AEL some years earlier), and when the implication was made that he might have to learn how to submit proposals with the assistance of AEL, he began to balk at further collaborative efforts with the Lab.

In the first place, the Clinch Valley Co-op is headed by a previous superintendent of Clinch County who earlier was a political rival of the current
superintendent. In addition, the Clinch County system has for years been quite
successful (according to the superintendent) in obtaining external monies: what
he perceived the district needed were not grant-getting *skills*, but avenues into
where the money is. Unfortunately, the RSS staff person who had been working
on the grant-writing angle with the superintendent first stopped coming into the
county to follow up on RSS activities in Spring 1989, and then she left the
project entirely to take another job.

Furthermore, the superintendent reacted negatively when he discovered in
Summer 1989 that the RSS project had set up an initial bank account of only
$1,200 for the newsletter (when he had heard that Charlotte County received
$5,000 for their feasibility study). Significantly, the superintendent had hoped
that AEL would donate enough money to the newsletter project that he could
use some of it for another purpose (e.g., purchasing some software for use by the
high school principal). Yet, when it became obvious (to him) that the AEL
connection was not going to lead quickly to important new revenues for the
entire system, he confided to us that he "had about had it" with AEL.

Thus, even by the official conclusion of Clinch County's RSS demonstration
project, no county school newspaper was ever produced. And while the teacher
charged with its production was still optimistic that the 1990–1991 school year
would see some publication, the lack of enthusiasm for the paper at the central
office suggested a dubious long-term future for this undertaking, which is all the
more disappointing, since such a project, seriously pursued, might have an
important impact.

The final system discussed in the evaluation report was Cave County,
Kentucky. As stated earlier, we had more difficulty penetrating the veneer of
how school leadership functions there, as few insiders (other than teachers or
ex-principals) would talk candidly (in our judgment) about system dynamics. On
paper, this is a good and progressive system. And by almost any account, the
Cave County situation had turned around dramatically during the 8-year
tenure of the current superintendent.

Yet, compared to each of the other systems, there were important differences
in Cave County with regard to leadership and direction. We judged system
innovation there to be very much under the direct control of the superintendent, to the extent that dissenting opinions about how things might work were
formally discouraged if not part of the superintendent's agenda. And as a
lifelong educator with definite opinions (and a clearly defined reference group in
the state department of education), educational innovation in Cave County was
more a function of extra classroom programs and special projects instigated by
him than a matter of sustained and building-coordinated activities sponsored by
principals or teachers.

As well, there was a politicized and nonconsensual style of decision making in the Cave County system uncharacteristic of similar processes in both Braxton and Charlotte Counties. Some board members, that is, those routinely on the wrong side of 3–2 policy votes/decisions, openly argued that they and their schools were treated as second-class citizens in the county. I was forcefully reminded of the politicized nature of school dynamics in Cave County in the late summer of 1990 when dedication ceremonies for the new high school sports complex were held. There, in front of a large community audience, the superintendent publically thanked (only) those three school board members who voted in favor of the complex in the years before. And only these three individuals were awarded a placque to commemorate the occasion, in front of the two other board members who had changed their minds about the project before its completion.

Similarly, it also appeared the case to us that the most professionally aggressive and talented elementary school building principals (with one or two exceptions) were routinely whisked away by the superintendent to the central office, where board members (who influence many if not most policy decisions involving hiring, firing, and building expenditure) could not stifle their creative efforts. It appeared to us that the Cave County superintendent wanted instructionally creative school leaders/administrators to stay where he could supervise them and direct their energies, as aggressive building-level innovation and independence had earlier led to some confrontations between previous principals and the superintendent.

Put another way, of the two aggressive and improvement minded school districts, one system (Braxton County) had strong, independent, and long-term building leadership, with central office staff providing support services. Meanwhile, the second system (Cave County) had a strong and carefully directed (primarily male) central office staff, but comparatively inexperienced building leadership. And in the latter case, the most aggressive and professionally minded principals appeared sooner or later to be either absorbed into the central office, or forced to resign.

The status of classroom teachers also appeared somewhat enigmatic in Cave County compared to the other three systems. While many very talented teachers believed in the programs instituted by the current superintendent, others felt intimidated and/or alienated by their treatment in the system. For example, the Cave County Educational Association was not formally recognized as a representative organization, even though more than 80% of county teachers belonged to the group. Similarly, differences of opinion with regard to several personnel and benefits policies in the system triggered several vocal and physical confrontations between board members, the superintendent, and a number of teachers, a fact which further alienated some staff members, including the president of the CCEA.

Nevertheless, as a superintendent with a long history of looking at innovative programs and one with a close professional friend affiliated with

AEL, the Cave County superintendent chose to participate in the RSS project in Winter 1987, and both AEL "evaluations" of the school district revealed few academic complaints about the system. Rather, parent involvement was chosen by the Steering Committee as a worthy project, particularly as it was hoped that such an emphasis could be directed at those parents (ostensibly more rural or of lower SES) without previously extensive track records of local school involvement.

Signifying (in our judgment) the lack of real commitment to the RSS project in Cave County, the school improvement efforts undertaken there consisted of a request by the superintendent to have the Lab sponsor an in-service program for teachers, and a request by the Steering Committee for AEL to provide money for individual teachers and schools to improve parent involvement in ways they (teachers) saw fit. Put another way, the parent involvement projects sponsored by the RSS project basically involved a series of motivational speeches and practical strategies directed at teachers, and numerous small scale grants to entice parents into schools and classrooms.

In effect, what the RSS program was offering to the Cave County system were suggestions/techniques for improving local communication *processes* in the county related to schooling. However, we judged that improving processes of decision making/collaboration both within the school governance structure and between schools and parents remained a less than urgent concern, as outcomes/results/special programs deemed of importance to the superintendent were more centrally valued.

Compared to either Charlotte County or Braxton County, there was relatively little active central office follow up on what, if anything, occurred in classrooms of teachers who took part in the RSS sponsored in-service program; furthermore, only half of the building principals involved in the project actively got involved in it, which led to an uneven pattern of school grant applications to the Lab from Cave County. Parenthetically, the principal who most aggressively urged his teachers to write for AEL grants was moved into the central office at the end of the 1988–1989 school year. And in 1989–1990, three (of five) elementary teachers were new to the principalship and to their schools.

To compound the relatively poor collaborative processes in the Cave County system, a major state accreditation report sent the system into a tailspin during Spring and Summer 1989. In this report, two of the county's five elementary schools were declared "interim" facilities (due to decreasing enrollments and the "need" to build a middle school), which was interpreted by many county parents as a failing of the superintendent and the school board. And given a history of behind-the-scenes decision making in the county, confrontations among some parents, some teachers, and the superintendent and several board members led the superintendent to downplay any further parent involvement initiatives for the foreseeable future.

THE MORE THINGS CHANGE, THE MORE THEY STAY THE SAME: 1990 COMES TO BRAXTON COUNTY, WEST VIRGINIA

There are probably several ways I could have updated and discussed significant school and community factors in each of the four counties earlier discussed. I could have ordered them according to the number of new events occuring in each; I could have discussed the one I felt most intrigued by and welcomed in first, and worked through the other three later; I could have returned to the first district described, and proceeded in the same order as in the first "go-round"; or I could have talked about the school system currently in the most precarious position, relative to emerging economic and educational issues.

Fortunately (or unfortunately, depending upon one's perspective), on almost every one of these counts, Braxton County, West Virginia, appears to me the best starting point in a review of important issues and discussion of significant school and community developments since my initial fieldwork.

In Chapter 2, I interpreted the Braxton County "situation" as one in which an early 20th-century boom in extractive industries and regional manufacture positively affected occupational opportunities and school building projects. Even though many in this county depended on small-scale agriculture and employment in extractive and lumber-processing industries, a diverse employment mix and large numbers of skilled workers (many employed in the railroad industry) appears to have made possible many educational opportunities and high expectations for the possibilities of education.

However, with the collapse of the coal industry, lack of acreage suitable for large scale agriculture, and inability of the state and county to construct a highway system suitable for commercial transportation, Braxton County's economy and the communities which depended on it went into serious decline by the 1940s, a decline which has yet to be significantly reversed.

Related to these facts, population outmigration in the county after 1940 was rapid, school closings were legion, and consolidation of remaining schools appears to have been at the forefront of the educational "story" in Braxton County during the 1940s, 1950s, 1960s, and 1970s. The last (I thought) significant chapters I would be able to talk about in Braxton County's "struggle with its history" involved the late-1960s consolidation of its three remaining community high schools into one (a consolidation still bothering many in Burnsville, Sutton, and Gassaway); and increasing state accountability measures intensified by the West Virginia legislature in the early 1980s, yet without general revenue increases by the state to pay for financial implications associated with these school improvement mandates.

Accordingly, we spent most of our time in Braxton County hearing about and/or observing several interrelated themes: continuing state economic crises as they affected public education there (signified by such factors as low teacher pay, late payment to local districts for the state share of school budgets, etc.); teacher and administration efforts (and controversies) in how best to facilitate educational performance of low-income and "at-risk" students; and continuing community and central office concern over leadership at the consolidated high school, particularly as the high school was meeting (or not meeting) the educational needs of potential high school dropouts.

To be honest, I expected that little of consequence would occur in Braxton County during late 1989 and 1990. While I expected that "leadership issues" at the high school would have been resolved during the school year, I assumed that state legislative efforts to hold back school-related expenditures would have been satisfied by Senate Bill 14, and economic improvements associated with I-79 would continue to proceed at a less than locally desired pace.

Instead, what I found in West Virginia was that the entire educational system in the state had remained in an uproar for almost the entire 1989–1990 school year, and that this uproar had seriously affected the Braxton County school system; that profound economic development (or at least talk of such development) was about to have (or may have) important consequences in the county; that the issues of improving high school dropout rates and high school leadership were not resolved during the 1989–1990 school year; and that school consolidation possibilities (now probabilities) in the county are likely to be as significant in the future of the county as they were 25 years ago, when BCHS was built.

While the general state of Braxton County's local economy remains currently in a marginal state, talk of big and serious changes (not all of which may be positive) are quite prevalent there. For example, the new steak house near McDonalds is now open, and a new Day's Inn is under construction on the hill overlooking the Interstate and all Flatwoods restaurants in one direction, and the forest in the others. The developer of the new motel/hotel argues, not only that will tourists find the new motel of great utility, but that the new facility is being designed as a convention center for state and regional groups seeking a site for regional conferences, etc.

As suggested in Chapter 2, talk about regional- and Washington, D.C.-sponsored prisons continues. While current plans call for downsizing the D.C. prison from 8,500 to 1,500 beds, it still appears that Gilmer County will be the location for the facility. Meanwhile, the regional jail to be built locally has been retargeted for a site in the approximate location of all the other current tourist developments, somewhere off the Flatwoods exit (and within a mile or so from BCHS). While there remains some concern about housing a population of criminals in the county, the fact that this population will be primarily of in-state origin (and theoretically incarcerated for less serious crimes) has led to less local resistance for the regional jail than for the D.C. prison when early discussions involved Braxton County as a location. For example, a widely publicized public hearing on the proposed jail site found only four citizens speaking against its proposed Flatwoods location in the summer of 1990.

As discussed at length earlier, the "immediate" policy concern at Braxton County High School involved the tension between the county central office and the building principal. We mentioned that, in Summer 1989, the principal of the high school left for vacation and did not return until the school year began, leaving preplanning and scheduling issues up in the air and eventually taken care of by others in the building.

As it turned out, however, the principal *never* really returned in a full-time capacity to the high school, yet he didn't formally resign either. Rather, he first took leave and went to Florida to continue his recuperation from cancer therapy. However, after a brief period of remission, the cancer was diagnosed as growing again, and his doctors announced that there was virtually nothing further which could be done to arrest it. Finally, after a rapid decline in early Spring 1990, Mr. M. died (in May 1990) while still officially principal of Braxton County High School.

As the Braxton County central office awaited the climax of the principal's illness, most school improvement projects, which focused on the continuing dropout problem, were delayed. And even though early 1989 data showed that Braxton County's dropout rate was among the highest in the state (approximately 29%), no major new efforts to address this problem were mounted during the school year. As stated before, the central office believed it inappropriate to go over the building principal's head or replace him against his will in his advanced stage of illness. Furthermore, no additional administrators could be brought into the high school under state funding formulas anyway, and the school vice-principal (who, as athletic director, arguably already had a full-time job) attempted to maintain the school as best he could during 1989 and 1990. Unfortunately (according to the superintendent), the lack of strong leadership at the high school was related to several burglaries and some vandalism at BCHS in the Spring of 1990. Although such a contention was disputed by many teachers at the high school, such events in any event probably further weakened its reputation, and it is still held in some contempt by residents of the three communities which had their high schools consolidated in order for it to be built.

As important as such economic and long-standing high school dynamics have been in the county over the past several years, two even bigger state-wide events with local implications occurred in 1990. One was the 1990 statewide teacher strike and school closures, and the second was the inclusion of Braxton County in a new middle-school building program, which is be funded out of newly approved state bond funds and which will consolidate the three current middle schools (formerly high schools) into one facility sometime in the early 1990s.

Returning to the first of these two themes, by mid-March 1990, all but eight

West Virginia County school systems were on strike for higher pay and increased health care benefits. Faced with (yet another) state budget crisis, incoming Governor Gaston Caperton, and the state legislature, announced in 1988 statewide cutbacks in the number of teaching positions to be funded under state law. In order to assuage concerned teachers then, some of the projected dollars saved from lost positions were promised to be set aside for salary supplements for remaining teachers. Yet not only did the Governor freeze earlier-promised (in 1988) 5% "equity" pay increases for teachers in the poorest local districts, he also announced that money saved from the teacher force reductions mentioned above would need to be spent on other state projects in 1990, contrary to earlier announcements and expectations. This lack of money for teacher salary increases came at about the same time that local teacher organizations were publicizing that West Virginia already ranked 49th out of 50 (nationally) in this area.

To say the least, teachers and their two professional organizations (WVEA and WVFT) were up in arms over these developments, and 6,000 teachers proceeded (on an official school day) to "greet" the state legislature when it returned to Charleston in Spring 1990. Following this, the governor met with teacher organization representatives (organizations which had supported him in his election bid) but failed to make any offer of restoring promised teacher raises. Upset by this lack of results, Mingo County teachers threatened to go out on strike on March 7 unless specific and immediate pay increases were made/ restored.

Seeking to head off a potential strike, the governor pledged to restore frozen teacher raises and benefits if county WVEA and WVFT representatives would call off strike activities organized at county levels. Yet, because leaders of the teacher organizations would only promise to delay the strike until the legislature concluded business (several weeks later), the governor withdrew his offer.

Importantly, one aspect of the West Virginia budget shortfall "discovered" in 1989 appeared related to the reneging of the state legislature on increased taxes on coal operations/holdings in the state. Earlier, funds to be generated by the change in coal taxes were to be used to balance the state budget and to help offset promised teacher raises. Yet critical observers were convinced that coal operators/owners (many companies of which are subsidiaries of out of state corporations) had applied pressure behind closed doors to rescind the new taxes targeted at them, thus forcing the budget crisis that earlier-designated teacher pay supplements would now be tapped to offset.

In any event, and in defiance of the state school superintendent and many county superintendents and school boards, teachers in all but eight West Virginia counties were on strike by March 16. According to the March 18th *Charleston Gazette*, approximately 15,000 teachers in the state (out of 21,653) were involved, and approximately 250,000 students were then out of school. Faced with this situation, the governor and legislative leaders in both the House and Senate agreed to immediately appoint a study commission for finding new monies for education (including salary improvements). The governor also promised to call the legislature back into special session "to adopt the plan." Apparently believing that the strike mood had crested and was about to receed, WVEA and WVFT leaders accepted this promise, and all teachers were back in their classrooms by the third week in March.

While almost 19,000 teachers (around 90%) in West Virginia belong either to the WVEA or WVFT, Braxton County has a much lower participating percentage, and several teachers in the county told us that they thought the local chapter was officially inactive. In any event, Braxton County teachers never voted to join the strike, although the last vote held was only one shy of joining (87–86). It seems likely the case that many county teachers feared the loss of income from such an action, which caused them to vote against the strike. The local WVEA (former) president, on the other hand, suggested a different reason for proceedings in her county: fear of the superintendent and his evaluations. In any event, had not some resolution to teacher demands around the state been met in Charleston, it appears quite possible that Braxton County would have joined the other striking 47, had the strike continued much longer, especially since teachers from surrounding counties had begun to drive in mid-March to Braxton County in an effort to persuade its teachers to become involved.

While some observers believe that the teacher strike in West Virginia signals a new era in the state for improving education (especially given that a special session to address short- and long-term educational needs is to be held), others believe things will get much worse before they get better. According to the Braxton County superintendent, for example, 1989–1990 "was the worst, most frustrating, most demanding, and most demeaning year that I have ever spent in education." Furthermore, according to him, "the forces which have kept education together here have completely disbanded. Retirements and cutbacks in central offices (due to the impact of Senate Bill 14 and other legislative acts) make all county school systems vulnerable to the whims of the legislature."

In the eyes of Braxton County's superintendent, lobbying for control of education funding (i.e., who is hurt the least when education budgets are routinely cut back) has turned in favor of the teacher organizations now (although the service worker's union also remains quite strong). Obviously speaking from his proadministration role and with deeply held convictions in favor of strong school leadership (which is consistent with our earlier analysis of dynamics in the county), the superintendent was almost as critical of statewide teachers' organizations in their ostensibly successful 1989–1990 lobbying efforts as he had been earlier of particular teachers he found ineffective at the high school. It seems too early to tell yet, but as of this writing, both the local and state educational mood remains highly confrontational. 1990–1991 could be a very interesting period in the history of West Virginia and in Braxton County High School, where the selection of a new principal by the board of education (as "advised" by the superintendent) has heightened the fears of many current teachers.

AND SCHOOL CONSOLIDATION

Amid all the West Virginia turmoil in public education related to general operating budgets and personnel, a new program for school building improvements was underwritten by the 1988 state legislature. Authorized under House Bill 2325, a state School Building Authority was created in 1989 and initially funded to spend up to $7.5 million for school building construction/ rennovation projects. These funds were over and above other school improvement monies targeted for county school systems dependent upon enrollment figures.

Significantly, the superintendent of schools for Braxton County was invited/ appointed by personal friend of his (a former county superintendent, then the head of the school facilities division in the state department of education) to be on the advisory committee charged with drawing up guidelines for project proposals to the state School Building Authority. As Braxton County's superintendent saw it, the success or failure of the School Building Authority's interest in improving education with new building projects lay in creating guidelines for new construction which were "politics proof." Subsequently, data-based protocols for submitting school construction/remodeling plans became a key component in the application process.

As well, rank ordering of proposed school building projects to be funded out of the first year's relatively small bond money occurred within each Regional Education Service Organization (RESA). School systems were to propose faciltes they would construct with Authority money, and they had to provide a data-based rationale showing how proposed projects would facilitate earlier-discussed state interests in increasing economies of scale and merging of schools. Proposals that in essence would spend Authority money to repair existing small schools or construct new small ones without significantly lowering instructional servies and/or administrative costs were at a competitive disadvantage, according to Braxton County's superintendent.

And, at least in his region/RESA, Braxton County's superintendent should have known how all of this worked, for not only was he an architect of the *state* guidelines for the School Building Authority, but he also was a voting member of the RESA which rank ordered county proposals for requested monies. Not surprisingly (to us), Braxton County submitted an elaborate and well-documented middle school construction plan, which met all the Authority guidelines and which was subsequently ranked first in the RESA (of six counties). The next step was to await decisions of the state Authority, which had to choose from among the first-ranked proposals in each region which could be funded with the first year's approved bond money.

Importantly, in Braxton County the proposal to build a new middle school without direct costs to county taxpayers was the "angle" used by the superintendent to have his board approve applying for the project. As well, the expressed unlikelihood either that the Braxton County project would be top ranked within its own region, or that, even if it became RESA IV's top ranked project, it would be one of the relatively few funded, made the application process go smoothly there. And the school board approved 5-0 to submit the central office's middle school building plan to RESA IV.

Local concern about the implications of getting new state monies for building a middle school didn't appear to generate much attention in Braxton County's until its plan received top ranking in its region. At this point a number of small town leaders (particularly those in Burnsville and Gassaway) began to understand the implications of Authority funding for the plan if granted: that construction of a new and modern middle-school facility would force the consolidation of the three middle schools (formerly high schools) into a new and modern facility near the enigmatic Braxton County High School. And, recognizing that this move would in essence close the chapter on three facilities that have served for over almost four generations as educational centers for all native Braxton Countians who have gone beyond elementary schooling, one board member voted against accepting state funding for the project after being heavily lobbied by his constituents.

Hoping to counter negative fallout from potential funding of the new middle school before any state decision was announced, public hearings on the process and proposal were held around the county in early Spring 1990. Curricular benefits, as well as cost savings involved in not having to renovate the existing middle schools (in various states of disrepair), were presented, as well as attempts to show how staff administrative positions (already being cut back at the state level) would be facilitated.

Interestingly, a strategy employed in public presentations to assuage some citizens was that mistakes seen in the construction of the high school would not occur this time, and that the new facility would not be close enough/arranged so that problems of the high school and/or its students would contaminate the middle school or its students (a situation and concern very unlike proposed construction of the new middle school in Charlotte County, where the hope was that the glory/success of Randolph-Henry High School would be shared by a closely interconnected middle school).

To conclude this Braxton County update, and to shorten what in itself will remain a very important focal point in this school system's "struggle with its history," the county's middle-school proposal was favorably reviewed by the State School Building Authority, and money set aside for its construction. In announcing this "success," the April 2, 1990 *Braxton County Citizens' News* ran this story, along with extensive quotes from the superintendent on why he believed it was necessary:

> 'From my standpoint, I'm tremendously pleased that the proposed consolidated middle school project has been funded,' said [the] Superintendent of Schools following last week's announcement that the state's School Building Authority had selected Braxton County as one of ten to receive funding. The local school system will receive $4.9 million in funding for the proposed consolidation project. Additional net enrollment proceeds, in the amount of $352,000 per year, for the next two years, bring the total amount available for funding for the new county-wide middle school to $5.6 million.

> 'I am also pleased with the turnouts we have had at all our meetings to gain public input into that proposal, as well as our long-range plans for facilities in Braxton County,' [he] continued. 'I think that by people showing up at those meetings they've demonstrated their interest in good schools in the county—both those folk who were opposed to the plan and those who favored it. . . . I think that the plan is good, it's solid, it's educationally sound, . . . it will allow us to continue to operate, I think, as a county unit. We've taken a couple of real tough stands in this county, number one, to get a consolidated high school, and now to get a consolidated middle school, that places us in a position where we can provide a better education for students in Braxton County in the years to come, because it's being asked of us by the Legislature and, I think, by the taxpayers of the state, to spend lesser amounts of money and do the job on fewer staff. I can see, in those counties that are not trying to become more efficient, to place themselves in the circumstances where they can operate their schools more efficiently, that their kids will suffer at some point in time. If I knew that we could adequately provide three libraries and three educational programs complete with all the courses that we think are needed, as well as those that are recommended, I would prefer to have three separate middle schools. However, that luxury probably does not exist, and it's not any longer realistic to expect it.'

1990 DEVELOPMENTS IN CHARLOTTE COUNTY

Critics of qualitative research are frequently frustrated upon reading work such as this, because few summary judgments or policy recommendations are necessarily part of the fieldwork focus and because subjective judgments and foci (while intentionally minimized) are admittedly infused into the research. I have talked earlier about the "leadership" focus of earlier case studies and why this was built into the evaluation project. On top of this, I have my own subjective preferences regarding which of the researched school systems and county contexts I most enjoyed during my fieldwork experiences.

For example, given my regional interests and personal values, and operating within the admittedly limited knowledge base gained from only 3 years of exposure to each of the four places discussed in this book, my "favorite" place to visit from among the four discussed here was probably Braxton County, West Virginia. On the other hand, if I had to choose a place where learner outcomes and a supportive (formal) educational ethos was important for (for example) my own children's educational opportunities, I'd probably choose Charlotte County, Virginia.

My "favorite" county is economically depressed, still relatively isolated, but with traditions broad, powerful, and complex enough to entice a culturally curious outsider in for more extensive investigation and participation. Braxton County's 20th-century "struggle with its history" has been a losing battle to date, both for many of its children and certainly for its three primary towns. But if there is any hope for what may in future occur there, it lies in the heart of many, many school and community people with whom we have spent considerable amounts of time.

Charlotte County, on the other hand, has weathered much better the 20th-century historical trials and tribulations it has faced. I cannot say that race relations in the county are ideal, or that equal opportunity is provided all students in the school division, even if by most of our limited experiences this might be the case. Nor can we suggest that future problems (some of which we make reference to shortly) will be easily addressed by Charlotte County citizens. What can be said, however, is that the isolation and overdependence on boom-and-bust 20th-century extractive industries has not overpowered Charlotte County, and that the educational and political traditions of its residents have served it comparatively well, even though times there have and continue to be difficult. Educational traditions and educational expectations remain high in Charlotte County; and educationally speaking, it probably provides the best overall schooling opportunities among our four districts.

With regard to education, Charlotte County's current struggle with its history involves battles between local citizens and citizen's groups over local funding shares of the school budget, particularly as this battle relates to general state mandates and budget issues. While 1988–1989 (discussed in Chapter 3) appeared to be building year in the county (educationally), the 1989–1990 school year has seen mixed results, but with nowhere near the intensity of activities experienced in either Braxton County or in Cave County. In terms of economic development, few new projects of note occurred in Charlotte County in 1990. Importantly, economic development stories there involve as much developments resisted as they do developments initiated. As suggested in Chapter 3, a medical incinerator and the construction of a new power plant on the Staunton River were being talked about in 1989; but both developments were rejected by the county on environmental grounds. While the power plant may still be built in an adjacent county and thus still have an adverse effect on Charlotte County (according to its opponents), local residents were able to force a regional discussion over the issue which has at least temporarily held this project up. Better yet (from a local standpoint), the medical incinerator (proposed by a former resident of New Jersey who has bought property in the county) now seems a dead issue. And the lawsuit against the Charlotte County Board of Supervisors has been dropped as of this writing.

There have been two relatively positive economic developments in the county recently, however, which deserve at least some mention. United Parcel Service (recognizing the strategic highway location of Charlotte County) has established a regional handling center on State Highway 360, which now employs a number of local citizens as drivers. Closer to home (i.e., the home of the Charlotte County school board office), a new locally owned restaurant opened in Spring 1990, which briefly provided an outsider like myself an opportunity to have lunch or dinner somewhere besides at the gas station or in a school cafeteria. Unfortunately, (ostensible) lack of clientele forced the Court-House Inn out of business in July 1990.

PEDAGOGICAL DEVELOPMENTS IN CHARLOTTE COUNTY SCHOOLS

Educationally speaking, the mood in the county at administrative levels appears to have been positive in 1989–1990. The Bacon District Principal lauded the superintendent's proinnovation stance in the division, claiming that the former ethos of "management" rather than "leadership" had been reversed during the new superintendent's second year in office. And, he claimed, programs and iniatives designed to aid the teaching of particularly empoverished (primarily Black) children in his school were being supported by the central office.

Of course, having a good school year in Charlotte County probably always means that Randolph-Henry had a good year. And 1989–1990 appears to have been no exception to this rule. Significantly, there was a principal change at Randolph-Henry this year, a change which saw the female division curriculum coordinator request to become the new principal. And this request was approved, making Mrs. L the first ever female principal of Randolph-Henry.

As mentioned in Chapter 3, Charlotte County's was the only high school to have an active PTO among the four counties we "studied" for the AEL project. For its 50th anniversary year, this organization helped to sponsor and procure other contributions for its monthly celebrations during 1989–1990. And the enthusiasm and dedication of Mrs. L to making the year one of celebration and success appears one reason that both the school and the community had the good school year that it had.

In addition to successful programs like those seen in 1988–1989, this year's announced accomplishments included significant gains in standardized test scores for eleventh graders, increased enrollment in the dual enrollment program with Keysville College (making it the largest dual enrollment program in Virginia), almost 100% participation in the state-developed family life program (which has caused great problems in other school divisions), the implementation of a large peer tutoring/counseling after-school program, etc. To cap off an already positive school year for Randolph-Henry, its dual-enrollment program was featured in a national television series (developed by PBS and entitled "Restructuring American Education") as an illustration of how one rural and poor school system could "achieve excellence."

Central Middle School also had a positive year, but its success was less associated with celebrating its existence than it was with addressing and improving learner outcomes for its sixth-grade classes. Specifically, lower than hoped for student success rates in some middle school subject areas had led the superintendent and the principal at Central Middle to look for new instructional methods in 1989. The program they chose (mentioned in Chapter 3) involved team teaching by all sixth-grade teachers. And the results so pleased the division administrative staff that they began talking about and/or planning to turn all three grade levels at Central Middle into team-teaching and teacher-directed operations. Apparently, some teachers, and even central office staff members, have suggested that, barring certification barriers, middle-school teachers in the near future may move through the three grade levels with student cohorts, rather than passing children along to new teachers at the next grade level year after year.

FINANCIAL CONSIDERATIONS

While the educational mood among Charlotte County citizens, teachers, and administrators appeared quite positive on our last visit to the county, school financing concerns and related confrontations with the County Board of Supervisors suggest that all is not upbeat there. The new state funding formula for Virginia, based on student enrollment, provides downwardly adjusted dollars for school divisions like Charlotte County. Unfortunately, as in Braxton County (and each of the others in this book), costs for maintaining school facilities are the same in a school with 100 children as they are in a school enrolling 105 children, unless schools are consolidated or teachers laid off. At the same time, new and improved state programs in Virginia under the Standards of Quality program (and under various other nomenclatures in the other states) almost always entail more costs, costs which school leaders in each of our four counties claim are not fully paid for by the state legislatures/school boards which mandate them.

According to the Charlotte County superintendent, state-mandated program improvements and additions in the county have added up to over $400,000 in new local costs (for the 1990–1991 school year), but less than 10% of these costs are being compensated for by the state. The *Mecklenburg Times-Dispatch*, an aggressive newspaper in adjoining Mecklenburg County which believes school news in Charlotte County is underreported by its local county paper, ran several stories in early 1990 regarding school funding issues there. It's story of March 14 included the following:

> The Charlotte system is struggling with state mandates that will cost about $480,000, an expense over and above the usual budget shortfalls that educators wrestle with every year. What's worse, said school Superintendent S, is that the state hands down mandates but hasn't given the system additional funds to work with. "We feel like we are getting a raw deal compared to some systems around us."
>
> Expecting to receive a sizeable sum from the state to pay for required items, the Charlotte school system got $34,706—a drop in the bucket compare to new expenses. "That much additional funding just doesn't begin to cover the costs of new mandates, not including the normal expenses we have to deal with," [the superintendent] said.
>
> Charlotte, which currently operates an $8.98 million school budget, . . . will have to spend $100,000 for new buses, $213,000 for teacher salary increases, $40,000 for asbestos removal and $125,000 to hire five more special education teachers (according to new state requirements).
>
> If the system has to make up a roughly half-million dollar shortfall on its own, some 25 teachers and other personnel could lose their jobs, [the superintendent] said. . . . [he] recently sent out letters to 25 teachers saying they could lose their jobs next year. However, he said he is hopeful that the county will step into the gap and make up perhaps as much as $250,000.
>
> That amount would probably mean personnel cuts of only about a dozen persons and the loss of the music program in the elementary schools, as opposed to steep cuts in an instructional force that numbers about 150 teachers.
>
> [Mr. S] said he didn't know why Charlotte received so little money from the state but conceded the county's relatively low level of local funding may have had something to do with it. He said in the last two years the county had funded the system above the minimum local level, but it was "traditional" for Charlotte to keep its contribution to the minimum.

One of the primary educational undertakings addressed in Spring 1990 by the local school board and superintendent involved putting together a budget which would appear lean enough to obtain approval from the county Board of Supervisors. According to local officials, the Charlotte County Board of Supervisors in 1990 is comprised of three members generally in favor of the school system's budgetary activities, and three who remain generally opposed to spending any more than necessary for educational programs. One of the three traditionally most skeptical of increasing school costs is the chairman of the board.

As suggested earlier, Charlotte County's primary (current) struggle with its history is related to how programmatically aggressive the county school board is, and to what extent it wants to wrestle/debate the Board of Supervisors (and raise public support) for the school money it requests. To its credit (in our view), the fashioning of the annual school budget by the division school board is a public event in Charlotte County, as is the subsequent presentation of this budget to the Board of Supervisors. As best I can interpret, public relations and a certain degree of gamesmanship are involved in the public discussion of the budget, and school officials make sure that public forums on budget discussions (as on other types of discussions) are well attended by sympathetic parents.

Not satisfied with asking for the minimum allowable funds from the local Board of Supervisors, the Charlotte County school board volunteered to cut several high school programs and over a dozen teaching positions throughout the system (the enrollment projection at the high school for next year is about 600 students, 11% fewer than for 1989–1990). In effect, they voluntarily deleted over $300,000 in teaching positions and programs from their budget, made necessary by state mandates without extra dollars. In return, they requested a 1.4% increase (approximately $200,000) in local support to make up for other programs which would also be lost without extra support. And (in a public forum filled with people asking for even greater local school budgetary support), the superintendent/school board pointed out such dollars could be transferred from existing county funds to the school budget without raising taxes.

Apparently impressed with the voluntary (and publically proclaimed) self-imposed budget cutbacks, the Board of Supervisors approved the school division budget, after much debate and questioning, on a vote of 4–2. One of the two voting against approving the budget was the board chairman. Another factor related to the Board of Supervisor's acceptance of division budget proposals was their apparent realization that state funding formulas are (according to Charlotte County officials) biased against small and rural Virginia school divisions.

In efforts to underscore what they perceive are inequitable financing protocols at the state level, 39 school divisions (as of May 1990) have joined together into a "Coalition for Equity in Educational Funding." Charlotte County is a charter member of this group, which is getting free research and legal advice from Virginia Tech; and the superintendent of Charlotte County schools is the Southside regional representative. In May 1990, the Charlotte County Board of Education voted to contribute 50 cents per student in their division as a membership contribution to the Coalition.

Responding to statewide concern over discrepancies in school budgets (where, for example very wealthy Northern Virginia school districts spend almost two times as much per student as do poorer districts), newly elected Governor Wilder has appointed a commission to study alleged inequities (the Governor's Commission on Educational Opportunity), a study group which was scheduled to meet with (among others) the Coalition for Equity Educational Funding. According to central office officials in Charlotte County, the state is not eager to be sued over its funding formulas (as has occurred in each of the other three states in this book during this decade). Their "legal advice" from VPI is that the Virginia constitution is much more explicit in specifying equal schooling opportunities under state law; thus, if the Virginia legislature doesn't voluntarily correct current funding formulas, they will lose when challenged in court.

AND THE FATE OF THE MIDDLE SCHOOL?

As discussed at length in Chapter 3, the agreed-upon school improvement plan for Charlotte County which AEL hoped to effect involved a feasibility study which might spur the county Board of Supervisors into applying for Literacy Funds for middle-school construction. And, as opposed to the newly proposed middle school for Braxton County, part of the appeal of the now officially accepted middle school feasibility proposal in Charlotte County involves a number of shared facilities with Randolph-Henry High School, and even some remodeling of the Charlotte County high school.

Unfortunately, the budgetary picture in Charlotte County was not good in 1989 and 1990, and since the school division even had to ask for a significant increase in local funding to maintain a number of existing programs, no new pressures/requests for middle school funding were made in the most recent budget hearings. The hope in the county is that pressures to be brought by the Coalition for Equity in School funding will improve state funding of local schooling costs, which will then make it possible for the Charlotte County school board once again to bring up the possibility of borrowing state Literacy Funds for building a new middle school.

However, several potential wrinkles in the "better wait until next year" approach to requesting Literacy Funds for the middle school lie at both the local and state levels. On the one hand, the Chairman of the Charlotte County Board of Supervisors is currently quite angry with the local school board and with the superintendent in particular. As in a number of small and rural communities (including all four in this study), many school employees are either related to other school employees or to occupants of other professional or business fields. As it happens, one of the teachers whose jobs were rearranged in the 1988–1989 school year as a result of an earlier round of budget cuts was the wife of the Chairman of the Board of Supervisors. Displeased with her 1989–1990 school assignment, she chose early retirement, a choice which her husband blames the school division with forcing her to make. At the current time he remains a self-proclaimed critic of the division superintendent and the school board and has vowed to make fiscal matters as difficult as possible for the local school division.

At the state level, financial conditions also appear ominous for short-term school improvements in Charlotte County. For example, the Virginia Literacy Fund, which has been used throughout the twentieth century for school building projects in places like Charlotte County and is to be the potential funding source for the county's someday middle school, is being "threatened" by other agencies. Specifically, as mentioned in Chapter 3, confiscated property involved in criminal acts has been a primary source of money for this Fund. Yet, with escalating costs to fight the "drug problem" in metropolitan Virginia, some law groups and legislators are attempting to tap into these monies for law enforcement efforts. To date, this has not occurred, but one has to wonder how much money for improving education in rural Virginia will be available in the years ahead if this funding source, which we have suggested may underlie much of that state's educational success, is diverted to other uses.

In a related development, newly elected Governor Wilder announced a projected $1.35 billion revenue shortfall for the state in the summer of 1990, and specified cuts for the 1990–1992 state budget. Among other cutbacks, the Governor announced that state funds for local governments would be scaled back by (at least) $375 million, and that $172 million would be cut from state aid for local school divisions. Therefore, since much of Charlotte County's regular school budget comes from both these sources (and be approved by the local board of supervisors), it appears quite likely that even keeping *current* school funding will be difficult in the years immediately ahead. And while Governor Wilder maintains that addressing the disparity in state funding levels for local districts is one of his concerns, I suspect that Charlotte County's history of being fiscally conservative paints a less than benign picture for school improvement hopes there, particularly the construction of a new middle school in the foreseeable future.

CLINCH COUNTY: THE HARD TIMES CONTINUE

More of the same, but with interesting possibilities on the horizon: This would probably be the best way of describing the educational and community state of affairs in Clinch County in July 1990. At the community economic level, truly little has happened of importance since the discussion in Chapter 4. The Hardee's restaurant appears to have grown in acceptance over the past year, and it has now become a favorite place for lunch among many of the people I interviewed during recent site visits to the county. It's also the only public place that stays open later than 8:00 P.M.

In earlier discussions of Clinch County, I suggested that real vestiges of older and more traditional Appalachian community life are still very visible there. For instance, I noted that church–school connections were still present in Clinch County, even more so than I detected in any of the other three sites. This fact was brought close to home on the last interviews completed there: Both female teachers I talked to (in different settings and belonging to different churches) had to cut short our discussions to go prepare for evening Bible school classes they were running for county children.

So too, I noted in Chapter 3 that, in the 19th and early 20th century, both distant and local churches frequently provided major support for social services in Clinch County, including local schools. And this relationship still exists. Even today, for example, distant churches eager to improve the physical and spiritual chances of local residents are working in the county. In Summer 1990, as they have for a number of years, the Methodist Church is running its "Appalachian Outreach" program in (among other places) Clinch County. Significantly, 80-plus college age volunteers from around the U.S. are rotated every 2 weeks into the county to build and repair houses and perform whatever technical and social assistance they can for its most impoverished citizens. And when they aren't working out in the county or riding around in their mini-busses, they are literally camped out in Clinch County High School, with the approval of the superintendent and the school board.

Local churches are also formally very visible in support of the school system too. For example, since the county school board and county commission expect that school fundraising will be a major source of income for particular schools, church groups still hold fundraisers in and for them. A gathering I missed but wanted to attend was the "Gospel Extravaganza" on June 9, 1990, at Clinch Central. Four gospel groups were headlined for this convocation, a "large family bible" was the door prize, and "all proceeds (were to) go to the Clinch School System."

While older forms of community organization continue, and while good rains in Spring 1990 augered high hopes for the small burley tobacco plots which boost the household incomes of many county residents, at least two more "modern" developments of county-wide interest have occurred, although neither has shown any dramatic impact yet. The greatly improved road from Sealsville which runs over through Bean Station, along Cherokee Lake, and towards Rogersville is now complete, which likewise makes commuting out of the county for employment just a little bit easier. So too, a new county Chamber of Commerce has been created by a group of local citizens. The hope among group members is that such a group will help stimulate some local economic growth: yet its relationship to other county political structures is not yet resolved.

And, speaking of politics, the Spring and Summer of 1990 have seen quite a scramble in Clinch County on issues and personalities extensively talked about in our earlier discussion. For example, the Republican primary in May saw the defeat of the County Executive responsible for expanding the county jail (which continues to house both state and D.C. prisoners). So, too, the county sheriff, who oversees the jail, also lost his primary election bid. While he will be running in August as an independent candidate, and while he is suspected of garnering moderate support based on the number of jobs he has given at the jail to his friends and relatives, he is still expected to lose.

Signifying once again the close ties that the county school system has with local governance structures, a former school teacher and son of the famous county political figure who controlled Clinch County schools for decades as superintendent and board chair will probably be the new County Executive. And the odds-on favorite to win the sheriff's race is currently the basketball coach at the high school (a position prominent and visible enough to garner many votes, in addition to whatever factional backing he may have gotten from behind-the-scenes forces).

Closer to the school system, two board races are being contested in the county in the August election, one of which presents some concern to the superintendent. While the potential winner of the County Executive race was not formally backed by Mr. A., these two figures are apparently not bitter enemies at this time. On the other hand, one of the board races which is reputed to be too close to call at this point contains an ally of school superintendent, and this individual is expected to lose to an outspoken critic of Mr. A. Furthermore, as Mr. A puts it, "every one of the county commissioners running for election this year is running against me." Which suggests that future working relationships between the school system and the county commission will remain difficult.

CONTINUING EDUCATIONAL CONCERNS

Clinch County 1990 educational issues also appear to continue in ways approximating those earlier discussed. For example, after over a year of talking and planning, there still has been no newsletter produced at the high school, even with the funds donated by AEL. The teacher who volunteered to undertake the project also volunteered to undertake many other projects, and the combined weight of all these initiatives basically overwhelmed her during the Spring semester. The newsletter is still in her mind and in her plans, but none have seen publication yet.

In other school-based matters, there was a staffing crisis at Clinch Central during the Winter, when two veteran teachers were hospitalized for different illnesses. Ostensibly, since no certified permanent replacements were available in the county, several teachers were "reassigned" to different grade levels by the school board without getting any input from them or the affected building principal.

One of the reassigned teachers (reassigned without her consent and against her will) was the former president of the county education association, which had lobbied the TEA in the Summer 1989 to sue the local board for nonpayment of teacher salaries. This same teacher decided that, given the "lack of professional respect" shown her by the school board, she would no longer lead the out-of-state senior trip which she had voluntarily done for the previous few years. According to her, this would not be missed by the superintendent anyway, because "it was becoming quite popular here, and everybody knew it wasn't even his idea."

Other "questionable" central office practices were also mentioned by current teachers in Clinch County. Some wondered where all the people supposedly served by several federally funded programs were. Claiming that many dollars were known to have come into the county for these programs, these informants suggested that few of the teachers they knew around the county had ever talked with people who were eligible for such programs but who had received any services.

On another front, questions regarding the expenditure of state summer supplement monies tied to Level III Career Ladder programs surfaced in my last interviews. According to county teachers, qualified Level III teachers would have first options on teaching summer classes to qualify for extra income. Only after Level III teachers declined to work extra weeks in the summer for these supplements could other teachers apply to teach, and then only after classes needing teachers were advertised around the county. Yet decisions on who and what would be taught appeared to come right from the superintendent's office without discussion. And keeping this information from county staff members is difficult in Clinch County, since the superintendent's office is literally located above the classroom of the President of the CCEA.

"Creative" bookkeeping and "creative" personnel management were also recently featured in Clinch County (and in a neighboring county) in more visible ways during the past several months. In the neighboring county, the County Commission forced the school superintendent to resign for fraudulent bookkeeping practices. In Clinch County, several state prisoners (allegedly at the behest of the County Sheriff and County Executive) are suing the County for overcrowding at the county jail. According to one of our politically well-placed County informants, the Sheriff and County Executive are hoping that all the controversy surrounding the jail will force the County to sell the jail back to the company that built it. Then, as a private venture, these two (soon to be former) County employees may become partners in privately managing the facility.

In the meantime, while litigation takes place, the state has held up its payments to the jail for state prisoners, and D.C. payments continue to be in arrears. Thus, the County Commission is behind in payments to the school system (according to the superintendent, they have literally "lost $170,000 somewhere"); and, yes, monies still being held for teacher checks already earned are being used to pay school system expenses this summer. Furthermore, even though July was supposed to be the month the County Commission reviewed and approved the school budget for 1990–1991, Mr. A. hasn't even submitted a budget to the commission. Instead, he has "only filled out a line or two of my next year's budget," and is waiting to see who will win all the contested seats in the August County Commission races. Furthermore, the superintendent has already announced that, if the county commission doesn't approve the budget he will submit to them in August, he plans on not reopening Clinch County schools in the Fall.

Personnel management in the county is also of some local concern in Summer 1990. For example, I mentioned that the high school basketball coach (and "building trades" teacher in the vocational program) appears likely to win the sheriff's race in August (although he isn't a certified classroom teacher *or* a certified law enforcement officer).

Given the expected vacancy, the former (second year) principal/teacher at Hickory Gap has been given the new job as high school basketball coach, and since he has no high school teaching certification, he must perform his part-time teaching at Clinch Central. Suggestively, this "promotion" typifies a major philosophical difference in Clinch County compared to all of the other three systems in this study, for only in Clinch County would a reputedly excellent teacher and successful principal be ushered out of an instructional role in which he had acclaimed success and into one requiring little or no certification (as basketball coach) and for which many aspirants were available.

So, too, the auto mechanics teacher at Clinch High school announced his retirement from the system at the end of 1990. Ordinarily, one might expect that both the building trades and auto mechanics programs would need replacements for the 1990–1991 school year and beyond. Yet citing the importance of getting local people (perhaps with histories of support for the superintendent and/or important board members), two new programs were approved without extensive discussion in the June board meeting at Sealsville. One of these new programs will be in "health occupations" and the other in "cosmetology." While it appears defensible that the "health occupations" program may provide skill training in growing health-care/retirement programs in Clinch County (a defense which the superintendent makes), how local and/or regional industries can use more cosmetologists is unclear. As discussed in Chapter 3, studies of Clinch County High vocational programs completed in the 1950s and 1960s (not commissioned by the school system) criticized the lack of planning involved in preparing county students for real and existing or emerging regional jobs. Some might argue that this tradition (also) continues currently in the county.

HOPING TO "CASH IN" ON THE BIG ONE

As stated at various points in this manuscript, each of the four county school systems studied for this book has been involved in some form of litigation and/or coalition for altering state funding formulas involving small and rural school districts. However, only in Clinch County (easily the poorest among the four) has the local superintendent become personally and politically involved in legal actions against the state.

In terms of getting local, state, and even national coverage for the case against current school-funding formulas in Tennessee, the "performance" of the Clinch County superintendent must be given high marks. For example, at least three times in the past year and a half either regional TV (i.e., Kingsport) stations, or those from Knoxville, have completed school documentaries featuring the visible poverty of Clinch County schools. So, too, a feature story in the highly polished state magazine (Fall 1989) profiled the lawsuit and superintendents of the state's three poorest county school systems. Mr. A was quoted at length in this story, which not only provided him a platform to tell about how little his system was able to provide, but also increased his visibility around the state and in the county.

Most recently (July 1990), the national Cable News Network (CNN) included coverage of the Tennessee lawsuit for educational equity as part of their week-long "Education Revolution" series. And one particular episode focused on the funding and programmatic differences between the wealthy Kingsport (city) school system (1 hour east of Sealsville) and that of Clinch County.

The televised differences between the schools was clear and graphic (even if somewhat staged). The Kingsport children were shown in exercise classes, art theory lessons, hands-on physics instruction, and computer-programming workshops. Countering this image, Clinch County's kids were shown assembling popsicle sticks for an art project, playing on dilapidated swings, being lectured on physics, and having a computerless library stocked with books laughingly out-of-date (ostensibly to comply with state laws mandating minimum *numbers* of book holdings per student). The main Kingsport newspaper in mid-June described for local citizens what would be aired about their schools on the CNN special:

> With the highest-paid teachers in the state, Kingsport is known as being the best-funded in Tennessee, according to CNN officials. On the other hand, rural Clinch County has some of the lowest teacher salaries and spends less per student. . . . At Johnson [elementary], the [CNN] crew filmed students using the Electronic Bookshelf and others who were practicing recorder in the music room. Cameras rolled at D[obyns]-B[ennett High School] during student orchestra practice and during physics lab and computer math lab demonstration.

What the Kingsport paper did not reveal in its story is that Clinch County has no Electronic Bookshelf, no separate music rooms, no orchestra (or band), no separate physics lab, and no computer math lab. These facts were demonstrated in the CNN newscast, which clearly suggested that lack of funding severely hampered equitable school programs in Clinch County.

Another controversy not profiled in most national coverage of the lawsuit for equal school funding in Tennessee, but which is implicitly suggested in the Kingsport story, is that several city school systems in Tennessee are opposed to the rural schools' suit against the state for more money. According to them (and illustrating what many claim is a century-long battle between urban and rural forces in the state), the suit is misguided, for it seeks to divide up current state appropriations for education by altering expenditure ratios for small and rural schools. Instead, the city school systems argue that new taxes must be generated across the state for improving educational financing for all schools rather than "taking from the rich and giving to the poor."

Signifying a possible state crisis over education funding, the Governor of Tennessee (as did the Governor of Virginia) campaigned across the state (and in Clinch County) this Spring for his "21st Century School Plan." According to the Clinch County superintendent, "the Governor knows we're going to win" efforts at improving school equity, which may be one reason why litigants in the suit have grown from 66 to 73 school districts.

To accomplish this "21st Century Plan," Governor McWherter "won't rule out a state income tax" along the way to increasing per-pupil expenditures "into the $3,800–4,500 range." Current expenses per student in Clinch county are approximately $2,900. Importantly, even *talking* about imposing a state income tax in Tennessee is potentially fatal politically; but while no Clinch County elected leaders are willing to campaign for increasing local taxes, many educators (at least) are quite pleased that the governor might.

A FINAL OBSERVATION

There can be little doubt that increased school funding would improve schooling opportunities in Clinch County. On the other hand, it may well be the case that "merely throwing money at the problem" (as national politicians phrase this possibility) won't make everything better. Governor McWherter's plan suggests that increased spending for education would be accompanied by fiscal control of school budgets by county school boards, increased account-ability safeguards, and the end of elected superintendents in Tennessee school districts. Based on our observations in Clinch County, such policies might positively affect educational improvement practices, but even these might take years to institutionalize.

More money in the Clinch County system would probably be used initially for the consolidating of one or more elementary schools (which was the plan Mr. A was working towards in 1988, when he believed federal Impact Aid might be bequeathed to the county). On the other hand, with regard to sustained and continuous local school improvement initiatives, only state mandates for future planning (coupled with their auditing) would probably force the central office in

Clinch County to approximate those of the other three counties in this study. Because school funding has always been low, and because the superintendent there importantly views himself as a politician, the school improvement "culture" of Clinch County is not strong. School improvement language, planning, and concern is not dominant there, and even the superintendent admits he isn't sure what "instructional leadership" really means.

This interpretation can perhaps best be concluded with reference to the last comment made by the superintendent in my final interview with him. When asked what increased state funding might mean for the County, he did not begin to talk about computers in the school, enhancing learner outcomes, or improving learning climates. Rather, he began to wistfully compare the (hypothetically) adequately state-funded superintendent's political future with that of the county road commissioner:

> It used to be [the case] around here that local taxes paid for road maintenance, and this made the commissioner's job real political. But then the state took over the funding of this job, and now Clinch County gets the same money as all the other counties. Well, the commissioner is now able to buy all the equipment he needs and it doesn't cost the local taxpayers a cent. He has become a hero . . . and is now [politically] impossible to beat.

CAVE COUNTY AND THE KENTUCKY SCHOOL REFORM ACT OF 1990

While Mr. A in Clinch County looks forward to the day that his state may increase its share of the funding of rural and poor schools, many superintendents and school boards who composed the Council for Better Education in Kentucky have probably had second thoughts regarding their "successful" suit for improving educational equity in their state.

Cave County, being the last of the four districts discussed in previous pages of this work, probably needs the least amount of "updating" since I last left it in Chapter 5. On the other hand, the arguable success of the Council for Better Education class-action suit in Kentucky has led to a school reform act which has the potential for dramatically transforming all school systems in the state over the next 5 years. And for Cave County, this transformation probably has as many sharp edges as it does positive opportunities, viewed from the perspective of the county superintendent's office. Put another way, if improving schools truly involves parent, teacher, and community involvement in education, and focusing on building level school enhancement, systems like that of Cave County may struggle as much with their futures as well as their histories.

As mentioned in Chapter 5, Fall 1988 and Summer 1989 saw both circuit court and Kentucky Supreme Court decisions/opinions which ruled that

Section 183 of the state constitution was being violated in Kentucky. Section 183 mandates that "The General Assembly shall, by appropriate legislation, provide for an efficient system of common schools throughout the state." As discussed earlier, defining just what an "efficient" system of education is has changed throughout the twentieth century in Kentucky. And in the 1988 and 1989 court decisions, plaintiffs suing the state for inefficient schooling opportunities won their case.

Importantly, inefficient schooling opportunities were tied in both court decisions to equity concerns, and to the extent that Kentucky school children at the time of the court case were not provided "uniform" schooling opportunities across the state. Furthermore, the Franklin Circuit Court decision (appealed by the state department of education) that financial inequalities required a "new funding system for public education" was greatly expanded by the subsequent state Supreme Court decision, in which the *entire system* of public education was ruled unconstitutional. According to the Supreme Court, the Franklin County Court decision was much more than just a decision over financial equity. As Judge Stevens stated:

> This decision applies to the entire sweep of the system—all its parts and parcels. This decision applies to the statutes creating, implementing and financing the *system* and to all regulations, etc., pertaining thereto. This decision covers the creation of local school districts, school boards, and the Kentucky Department of Education to the Minimum Foundation Program and Power Equalization Program. It covers school construction and maintenance, teacher certification—the whole gamut of the common school system in Kentucky. . . . Since we have, by this decision, declared the system of common schools in Kentucky to be unconstitutional, Section 183 places an absolute duty on the General Assembly to recreate, re-establish a new system of common schools in the Commonwealth. . . . The General Assembly has the obligation to see that all [taxable] property is assessed at 100 percent of its fair market value. . . . We view this decision as an opportunity for the General Assembly to launch the Commonwealth into a new era of educational opportunity which will ensure a strong economic, cultural and political future. (LRC, 1990, pp. 3–4)

THE PUBLIC/POLITICAL ORIGINS OF KENTUCKY SCHOOL REFORM

It appears quite likely that court decisions related to Kentucky school reform were probably influenced by both the national and state school reform climates prevalent in the 1980s. My own work on late 20th-century educational perspectives equating school improvement with "investing in human resources" is articulated in DeYoung (1989). In Kentucky, the climate of educational reform was heavily fueled by both of the state's largest newspapers (the *Lexington*

Herald-Leader and the *Louisville Courier-Journal*) and by the Prichard Committee for Academic Excellence (which was discussed in Chapters 1 and 5).

More importantly, Governor Martha Collins (1984–1988), and then Governor Wallace Wilkinson (1988–1992) both claimed to be crucially concerned about education reform in the state. Yet, as in earlier school reform movements in each of the other states discussed, reform laws legislated under the former of these two governors were not completely funded during her administration, and the subsequent governor refused to sponsor their funding once he became elected. In particular, Governor Wilkinson had promised that no new taxes would be passed in order to improve Kentucky schools; rather, he ran for office and was arguably elected on his promise to institute a state lottery (which he did), the proceeds of which would (primarily) be used for education.

One dramatic appointment by Governor Wilkinson in early 1988 was his new Secretary of Education, an individual much enamored with late-1980s school reform proposals like "site-based management, performance-based incentives," and so on. And during 1988 and 1989, Governor Wilkinson promised a new round of school reforms would be proposed by his administration for legislative action, proposals which would be developed by his Secretary of Education.

However, most statehouse pronouncements and proposals about future school improvement efforts were muted and/or legislatively killed following the court decisions of 1988 and 1989. Rather, under pressure from the Court decisions, a Task Force on Education Reform was chartered in July of 1989 to come up with a new plan for educating Kentucky's children for the following Spring legislative session. No doubt recognizing that they would have to have the cooperation of the governor's office in order to pass significant school reform (and tax) legislation, the Task Force on Education Reform was put together by the General Assembly, and it comprised both Senate and House representatives (e.g., members of education committees and leaders of both houses in the General Assembly), as well as representatives appointed by the governor.

PROVISIONS OF THE EDUCATION REFORM ACT OF 1990

In March 1990, the Task Force on Education Reform brought to the General Assembly a massive document full of proposals for reforming the state system of education. Most of this document, large portions of which had been engineered with the help of national consultants, subsequently became House Bill 940. Surprisingly, after having downplayed the significance of the Task Force, and after almost 2 years of suggesting that his administration would not raise taxes for the General Assembly's school reform plans, the governor switched his position on both matters. The net effect was that, with full backing of both the state legislature and the governor's office, House Bill 940 became law in April 1990, and it is argued by most contemporary legislative observers (including the state media) as the most revolutionary and comprehensive educational reform package to ever be seen in the state.

There were three separate educational areas to be "restructured" under the Kentucky Educational Reform Act of 1990. These include the Curriculum, Finance, and Governance. Given the "postscript" nature of this Cave County discussion, I am unable here to completely overview the many mandated changes and new programs to be phased in over the next 5 years in the state. Thus, interested readers may want to obtain the Legislative Research Commission (1990) booklet cited in the references, which outlines many of these programs. On the other hand, many programs to be instituted in Kentucky have rarely been comprehensively tried anywhere, and how, or whether, they will work at all remains to be seen.

This perspective was concurred with by the Cave County superintendent, who noted that the primary consultant for curriculum reforms passed in House bill 940 was an "out-of-state minister who never had a church . . . (who also) had a law degree but never practiced law." So, too, he observed that the State Secretary of Education "is a criminologist . . . neither one of those two has ever taught in or run a school."

FINANCE REFORMS

In view of the themes and issues discussed earlier for Cave County, only one will probably serve interests of both the county and the central office. At the state level, guaranteed state minimum per pupil expenditures for 1990–1991 (entitled the Support Educational Excellence in Kentucky fund) were set at $2,305 for each student and are to increase gradually for the next 5 years. In addition, extra monies for each district based on the number of children receiving free lunch were established, additional monies for the newly mandated 4-year old program and for "technology education" were provided, and limited funds for professional development activities were also set aside. Also, funds for rewarding "successful schools" were budgeted, although at the current time the standards for judging "success" have not been proposed (see the Curriculum discussion below).

In order to receive these various funds, local districts are required in 1990–1991 and thereafter to raise minimum local support for schools to 30 cents per $100 assessed valuation (up significantly for Cave County, as we discussed in Chapter 5). Furthermore, in order to participate in the state school building enhancement program (which lends money to local districts for building purposes), school tax rates must be set at 35 cents on $100. As another incentive, the state promised that locally generated per-pupil increases over and above those mandated by the SEEK program would be matched by the state at 150% of the state per-pupil average assessment.

Importantly, costs of the above programs could not be accommodated by existing tax levies in the state of Kentucky, and a large increase in state taxes accompanied HB 940. Among the new taxes were a 1% increase (to 6%) in the state sales tax and a rewriting of the state income tax to make it conform with federal tax guidelines. Also, a complete overhaul of property values was mandated by the General Assembly, to assure consistency and accuracy in the assessments local school districts were to draw upon for their shares of school taxes. At the time of this writing, furthermore, 25 (of 120) county tax assessment offices have been taken over by the state under suspicion that local property value administrators are underassessing local properties. With these several tax assessment improvements and rate increases, the state estimated that over 1.3 billion new dollars would be generated for Kentucky education.

In Cave County, appreciation and confusion over the financial implications of HB940 were both visible in the summer of 1990. Cave County's superintendent believed that somewhere around $900,000 dollars for the school system would end up coming there through the SEEK funding mechanisms, which was a substantial increase from state monies provided under the old minimum foundation program. On the other hand, much of this money was already tied to specific state mandates: local districts were told to increase all teacher salaries by at least 10% (raises were 11% in Cave County), and extra transportation costs are involved in the pre-primary-program mandates of the state. SEEK monies left over after these new costs were factored in for Cave County approximate less than $300,000.

Mr. G in Cave County welcomed the new funds but confided that figuring exactly how much extra money was available to Hart County was more difficult than the state legislature had indicated when the SEEK program was first announced. Specifically, he argued that the state had underbudgeted the "matching-funds" sections of the SEEK proposals, because they had failed to plan for the large number of counties which would pass local tax increases in order to participate in the state incentive programs. Therefore, the pool of money set aside to match local tax initiatives was too small to match them at 150%, and not until all districts are finished applying for these monies will final figures be available to local districts. And the same miscalculation, he suggests, accompanies building fund set-asides for the (many) counties that wish to raise local appropriations to $0.35.

GOVERNANCE AND CURRICULUM
REFORMS ISSUES

While Cave County's financial future is probably better (if not completely predictable) under the Kentucky Educational Reform Act of 1990, I suspect that school governance and curriculum issues will be somewhat troublesome for the Cave County central office. And even the superintendent is not particularly happy about most reforms proposed, with at least one noteworthy exception. Specifically, under the new state law, local school consolidation can only take place in Kentucky if and when local boards vote to close schools: The state cannot condemn a school to close just because it has low enrollment. Thus, the likelihood is that the two proposed "interim centers" in Cave County talked about earlier will be reclassified as "functional centers" once the state returns to restudy Cave County school facilities, for there are no longer "interim centers" under Kentucky school law. Thus, while the school consolidation issue in Cave County is not dead (i.e., obtaining money for a middle school someday may cause new pressures to close schools), at least the current superintendent is glad to leave this potential next round of school-closing discussions to a future holder of his office.

On the other hand, most governance reforms which became law on July 13, 1990, I would argue, threaten many of the central operating principles I focused on in earlier discussions of Cave County schools. For example, the State Department of Education was abolished by HB940, and the State Superintendent of Public Education "demoted" to virtual figurehead status. Replacing these two state agencies are (to be) a newly constituted State Board for Elementary and Secondary Education, and a new Commissioner of Education. All appointments under the new system are heavily influenced by the Governor's office, and the new chief state school officer (the Commissioner) for the first time in recent history will be appointed rather than elected. Whatever the long-term positive (or negative) consequences of this move, in the short term this has thrown Cave County into something of a turmoil; for as I discussed earlier, relationships between the (former) state department of education and Cave County were quite "cozy." What the new relationship might be remains to be seen, but it will certainly have to be recultivated: Even now, county school officials complain that many of the usual contacts in the state department have begun to "jump ship" in search of more stable employment.

Governance changes at the district level are also affected by the new state law. For instance, school board members in Kentucky can no longer hire their relatives for the school system. In fact, school board members can no longer hire *any* school employees. Such a function in the future resides completely with the superintendent. And should a superintendent find school board disfavor in his or her school appointments, they cannot even fire him or her without first gaining approval of the new Commissioner of Education.

In Cave County, critics contend, this new relationship will lead to a redefinition of power, since the old 3–2 board majority rested primarily upon the superintendent accommodating to the board many school-hiring decisions in exchange for their support of his policies. These same critics also note that all local school boards are big losers in local school decision-making ability; for in addition to not being able to hire new school employees, relatives of school board members are not allowed to work anywhere in the school system. This new law also applies to relatives of the superintendent, but in Cave County the seniority of the superintendent's wife nullifies this provision for current employees. Yet these antinepotism factors, combined with some serious erosion of local school board powers to make tax-rate decisions (i.e., they must raise rates to at least the new state minimum) effectively removes boards from making many important decisions related to local school system functioning, which was arguably one exact intent of the Kentucky Education Reform Act of 1990.

Curriculum reforms made mandatory by HB940 are likewise viewed with much skepticism in Cave County. Importantly, it was in the curriculum area where outside consultants had their greatest impact, and many school "improvements" which became law in HB 940 have never (or rarely) been seen in the state before. For example, an ungraded primary (grades 1–4) is specified in the School Reform Act of 1990, as are Family Resource Centers, Youth Service Centers, preschool programs, and mandatory kindergarten.

While several of the above listed programs are viewed as *perhaps* beneficial by Cave County school people I interviewed in July 1990, three related curricular reforms predictably concern the central office at Cave County. One of these involves "site-based management"; a second mandates that, by 1995–1996, a completely new state assessment program will be instituted; and, under a third, individual schools that are either "successful," or "unsuccessful" (as determined by the state) will receive differential rewards/sanctions as a function of their school's performance.

The problem of adapting to new performance standards set forth by the state will probably not be difficult in Cave County, only time consuming. School-based management, on the other hand, may be very problematic. As discussed earlier, the Cave County system is *not* one where building-level initiative has any long standing appreciation, and where teacher organization(s) have been openly criticized. The new Education Reform Act specifies that one site-based school must be identified and in operation by Fall 1991, and all others by July 1996. To date, however, no principal or school staff has volunteered to go first. And to compound matters, building principals lost their "fair demotion" protection under HB 940, which means that the superintendent can remove them without board approval if he so chooses.

Yet, while Kentucky superintendents seemingly retain some power to influence principals in the future regarding how they will manage school-based decision making, the Cave County superintendent may have to contend seriously in future with the "parent involvement" issue we judged that he earlier avoided. For, under new state law, school-based decision making councils (who will theoretically structure curriculum, staffing and scheduling matters) will include *both* of the groups excluded previously in Cave County educational policy: teachers and parents.

With the exception of finance reforms already being calculated in the Cave County central office, a "wait-and see" attitude seems as of this writing to dominate its procedures. The superintendent seems particularly chagrined at the concept of school-based decision making. In my last interview he suggested his opposition this way:

> I don't agree with site-based. At some point in time, somebody has to be the chief and the others have to be Indians. I've never believed that a committee can make good decisions. . . . I question what ability two parents can have to come in and look at my son's folder and make educational decisions for him and for his school.

Some advocates of improving education around the nation insist that future changes call for "restructuring" schools, not just "improving" them, which of course begs some question about the underlying rationale of this larger work. The Cave County superintendent probably feels that school restructuring is a bad idea. Apparently, others familiar with the Cave County school system also believe (as I do) that many parts of the Kentucky Educational Reform Act of 1990 will be slow in coming to Cave County—perhaps not until the current superintendent does in fact retire and becomes replaced by one more in tune with the intent of state educational restructuring hopes.

A former resident with deep roots in the county and who is currently recognized statewide for her commitment to civic projects wrote the *Cave County News* in May on this theme. She had this to say in "Letters to the Editor," with which I conclude this book. For now.

Dear Editor:

Yesterday I was in a meeting of people, like myself, who have been involved in the education reform movement. The discussion turned to which school districts would be most resistant to the reforms recently acted.

I expected to hear the name of one of those notoriously corrupt eastern Kentucky counties. But no. The first district named was Cave County.

I was aghast.

This was my home county they were talking about. The students they said were the least likely to receive the benefits of the most far reaching educational improvements in the history of the State are the children and grandchildren of my childhood friends.

It shocked me that Cave County led the worst list.

Although I have been away all my married life, I know that there are good teachers doing good work in Cave County because I saw evidence of that when I spoke at the Cave County High School graduation last May.

So, what is going on?

How has Cave County come to be labeled as a district where the students are most likely to suffer from administrative refusal to comply with the new State laws?

I surmise that highly placed school personnel have expressed negative views of the reforms, either in person or on the phone, to colleagues outside of Cave County. Based on the attitudes expressed by a few, educators across the State sense that a potentially poisonous atmosphere exists in Cave County. Thus, Cave County has been labeled as "kicking and screaming" against the ideas in the education program.

This is bad.

This is intolerable.

This must be turned around.

Every student in Cave County has a Constitutional right to the kind of education mandated in the Education Reform Act of 1990.

REFERENCES

DeYoung, A. J. (1989). *Economics and American education: A historical and critical overview of the impact of economic theories on schooling in the United States.* New York: Longman.

Legislative Research Commission. (1990). *A guide to the Kentucky Education Reform Act of 1990.* Frankfort, KY: Author.

Author Index

285

Subject Index